The
Mind
and
Will
of the Lord

JOHN TAYLOR

Photo Credits

Cover picture: William E. Berrett, *The Restored Church*, Tenth Edition,
(Deseret Book Company) p.418.

Black and white photo: Emerson Roy West, *Profiles of the Presidents*,
(Deseret Book Company) p.106. Photo by Fredrick Piercy.

ISBN: 1-55517-432-9

v.1

Published and Distributed by:

WestWood Books

115 E. Calvin
Taft, CA 93268
(661) 765-2241
www.westwoodbooks.com

Cover design by Corinne A. Bischoff
Lithographed in the United States of America

The
Mind
and
Will
of the Lord
JOHN TAYLOR

Compiled and Indexed by
Harold W. Pease, Ph.D.

JOHN TAYLOR

JOHN TAYLOR STANDS AGAINST THE MOB

Near Columbus, the capital of Ohio, they [John Taylor and his companions] stayed at a town where a number of brethren resided, and all were anxious to hear Elder Taylor preach. As they had no hall, it was arranged that he should speak in the open air.

A little before meeting time a number of the brethren came running to the house where he was stopping with the information that the whole town was gathering and that a number of men had proposed tar and feathers, and boasted they would dress him with them if he undertook to preach. The brethren advised him not to attempt it as they were not strong enough to protect him. After a moment's reflection, however, he decided to go and preach. The brethren remonstrated; they knew the tar and feathers were prepared and that he could not escape. He replied that he had made up his mind to go; they could go with him if they chose, if not, he would go alone.

A very large concourse of people had assembled to listen to him. He began his remarks by informing them that he had lately come from Canada—a land under monarchical rule; that standing as he then did on free soil, among free men, he experienced peculiar sensations.

"Gentlemen, I now stand among men whose fathers fought for and obtained one of the greatest blessings ever conferred upon the human family—the right to think, to speak, to write; the right to say who shall govern them, and the right to worship God according to the dictates of their own consciences—all of them sacred, human rights, and now guaranteed by the American Constitution. I see around me the sons of those noble sires, who, rather than bow to the behests of a tyrant, pledged their lives, fortunes and sacred honors to burst those fetters, enjoy freedom themselves, bequeath it to their posterity, or die in the attempt.

"They nobly fought and nobly conquered; and now the cap of liberty is elevated on the tops of your liberty poles throughout the land, and the flag of freedom waves from Wisconsin to Louisiana—from Maine to Missouri. Not only so, but your vessels—foremost in the world—sail over oceans, seas and bays, visiting every nation; and wherever those vessels go your flag flutters in the breeze, a hope is inspired among the down-trodden millions, that they, perchance, if they cannot find liberty in their own land, may find it with you.... Gentlemen, with you liberty is more than a name; it is incorporated in your system; it is proclaimed by your senators, thundered by your cannon, lisped by your infants, taught to your school-boys; it echoes from mountain to mountain, reverberates through your valleys, and is whispered by every breeze. Is it any wonder, gentlemen, under these circumstances—having lately emerged from a monarchical government—that I should experience peculiar sensations in rising to address you?

"But, by the by, I have been informed that you purpose to tar and feather me, for my religious opinions. Is this the boon you have inherited from your fathers? Is this the blessing they purchased with their dearest hearts' blood—this your liberty? If so, you now have a victim, and we will have an offering to the goddess of liberty." Here he tore open his vest and said: "Gentlemen come on with your tar and feathers, your victim is ready; and ye shades of the venerable patriots, gaze upon the deeds of your degenerate sons! Come on, gentlemen! Come on, I say, I am ready!"

No one moved, no one spoke. He stood there drawn to his full height, calm but defiant—the master of the situation.

After a pause of some moments he continued his remarks and preached with great boldness and power for some three hours.

At the conclusion of his discourse, he was waited upon by some of the leading citizens of the place who expressed their pleasure at what they had heard, and disclaimed, in behalf of the people, any intention of tarring and feathering him; but the brethren still insisted that such was the intention of the crowd, and that the tar and feathers had been provided; but they had been awed into silence by the boldness of Elder Taylor.

B. H. Roberts, *Life of John Taylor* (Salt Lake City: Bookcraft, 1963), pp. 53-55.

"And whatsoever they shall speak when moved upon by the Holy Ghost shall be scripture, shall be the will of the Lord, shall be the mind of the Lord, shall be the word of the Lord, shall be the voice of the Lord, and the power of God unto salvation."

Doctrine and Covenants 68:4

PREFACE

The Mind and Will of the Lord initially was compiled and indexed entirely for my own use many years ago. I wanted to know the past prophets personally and could think of no better way to do this than to assemble and read their general conference addresses. Prior to this time there was no place that one could go for the voice of the presidents of the Church collectively when each, in his time, was clearly, indisputably speaking as the prophet of God. Such is the case at General Conference. If man is indeed to live by every word proceeding forth from the mouth of God, as we are told, then it seemed to me that he should have available what has been said and what is being said by the holy prophets of this dispensation as well as those of earlier times. John Taylor's portion, published herein, is an important part of this work. The entire project took several years to finish, but I loved every minute of it.

Indexing the remarks, after gathering only those specifically associated with a general conference, became the most spiritual long-termed experience of my life. Given the voluminous quantity of materials gathered, it was obvious that the index must reflect accurately every notion expressed or that precious thought would be lost as most people would never take the time to read each address separately in its entirety.

What was needed was an index that could be used easily and quickly in church meetings to find the words of the latter-day prophets on any subject. The idea came to me to index by paragraph rather than by page. Each notion must be captured and reduced to a few words—the same words one would use in relocating the idea. No computer could do this. It had to be done one sentence at a time by human hand capable of being guided by the spirit. Some ideas were obvious, most came easy, many required a struggle, and not a few could never have been encapsulated without prayerful consideration. Those were by far the most rewarding as the spirit was always very strong. This was no ordinary book. In fact, it was the mind and will of the Lord. It was sacred. It had to be perfect!

Often I carried the word of the modern prophets with me to priesthood and Sunday School classes where, because of the unique way of indexing by paragraph rather than by page number, I always was able to find information within seconds on any subject to supplement the topic at hand even if the instructor drifted off the subject. To know the mind and will of the Lord almost instantaneously on subjects not addressed in the Doctrine and Covenants was awesome and now is so very easy.

Until I saw how useful this material was to me, it never occurred to me to make it available to others or to market the same. Also, the obstacles involved in publishing seemed insurmountable. Its utility and the need to make it available to all Saints became even more apparent when the Church began to focus on the prophets of this dispensation for priesthood and relief society classes beginning with Brigham Young. In doing this the brethren demonstrated that the words of past prophets still have great value to us today.

General Conference addresses rendered only by the president of the Church while serving as such were selected obviously because of the size limitation but also because the voice of the prophet is the single-most-important voice on earth during his tenure as president. It best represents the mind and will of the Lord during a prophet's portion of time, and we have been taught from our youth to accept it as scripture. Outside the Standard Works no assemblage of words better expresses the mind and will of the Lord than those spoken by the prophet of God at General Conference; yet until now these have not been separated, indexed, and shared with the Saints as in this single volume. Taken collectively *The Mind and Will of the Lord* series, I believe, is the single greatest source of light and revealed truth since the Standard Works.

Certainly President John Taylor considered what was said in General Conference as the mind and will of God. He said that the purpose of General Conference is "to correct whatever in doctrine or in practice is not in strict conformity with the mind and will of God and that we may endeavor to instruct and strengthen each other in every virtue and integrity that will be approved before high heaven" (*Millennial Star*, November 1, 1880, p. 690). His counselor in the First Presidency, George Q. Cannon, was once even more blunt. He declared boldly that the *Journal of Discourses*, a church publication housing the addresses of the brethren for over three decades, "deservedly ranks as one of the standard works of the Church..." (*Journal of Discourses*, Vol. 8, Preface).

Obviously each prophet speaks to his time, and *the messages of past prophets should never be taken as having greater value or meaning than those of the present prophet*, but as in past dispensations the messages of all are consistent with all. They support and clarify one another. For this reason the Church has decided to reemphasize the messages of the past prophets of our day.

Readers will find President Taylor to be far more tactful than was his predecessor. One was not easily offended by this prophet. What bleeds through the pages of this historic time period is that of a gentle, kind, and especially forgiving prophet. The reader will easily notice the numerous breaks in his addresses accommodating public laughter, yet the script itself is not particularly funny. Body language has to be the missing element, but unfortunately no video recording exists showing us this special side of President Taylor.

Probably the most profound character trait so consistently demonstrated throughout his life and making him especially suited for church leadership during one of the most persecutory time periods in church history was his boldness in defending the faith from all enemies. Whether single-handedly facing a mob that had promised to tar and feather him if he tried to speak to them, as in the story selected to introduce this great man, or when in Carthage Jail offering to escape and bring back an army to free the prophet Joseph Smith, or in leading the Church when so many of its leaders were in the penitentiary, or when a wanted poster was circulated even for members of the First Presidency, who had to go into hiding for many months, he stood as a rock against the storm. Probably only Joseph Smith faced greater opposition while leading the Church than did John Taylor.

Readers are also unlikely to emerge from their perusal of John Taylor without noticing his unusual and profound command of the English language. Such usage conveys the impression that one is dealing with one of the most highly literate prophets of this dispensation.

Each of the characteristics above noted plus the time period in which President John Taylor served makes the study of this prophet especially interesting and rewarding. Judicial tyranny again raged, as it had in Missouri and Illinois, yet throughout it all the loyalty of the Brethren to the Constitution as implemented by the Founding Fathers stood out.

Some minor changes in the formatting of the text were made. Spelling, for example, was updated. President Taylor occasionally used words that do not now exist. These were left without change. Older English words such as vail, to-day, to-morrow, fulfil, merchandizing, utilise, furore, sceptre, defence, centre, etc. were updated to veil, today, tomorrow, fulfill, merchandising, utilize, furor, scepter, defense, center, etc. Excessively long paragraphs, some a page or more with multiple subjects, were segmented into shorter paragraphs and numbered to enable readers to find more easily the exact phraseology they seek. No changes have been made to alter the emphasis or meaning intended by the prophet.

My research has been exhaustive. I have spent over seven and a half years gathering and indexing the addresses of the brethren. Some addresses given in the early days were either not recorded or are not now existent. If one should surface later on and can be verified to have been given by John Taylor at a designated General Conference, it will be included in any subsequent publication of this book.

Acknowledgments are extended to a number of persons whose assistance has made this work possible. My lovely wife Jeannene sacrificed hundreds of hours with me and willingly diverted family income to make possible the publishing of this book. Her encouragement has been priceless. Murray Rawson, two-time mission president, was one of the first to see the vision of this book and to encourage me to make it available to all. Ferrel G. Roundy, long-time colleague and friend, willingly offered his proofreading skills. Bobbi Jones and Barbara Moench devoted considerable time proofreading and correcting this manuscript. Each of these persons was a gift from God. The longer I live the more certain I am that real wealth is measured by the friends surrounding one. On that score I am a very rich man.

CONTENTS

The power of this book is its unusual index. For a specific topic indexed by paragraph please refer to it. Normally President Taylor treated multiple topics in each address. The contents would have been too detailed and cluttered for all to have been noted. Preference has been given to the most relevant and interesting topics.

ADDRESS   **PAGE**

ADDRESS 1

Remarks made by John Taylor, President of the Quorum of the Twelve Apostles, at the Saturday afternoon session of the 47th Semiannual General Conference of The Church of Jesus Christ of Latter-day Saints convened October 6, 1877, in the New Tabernacle, Salt Lake City, Utah.

1. I am very happy to find so great an unanimity of feeling in the voting, as has been manifested at this Conference. There is a very common axiom in the world, "Vox populi, vox dei," or, "The voice of the people is the voice of God." Although the voice of the people is very important, we do not believe in that action separate and alone. It was usual among ancient Israel for the Lord to speak, presenting his laws, ordinances, and commandments to the people, then they were presented to the people, and then all the people said "Amen." Then it was the voice of God and the voice of the people; or, in other words, the voice of the people assenting to the voice of God.

2. In relation to the duties devolving upon the Twelve, in consequence of the changes that have recently taken place, I can say, in behalf of myself and my brethren, that their full weight and responsibility are felt by us. Unless we had the sanction of the people we would be unwilling to assume them, and, were it not that these things are plainly laid down in the law of God, we would not have accepted the situation that we find ourselves placed in today. We feel now that unless God is with us we can accomplish nothing that can in anywise be for the welfare of Zion, or the building up of his kingdom on the earth. Those are my feelings, and those are the feelings of my brethren. It is not with us as viewed by the world generally, that there is something so very honorable in office, for we have learned that in order that any office in the government of the Church and kingdom might be made honorable, the office itself must be honored, and that, too, by faithfully complying with the laws of God governing it. Then it is a high honor conferred upon man from the Lord, and the Twelve so appreciate it. Whilst they thank you for the confidence which you have manifested in them, at the same time they feel to

rely upon God, and to ask that you will remember them before the throne of our heavenly Father in your prayers and daily supplications, that we may be guided by that wisdom and intelligence that flows from above, for without the aid, guidance, and direction of the Almighty, we can do nothing acceptably to him.

3. I have said very little, very little indeed, since the death of our esteemed President, Brigham Young. I have had various reasons for that. One is, my heart has felt sorrowful and pained, for we have lost a man who stood prominent in Israel for the last thirty-three years, yes, for upwards of forty or forty-five years. He is taken away, and all Israel felt to mourn the event. This is one reason why I have been so silent. Another is, a great many questions have had to be decided, arrangements made and investigations had, in regard to the proper course to pursue pertaining to these very important matters. Still another reason is, I did not wish to put myself forward, nor have I, as the Twelve here can bear me witness. [The Twelve unanimously gave their assent.] I have not had any more hand in these affairs than any of the members of my Quorum; but I am happy to say that in all matters upon which we have deliberated, we have been of one heart and one mind.

4. When brothers Pratt and Smith returned from England, as you will have learned from their published letter, their sentiments were precisely the same as ours, and also the Counselors of President Young, whom we esteem and honor in their place, are also united with us. We are glad to have them with us, as our friends and associates, and Counselors to the Twelve. I pray that the blessing of God may rest upon them, and lead them in the paths of life, and that they with the Twelve may unite together as a grand phalanx, not in our own individual interests, but in the interests of the Church and kingdom of God, and

the building up of his Zion on the earth; for the Priesthood is not instituted for the purpose of personal aggrandizement or personal honor, but it is for the accomplishment of certain purposes of which the Lord is the Author and Designer, and in which the dead, the living and the unborn are interested.

5. We ought, brethren, all of us, to feel and act as though we were the servants of the living God, feeling in our hearts an honest desire to do his will and establish his purposes on the earth. If we can be united in our faith, our acts and labors, as we have been in our voting, as manifested at this Conference, the heavens will smile upon us, the angels of God will manifest themselves to us, the power of God will be in our midst, and Zion will arise and shine, and the glory of God rest upon her.

6. [By request, Elder Geo. Q. Cannon read from the Doctrine and Covenants the following extract from a communication entitled, A Prayer and Prophecies, written by Joseph, the Seer, while in Liberty Jail, Clay County, Missouri, March 20, 1839, commencing at the 34th paragraph:

7. "Behold, there are many called, but few are chosen. And why are they not chosen?

8. "Because their hearts are set so much upon the things of this world, and aspire to the honors of men, that they do not learn this one lesson—

9. "That the rights of the Priesthood are inseparably connected with the powers of heaven, and that the powers of heaven cannot be controlled nor handled only upon the principles of righteousness.

10. "That that may be conferred upon us, it is true; but when we undertake to cover our sins, or to gratify our pride, our vain ambi-

tion, or to exercise control, or dominion, or compulsion, upon the souls of the children of men, in any degree of unrighteousness, behold, the heavens withdraw themselves, the Spirit of the Lord is grieved; and when it is withdrawn, Amen to the Priesthood, or the authority of that man. Behold! ere he is aware, he is left unto himself, to kick against the pricks, to persecute the Saints, and to fight against God," etc.

11. I wanted to have this excellent instruction read over in your hearing, for it was true and profitable at the time it was written, and it is so today. If we possess the Spirit that flows from God, and that dwells in his bosom, we shall possess the spirit of kindness and love and affection, that will eventually bind us in the bonds of eternal union. It becomes us, as servants and handmaidens of God, to seek after these things, that we may be full of light and life, and the power and intelligence of God, and feel that we are indeed children of the Most High, that he is our Father, and that, with the ancient Prophets and Apostles, and the Gods of the eternal worlds, we will unite in accomplishing the work God designed from the commencement of the world. No man or set of men need think that the work will stop, for God has decreed that it shall go onward, and no power this side of hell can stop its progress. The Lord is with us, the great Jehovah is our shield and our buckler; the Lord is our Judge, the Lord is our King, the Lord is our Ruler, and he shall rule over us.

12. May God help us to be faithful in the observance of his laws, that we may secure to ourselves eternal lives in his kingdom, is my prayer in the name of Jesus. Amen.

ADDRESS 2

Discourse delivered by John Taylor, President of the Quorum of the Twelve Apostles, in the Sunday afternoon session of the 47th Semiannual General Conference of The Church of Jesus Christ of Latter-day Saints convened October 7, 1877, in the New Tabernacle, Salt Lake City.

1. There are one or two items I wish to present before you in relation to the Trusteeship. I have been appointed to that office, and I feel that I need some assistance in regard to the duties devolving upon me in that capacity. I am desirous to have the matter laid before this Conference. One thing I refer to is the auditing of the accounts of the Trustee-in-Trust. I therefore beg to present three names, as an auditing committee, for the sanction of this Conference—namely, Wilford Woodruff, Erastus Snow, and Joseph F. Smith. [On motion, they were unanimously sustained.]

2. There is another subject that I wish to present, one which pertains more particularly to my brethren of the Twelve. I suppose that most of you know that they have traveled and labored for a very long period, some of them for forty years and upwards, without purse or scrip, while almost everybody else has been paid for his services. It does seem proper to me that they should be placed, at least, on an equal footing with other people, particularly as their labors necessarily increase. In consequence of our present organizations, necessitating their frequent visits to our quarterly Conferences, in addition to other duties accumulating upon them, rendering it impossible for them to pay any attention to their own private affairs. My proposition, and I know it will meet with the hearty response of the brethren generally, is that they have a reasonable recompense for their services, and that the Trustee-in-Trust be authorized to arrange this matter. I would wish these same remarks to apply also to the Counselors of the Twelve. [The motion was put and unanimously sustained.]

3. As has been remarked, the condition we occupy today is a very important one. There has been a change of Presidency, and necessarily a change of administration. In the providence of God our Heavenly Father, he has seen fit to take from us our beloved President Brigham Young, who has so long labored in our midst. It is one of those occasions that cause reflection and thought, casting a degree of gloom among this whole people. We have felt sorry to lose his counsel, to be deprived of that wisdom and intelligence that have characterized him in all of his administrations. For they have been of such a nature as not only to interest the Latter-day Saints, but his name has become famous throughout the world. Brigham Young needs no factitious aid to perpetuate his memory; his labors have been exhibited during the last forty-five years in his preaching, in his writing, in his counsels, in the wisdom and intelligence he has displayed, in our exodus from Nauvoo; in the building of cities throughout the length and breadth of this Territory, in his opposition to vice and his protection of virtue, purity and right.

4. These things are well known and understood by the Latter-day Saints, and also by thousands and millions of others. But, as with his predecessor, Joseph Smith, who had to leave, while we are called upon to mourn a President dead, angels announce a President born in the eternal worlds; he has only gone to move in another state of existence. But then in speaking of these things we would not eulogize only the man, for Brigham Young, although so great a man could have done nothing towards developing the purposes of God unless aided and sustained by him. Joseph Smith could have done nothing, neither, as I have already said, can the Twelve Apostles accomplish anything unless they receive the same divine support. The work we are engaged in emanated from God, and what did Joseph Smith know about it until God revealed it? Nothing. What did President Young, or the Twelve, or anybody else, know about it before the heavenly messengers, even God himself, came to break the long, long silence of ages, revealing through his Son, Jesus Christ, and the holy angels, the everlasting Gospel? Nothing at all. We were all alike ignorant until heaven revealed it.

Then in the administration of these things the heavens are interested.

5. These my brethren before me, this Priesthood that assembled yesterday in their various quorums, all of them have assisted in this work, all have more or less been preaching and laboring in the interest of Zion, in the building up of this the kingdom of God upon the earth. So that it is not by any means an individual affair, as many totally ignorant of it suppose and say it is; it is not in the wisdom of this man or the intelligence of the other, but it is the wisdom and guidance of God, and by his sustaining hand, that this whole people are led forward, and that this kingdom has an existence upon the earth.

6. For my part, I would say today as Moses did on a certain occasion, when God said he would not go up with the children of Israel because they were rebellious people, "If thy presence go not with us, carry us not up hence;" or, in other words, I want nothing to do with so great an undertaking as the leading forth of this people without the Lord's assistance. I would say today, if God be not with us, if we are not sustained by the almighty power of Jehovah, if his guiding and protecting hand be not over us, I want nothing to do with it. But he is with us, and we know it.

7. The feeling that was manifested here yesterday, is most creditable to Israel, it is approved of by the Gods in the eternal worlds; and if we carry out in our practice and daily lives that union which we manifested in our voting, the Lord God will continue to pour upon us his blessing until we shall be united in all things, temporal and spiritual, which unity we have got to come to. When this is achieved, Zion will arise and shine, and then the glory of our God will rest upon her, then his power will be made manifest in our midst.

8. You heard this morning a good deal said, and that very correctly too, in relation to Priesthood and the organization thereof, and the position we occupy in relation to these matters. You voted yesterday that the Twelve should be Prophets, Seers, and Revelators. This may seem strange to some who do not comprehend these principles, but not to those who do. The same vote was proposed by Joseph Smith and voted for in the Temple in Kirtland, so long ago as that; consequently there is nothing new in this. And, as you heard this morning, this is embraced in the Apostleship, which has been given by the Almighty, and which embraces all the keys, powers and authorities ever conferred upon man. I do not wish to enter into the details of this matter; you will find them in the Book of Doctrine and Covenants, very clearly portrayed, and I refer you there for the evidences on these points.

9. You heard too that although the Priesthood held certain powers and privileges, the manifestations and powers thereof were only conferred according to the exigencies of the case and the necessities and requirements thereof. God has conferred upon us these blessings, but here are certain manifestations and powers that must come directly from him, and it is the duty of the Twelve to hunt up, search after, pray for and obtain them; and it is also the duty of these Presidents of Stakes, Bishops, High Priests, Seventies, and all men holding prominent positions, to seek after and comprehend God, whom to know is life everlasting.

10. We need, all of us, to humble ourselves before the Almighty, for we are before him, and all creation is, and hell and destruction are also without a covering before him. As mortal and immortal beings, as men holding the holy Priesthood that the Lord has conferred upon us for the establishment of his kingdom the building up of his Zion, the redemption of the living and the dead, it is of the utmost importance that we stand forth, everyone of us, and magnify our several callings; for with all our weakness, with all our infirmities, God has given unto us great treasures, which we hold in these earthen vessels.

11. As has been referred to, the President was operated upon to organize the Church throughout the Territory more completely; the Twelve were called upon to visit every part of the Territory and organize it, which they have done. There are now twenty different Stakes fully organized with their Presidents and Counselors, with their High Councils, with Bishops and their Counselors, who operate as common judges in Israel, and with High Priests, Seventies, Elders, and the lesser Priesthood, that they may administer in all things in their several Stakes under the direction of the Twelve. As was remarked this

morning, the Church never since the day of its organization was so perfectly organized as it is today. What has this been done for? Is it to place some men in positions of honor or emolument? No, but it is to organize the Church and Kingdom of God according to the pattern that exists in the heavens, that we may be prepared to comply in all things with the ordinances of God, for, as we are told, "In the ordinances, the power of godliness is manifest, and without the ordinances thereof, and the authority of the priesthood, the power of godliness is not manifest unto men in the flesh; for without this no man can see the face of God, even the Father, and live."

12. It is expected that these Presidents of Stakes be full of the Holy Ghost and the power of God, that they feel and realize that they are the servants of Jehovah, engaged in his work, and that he will require at their hands an account of their stewardships. It is necessary also that the High Councils and the Bishops act in the same way, together with the High Priests, Seventies, Elders, and all those of the Aaronic Priesthood, and that all operate together in the fear of God, for his eye is over you, and he expects you to work righteousness and purge the Church from iniquity, and teach the people correct principles and lead them in the paths of life. This is what God requires at your hands.

13. Hence, while we are looking at these things and are engaged in these organizations, there are other things necessarily connected therewith. There has been a feeling working gradually upon the minds of the Saints that many could not comprehend, nor tell where it came from, and that is to build Temples. President Young, the Twelve and the people generally have felt drawn out in their feelings with an almost unaccountable desire for the accomplishment of this object; and why? Can you tell me the reason? It is very difficult sometimes to explain some of these matters to the human mind.

14. You heard this morning about Moses appearing in the Temple at Kirtland, committing to Joseph Smith the Keys of the Gathering Dispensation, over which Moses presided anciently, and over which he presides today. Unless those keys had been restored and you had partaken of that influence and spirit, would you have been here today? No, you would not. When the Gospel went forth among the people, after the appearing of Moses in the Temple, and the committing of the Keys of the Gathering, when you Latter-day Saints received the Gospel of baptism for remission of sins and the laying on of hands for the reception of the Holy Ghost, you also received the spirit of the gathering. You Elders before me today might have preached until your tongues had cleaved to the roof of your mouth, but if the Spirit of God had not accompanied your administration in this regard, you could have accomplished nothing of any worth.

15. At the time this messenger came, there appeared another, even Elijah, whose mission was to turn the heart of the fathers to the children, and the heart of the children to their fathers, lest (says the Lord) I come and smite the earth with a curse. He committed these keys. But before they were committed, what was done in the Temple? Did we baptize for the dead there? No, we did not. Why? Because the keys were not given. When they were given and afterwards when the Temple was built in Nauvoo, then that spirit accompanied it, and we began to feel after our fathers behind the veil, and they likewise began to feel after their children. Brother Woodruff, who has been ministering in the St. George Temple, could relate to you if he had the time, many things of great importance, associated with these matters.

16. Suffice it to say that the purposes of God pertaining to the human family, which he had in his mind before this world rolled into existence, or the morning stars sang together for joy, all have to be accomplished in the salvation of the living and in the redemption of the dead. These things you are acquainted with: it is not necessary for me to talk much upon these subjects. But I merely wish to refer to the spirit and influence and power that have operated upon the Saints, and which are operating upon them throughout the length and breadth of this Territory. That comes from the Priesthood which existed before; it comes because the keys of that Priesthood have again been restored to man. What is the result? Why, a desire to build Temples. What for? That we may administer therein in those ordinances in which they and we are so greatly interested.

17. You heard through Brother Woodruff how many more administrations there had been for the dead than for the living. This is because Elijah has been here and has delivered the keys that turn the hearts of the children to the fathers, and we are beginning to feel after them. Hence we are building a Temple here, one in Sanpete, another in Cache Valley, and we have one already built in St. George, all of which I think will be quite creditable buildings, which the Lord and holy angels will accept.

18. Do we devote our labor and our means? Yes, we do; and it is this spirit which rests upon us that is prompting us to do it, and it will not let us rest until these things are done. Why? Because the keys of the Priesthood have brought us in connection with the Priesthood in the heavens, of which we are a part, belonging to the Church of the First Born, whose names are written in heaven. They are interested in their children, whose children are our fathers. We have been called together for the purpose, among other things, of operating with them in this work; for they without us are not made perfect, as the Scripture tells us. Therefore it is necessary that we should be here, building Temples and ministering therein, that their seed and posterity may be hunted up and looked after. We without them cannot be made perfect, for we need the help and assistance and the power of God to sustain and guide and direct us in our labors and administrations.

19. This is the thing Prest. Young has been engaged in with all his might, mind and strength; this is the thing my brethren of the Twelve have been engaged in, and what we are engaged in today. This is the thing that all Israel ought to be engaged in, for we are living only for a short time here, and by and by we shall pass away, as our President has done but it will only be to associate with another Priesthood, or the same, if you please, in the eternal worlds, for the one is combined and united with the other.

20. The Priesthood that has lived before, and that which lives now are eternal, and administer in time and in eternity; and the principles which God has revealed to us draw aside the curtains of the eternal worlds, giving us a glimpse within the veil, where Christ, our Forerunner, has gone. We are gathered together, "one of a city and two of a family," as the Prophet said they should be. And he says, "I will bring you to Zion." What will he do with them when he has brought them there? "I will give them pastors after my own heart, which shall feed them with knowledge and understanding." Again, "Saviors shall come up on Mount Zion, to judge the Mount of Esau; and the kingdom shall be the Lord's." Some talk about empires and kingdoms being built up by man. This is the Lord's kingdom and not man's. The Lord is our God, he is our king and our lawgiver, and he shall rule over us; and we will seek for and obtain his help and power.

21. Saviors shall come up on Mount Zion, say the Scriptures. What is a Savior? One who saves another, is it not? How could any man save people if he knew not how, and how could he know except the Lord teach him?

22. The world often finds fault with us. There are no greater benefactors to the world in existence than the Latter-day Saints are. There are no persons who have done more for the benefit of mankind, according to their number, than this people have. President Young, who is dead, and a number of others who have passed away, as well as the Twelve and thousands of others who still tarry, have traveled the length and breadth of the earth, without purse or scrip, to preach the glad tidings of salvation which heaven revealed to them. Do you find anybody else that has done it, or that is doing it, outside of this Church? No, such a thing is unheard of. We have gone forth, as the Scriptures say, bearing precious seed, and have returned again rejoicing, bringing our sheaves with us. Is this anything to hurt anybody? Does it interfere in the least with the rights of any? No. Are there any in this city, who are not of us, that can show that their religious rights, privileges, or principles have been interfered with or infringed upon by the Latter-day Saints, or by the authorities of this Church? No, not one. If I knew of any that were in any way being interfered with, I would be the first to protect them. These are our feelings towards the world, and to those who say all manner of evil against us.

23. We have expended millions upon millions in gathering the poor to this land, by what is known as the Perpetual Emigration

Fund. We may ask why did this people in these valleys expend such large sums? Was it because they were sending for relatives and friends? No, but because they were of the family of Christ, the sons and daughters of God, and desired to come to Zion. We have sent as much as five hundred teams at a time to help out the poor. You have done it, and many of you have either sent your sons or gone yourselves, and you have carried provisions for them as well as bringing them here. I do not think there is very much harm in that.

24. And what then? When these same men who had received the message of truth in far off lands, and who had been gathered here, had been further instructed, we have sent them back again to the nations from whence they came, to proclaim to their kindred and friends, to their tongue and nation, what God had done for them. After fulfilling their missions they return again. What to do? To slumber and sleep away their time? No, but to continue their work in reclaiming the waste places, and to build Temples in the interest of humanity, as the friends of God and of the world.

25. There are, today, engaged working on our Temple, one hundred and fifty men. What for? That a place may be found that will be acceptable to God, and in which we may administer, in the name of the Lord, for our dead as well as for our living. We do not want to do this grudgingly, but with willing hearts, desiring to operate, with the Priesthood behind the veil, in building up and establishing the kingdom of God upon this earth. These men, after preaching and returning again, can then go into these Temples and minister in them as representatives of the nations form whence they came, and in the interest of these nations we are operating. Will God be pleased with this work? Yes, if we continue faithful in well doing. There are not less, I presume, than 500 men at work on the Temples now being erected in this Territory, and probably more than that. This seems foolish to the outside world; but we know in whom we have believed, and we know the work in which we are engaged—and who is injured by it? None.

26. Some of our brethren feel sometimes that these things draw heavily upon them. Of course they do; and God expects to try us, to see what we are made of, and see whether the right ring of metal is in us or not, and whether we are prepared to stand up to the rack and walk forth in the name of Israel's God. Is it the desire to oppress anybody? No, never, nothing of that kind.

27. In speaking on this, I would say to the Presidents of Stakes, and to the Bishops, see that there is no oppression of any kind, or anything approaching arbitrary measures, or anybody interfered with; let everything be done righteously, properly, and voluntarily. Instead of oppressing the poor, feed them. Instead of taking from the naked, clothe them. Be merciful to the widow and the fatherless and the orphan, and all who may be in distress; dry up their tears, and pour balm into their wounds, and be full of compassion, and kindness, and the love of God, and let it bubble and flow from you like a river of life. These are the feelings that ought to exist among the Saints; nothing like oppression or wrong of any kind should find place in our hearts.

28. Let me pass from this to another thing which was touched upon this morning, which is, but which I really wish was not, true. Many of these my brethren have sent out their teams, and have subscribed their means to send for the poor, bringing them to these valleys. According to the provisions of the Perpetual Emigration Fund, the people who are thus assisted are expected to repay the means advanced to them when they have earned it, so that others may be helped with the same money, and thus that the fund in its operations, as was desired, may be perpetual. I am told that there is upwards of a million dollars of indebtedness to this fund today. This is a sad reflection upon the gratitude of men thus assisted. I am afraid the heavens will not smile upon such proceedings, and that God will not sanction it. It is time we waked up and attended to these obligations and duties, and felt that there was somebody else in the world besides our own selves; and if we have been assisted that we will be at least honest enough to meet that amount, and others who need its assistance may find it through the proper channel.

29. We are engaged in this place in building a Tabernacle, in which we can meet during the Winter season. We do not call upon you

outside brethren to assist us in this undertaking, because it is local and belongs to this Stake. This is a matter that was designed by President Young before his death; and we have been desirous, as Brother Cannon said this morning, to carry out the views of our venerated President, as far as we can. We have commenced to build this house, we want to put it up without delay. In this, as in every other matter, we do not wish anybody to contribute his means or labor towards it, unless he feels free to do it; for there are plenty that will do it willingly, and it will be built; and we shall have a nice, comfortable place to worship in through the Winter, and it will serve the Priesthood for all necessary purposes, as well as the public. The building will be 116 x 64 feet inside, with gallery all around. It will be a little larger than was at first contemplated; and we have also departed a little from the original intention respecting the kind of building material. Instead of adobe, we have concluded to use rock. I now invite the people of this Stake and the masons especially to come forward and exert their energies, and let us do the work. It will be done by voluntary donations and by utilizing labor tithing. Some people may say, "Why do it by voluntary donations?" "Why not use the tithing for all such purposes?" "Is not that sufficient?" Yes, if all of you strictly paid it, but then you do not all do this, and consequently we have to resort to other means. But, as I have before said, in this and everything else, we do not wish to press the people, nor place any in unpleasant positions; but as we sometimes sing, it's "all free grace and all free will."

30. I wish to make a few remarks in relation to what we term the United Order. We are united today with God, and with the holy Priesthood that existed before us, with Jesus the Mediator of the New Covenant, and with the ancient Prophets and Apostles and men of God, in building up the Zion of God upon the earth. They, in their different spheres and callings, are operating with us, and we with them, and the whole thing is a grand Cooperative Society; and everything we do here should be with the view of uniting our earthly interests, that we may be one in things temporal and one in things spiritual, one on the earth and one with those in the heavens, helping with our united efforts to roll on the Kingdom of God according to his purposes, and not according to our erratic notions.

31. In speaking of these things I would address a few words to our sisters of the Relief and of the Mutual Improvement Societies. You are performing a good work in Zion. I am pleased with the paper you publish, and have been very much interested in the reports you have made, in witnessing the energy and zeal you display in endeavoring to introduce home-manufactured goods and articles of different kinds, in looking after the poor and necessitous, and in trying to elevate the community generally. To our Young Men's Mutual Improvement Societies I say, God bless you, and all who are operating in the interest of Zion, forever.

32. Now let me say to parents, let us see that our youth are properly cared for and taught, and that honesty, truthfulness, virtue and good morals are inculcated, that they may grow in the faith of the Gospel and in the fear of God, to be useful in their day, to carry on the great work in which we are engaged. We already perceive a great improvement among our young men in their administrations; they are stepping forth, manifesting an excellent spirit, and many of them promise to become mighty men in Israel, who will roll forth the work when we get through. I will say to the Presidents of Stakes, encourage and foster these institutions; and to all the people I would say, love God and fear him and keep his commandments. Be honest with yourselves, honest before God. Be virtuous, be truthful and full of integrity, and fear the Lord your God in your hearts, and his blessing will be with you, and his Spirit will attend you, and your generations after you, worlds without end. Amen.

ADDRESS 3

Discourse delivered by John Taylor, President of the Quorum of the Twelve Apostles, in the Sunday afternoon session of the 48th Annual General Conference of The Church of Jesus Christ of Latter-day Saints convened April 7, 1878, in Salt Lake City. Some discrepancy exists as to whether this address was given on the 7th or the 8th of April with the *Deseret News* noting the 8th and the *Journal of Discourses* sighting the 7th.

1. I shall feel very much obliged, while I attempt to address you; if you will keep as quiet as possible; because it is quite a labor to speak to so large a congregation, and unless quiet and order is preserved, it is impossible for all the people to hear.

2. I have been very much interested and edified in listening to the remarks made by the brethren since we have assembled together in this Conference. And I have been very much pleased in witnessing the union and general feeling of interest manifested among the people to attend these meetings. It is evidence to me that the people feel interested in these great and eternal principles developed through our holy religion, and that they have a desire to yield obedience to the law of God and to keep his commandments. And in that alone is our safety, our happiness, our posterity, and our exaltation, as a people; for we derive every blessing we enjoy, whether of a temporal or of a spiritual nature from our Heavenly Father; and without him we can do or perform no good work, for in him "we live and move and have our being," and from him, and through him we receive all blessings pertaining to this life, and we shall hereafter, if we possess eternal lives, inherit them and obtain them through the goodness, mercy and long-suffering of God our Eternal Father, through the merits and redemption of Jesus Christ our Savior.

3. It is not in man to direct, to manage and control affairs of the Kingdom of God. No man ever did possess that power, nor will he, unaided by the power of the Almighty. All nations and all peoples are more or less under his direction and control, although many of them do not know it. He raises up one nation, and puts down another, he debases the proud and exalts the humble at his pleasure, and he pursues that course among all the peoples and nations of the earth, as seemeth best unto him;

and all nations and all peoples are his offspring and he is the God and Father of the spirits of all flesh, and feels an interest in the welfare of all the human family. He has been in the ages that are past, and he is in the present age doing all that he can to promote the happiness and well-being of the human family. This does not always appear to men of superficial minds, the dealings of God with man are not always comprehended. But he nevertheless does control the destinies of all peoples; and if in many instances it does not seem for their present benefit, yet as mankind are eternal beings, having to do with eternity as well as time, when the secrets of all hearts shall be developed and the actions of gods shall be made known and fully comprehended in the future destinies of the races of men, it will be found that the Judge of all the earth has done right.

4. The Lord has in these last days, for his own special purpose, and also in the interest of humanity, revealed himself from the heavens, made manifest his will to man, sent his holy angels to communicate and reveal unto us his children certain principles as they exist in the bosom of God, and he has pointed out the way whereby we may secure our happiness and an eternal exaltation in the celestial kingdom of God. He has been pleased to restore again the everlasting Gospel in all its fullness, with all its riches, and blessings, and power, and glory. He has organized his Church and Kingdom upon the earth; he has chosen men as he did in former times to be the bearers of his message of life and salvation to the nations of the earth. He has, through these instruments, instructed us, and gathered us together, as we are found here today, from the different nations where the Gospel reached us. He has brought us here according to certain eternal principles which he had in his mind before the world was, and

according to certain councils that existed in the heavens among the gods, who have been operating upon and with the human family from the commencement to the present, and will until the winding up scene.

5. The work that we are engaged in is not the work of man, it did not originate with man, it was not found out by him. It is the work that has been prophesied of by all the holy prophets that have lived on this continent, on the continent of Asia, and in the various portions of the earth. As the Apostle Paul describes it, it is "the dispensation of the fullness of times spoken of by all the holy prophets since the world was." And anything that we may have received—any light, any intelligence, any knowledge of the things of God, have emanated and proceeded from him. He saw and comprehended the fitting time for this work to commence; he prepared the way by once more opening the heavens, by revealing himself and his Son Jesus, and by afterwards sending holy angels to communicate his will and his purposes and designs to the human family. It therefore did not originate with us, nor with any sect or party or people, for nobody, not even Joseph Smith, or Brigham Young, or any of the Twelve Apostles knew anything about the great principles that were stored up in the mind of God.

6. It was the mind and will and revelations of God, made known to the human family, in the first place to Joseph Smith, and through him to others. And when the Elders of this Church went forth to the nations of the earth, as bearers of the gospel message, if they had gone upon their own responsibility they could have accomplished nothing. But having been chosen and set apart of the Lord, they went forth as his messengers, without purse or scrip, trusting in Him. And he opened up their way and prepared their path, as he said beforehand that he would. "Behold," said he, "I send you forth to the nations of the earth, and my Spirit shall go with you, and my angels shall prepare the way for you." I send you forth not to be taught, but to teach, not to be instructed by the world of mankind or the intelligence of the world, but by the wisdom and intelligence and power and spirit which I shall give you, and it is through and by this influence that we have been gathered together.

7. And why are we gathered? These Elders could not have gathered you unless God had been with them; they could not have influenced you to come here unless the Spirit and power of their mission had been with them. But the Lord said in former years through his prophets, "I will take you one of a city, and two of a family, and I will bring you to Zion. And I will give you pastors according to mine heart, which shall feed you with knowledge and understanding." And through the operation and influence of the Spirit of the living God, manifested through the priesthood, God's ministers on the earth, you have been brought together as you are today.

8. But why should we be thus gathered together? That there may be a body of people found to whom God can communicate his will, that there might be a people who should be prepared to listen to the word and will and voice of God: that there might be a people gathered together from the different nations who, under the influence of that spirit should become saviors upon Mount Zion; that they might, under the inspiration of the Almighty, and through the power of the Holy Priesthood which they should receive, go forth to those nations and proclaim to the people the principles of life, that they might indeed become the saviors of men.

9. And if we could fully comprehend our position, we should see things very differently from what we now do. If we could comprehend our relationship to God, to each other, to his church upon the earth, and also the greatness and magnitude of the work in which we are engaged, and the responsibilities that devolve upon us as Elders in Israel, as Saints of the Most high God, we should see things in a very different light from what we now do. We are not here, as they say in the Church of England, to "follow the devices and desires of our own hearts;" we are not here to pursue our own individual interests and emoluments, we are not here merely to attend to our own secular affairs, but to learn the laws of life, and then teach the people the way of salvation. There was an old saying among ancient Israel: "Hear, O Israel, the Lord our God is one Lord, and thou shalt worship the Lord thy God with all thy heart, with all thy mind, with all thy soul, and with all thy strength, and him only shalt

thou worship." And Jesus, in after time, added a little more to this: "Thou shalt love thy neighbor as thyself." God is one, and they who dwell with him are one. Those who will inherit the celestial kingdom will be one when they get there; and we, as a people, ought to be one—one in faith, one in principle, one in practice, one in our interests, one in our associations with each other and in our families, one with God, one with the holy angels, one in time, and one in eternity.

10. To bring about a union of this kind, the principle of baptism has been introduced that we all might be baptized into one baptism, by the laying on of hands, and through the various orders of his Priesthood, we all partake of the same spirit; and being brought into union and communion with God, that we all might feel after God, that the tens of thousands, and hundreds of thousands might be brought into connection with the Almighty, whose prayers could ascend into the ears of the Lord of Sabbath.

11. And for the accomplishment of this purpose, he selected Joseph Smith to be the first Apostle in his Church: he was called "not by the will of man," nor by the power of man, nor by the intelligence of man, but by God who revealed himself unto this young man, as also the Savior, committing unto him a mission to perform to the inhabitants of this earth. He was endowed with power and authority which was given him for that purpose, that he might be the legitimate representative of God upon the earth. He also taught him how to organize his Church, and put him in communication with many of the ancient Prophets who have long since passed away, who also communicated with him, and revealed unto him further the plan and design of the Almighty in relation to this earth, and the salvation of all who would listen to the principles of truth.

12. The nations of the earth have their representatives, their ministers, their plenipotentiaries, empowered and sent forth by the recognized authority of the several nations. He was the representative of God, his credentials came from God, and his mission extended not to one nation only, but to all nations; and he was authorized to establish and organize what was termed the Church and Kingdom of God upon the earth. And every step that he took, every principle that he inculcated, and every doctrine that he taught, came from God by the revelations of God to him, and through him to the people. He selected others by revelation—Apostles, High Priests, Seventies, Bishops, Elders, Priests, Teachers and Deacons, also High Councils, and Bishops' Councils, and Patriarchs, and all the various authorities and organizations of this Church. Joseph Smith neither knew how to select men, whom to select, nor what their offices should be until it was communicated by the Lord.

13. And yet we find that these principles revealed to him, agree with those that existed in former ages whenever God had a Church or people on the earth. And hence the ushering in of the Gospel simply means the revelation of the will of God to man; it simply means the placing of mankind in communication with the Lord that he may not be governed by his own follies or notions or theories, but by the will and word of God. And the examples that you heard referred to here, of our Stakes, with their Presidencies, together with the Bishops and their Council, etc., is a part of the system of heaven, as it exists in the eternal worlds; and the Priesthood that we hold is the everlasting Priesthood, and it administers in time, and it will administer in eternity; and a knowledge of the works that we are now engaged in, in regard to the building of Temples and administering therein, all came from God, and are a part of the eternal system. Who knew about them until God revealed it? Nobody. Who knows how to administer acceptably in these Temple without revelation? Nobody but those to whom it has been communicated, it came from God. And our preaching to the living, and our administering for the dead are all of them parts and parcels of the same concern.

14. The fact is, we are in a state of probation; we have enlisted under the banner of the Almighty; we have dedicated ourselves to him for time and for eternity, and he expects it at our hands that we be true to the trust conferred upon us, that we be faithful to our obligations and fulfill them, that we honor our God, that we magnify our callings and Priesthood, and that we stand forth among the people and before the nations, as the representatives of God upon the earth. We have a similar view to that of the Apostle Paul, who said

when addressing himself to the Corinthians: "Ye are not your own, for ye are bought with a price; therefore glorify God in your body, and in your spirit, which are God's." We have enlisted in a work, have engaged in a warfare that will last while time shall be, and if we live our religion and keep his commandments, the principles that we are in possession of will bear us off triumphant over death, hell and the grave, and land us among the just, among the celestial host that dwell with our Father in heaven. We really have no time to attend to those trivial affairs, that some people seem to think ought to occupy so much of our time.

15. I wish now, while we are together to talk upon some general principles associated with the Priesthood which has been conferred upon us. It was said of ancient Israel, if they had kept the commandments, that he would have made out of them a kingdom of Priests. We are literally a kingdom of Priests today. Our business is not to follow our own will, our own desires and plans, but to seek to know and to do the will of God, to carry out these principles which he has revealed, and in this is our happiness and exaltation in time, and will be throughout the eternities that are to come.

16. We ought to be operating with God, and with the holy angels; we ought to be feeling after them, we ought to be operating with the ancient Priesthood that have lived before— the Patriarchs, the Prophets, the Apostles, and all those men of God who have lived and died in the faith who act with God our heavenly Father, and with Jesus the Mediator of the new covenant. We ought to be operating with them in establishing righteousness throughout the earth, not nominally, but really; we ought to be laboring in conjunction with them in saving the living, not to make it a hardship and a trouble and a toil; something that we can hardly endure to go through; but on the contrary, feeling it an honor to be associated with the interests of God and bearers of the message of life and salvation, and also seeking for wisdom, and intelligence, and power, and revelation from God to carry out his will and designs, and to accomplish his purposes upon the earth.

17. Will his purposes be accomplished? They will. Will the Gospel grow, spread and increase? I tell you, in the name of Israel's God, it will. Will the time come when every

fictitious thing will be removed, when light and truth shall prevail, and when the kingdoms of this world will become the kingdoms of our God and his Christ? I tell you it will, and God will hasten it in his time. And this priesthood and this people are to be the instruments, in the hands of God, in connection with the priesthood who have gone before, who are now operating in their sphere, as we are in ours. The Lord hath so ordained, says the Apostle, "that they, (referring to the dead) without us should not be made perfect;" neither can we without them be made perfect. There needs to be a welding and uniting together, that in all of our doings as God's servants and representatives, we may be influenced and directed from above, being united with the Gods in heaven we may become one in all things upon the earth, and afterwards one in the heavens. And says the Lord, "If ye are not one, ye are not mine."

18. Everything that tends to divide the people, as you heard this morning, proceeds from beneath, and those that are engaged in it are the emissaries of the devil; for as he is the father of lies, so he is the father of division, strife and discord. But union, peace, love, harmony, fellowship, brotherhood and everything honorable, noble and exalting, proceeds from God; these are the principles that we ought to seek after and to disseminate as far as we can everywhere and among all peoples. And then when we have done that work, turn our attention to the building of temples and minister in them for the dead, that we may operate with the fathers in the interest of their posterity, helping them to perform that for their posterity which they were not able to do.

19. And in regard to the world, what ought our feelings to be towards them? A feeling of generosity, a feeling of kindness, a feeling of sympathy, with our hearts full of charity, long-suffering and benevolence, as God our Father has, for he makes his sun to rise on the evil as well as the good; he sends his rain on the unjust as well as the just. And while we abjure the evils, the corruptions, the fraud and iniquity, the lasciviousness and the lyings and abominations that exist in the world, whenever we see an honorable principle, a desire to do right, whenever we see an opening to promote the happiness of any of these people, or to reclaim the wanderer, it is

our duty to do it, as saviors on Mount Zion.

20. Will they have trouble? Yes. Will there be tribulations? Yes. Will nation be arrayed against nation? Yes. Will thrones be cast down and empires destroyed? Yes. Will there be war, and carnage, and bloodshed? Yes. But these things are with the people and with God. It is not for us; we have a mission to perform, and that is to preach the Gospel and introduce correct principles, to unfold the laws of God as men are prepared to receive them, to build up his Zion upon the earth, and to prepare a people for the time when the bursting heavens will reveal the Son of God, "and when every creature on the earth and under the earth will be heard to say, blessing and glory, and honor, and power, and might, and majesty, and dominion be ascribed to him that sits upon the throne, and unto the Lamb forever."

21. Will this people grow and increase? Yes. And the time will come—it is not now, we are not prepared for it—when calamity and trouble and bloodshed, confusion and strife will spread among all the nations of the earth. The time will come, and is not far distant, when those who will not take up the sword to fight against their neighbors, will have to flee to Zion for safety. That was true some time ago, and it is nearer its fulfillment by a great many years than at the time it was first uttered.

22. What are we here for? To build up or aggrandize ourselves? No, but to build up the Church and kingdom of God upon the earth, and to spread the light of truth among the nations. That is our duty, and also to pray for the revelations of God, that the Spirit and power of God may rest upon us, that we may comprehend correct principles and understand the laws of life, to guide and guard and protect the ship Zion from among the rocks and shoals and troubles that will sooner or later overcome this nation, and other nations, and prepare ourselves for the events that are to come. We ought to be men of honor, of honesty, of integrity, having our eyes single to the glory of God. That is the duty of these Apostles, and not to act with a view for their own aggrandizement, and for the obtainment of filthy lucre, or anything else pertaining to this world. We brought nothing into this world, we can take nothing out. It is for us to operate for God and in the interests of his Church and kingdom.

23. And what of these other brethren, the High Priests? They have a mission to perform, and that is to make themselves acquainted with the laws, doctrines, ordinances and government of the Church of God upon the earth, that they may be prepared, when called upon, to fulfill the duties and responsibilities devolving upon them. I will here read part of a revelation which indicates the nature of these duties. "And again I give unto you, Don C. Smith, to be a President over a Quorum of High Priests, which ordinance is instituted for the purpose of qualifying those who shall be appointed standing Presidents over the different stakes scattered abroad." Hear it, O ye High Priests! This is the prominent duty devolving upon you. The position you occupy is a sort of a normal school, if you please, to prepare those who are in it and are taught in it, that when they shall be called to hold official places in the various stakes of Zion, they may be prepared to magnify them.

24. How was it when we were engaged organizing these stakes, were these brethren prepared? No, many of them were not by any means. One was engaged on his farm, another was tied up in his merchandising, another had bought five yoke of oxen and had to prove them, and another had married a wife and he could not come. And we, therefore, had to go outside of the High Priests, whose legitimate business it was to occupy these positions, and call other men and ordain them High Priests, and set them apart to preside in these stakes, as Presidents and Bishops and Councilors, having to take them from among the Seventies' and Elder's Quorums, because the High Priests were not prepared to magnify their legitimate calling; whereas, if they had been doing their duty, living their religion, and meeting together in prayer, and examining the doctrine of Christ, instead of being engaged almost exclusively in many of these other matters, they would have been prepared to step forward and magnify their calling. There are many other stakes to be organized. Prepare yourselves, you High Priests, for the duties and responsibilities that may devolve upon you, that the Church of God may be strengthened in all its parts, and every man in his place, all prepared to magnify their calling.

25. Then, again, there are seventies; I think there are some seventy-six quorums of sev-

enties. Does their duty consist merely in making their own plans and calculations, such as to go on a farm and live there all their life time, attending to their own individual affairs, or pursue any other avocation without considering the obligations they are under by virtue of their Priesthood, and calling? I tell you nay. We have something else to do. I read in the revelation touching this matter, when the seventies were ordained, "they were to ordain more seventies until there should be seven times seventy, if the labor in the vineyard required it. "They were to do this if the labor in the vineyard required it." In whose vineyard? Their orchards and farms? I do not read it so. Does this refer to their merchandising? It does not so read. In looking after their own affairs or emoluments? That is not what I read; but for the labor of the vineyard. Whose vineyard, then? The vineyard of the Lord. But it seems that a great many of the Seventies have no more idea of going into the vineyard of the Lord, than if they held no such Priesthood or calling; they do not seem to comprehend their duties, nor their responsibilities.

26. Hear it, O ye Seventies! You are called and set apart by the Priesthood, to act under the direction of the Twelve, to go forth as His messengers to the nations of the earth. Do you believe it? This is your calling. Prepare yourselves for it. I do not want Elders coming to me, as some have been doing, after having been called upon missions saying, I pray thee have me excused. And I call upon the first President of the Seventies to instruct the various Presidents of Seventies, and they in turn the members of their several quorums, in regard to their duties; and to live themselves so that the spirit of the living God may rest down upon them, that they may indeed be qualified to teach their brethren what their duties are, that they may prepare themselves to magnify them. Instead, therefore, of every one seeking his own individual gain from his own quarter, let every man feel that he is a servant of the living God, a messenger to the nations of the earth, and that when the Lord calls upon him, through the proper authority, to do a certain work, he must obey, and that readily and willingly! These are the duties and responsibilities that devolve upon you, my brethren of the Seventies.

27. And it is the duty of the Elders also to magnify their callings; to feel after God and to seek instruction from Him, and to magnify their calling and Priesthood at home or abroad, being governed by the Holy Priesthood, in regard to their duties, that they may be acceptable to the Lord, and magnify their callings with all diligence and fidelity.

28. And then it is the duty of the Presidents of Stakes to look after the interest and welfare of their own people under their Presidency, not in a formal manner, but as interested in their welfare, having a lively desire to benefit and build them up, both spiritually and temporally, and perfect them in righteousness, purging out when necessary the ungodly, lifting up and exalting the poor, and blessing and benefiting everybody according to the principles of righteousness and truth, guarding their virtue and their honor, and see that men are honorable, that they regard their word of more value than their bond, that all people may rely on them; men who, in the language of the Prophet, will swerve to their own hurt and change not, and who will do that which is right and equitable before God. It is their duty, and the duty of the Bishops and also that of the High Priests and Seventies and Elders operating with them, to look after the poor and see that they are provided for. Do not let us have anybody crying for bread, or suffering for the want of employment. Let us furnish employment for all, divide up our farms and plan and devise liberally that all who need work, and want to be employed, may find labor. And I now call upon the Presidents of Stakes throughout Zion to give this matter their serious and earnest attention. We have land in abundance, water in abundance, and means in abundance; let us utilize them for the common wealth. Talk about financiering! Financier for the poor, for the working man, who requires labor and is willing to do it, and act in the interest of the community, for the welfare of Zion, and in the building up of the kingdom of God upon the earth. This is your calling; it is not to build up yourselves, but to build up the Church and kingdom of God; and see that there is no cause for complaining in all your villages and cities and neighborhoods. Let us take hold together for the accomplishment of this object, and pray God

to give us wisdom to carry it out, and he will pour upon us blessings that there will not be room enough to contain.

29. Again, we have what is called a Perpetual Emigration Fund. I wish to draw the attention, not only of the Presidents of Stakes but of the Bishops of the various wards, and of the whole people, to the responsibilities that devolve upon us in relation to this matter. We seem to be dwindling down in some of these matters, and I am sorry to say that there is a great lack of that integrity and interest that we would like to see manifested among our brethren. There are those here who have assisted with their means to the amount of upwards of a million dollars, which is unpaid by those who received the benefit of it. It was the calculation that this means should be used to bring those of our brethren to this land, who needed and were worthy of this assistance, and when you who were thus assisted were in distant lands praying and wishing to be gathered to Zion, this help came to you and you were brought here; and instead of paying this your honest debt, you go to work and build up yourselves, without meeting your obligations, what is the result? Those of your brethren who still remain, who are just as worthy as you to be gathered to Zion, are left to cry for assistance. I am daily in receipt of letters from different parts of the earth, asking to be thus assisted pleading: "we want to gather with the Saints, can't you help us?" Yes, we can if you who owe the Fund will pay your honest debts, we can then meet all these requirements. And I call upon the Presidents of Stakes and upon the Bishops to look after these things, and see that these obligations are met, that the poor from abroad may not cry in vain; but that we may help them, and then they return the amount advanced to them to assist others, and thus keep the work rolling in the same direction. And if this duty is not performed, how can we expect the blessing of God to rest upon us?

30. We are engaged quite extensively in the erection of Temples. We are building one here, and also one in Cache Valley, and another in Sanpete, and if we had time, and it was considered advisable, we could read the report read setting forth the receipts and disbursements of these places; and I presume we shall, before the Conference adjourns. Suffice it to say, with all our backwardness in some other things, there are a great many of the Latter-day Saints who are doing all they can in every laudable enterprise. I presume at the present time there is not less than 500 men engaged in rearing the walls of these Temples. And men are taking hold of it with energy, doing all they can in many instances, but not in all by a great deal.

31. Then in regard to our Tithing operations, Bishop Hunter informs me that many of the people are very negligent in regard to this matter. Now, I would say in behalf of the people, that perhaps there may be a partial excuse for some of these things. We have had a very stringent time for a number of years past, a financial crisis has prevailed in the eastern States for some years now, and almost every paper reports the failure of mercantile and business institutions—of the failure of one firm after another; and we have been subject, more or less, to these depressions. The fact also must be considered that great exertions have been made in the building of the St. George Temple, and also the three Temples now under way, which have already exhausted considerable means furnished chiefly by the people residing in those Temple districts. I must give the people credit for their zeal and energy in this direction, which we must all acknowledge is very commendable and praiseworthy. And, perhaps, in the performance of this labor many have done the best they could, and possibly circumstances have so overruled that they find themselves hardly able to meet their Tithing, for as a rule it is those who take delight in observing the law of Tithing that subscribe to these other calls.

32. We do not wish to crowd or press upon the people; but rather let us take things easily and deliberately, seeking always to break off the yoke of him that is bound, letting the oppressor go free. And let our sympathies be extended towards the widow and the orphan; and while we are building Temples, paying our Tithes and offerings, and doing the best we can before God and man, we will let that go for the present, and when we get into more favorable circumstances we will do better. At any rate, we will keep doing with a long pull and a strong pull, and a pull altogether, as one

in the interests of all Israel. But we must not forget our duties to the Lord.

33. I would say in this connection that there are three of the Twelve appointed to superintend the erection of these edifices in these outside districts, and then there are those residing here attending to home affairs. And we are seeking to act in concert and do the very best we can. Some people have an idea that these Temples ought to be built from the proceeds of the Tithing; I do not object to it in the least, providing you will only pay your Tithing. But we cannot build Temples with something that exists only in name. You deal honestly with the Lord, handing over in due season that which belongs to his storehouse, and then we will show you whether we can not build Temples, as well as do everything else that may be required with it. In the mean time, we have got to do the best we can in these matters; and as we are personally interested in these things, as well as our brethren, the departed dead who have gone before us, and who depend upon this being done, we feel a strong desire to carry out these projects; and this feeling, I am happy to say, exists throughout all Israel.

34. We want also to be alive in the cause of education. We are commanded of the Lord to obtain knowledge, both by study and by faith, seeking it out of the best books. And it becomes us to teach our children, and afford them instruction in every branch of education calculated to promote their welfare, leaving those false acquirements which tend to infidelity, and to lead away the mind and affection from the things of God. We want to compile the intelligence and literacy of this people in book-form, as well as in teaching and preaching; adopting all the good and useful books we can obtain; and what we need and cannot obtain, make them. And instead of doing as many of the world do, take the works of God, to try to prove that there is no God; we want to prove by God's works that he does exist, that he lives and rules and holds us, as it were, in the hollow of his hand. For it is very unfair for man to take the works of God to try to prove that there is no God. But then it is only the fool that has said in his heart, there is no God. I would like to talk upon this subject if time would permit.

35. I am pleased to see the exertions made by the young men's and young women's mutual improvement associations, to benefit and bless the rising generation of our people. And I am also pleased to witness the degree of intelligence and studiousness manifested by our young people; it is creditable and praiseworthy. We want to lead them on and encourage them in the study of correct principles, so that when the responsibility of bearing off the Church and Kingdom of God shall pass from us to them, they may be prepared for it, and carry on the work to a glorious and triumphant consummation. And that we may stand in regard to education and literacy, the sciences, the arts and intelligence of every kind, as high above the nations of the earth, as we do today in regard to religious matters.

36. And before closing I would refer briefly to the ladies' Relief Society. We are told that, "the man is not without the woman, nor the woman without the man in the Lord." She is spoken of as a helpmeet to her husband. I remember the organization of the first Relief Society in Nauvoo, by the Prophet Joseph Smith; today we find them spreading all over the land, and the benefits of their labors are widely realized. Our sisters are doing a noble and commendable work in writing and publishing, in visiting the sick and needy, and ministering to their wants, and showing kindness and benevolence towards the suffering and distressed, and also advocating principles that are honorable and praiseworthy before God and man, calculated to elevate and bless their sex. And I say to the sisters, God bless you in your labors of love, and in your enterprise, continue to press forward in your good work, and the Lord will bless you and your posterity after you; for you are mothers in Israel who are raising up kings and priests unto the Most High God. See that your children are taught aright, and that they grow up in virtue and purity before the Lord. Teach them good principles, never mind so much about the fashions; but let economy, industry, charity, kindness and virtue be early impressed upon their minds, and try to love your sons and daughters, and to lead them in the paths of life.

37. I should like to speak of our Sunday Schools and other institutions, but time will not permit. I have talked long enough. God bless you, in the name of Jesus. Amen.

ADDRESS 4

Discourse delivered by John Taylor, President of the Quorum of the Twelve Apostles, at the 49th Annual General Conference of The Church of Jesus Christ of Latter-day Saints convened April 8, 1879, in the new Tabernacle, Salt Lake City.

1. I will state that I feel very much obliged to my brethren for the generous feeling manifested to myself. Permit me, however, to say, with regard to some of these ideas presented to the Conference by Brother George Q. and which he has said, he has frequently presented to me and others of the Twelve, that while I duly appreciate the feelings and views of my brethren, and am not ignorant of the proprieties of life, individually I would not wish to change my position. Personally I care nothing about the outside show, the glitter and appearance of men; but I do care about the great eternal principles associated with the Church and Kingdom of God upon the earth. And as has been stated, it was some time before I could make up my mind to accept a proposition of this kind. And I accept it now simply in the capacity of your servant for Christ's sake for the benefit of the Kingdom of God and that all things may be conducted in a proper manner.

2. Now we will let this pass, and talk about something else.

3. I have been very much interested in the remarks that have been made at this Conference. It is now forty-nine years since the Church of Jesus Christ of Latter-day Saints was organized. There were then, as you heard stated and as we very well know, six members organized. There were however, more than six persons in the Church, as was remarked by Brother Snow, the organization being effected for the purpose of legal recognition, still there were only a very few, and as the spirit of revelation rested down upon God's servant Joseph in these early days, who like Adam, Moses, Abraham, Jesus, Jared, Nephi, Moroni and others, had the heavens unfolded to his view, and although the Church was so few in number the principles and purposes of God were developed fully to the vision of his mind, and he gazed upon the things that are to transpire in the latter-days associated with the dispensation that he was called upon by the Almighty to introduce.

4. He learned by communication from the heavens, from time to time, of the great events that should transpire in the latter days. He understood things that were past and comprehended the various dispensations and designs of those dispensations. He not only had the principles developed, but he was conversant with the parties who officiated as the leading men of those dispensations, and from a number of them he received authority and keys and priesthood and power for the carrying out of the great purposes of the Lord in the last days, who were sent and commissioned specially by the Almighty to confer upon him those keys and this authority, and hence he introduced what was spoken of by all the prophets since the world was; the dispensation in which we live, which differs from all other dispensations in that it is the dispensation of the fullness of times, embracing all other dispensations, all other powers, all other keys and all other privileges and immunities that ever existed upon the face of the earth.

5. At that time he was a feeble youth, inexperienced, without a knowledge of the learning of the day. But God put him in possession of that kind of intelligence, and what may be termed as scientific knowledge of all things pertaining to this earth, and the heavens, if you please, which was altogether ahead of all the intelligence that existed in the world. He commenced as opportunity presented by following the education he had received from the Almighty, by teaching the principles of life and salvation, the principles of the everlasting Gospel, by conferring upon others that priesthood which had been conferred upon him, and by organizing a state of things that was after the pattern of the heavens, that was calculated to live and grow and increase, that had the principle of

life and vitality within itself, and that was calculated to draw together the honest in heart and assimilate them in their ideas and views and feelings and faith, and empower them to operate with him and with the Lord and with the holy priesthood that had existed in former ages.

6. And thus he commenced to organize the Church with all its various offices under the direct inspiration, guidance and revelation of the Lord. The First Presidency was pointed out, the Twelve were also pointed out and designated, and these quorums were ordained. The high priesthood was organized, however, before these other quorums took shape. Then there were the quorums of Seventies, then the quorums of Elders, then the Bishops, then the quorums of Priests, Teachers and Deacons, together with the High Councils and all that we know about these things. He taught us all that we know about them; God taught him. Hence in the various organizations of the several quorums of priesthood whether it relates to the Melchizedek, Aaronic or Levitical priesthood, all of these, together with the duties devolving upon each, were given by the Lord. And hence the church that we are associated with is called the Church of Jesus Christ of Latter-day Saints.

7. Hence Jesus Christ is the medium through whom we are to approach the Father, calling upon him in the name of Jesus; for there is no name given under heaven, nor known among men, whereby we can be saved, but the name of Jesus Christ. And although they do not do it now, yet the time is approaching when to him "every knee will bow and every tongue confess that he is the Christ, to the glory of God the Father." And hence the religion we profess is one that has been given us from the heavens. We cannot dispense with it; we cannot dispense with any part of it. It is not of man, but from the Lord God, our Heavenly Father, through our Lord Jesus Christ, making use of his servant Joseph and those whom he should call by revelation as the instruments to carry out the purposes of God upon the earth.

8. The priesthood we have received we received not of man nor by man, but by revelation. And latterly President Young, a little before his death, organized all the various branches of the Church into Stakes, with the officers thereof, carrying out the design of God and his revelations to Joseph Smith; and placed them upon the foundation that was first laid by Joseph Smith under the immediate revelations of the Lord.

9. And God expects it at our hands that we magnify our calling, and that we cleave unto him as his servants upon whom he has conferred this priesthood. He expects it at our hands that we shall magnify it, and not operate according to our peculiar notions, but according to the will and law and guidance and revelations of God in all things and under all circumstances; for we are here as Jesus was here—not to do our own will, but the will of our Heavenly Father who has sent us, and who has called us to this high calling, and has made us to sit together in heavenly places in Christ Jesus.

10. In accordance with the order of God, the Twelve, the Seventies, the High Priests and Elders have been abroad among the nations of the earth, delivering the testimony which God gave to them, and the Spirit and power of God has operated with us in our ministrations; and the results of these operations and these labors, and the faith and the self-abnegation and self-denial and the desire to do the will of God, and the testimonies that have been borne, are manifested in the Saints gathered today as we are in the valleys of the mountains. These things have been brought about by the interposition of the Almighty; we are, as such dependent upon him today, and as we ever were in all the days of our lives, for guidance, for support, for revelation, for the Spirit of God to guide us that we may not make any false steps; but as a people we must magnify the Lord our God in our hearts and honor him and observe his laws and keep his commandments.

11. There has quite a change taken place since this Gospel was introduced, as the thousands of people who inhabit these valleys sufficiently attest. And if we continue to progress in faith, in union, in intelligence, in virtue, in purity, in knowledge, and especially in the knowledge of God and in the observance of his ordinances, the work of the Lord will continue to roll with tenfold rapidity. We are just commencing our labors, and are just getting ready to perform the work that God has laid

upon our shoulders, and are just commencing to perform the work that God intends us to accomplish; everything that has been prophesied by all the ancient prophets, as contained in the Bible and the Book of Mormon, and those things predicted by Joseph Smith, and every other prophet of God, will as surely be fulfilled as we are here today, without any faltering, or flagging, or hesitation.

12. We go on and attend to many things. Our organizations are very good; but we need, I think sometimes, the breath of life from God breathing into them all through, that the Spirit and power of the Most High may be in our midst, and that the power and blessings of God that come through the ordinances may be in our midst, and that the power and blessings of God, that come through the ordinances may be imparted to us; and such will be the case if we are faithful in the performance of the duties devolving upon us. It is not with us a question of what we shall eat, or what we shall drink, or what kind of houses we shall live in; it is not a matter of so much importance as it is to be doing the will of God, to have our hearts engaged in his service, to feel that we are building up the Zion of the Lord of Hosts, to feel that we are recognized of the heavens, to feel that we are associated with the priesthood behind the veil who have lived and operated in time and are now operating in eternity; for they without us cannot be made perfect, neither can we without them be made perfect. We need their assistance from the heavens, and we ought to seek it all the time.

13. Let me speak of this not only to the Twelve, but to the presidents of Stakes and their counselors, and to all men holding authority, to seek to God, seek for wisdom, seek for faith, and learn to approach God, that we may draw down blessings from heaven and partake of that faith which was once delivered to the Saints. We are trying to do some things and are doing them pretty well. Do I wish to find fault? No. Or to censure anybody? No. But I wish everybody would so live and act that they would not censure themselves, that their minds would not condemn them; for if your own hearts condemn you, God is greater then your hearts.

14. We are doing pretty well. We are building our Temples, and there is a laudable spirit manifested in relation to these things generally. Do all do it? No. Have all this spirit? No. I wish they had; but then we would be expecting too much perhaps. But there is a growing interest in these things, which I am glad to give the Saints credit for. And in speaking of our Temples, I suppose there are no less than 500 men engaged today in building Temples in this Territory. Some people would consider this quite a tax upon them, and, I may say, we have some who call themselves Latter-day Saints who have a little of this feeling, not much, but a little of it. But men who feel right, they feel that they and all they have belong to the Lord; they feel that they are on hand to perform the work of God, to build up his kingdom, to operate with him and with the holy priesthood, and to prepare Temples to administer for the living and for the dead; that we may indeed be not poor and helpless dolts; but feel that we are saviors upon Mount Zion, and that the kingdom is the Lord's.

15. There is a good feeling manifested among the brethren and also among the sisters, who are quite as zealous in most interests as the brethren are. Notwithstanding the immense labors we are performing in our building, for we are doing a good deal, we are not unmindful of other matters. There is constant labor going on in the Temple at St. George, with very little intermission, and a corps of persons steadily engaged administering in the ordinances of the Lord's House there; while in these other places, as you have heard read over, according to the financial accounts pertaining to the Temple being built in Manti and Logan—there has been expended in a short time on these two Temples nearly two hundred and fifty thousand dollars. The brethren have taken hold of it with a will, and there seems to be a feeling among many of them to see who shall do the most, instead of who can do the least. And notwithstanding this there is about fifty thousand, I think, in round numbers, more tithing paid this last year than there was before these things commenced. I speak this for the credit of the Latter-day Saints. Honor, as the Scriptures say, to whom honor is due. And I am pleased to see a spirit of that kind grow and increase among the brethren.

16. There has been a good deal of care bestowed on the sending forth of missionaries whom we have sent forth among the different nations abroad and to this nation. There is a duty devolving upon the Twelve and the Seventies especially, to see that this work is performed; and we have been alive to this matter, and have aimed to call men that would not be embarrassed or perplexed in their minds, but such as would go forth as the servants of the Living God, who would not, when they got about two hundred miles from home, commence to think when it would be time for them to return; and the fruits are fast beginning to be borne in the European, the Scandinavian and other missions, and also in the United States.

17. And we wish it to be understood among the Elders and Seventies that we do not want men to go on missions who look upon it as a painful duty for them to fulfill; we would rather such men stay at home. But he that hath a desire to preach the Gospel to the world, whose life is upright, pure and virtuous, and who is capable of presenting the principles of the Gospel to the world; he is the kind of man we are desirous to send. We do not want anybody to go simply because it might be thought that a mission would do him good, or that it might save him from some evil he might be likely to fall into. We do not want men to go abroad representing the Captain of our salvation to reform themselves; let the work of reformation be done at home. We want men to preach the Gospel who are honorable and upright men, and full of the Holy Ghost; and when such men go they go with our faith, carrying with them our esteem and love and affection; and if they need anything, we will give it to them.

18. If their families need anything, we will have them looked after, we will feed them and clothe them and take care of them, and consider that they are our brethren and not that they are poor, miserable paupers, or that their wives and families are a trouble to us; we want to do away with all such feelings. Let us cultivate the spirit of magnanimity and kindness, and as the Lord blesses us, let us bless others; and that is all the things of the earth are worth. Do good to all men, especially to the household of faith. And by and by, as was the case formerly, those who go forth weeping, bearing precious seed, will return rejoicing, bringing their sheaves with them.

19. Furthermore, we have an auxiliary among our sisters here. Brother Geo. Q. Cannon represented how they were imposed on in many lands and how they had been. Why should they be? Are they not our mothers? Are they not our wives? Are they not our sisters? Are they not our children? Should we not protect them? Do we profess to be in the image of God, holding the holy priesthood of God, and then would we treat the fair daughters of Zion with contempt, or permit them to be injured or imposed upon in any way? God forbid. They are flesh of our flesh, bone of our bone; they are our helpmeets, and our associations and our relations with them ought to be pleasant and agreeable and with all long suffering and fidelity. And then the sisters should turn round and help to bless one another, and act as our teachers are doing in other respects— teaching their sisters, looking after the poor and assisting the bishops in the performance of their labors. And the Relief Societies which have been organized have been of very great benefit to the Saints of God.

20. And I say, God bless the sisters, and inspire them with more of that heavenly spirit, that they may assist their husbands and their brethren and their children—their sons and their daughters—to promote correct principles, to stem the tide of iniquity, and to promulgate virtue, truth and purity among the Saints of God. And I would say, it is the duty of the bishops and presidents of Stakes to assist them all they can, which I believe they generally do, to carry out everything that is good and praiseworthy.

21. There is another class of people among us doing a great deal of good; that is our Mutual Improvement Associations; both Young Men's and Young Women's. How much more pleasant it is to see our youth grow up in the fear of God, trying to instruct one another in the principles of life and salvation, than to see them ignore the laws of God. How pleasing to us! How pleasing to God and the holy angels! Let us encourage these things and instruct our sons and daughters, that they may grow up in intelligence, virtue, purity and holiness before the Lord.

22. And then we want to study also the principles of education, and to get the very best teachers we can to teach our children; see that they are men and women who fear God and keep his commandments. We do not want men or women to teach the children of the Latter-day Saints who are not Latter-day Saints themselves. Hear it, you Elders of Israel and you school-trustees! We want none of these things. Let others who fear not God take their course; but it is for us to train our children up in the fear of God. God will hold us responsible for this trust. Hear it, you Elders of Israel and you fathers and you mothers! Talking about education, as I said before, Joseph Smith knew more in regard to true educations than all the philosophers and scientists of the earth; and he knew it by the revelations of God. We want to get together to train our children up in the fear of God, to teach them correct principles ourselves, and place them in possession of such things as will lead them in the paths of life.

23. I find it is time for me to quit. I feel to thank you for your attendance at this Conference, and for the kind of spirit that has been manifested here; and to thank the members of our choir who have made for us sweet music; and I would say that our choir is a credit to our Territory and to our people. And furthermore they are meeting together for the purpose of cultivating the art of music, and that we may be organized and be more perfect in relation to these things.

24. I would like to have said something about our Sunday Schools. I do not believe we are behind any people on the face of the earth in relation to these matters. I am informed by the general Superintendent that we have 29,000 children attending Sunday Schools; and I would not be afraid to say that that is more than attend the Sunday Schools in all the Territories put together, outside of Utah. (A voice from the stand—"And in half the States.") Some one remarks, and in half of the States. I do not know how that is. But they do say our children are Utah's surest and best crop. Let us try to train them up in the fear of God, that we may have his blessing to be with us.

25. I would like to have said something, too, about our cooperative associations. I am pleased to inform you that the Cooperative Institution of this city is doing remarkably well; it is on a solid foundation and everything is moving along pleasantly and agreeably. We have organized for some time a Trade's Union, through which all the people of Utah can be represented. And while the Co-op calls upon us to sustain them, which is right and proper, we want the Co-op to sustain us. There are two sides to this question, hence we have an organization called a Board of Trade in a number of the Stakes, and expect to perfect them in all the Stakes, that the whole people may be represented at our general board. Then we expect to spread and grow in manufactures of all kinds, that we may become a self-sustaining people, a people who shall be independent, under God, of all other powers.

26. I will not detain you. God bless Israel, and all that bless Israel, and let our enemies be confounded. And God grant unto us power to serve him and observe his laws that we may have a claim upon his blessings, and at last obtain eternal life in his kingdom, in the name of Jesus. Amen.

ADDRESS 5

Discourse delivered by John Taylor, President of The Quorum of the Twelve Apostles, at the 49th Annual General Conference of The Church of Jesus Christ of Latter-day Saints convened April 9, 1879, in the new Tabernacle, Salt Lake City. Some discrepancy exists as to when this address was actually given. The *Journal of Discourses* gives the above date while the *Deseret News* gives the delivery date as October 8, 1878, six months earlier.

1. It has been very properly remarked that we are becoming a great people, and there are a great many interests of a temporal, as well as spiritual nature, that must necessarily be attended to—in fact it has been so contemplated from the beginning. We talk sometimes of earthly things: at other times we speak of heavenly things. Sometimes we speak of things pertaining to time, and at other times of things pertaining to eternity. We have to do with both or we could not have been here. And being here it is proper we should come to a right understanding in regard to the position we occupy; and especially that we should comprehend our duties relating to our temporal affairs and by acting truthfully, honorably and conscientiously avoid so much annoyance, trouble, litigation and difficulty that so frequently exists.

2. In relation to the Gospel of the Son of God, it gives us information pertaining to our existence and to our general relationship to God and to each other, pointing out our various duties and responsibilities. Associated with it is a priesthood which among other things is to promulgate the will of God to the ends of the earth; it has taught us principles pertaining to our future, both in relation to the living and the dead, relative to the present, past and future. We talk a great deal about our Gospel, about our spiritual affairs; we have our church organized according to certain principles associated therewith. We have a priesthood organization, embracing our Stake organization; we have organizations pertaining to spiritual things, if you may so call them, and also for temporal things, for we have to do both with time and with eternity, both with earthly and with heavenly things, and consequently it is necessary we should be interested in all.

3. When we reflect upon our position, there is something peculiar associated with it. At first the Elders of this Church were told to go forth and preach the Gospel to every creature; then they were instructed to gather together those who believed. According to the Scriptures, "I will take you one of a city, and two of a family, and I will bring you to Zion. And I will give you pastors according to mine heart, which shall feed you with knowledge and understanding."

4. We are gathered together; but being gathered together there is something more than spirituality associated with our existence. We brought our bodies with us when we came, and we necessarily have to eat and drink and to have houses to live in, etc.; in fact, we require the common necessaries of life just as much as any other people. And then, if we have children, as Bishop Hunter says, "there are none of them born with shoes and stockings;" but these things have to be provided.

5. Furthermore, being gathered together, we necessarily form a body politic, if you please, and we cannot help ourselves if we would; but we do not want to. We frame laws according to the usage of the nation we are associated with; for being here and finding ourselves in the territory of the United States, we necessarily have had to organize a government which has assumed a territorial form; and that means a legislature with its enactments and all the various adjuncts of a government. Laws have to be made, officers must be created to execute those laws; and we necessarily become an integral part of these United States, and have to perform all the political functions associated therewith.

6. These things naturally flow unto us, and they will continue to grow and increase, if it be true what the Scriptures say, and if it be true what many of our brethren have

preached to you since the assembling of this Conference. Then it becomes a matter for us to reflect upon that we understand our true position, how we can best sustain ourselves religiously, socially, politically and financially, and among other lessons learn to produce at home those articles we stand in need of.

7. We have been brought up in the world, and have imbibed many ideas in common with mankind generally pertaining to commerce, trade and manufactures. But we need the inspiration of the Almighty in all of the affairs of life; for we profess emphatically to be the people of God, and as it is with us in our religion so it ought to be with our politics, our trade and manufactures. They ought, in all things, to be subservient to one grand principle, and that is the acknowledgment of God and his laws.

8. Permit me here to state that before the revelations of God to man in these last days, there were no people that had a correct knowledge of God, that we have any knowledge of, anywhere upon the earth. All were without prophecy, without revelation, without a knowledge of the doctrine or ordinances of the Gospel.

9. And to whom are we indebted for a knowledge of these things? Certainly not to ourselves, and as assuredly not to any earthly body or system in existence. We are indebted alone to God for a knowledge of these things; through His revelations made first by himself and by his well beloved Son, and then by the ministering of holy angels, by communication from the heavens to the earth. We are indebted to him for all the light and intelligence we possess in relation to these things. What did we know about the first principles of the Gospel? Nothing. What did we know about the gathering, or about Zion, or about the ordinances of the Gospel or about the holy priesthood? Nothing at all. Nor did we know anything about the building of Temples, or about the mode of administering in them until directed by the Almighty; it was He who revealed the necessity of the construction of those sacred edifices and the mode of administering therein. What does the outside world know about these things? Nothing. And if they had our Temples they could not administer therein. We are indebted to God alone for the light and intelligence we have received.

10. Again in regard to political matters, where is there a nation today, under the face of the whole heavens that is under the guidance and direction of the Lord in the management of their public affairs? You cannot find one. It is true that the founders of this nation, as a preliminary step for the introduction of more correct principles and that liberty and the rights of man might be recognized, and that all men might become equal before the law of the land, had that great palladium of liberty, the Constitution of the United States, framed. This was the entering wedge for the introduction of a new era, and in it were introduced principles for the birth and organization of a new world.

11. The Prophet Joseph Smith said that "The Constitution of the United States was given by the inspiration of God." But good, virtuous and holy principles may be perverted by corrupt and wicked men. The Lord was opposed by Satan, Jesus had his Judas, and this nation abounds with traitors who ignore that sacred palladium of liberty and seek to trample it under foot. Joseph Smith said they would do so, and that when deserted by all, the elders of Israel would rally around its shattered fragments and save and preserve it inviolate.

12. But even this, good as it was, was not a perfect instrument; it was one of those stepping stones to a future development in the progress of a man to the intelligence and light, the power and union that God alone can impart to the human family. And while we acknowledge, as citizens of the United States, the laws and institutions thereof (which by the way are very easily complied with), we have a higher law, more noble principles, ideas that are more elevated and expansive; principles that reach to the whole human family, and which he will continue to reveal to us. Does that prevent us from obeying the laws of the land? Certainly not. But then, is that a perfect system? I do not think that many of you will say it is, nor do I think that the people of the United States of any political party will tell you it is. I do not wish to cast any reflections or refer to any events that have taken place; I am merely speaking on religious principles, and principles too in which we as Latter-day Saints are interested.

13. We are united, then, as a body politic, as an integral part of this Government, and it becomes our duty to submit to the laws and institutions of that Government—to all that are constitutional, framed and based upon correct principles, and not in violation of what the fathers of the country instituted.

14. But have we any higher aim than this? We have. Do any object? If so why should they? Do we in anywise interfere with any man's rights, Government, or make war upon any parties? No, but we are interested in the preservation of justice, equality and the rights of man in the development of peace, the further establishment of correct, more elevated, refined and exalted principles, in placing ourselves in a position more in accordance with things as they exist in the heavens, for the welfare and happiness of the human family. God has given unto us certain principles which we feel bound to observe. Is there anything wrong in this? I think not.

15. We have all kinds of institutions here in the United States and in other nations, such as Odd Fellows, Free Masons, and others; and they have a right to their ideas and manner of doing things as long as they observe the laws, and so have we, and have a right to be protected also in those rights. But to say we must stand still is a thing not connected with our creed. If others do not desire to accompany or keep pace with us, we must still go on under the guidance of the Lord. As was said of ancient Israel, "The Lord is our God, the Lord is our King, the Lord is our judge, and he shall rule over us," so we say. We need information and revelation in regard to out religious matters, we also need information, intelligence and revelation in regard to our political, social and all temporal matters.

16. If we humble ourselves and purify ourselves, and magnify our callings as the Elders of Israel, according to the Scriptures, we will yet teach the princes of this world wisdom and their kings knowledge and understanding; for these things that are spoken of will assuredly come to pass when "out of Zion shall go forth the law, and the word of the Lord from Jerusalem." The purposes of God shall yet be fulfilled in relation to these matters; God's work will most assuredly progress, until "the kingdoms of this world shall become the kingdoms of our God

and his Christ, and he will rule for ever and ever," not in war, not in confusion and strife and discussions, not in evil and corruption; but in the interests of humanity, according to the laws of life and in accordance with the intelligence that dwells in the bosoms of the Gods, and in the interests of a fallen world.

17. Now we come to other matters pertaining to our mercantile associations, I might talk further about our social relations, etc., however, these are subjects we hear a good deal about; we are pretty well informed in relation to them. The information we have pertaining to our associations with our wives, and wives with their husbands has been revealed to us by God, and we are striving to carry out those eternal principles,—principles that will exalt us, our progenitors and our posterity in the celestial kingdom, where we can enjoy the presence of God and that of the celestial hosts who have gone before.

18. We come again to our temporal interests. Has the world been our exemplar with regard to any of these things that I have mentioned? No, the Lord has been our teacher, He has been our guide and director; without him we could have accomplished nothing, for we knew no more naturally than anybody else did.

19. In relation to temporal things. Are we capable, as Latter-day Saints, of fulfilling our destiny on the earth, and procuring a full temporal salvation and sustaining ourselves, on temporal principles without the interposition of the Almighty? I tell you no, we are not, no more than we are in regard to any other things.

20. We read in the Scriptures of a time that is coming when there will be a howling among the merchants in Babylon, for men will not be found to buy their merchandise. This is in accordance with the prediction of John the Revelator. And the gold and the silver and the fine linen, etc., in Babylon will be of no avail. But before that time comes, we as a people must prepare for those events, that we may be able to live and sustain ourselves when in the midst of convulsions that by and by will overtake the nations of the earth, and among others, this nation. The time that is spoken of is not very far distant. "He that will not take up his sword against his neighbor, must needs flee to Zion for

safety." And Zion herself must flee to the God of Israel and hide herself in the shadow of his wing, seeking for his guidance and direction to lead her in the right path, both as regards spiritual and temporal affairs; things social and things political, and everything pertaining to human existence. We are not prepared as a people today for the accomplishment of this object; we need the interposition and guidance of the Almighty.

21. It is just as necessary that we be under his guidance in relation to these matters, as it is in regard to any other matters. Who made the earth? The same being that made the heavens. Who made our bodies? The same being that made our souls; and it takes the "body and the spirit to make the soul of man." We need not arrogate to ourselves any particular intelligence, whether of mercantile, manufacturing, chemical or scientific nature, for if there is anything good or intelligent, it is the Lord who has imparted it, whether man acknowledge it or not. We want to acknowledge the Lord in all things, temporal as well as spiritual.

22. I wish now more directly to touch upon some other principles associated therewith. Some of us seem to be very much confused in our minds as to how we shall operate in regard to temporal affairs. We have brought with us the feelings, views and ideas of the people from whence we came, which are conflicting, and which tend to disintegration and division, and lead to covetousness and fraud, which ought not to have an existence among the Saints of God. We have advertisements published in our newspapers by the Latter-day Saints too, things that are infamous, that are untrue, that are a shame and a disgrace among honorable people, and stand as a living lie. The community at large should not countenance such things as we see daily in our papers to attract the attention of the unwary and bring what they call grists to their mill, in the interest of the individual.

23. We as a people are not called together to act in individual interests; we are called together as Saints of God to operate in the interests of the Zion of God, for the welfare of Israel, and not let ourselves float along with the balance, and all swim together, or all sink together. We ought to be governed by principles of union, fellowship and right feel-

ing, carrying out honorable and upright principles that should be acknowledged before God, the holy angels and all honorable men.

24. Now after speaking so much upon general principles, let me touch upon some things referred to here about these reports, etc. We have long talked about the united order and about cooperation; and we have started in a good deal like some of our little boys when they begin to run—we have made a great many stumbles in this matter. Little Willie and Annie often think they can manage things better than Daddy and Mammy; and we, like them, have assumed to ourselves strength, and the first thing we know are pulling this way, that way and the other. Then, have the institutions been exactly right? No, all kinds of foolishness and all kinds of blunderings have occurred in their administration. But shall we quit? I think not; that is just what the devil would like, just what many of our merchants want, and it would be the very thing that would suit the world, and the devil would laugh at us.

25. What we want to do is to purge out the things that are wrong, and correct them and place them upon a correct basis, and then adhere to them as we would any other part of our religion. In the Church, if a man lies or swears, or commits adultery, or does anything wrong, we deal with him according to the laws of the Church. But because men do wrong, we do not abandon our principles, nor leave the Church, but we turn such individuals out that will not be righted, and we aim to adjust all things and place them on a proper basis.

26. Why not do the same in temporal things? We have, for instance, Zion's Cooperative Mercantile Institution; it is called the Parent Institution, and it ought to be the parent of all these institutions and act as a father and protector and benefactor, doing all it can to promote the welfare and prosperity of the people. And then the people, on the other hand, ought to protect it and sustain it by doing their business through that institution and act prudently, wisely, orderly and unitedly in regard to these matters, that we may be one; for our revelations tell us, If we are not one, we are not the lord's. And if we are not the Lord's, whose are we?

27. We talk sometimes about the United

Order. I do not propose to read to you on this occasion from any of the revelations bearing on this subject, but will quote to you in substance from one of them. The Lord has told us that those who would not comply with the requirements connected with this order should have their names erased from the book of the law of God, and their genealogies must not be found on any church records or history, their names shall not be found nor the names of the fathers, nor the names of the children written in the book of the Law of God. These words are to us, Latter-day Saints; they are true and are binding upon us.

28. Another thing; what did we do when President Young was among us, urging these things upon us? Did we not enter into covenant by re-baptism to be subject to the Priesthood in temporal as well as spiritual things, when we took upon ourselves the obligations of the United Order? Let me ask you, what do we mean by doing this? Is it a mere form, a farce, or do we intend to carry out the covenants we made? I tell you in the name of Israel's God they will be carried out, and no man can plow around these things, for God has decreed that they shall be accomplished; and any man who sets himself in opposition to these principles which God has established, he will root him out; but the principle itself will not be rooted out, for God will see that it is accomplished. And in the name of Israel's God we will help him to do it; and all who feel to do it, say amen. (The large congregation responded with a loud, "Amen.")

29. We have started cooperative institutions, and I will touch on a principle now, showing how they ought to be governed. God has ordained two priesthoods upon the earth—the Melchizedek and the Aaronic. The Melchizedek presides more especially over the spiritual affairs of the Church, and has done in all ages when it has existed upon the earth. You will find this provided for in the Doctrine and Covenants; you can hunt it up at your leisure, I do not wish to stop to make the quotation now. The Aaronic priesthood is presided over by the presiding bishop. If we had a literal descendant of Aaron he would have a right to preside over the bishopric, and to operate and manage and direct these things without the aid of counselors. In the absence of such men the Lord has directed us to take men from the high priesthood and set them apart to be bishops to administer in temporal things. This Aaronic priesthood is an appendage to the Melchizedek priesthood, and its province is to administer in temporal affairs. One reason why we want men of this class to administer in temporal things is because there is a special provision made for it. Nevertheless a High Priest that is after the order of Melchizedek may be set apart to administer in temporal things, having a knowledge of them by the Spirit of truth. And before a man attempts to administer in Zion in temporal things, he ought to obtain a knowledge of that spirit of truth to administer according to the intelligence which that spirit of truth imparts. Thus we have the Aaronic priesthood in its place; the Melchizedek priesthood in its place. And in all the various functions it is necessary to enter into all the various organizations. It is on one or two particular points that I wish to speak now.

30. In the first place the Lord requires certain things to be done to meet his approbation; and everything has to be done under the direction of the presidency of the Twelve, both temporal things and spiritual things. The bishops and the presidents of Stakes and all the officers in the Church of God are subject to this authority and they cannot get around it. And when any officer of this Church who by virtue of his calling does things without counseling with the proper authorities of the Church, he takes upon himself things that he has no right to do, and such a course cannot be acceptable before God and the Priesthood.

31. Now then, we come to the bishopric. Ought the bishops to be consulted in regard to temporal things? Yes, they ought. And as an example, let me tell you that for the last year Bishop Hunter has associated with the Council of the Twelve whenever they have met to consider temporal matters. And I may say we have been pleased to have his company, because it was his place to understand the position of temporal things, that we may know his feelings, and counsel with him and he with us, that everything may be done according to the order and laws of God, that there may be perfect unanimity. With this view he was placed as one of the counselors to the Trustee-in-Trust—because the Trustee-

in-Trust thought it belonged to him to hold that position, and thinks so today. But then, does he preside over the Melchizedek Priesthood? No, he does not. Who and what is he? A high priest ordained and set apart to the bishopric. By whom? The Presidency. Does he control the Presidency? No, he is set apart by them; as bishop he is an appendage to the higher priesthood, and does not control it. No man controls it.

32. I remember a remark made on one occasion by Joseph Smith, in speaking with Bishop Partridge, who was then Bishop. He was a splendid good man, as Bishop Hunter is. But he got some crooked ideas into his head; he thought he ought to manage some things irrespective of Joseph, which caused Joseph to speak rather sharply to him. Joseph said, I wish you to understand that I am President of this Church, and I am your president, and I preside over you and all your affairs. Is that correct doctrine? Yes. It was true then and it is true today.

33. Well, it is necessary that we should have an understanding of these things, that we may make no mistakes in our administration. I want, then, in all our operations to confer with our bishops. And if this institution of ours is "Zion's Cooperative," then it should be under the direction of Zion, under the direction of the Priesthood; and if it is not "Zion's" Cooperative, then it is a living lie. But do we wish to interfere with them? No, we do not. Do we wish to interrupt them in any of their operations? No, we want to help them; we want to unite them and all the people into one, with God at our head, governed by the holy priesthood. Have they rights? Yes. Do we respect them? Yes. Have the people rights? Yes. Shall the people be respected in their rights? Yes, they shall, all the people in all the Stakes; and while we sustain them they must sustain us; and if they expect to have our support, they must give us theirs.

34. Having said so much, I will tell you that I believe sincerely that the men managing our Cooperative Institution are doing just as well as they know how. And I will state further, that I don't know of any persons in this community who know how better than they do. And I have been now for some time associated with them, and am acquainted with their proceedings.

35. There are other principles besides this; we want to learn to manufacture our own goods. And while on the one hand we use the best talent and financial ability we can get to attend to our mercantile institutions; on the other hand, we need to cherish a spirit to encourage home manufactures of every kind, and we want to get this institution to help us do it. If we manufacture cloths and boots and shoes or anything else, we want the institution to dispose of our goods. If we need encouragement in regard to the introduction of any manufactures of any kind, we want them to help us, and we have a right to expect this of them so far as is wise, prudent and legitimate. I will state that the directors of ZCMI feel interested in the very things that I am talking about, and I say it to their credit and for your satisfaction. I do not think there is an institution in the United States in a better condition than that is today; and it is improving all the time, not after any fictitious manner, but on a solid, firm, reliable basis.

36. Now then, I have proposed to these brethren, which they quite coincide with, that when they shall be able to pay a certain amount as dividends on the means invested, after reserving a sufficient amount to preserve the institution intact against any sudden emergency that may arise, which is proper among all wise and intelligent men, that then the profits of the institution outside of this, should be appropriated for the development of the home manufactures, the making of machinery, the introduction of self-sustaining principles and the building up of the Territory generally, and they acquiesced in this feeling; and I say it to their honor and credit. And I will tell you again that the Church has got a large interest in that institution, consequently we wish to see everything go aright, not on any wild erratic principle, but on a solid, firm, reliable basis, that can be carried out and that will elicit the admiration and confidence of all good and honorable men.

37. Sometimes little difficulties have arisen outside through interested individuals who have resorted to a good deal of trickery; other times perhaps from just causes. And I will say too that complaints have been made that we have not sufficiently sustained our

home manufactures. I will say however that the Institution has stood in a very delicate position. We have been struggling with the financial crisis that has cast a gloom over all this nation for the last number of years—since 1873. But we are now getting into a solid firm position, and when we declared 3 per cent for the six months dividend, it was because the Institution was able to do so. And when we are able to extend this a little farther we will be quite willing to do so.

38. Some of the complaints that have been made against the institution we have heard; and we have thought best to have a board and refer to that board any complaints that might be made from any part of the Territory. This board that has been temporally organized has given us these various reports which have been read in your hearing, which indicate their views and feelings in regard to these things. We wish a board of that kind to be organized upon a correct basis according to the order of this Church and Kingdom of God; and then as the people throughout the Territory send to purchase their goods from them, let the people that make these purchases be represented; and if there is anything not straight in their operations let them be made straight. And this is what this committee is for, that the people may be protected as well as the Institution.

39. Then Stake organizations are recommended, with a representative from each Stake at the general or central board, and it will make it much more pleasant for the management of that Institution to have a criticism of that kind. And it will also tend to allay many of these foolish things which are frequently put in circulation in different parts of the Territory. The object then, of this Board is that the people may be represented, and that Zion's Cooperative may also be properly represented, that it may serve as a balance wheel to adjust and correct any matters of difficulty that may arise.

40. I am happy to say that in many parts of the Territory they are introducing the manufacture of leather and boots and shoes and a variety of other articles. And suffice it to say that, according to these reports, the Parent Institution has sustained the manufacturers of these homemade articles quite liberally; and we want it to be in that position that everything we use can be bought there. This is, too, the feeling in relation to this matter. And when we get things into a proper fix we will pull with a long pull and a strong pull and a pull altogether. We will strive to be one; and if we cannot go so far as to sustain cooperation in regard to these things, how in the name of common sense are we ever going into the United Order? But we will begin with this, and then cooperate in all the different Stakes, not only in your merchandising, but in your manufacturing affairs and in your producing affairs; and in every thing it will be the duty of this general Board of Trade to regulate the interests of the whole community, honestly and faithfully, at least we will do it according to the best ability we have; and if there should any mistakes arise, we will try to correct them; if they are on the part of the people, we will talk to them about it, if on the part of the institution, we will talk to its management about it. And we will keep working and operating until we succeed in introducing and establishing these things that God has desired, and until Zion shall be a united people and the glory of all the earth.

41. God bless you and lead you in the path of life, in the name of Jesus. Amen.

ADDRESS 6

Address delivered by John Taylor, President of the Quorum of the Twelve Apostles, at the 49th Semiannual General Conference of The Church of Jesus Christ of Latter-day Saints convened October 6, 1879, in the Tabernacle, Salt Lake City.

1. I have been interested in listening to the remarks of the brethren this afternoon, and I am thankful to find that good old-fashioned Mormonism, or Latter-day-Saintism is not altogether dead yet—that there is a little of it living in the bosoms of the Saints, in our speakers, and in those who hear. The Methodists, you know, used to have a prayer to the effect that "His Spirit might pass from heart to heart as oil passes from vessel to vessel," and I have thought that that kind of a spirit has been exhibited more or less here today, whether we have any Methodists among us or not.

2. We have come here, as has been stated, to worship Almighty God in accordance with his commands. Most of this congregation were good citizens before they came here. Some are from the various parts of Europe and from other parts of the earth, and a great many from different parts of the United States. They were good citizens and observed the laws of the land to which they belonged. They have observed every law of the United States, except one that was made on purpose to make them disobey God, and therefore, so far as political affairs are concerned, and the duties pertaining to citizens of the United States, they have been maintained in their integrity up to the present time.

3. I remember being asked in a court here some three or four years ago—I do not remember the time precisely, but the court seemed to be very fond of interfering with religious matters, it was not always so; but I suppose civilization has extended—I was asked, "Do you believe in obeying the laws of the United States?" "Yes I do, in all except one"—in fact I had not broken that. "What law is that?" "The law in relation to polygamy." "Well, why do you except that one?" "Because," I replied, "it is at variance with the genius and spirit of our institution; because it is at variance with the Constitution of the United States; and because it is in vio-

lation of the law of God to me." The United States Supreme Court, however, since that time has made it a law of the land, that is, it has sanctioned it; it was not sanctioned at that time, that question was not then decided.

4. We are here today, gathered together according to the word and law of God and the commandments of God to us. "Gather my Saints together unto me," says one of the old prophets, "Those that have made a covenant with me by sacrifice." "I will take you," says another, "one of a city and two of a family, and I will bring you to Zion, and I will give you pastors according to mine heart, which shall feed you with knowledge and understanding." Now, the servants of God in these last days have been sent out as they were in former days to gather the people, and the Lord has given us this law—the law of polygamy—among other things, and I know it before God and can bear testimony of it, if nobody else knows it. I know that it came from God, and that God is its author. But there are hundreds and thousands of others who have a knowledge of the same thing; but I speak of it in this wise to testify before God, angels and men, before this nation and all other nations that it came from God. That is the reason that I speak of it, that I may bear my testimony to you and to the nations of the earth.

5. Now, then, about the result of it; that is with God and with the people. It is for us to do the will of God; it is for the Lord to bring about the results in his own way. But one thing I can assure all men, in the name of Israel's God, that neither this nation, nor any other nation, can do anything against the truth, but for the truth. Do their very best, help themselves as they may, they cannot help themselves in regard to these matters, for the Lord will say unto them, as he did unto the waves of the mighty ocean, "Hitherto shalt thou come but no further: and here shall thy proud waves be stayed." Now, that is how the thing is. The prophet in anoth-

er place says, "Surely the wrath of man shall praise thee; the remainder of wrath shalt thou restrain." He will manage the other. He will put a hook in the jaws of men and of nations, and lead them just as he pleases. They are all in his hands, as we are in his hands.

6. Need we be surprised that people should feel inimical to the Gospel of Jesus Christ? No. Need we be surprised that men, as the scriptures say, "should wax worse and worse, deceiving and being deceived?" No. We have preached it—I have preached it upwards of forty years in this nation and in other nations. Need we be surprised that they should trample under foot the Constitution of the United States? No; Joseph Smith told us that they would do it. Many around me here knew long ago that they would do this thing and further knew that the last people that should be found to rally around that sacred instrument and save it from the grasp of unrighteous men would be the Elders of Israel! When, therefore, we see these things progressing need we be astonished? I do not think we need be.

7. Some of our people you know, who are a little shaky and get how? Why, a little astride of the fence, and say "good Lord and good devil," not knowing into whose hands they will fall; when they see some of these things transpiring they are filled with amazement; but men who understand themselves, and who are in possession of the gift of the Holy Ghost and the Spirit of the living God, are looking for such things and they are not at all surprised.

8. Were we surprised when the last terrible war took place here in the United States? No; good Latter-day Saints were not, for they had been told about it. Joseph Smith had told them where it would start, that it should be a terrible time of bloodshed and that it should start in South Carolina. But I tell you today the end is not yet. You will see worse things than that, for God will lay his hand upon this nation, and they will feel it more terribly than ever they have done before; there will be more bloodshed, more ruin, more devastation than ever they have seen before. Write it down! You will see it come to pass; it is only just starting in. And would you feel to rejoice? No; I would feel sorry. I knew very well myself when this last war was commencing, and could have wept

and did weep, over this nation; but there is yet to come a sound of war, trouble and distress, in which brother will be arrayed against brother, father against son, son against father, a scene of desolation and destruction that will permeate our land until it will be a vexation to hear the report thereof. Would you help to bring it about? No, I would not; I would stop it if I could. I would pour in the oil and the wine and balm and try to lead people in the right path that will be governed by it, but they won't.

9. Our Elders would do the same, and we are sending them forth doing all that we can, selecting the very best men we can put our hands upon—men of faith, men of honor, men of integrity—to go forth to preach the Gospel to this nation and to other nations. And how do they receive them? Not long ago they killed one and mobbed others. Well, we cannot help that. They are in the dark; they do not realize the position they occupy; they know not what spirit they are of. But it is our duty to have our bowels full of compassion extended to them, to send forth the message of life. But when our Elders go among these people they have to take their lives in their hands and trust in the living God. Nevertheless, we need not be afraid, we need not be troubled about any of these matters. "Fear not them which kill the body, but are not able to kill the soul: but rather fear him which is able to destroy both soul and body in hell."

10. Yea, I say unto you fear Him; and we feel today, while we would submit to every ordinance of man that is just, equitable and right, observe every law and interfere with no man's rights, we are not ignorant of the fact that it is unjust for legislatures and courts to make and enforce laws to entrap and destroy us; that a magnanimous and just government would protect all its citizens; but we feel, at the same time, that the Lord is our God, the Lord is our judge, the Lord is our Law-giver, the Lord is our King, and he shall rule over us; and all that feel like saying that say Amen. (The vast congregation responded "Amen.")

11. It is an historic fact, written in letters as of living fire, that neither nations, peoples, emperors, kings, or presidents, nor the combined powers of the earth, are able to regulate the conscience or change the faith

of man. Noah maintained his faith alone, as against that of a world. Abraham could not be swerved by the most unnatural and forbidding circumstances. Moses, at the behest of God, alone withstood the power of Egypt's king and nation. Daniel unflinchingly bowed his knee to Israel's God, in the face of a prohibitory regal decree, passed by the intrigues of the combined powers of the kingdom of Babylon, who were his enemies. Job, when tried, maintained his integrity, even as against God, and said, "Though he slay me, yet will I trust in him;" and he further said, "I know that my Redeemer liveth, and that he will stand at the latter day upon the earth; and though worms destroy this body, yet in my flesh shall I see God." The three Hebrew children could not be made to bow to the image set up by the King of Babylon; but rather than deny their faith chose the penalty of the fiery furnace, in which they walked accompanied by the Son of God. Jesus came to do the will of his Father, and though in doing it he sweat great drops of blood, and begged of his Father to let the cup pass if possible, yet "not my will," he said, "but thine be done;" and when groaning in mortal agony he cried, "My God, my God, why hast thou forsaken me." And though he could have commanded twelve legions of angels, who would have obeyed him, yet in obedience to the mandate of his Father, he quietly said "It is finished," and gave up the ghost.

12. And this nation may yet learn that under no fictitious pleas, as used by the Babylonish nation against Daniel and others, can they pervert or overthrow the faith and religion of the Latter-day Saints; and that no legislative enactment, nor judicial rulings, can pluck from the mind of man his undying faith, or legislate away the scrupulous exactions of an inexorable conscience. The rack, the gibbet, the faggot, and death in all its horrid forms has never accomplished this, nor never will. And in free America, the land of boasted toleration, it will be as impotent under the guise of liberty as it has been in other ages under the name of despotism. And Congress to cover their shameless infraction of the Constitution of the United States, which guarantees religious liberty to all—in order to avoid the odium of religious persecution, which naturally attaches

itself to them, may pervert an institution of God by misnaming polygamy and calling it bigamy and not religion, and though the Supreme Court of the United States may confirm their acts, yet there are more than one hundred thousand persons who know better than they do, who will declare that polygamy is a part of their religion and a command and revelation from God.

13. These are our feelings and we will try to acknowledge the Lord in all things. And then, on the other hand, we do not wish to treat anybody disrespectfully. Have we any quarrel with this nation? No; they are seeking to quarrel with us; don't let us give them the opportunity. They are like the boy strutting along the street with a chip on his shoulder, asking us to knock it off. But we won't knock if off, but let them strut. It is true they try all they can to annoy and provoke us— that is, a few mean men do, although that is not generally the feeling of the nation, but is confined in great measure to religious fanatics and corrupt politicians, some of them holding positions under government, are trying to stir up strife. What for? Well, they want to get a certain "ticket" elected. A great amount of this "fuss and feathers" that we have today is simply a political ruse in the interest of party politics. What for? Why, the brethren have told you. Mormonism is very unpopular, and if they can only do something that will be in opposition to Mormonism it will satisfy the howling priests throughout the land, and a great many of their flocks. As was remarked by one of the brethren, when Jesus was crucified, Pilate and Herod could be made friends.

14. When Mormonism is to be opposed, all men, or at least a great many men, can unite in opposing it. And they want to go before the people and tell them that they have rooted out slavery, and now they are after Mormonism, and wont you religious fanatics join in? No, excuse me, I mean, you pure and holy religious people, who are so humble and posses so much of the spirit that dwelt in the lowly Jesus, won't you help us to do this thing—won't you vote for us because we are doing this thing? Why, bless your souls, they would not hesitate to sweep us off the face of the earth to get elected. That is their feeling. They care nothing

about human rights, liberty, or life, if they can bring about the results desired. They would despoil, destroy and overthrow this people to accomplish their own end. Well, the other party, it is true, would not be very well suited about it, but they would not care to see it politically. However, it is for us to do the best we can. We have got to put our trust in the living God.

15. We might ask—Will they derive any benefit from any course taken against the Latter-day Saints? No, a thousand times no!! I tell you that the hand of God will be upon them for it, and every people, be it this nation, or any other nation, that shall lift up their hands against Zion shall be wasted away; and those that want to try it let them try it, and it is them and their God for it. But it is for us to fear God, to keep his commandments; we can afford to do right whether other people can or not.

16. Respect all men in their rights, in their position, and in their privileges, politically and socially, and protect them in the same; but be not partakers of their evil deeds, of their crimes, nor their iniquities, that you have heard spoken about here today. We do not want them to force upon us their drinking saloons, their drunkenness, their gambling, their debauchery and lasciviousness. We do not want these adjuncts of civilization. We do not want them to force upon us that institution of monogamy called the social evil. We will be after them; we will form ourselves into police and hunt them out and drag them from their dens of infamy and expose them to the world. We won't have their meanness, with their foeticides and infanticides, forced upon us. And you, sisters, don't allow yourselves to become contaminated by rustling against their polluted skirts. Keep from them! Let them wallow in their infamy, and let us protect the right, and be for God and his Christ, for honor, for truth, for virtue, purity and chastity, and for the building up of the kingdom of God. Amen.

ADDRESS 7

Discourse delivered by John Taylor, President of the Quorum of the Twelve Apostles, at the 49th Semiannual General Conference of The Church of Jesus Christ of Latter-day Saints convened October 7, 1879, in Salt Lake City.

1. I will state to the Conference that we have no financial account to present, because we do not get our returns from the various Stakes until the close of each year; in consequence of this we find it impracticable to present a satisfactory account to the General Conference oftener than once a year.

2. The Lord has given us a certain work to accomplish; and the feelings or ideas of men in the world in relation to this work have but little to do with us. We are gathered here for the express purpose of building up the Church and Kingdom of God upon the earth. We are endeavoring to do this—that is, a great many of the people are, to the very best of their ability; and we consider ourselves responsible to God for the action we take and for the course we pursue in relation to the fulfillment of His purposes. We think that in building Temples, sending the Gospel to the nations of the earth and prosecuting our other labors that we are carrying out the word and will, and the commands of God. Yet it not infrequently happens, that when we are doing our very best to promote correct principles among ourselves, as well as to spread them abroad, even to all nations, that we meet with determined and unrelenting opposition. This we cannot help. We do not seek it, but we do not fear it.

3. There has existed a principle of antagonism ever since the dawn of creation, namely, the powers of God have been opposed by the powers of the Evil One. Satan and wicked men have operated to subvert the plans and designs of Jehovah. And if we have a little of such opposition to contend with in our day, there is nothing new in it. The martyr Stephen when arraigned before "the Council" to answer to a charge of blasphemy, said, "Which of the prophets have not your fathers persecuted? And they have slain them which showed before of the coming of the just One; of whom ye have been now the betrayers and murderers." We have always expected that there would be a spirit of antagonism to the Church and Kingdom of God, and our Elders have been telling us, more or less, during the last fifty years, that this feeling still existed and, indeed, every now and then, we have occasion to believe them; or, to use an old saying, "The devil is not dead yet;" and he uses his influence now, as in former days, to oppose the principles that God has revealed.

4. We are gathered here from many nations in order that God may plant among us the principles and laws of eternal lives; that we may operate in the Priesthood with the holy men who held it in former ages, and with God the Father, and with Jesus the Mediator, and with the holy angels in the interests of mankind, not only in things pertaining to ourselves individually, but in those that concern the whole world; not only to the people that now live, but also to those who have lived; for the plans of God reach back into eternity and forward into eternity, and we are being taught and instructed through the holy Melchizedek Priesthood, which holds now, as in past ages, the keys of the mysteries of the revelations of God. It is our privilege to operate through this order, with men who have held the same keys and possessed the same powers and have had the same communication with God, and who have looked forward to the time, with joyful anticipation, that we now live in, namely, to the dispensation of the fullness of times.

5. For this purpose we are gathered together, for this purpose we are building Temples according to the order and revelations of God—for until He revealed these things to us we knew nothing about them. And the world of mankind today know nothing about Temples and their uses. If we were to build Temples for them according to the order of God, they would not know how to administer in them; neither could we know had the Lord not revealed to us how to do it, which he did through the Prophet Joseph. We are acting upon this revealed knowledge today, seeking to carry out the will, the designs and the purposes of God, in the interest of common humanity, not for a few people only, not for the

people of the United States only, nor for those of two or three nations, but for the people of the whole world. And the hearts of the people are being drawn after these principles; or, in other words, the hearts of the children are being turned towards the fathers, as well as the hearts of the fathers towards the children.

6. The spirit that is being manifested in the various Stakes of Zion is very creditable in this respect to the Latter-day Saints. And we purpose, God being our helper, and the devil not hindering us, to go on with our work, to build our Temples and to administer in them and to act as the friends of God upon the earth. And if we are not His friends, He has none, for there is no people anywhere, except the Latter-day Saints, who will listen to His laws—and as they say sometimes, "it's a tight squeeze" for us to do it. The question is, Shall we falter in our calculations; I think not; but I think we will say, as the ancient servant of God said to a man who was seeking to hinder the progress of the building of a Temple to the Lord of Hosts: "I am doing a great work; hinder me not." We are doing a great work, and we would say to our outside friends and to people generally who are not conversant with our affairs, will you be so kind as to let us alone and hinder us not; so that we may go on with our labor of love in the common interests of humanity and in our efforts to promote the welfare of the world at large. This is one thing we have to do, and we will try to do it, the Lord being our helper.

7. Then another thing we are called upon to do is to preach the Gospel to every creature throughout the world. "Why, the people will oppose you?" That they always did. But Jesus said, and I will say by way of repeating His words—for they are as true today as they were in His day—"Blessed are ye, when men shall revile you, and persecute you, and shall say all manner of evil against you falsely, for my sake. Rejoice, and be exceeding glad, for great is your reward in heaven; for so persecuted they the prophets which were before you." Therefore we need not be troubled about it. When we first started out in this work we never looked for anything else, and we have not looked in vain either; we have found an abundance of it, and we have commenced to regard it as a natural thing.

8. But we must not forget that we owe a duty to the world. The Lord has given to us the light of eternity; and we are commanded not to conceal our light under a bushel, but on the contrary we should let it shine forth as a city set upon a hill that cannot be hid. We need not try to get into an out-of-the-way corner from the gaze of the public eye, for we cannot. We thought we had wandered a long way from civilization when we came here; but, according to the remarks of the speakers this morning, a certain degree of it has followed us, and we are not quite out of it yet.

9. But there are some things we can do. We will let them pursue their course, and we will ask them, if they will be so good and so kind as to let us worship God according to the dictates of our consciences. This is not a very great boon to ask of anybody. Still we do ask that we may be permitted, in this land of liberty, in this land which we call the home of the brave and the land of the free; the asylum of the oppressed of all nations, we ask that we may have the simple privilege of worshipping God according to the dictates of our own consciences. Then, while they are trying to injure us, we will try to do them good. We will teach them good principles at home, and we will send the Gospel abroad.

10. And the kind of men we want as bearers of this Gospel message are men who have faith in God; men who have faith in their religion; men who honor their Priesthood; men in whom the people who know them have faith and in whom God has confidence, and not some poor unfortunate beings who are wanted to leave a place because they cannot live in it; but we want men full of the Holy Ghost and the power of God that they may go forth weeping bearing precious seed and sowing the seeds of eternal life, and then returning with gladness, bringing their sheaves with them. These are the kind of men we want. We do not want the names of men of the former class presented to us to go on missions; if they are and we find it out, we shall not send them; for such men cannot go with our fellowship and good feeling. Men who bear the words of life among the nations, ought to be men of honor, integrity, virtue and purity; and this being the command of God to us, we shall try and carry it out.

11. Some imagine that we have almost got through with our work; when the truth of the matter is, we have hardly commenced yet. Here is Brother Joseph Young, who represents the Seventies,—Brother Joseph, how many

Seventies are there enrolled? [Brother Young replied that there were 5,320]. I am told that there are 5,320 Seventies; we expect to call upon a great many of these men to go abroad and proclaim the fullness of the Gospel. We received a small order lately—you know, we talk business sometimes—for forty missionaries to go and labor in one place; they did not send the money to pay their fares; but then, we have the missionaries, and we will trust in God for our pay and we shall get it if we are found doing His will and carrying out His purposes.

12. Again, another duty we have to do is to preserve the order of God among ourselves. And here is a great responsibility resting upon the Presidents of Stakes and their Counselors, and upon the Bishops and their Counselors, and upon all men holding authority in the Church and Kingdom of God, and upon the Twelve specially, to see that the order of God is carried out, and that iniquity does not exist among the Saints of the Most High God.

13. We talk sometimes about the outside world, and we sometimes indulge in casting reflections upon them—and there is plenty of room for it, no doubt; but then, what of ourselves? What do we do? Do not our own members keep some of the very saloons we talk about? And do not we engage in this business because we are afraid somebody else will? Why, that is the argument of the thief. He says, "If I do not steal, somebody else will." But, besides, say these brethren, "We want to get a living." But before I would live in that way, I would die and make an end of it; I would not be mixed up with such concerns nor have any hand in them, but pursue another and more honorable course to get a living than in seeking to put the cup to the mouth of the drunkard and in leading our youth and others who may be inclined that way, in the path that leads to death.

14. What else do we do? Why some of us Elders, and some of us High Priests and Seventies, frequent these places and get drunk and disgrace ourselves and our families, and the people with whom we are associated. And what else do we do? We are commanded to remember the Sabbath day to keep it holy; and yet we find that our trains leave this city every Sabbath, until the weather gets too cold to bathe, carrying many of our people, who indulge in all kinds of amusements and thus violate the Sabbath, which we are commanded to keep holy, which many respectable Gentiles would never think of doing. And yet you are Latter-day Saints, are you? You are a good people, and you will talk about the gift of the Holy Ghost and the Spirit of God being in you, while you are violating some of the plainest everyday principles of the Gospel of Christ.

15. And what then? Why, we have been told about the Gentiles introducing into our midst what is termed the social evil; and we find some of our youth, and older ones too, contaminating themselves with it, thereby breaking their covenants and forsaking their God, and disgracing themselves before God, angels and all good men. Such men are a disgrace to any community, much less to a community professing, as we do, to be Saints. Are such persons Saints? No, they are not. Can we fellowship them? No, we cannot. God requires it of us before we talk of cleansing the outside of the platter, to see that the inside is clean, to place ourselves right upon the record. Do we do it? Well, sometimes—I was going to say, "hardly ever." Sometimes we do it, but in a great many instances we do not do it. What is the matter? Good men have mean sons, and the sons must not be handled. Why so? God, you will remember, had a host of sons in heaven who did not do right, and they were cast out, even a third part of His entire family. That is the way I read it. Again, there are some sons who are good men, who have disreputable fathers, who have departed from correct principles, but out of respect to the fathers in the one instance and the sons in the other, we allow evil way to go unchecked. Well, you Presidents and you Bishops and you Priests and Teachers may do that if you please, but their blood will be upon your heads, not upon mine. And we call upon you to honor your calling and Priesthood and purge from your midst corruption of every kind. And we call upon the Presidents of Stakes and their Counselors, upon the Bishops and their Counselors, and upon the Priests, Teachers and Deacons, to magnify their offices, and not to be partakers of other men's sins. For as sure as I live and as God lives, if you do God will require it at your hands. And therefore, I call upon Presidents and men in authority, where men do not magnify their calling to remove them from their positions of responsibility and replace them by men who will; and let us have correct principles and the order of God carried out in Zion.

16. Apostles, Prophets, Pastors, Teachers and Evangelists were placed in the Church of old for what? "For the perfecting of the Saints, for the work of the ministry, for the edifying of the body of Christ, till we all come in the unity of the faith and of the knowledge of the Son of God, unto a perfect man, unto the measure of the stature of the fullness of Christ." It is so today.

17. My brethren who have spoken have told you plainly of many evils that exist in our midst; but we can scarcely perceive them, many of us. Sometimes it is very difficult to discern between a Saint and a sinner, between one who professes to fear God and one who does not. It is for us to straighten out these matters; and you men in authority will be held responsible, and the Twelve will be held responsible, and I hold you responsible, and God will hold you responsible for your acts.

18. The great difficulty with us is that we are too fond of catering to the world, and too much of the world has crept into our hearts? The spirit of covetousness and greed, and—what shall I say—dishonesty has spread itself like a plague throughout the length and breadth of the whole world in every direction, and we have drunk more or less into that spirit. Like a plague it has pervaded all grades of society; and instead of being governed by those high, noble, and honorable principles that dwell in the bosom of God, we are after the filthy lucre which is spoken of as being the root of all evil; and instead of setting our affections upon God, we set our affections upon the world, its follies and vanities. Come ye out from the midst of her; be ye clean, that bear the vessels of the Lord; and honor your Priesthood and calling, and show and prove to the world, to angels and to God that you are on the side of truth and right, of honesty, purity and integrity, and that you are for God and His Kingdom, let other people do as they will.

19. We sometimes talk of the affairs that are taking place around us. There is now a little commotion that interested parties are getting up about the "Mormons" for the purpose of forwarding their political operations. Bless your soul, we knew about that long, long ago, and also knew what it would be for. It is about the same with these parties as it was with the editor I have read of; the printer asked for "copy," it was handed to him, but it was not enough, he wanted more. The editor told him that he had not time to prepare any more then, but to pitch into the "Mormons." That was a kind of standing matter they kept on hand. The move that is being made now is simply a political scheme, out of which to make political capital. It was started by interested demagogues for that purpose, in order that they might have the honor of putting down "Mormonism," and sailing into power on the current of incensed public opinion. Now they can have all the honor they can get on that score; and I guess it will be the same as Stephen A. Douglas and others have attained to by pursuing that course, and I think no more.

20. We are here to serve God and keep His commandments; and if we will purge ourselves from our iniquities, live our religion and keep the commandments of God, there is no power on this side of hell nor on the other, that can harm us, for God will be on our side to protect us in the position we occupy.

21. There is one thing I wish to speak to you about that you are well acquainted with. We had a little commotion gotten up about some of our money matters associated with the heirs of the late President Young, and it has been talked about generally. We thought we had made a settlement with them at one time, which we did, and the executors of the estate took their releases which exonerated them from all blame, and they avowed themselves satisfied with the settlements made. But then, some men's word and some men's signatures do not amount to much. What next? Why, some of our very pure and high-minded lawyers are not above entering into such things because of a little monetary inducements. It would not be proper to say they were anything but pure, high-minded and honorable men, for it is understood that all lawyers are, is it not? Well, we knew we had treated them very liberally before; and so did you. We knew we had given them all we ought to give them, and more too. But we felt to be generous to the heirs of President Young; and we did what we could to promote their welfare. Still these things came out. No matter. Bonds and writings and signatures and releases amount to nothing with some people. So they started in, and we have had a legal fight about it. Some of the Apostles have had to be confined in the penitentiary; and it was a pretty narrow squeeze with me. [Laughter.] But then I have been in such places before, and was shot at while there

and hit, and therefore it would have been nothing new, and I was not much concerned about it. When they wanted to get hold of some of your means and property which I held in trust, and which they had no right to, I told them No, they could not have it. "Well," said they, "you will have to go to jail." "Well," said I, "jail it is then. Some folks go off to rusticate at Soda Springs and other places; I think I will go and rusticate in the penitentiary." But they would not have me. [Laughter.] They took Brother Cannon, Brother Brigham and Brother Carrington; I suppose they considered them worthier men, and that I had better stay out.

22. There are all kinds of curious things started up; and among other things that have grown out of this contest is what is termed a cross suit; and because of this movement some people think we are going to law. I will tell you how much. We were merely attempting to put the complaining heirs in the same position as they had put us; thinking that by doing so they might be led to reflect that there were other people in the world besides themselves, and that other people might be placed in jeopardy besides some of our brethren. "But," say you, "was it not contrary to a law of the Church to go to law with your brethren?" We did not exactly do it; we merely started in.

23. I will tell you what we would have done if this settlement had not been made. We would have called upon all those who were good and honorable of President Young's family—and I am happy to say that with very few exceptions they are of that class and are desirous to carry out and fulfill their obligations, and stand by the covenants they have entered into—we were going to call upon them to turn over to our side, and then we were going to cut the others off the Church, and then go to law with them and sue for their property as they had for ours. That is all.

24. I thought I would explain this because it is not generally understood by the people. It is really one of those things called a legal fiction, which had to arise to meet certain technicalities of the law, in order that the proper releases might be given, releases that would stand, and also a decree from the court to settle these difficulties.

25. This compromise was talked of, but it could not be reached very readily, for some of them wanted a little more money, and the lawyers wanted a little, and of course such honorable gentlemen should have it. Well, the compromise was at last effected. We thought it better to furnish them a little means than to have these unpleasant things going on month after month, and perhaps year after year; and we could see that we would have to be very smart indeed to prevent some of these men of honor from running away with the balance of it. That being done, we have done all we could to try to promote peace in our midst. We have taken the best of counsel, and have acted in this matter according to the very best of our judgment.

26. And now about the money involved. It is a large amount? Yes, some seventy-five thousand dollars paid by the Trustee-in-Trust in behalf of the Church, beside a further amount paid by the administrators. That would be just a dollar apiece from 75,000 people. It is quite a little sum; but then, did you ever know of people giving a bone to a dog? And after you had done so, you did not think you had lost much, did you? We thought it better to take that course than to be mixed up any longer with such miserable doings; and we agreed to do it. And I would like to know whether you approve of this act or not. You who do, please signify it by holding up your right hands. [A forest of hands was raised; and a unanimous vote declared.]

27. Well, some have asked what we were going to do with these complaining heirs. I think we will have to deal with them according to the laws of the Church. Are you going to bring their case before the Conference? No, I think not; there are the proper officers in the Church to attend to such things, and we say to them, go, and do your duty. We are very sorry that they should have placed themselves in that position; and we are very sorry that a great many other people should, and we are very sorry that a great many of these evils referred to should exist in Israel. But they do; and what shall we do about it? Go to work and cleanse the inside of the platter, and then we can go before our God in good faith, and stand approved of him, and rejoice in the fullness of the blessings of the gospel of peace.

28. There are some other things I would like to touch upon, but as the time has already expired, and as there will be a Priesthood meeting tonight in this tabernacle, to which the young and the old of both sexes are invited, I will defer speaking further until then.

ADDRESS 8

Closing Remarks made by John Taylor, President of the Quorum of the Twelve Apostles, at the 49th Semiannual General Conference of The Church of Jesus Christ of Latter-day Saints convened October 8, 1879, in Salt Lake City.

1. I think we are now pretty much through with the business of this Conference. I am very pleased to have witnessed the feeling and spirit that have been manifested in our midst and I would again call upon the presidents of stakes, the bishops, the high councils, the priests, teachers and deacons, to carry out the instructions that have been given here in their several stakes; and to see that the order of the Kingdom of God is sustained and maintained; that we individually and collectively seek for a closer union with the Lord; that we see that the principles of honesty, truth, integrity and virtue are maintained in the several stakes; that we operate in a way that we may always have the smile and approbation of God.

3. See that in your several stakes you maintain pure principles and put down anything that is contrary to virtue, contrary to righteousness, contrary to integrity, and see that the laws of God are maintained, that the Church is purged from iniquity, that we may be prepared to present ourselves before the Lord with confidence that he may sustain us in all our acts; that we may approach near to the Lord instead of getting further off; and that we may follow the counsel given in regard to cooperation, and more especially in regard to manufacturing. We want to encourage home manufacture, in all its various branches, that we may be self-sustaining. And let us try to live our religion and keep the commandments of God, and the blessings of God will rest upon us, but if we neglect these things they will not.

3. I want to repeat again what I said yesterday in relation to this matter, that no president, no bishop, no priest, or teacher, no deacon can be justified in allowing the laws of God to be trampled upon with impunity within his jurisdiction. If they do—if they wink at iniquity of any kind, God will require it at their hands, and if they have a mind to bear the iniquity of other men, all right, but I will not, and the Twelve will not. It is for us to do the will of God and keep His commandments, and if we do, the spirit and blessing and power of God will be with us from this time forth, but if we do not, we may expect his hand to be over us for evil. Let us then look for men that occupy offices to be men of honor, of truth and of integrity. We do not care for the covetous and fraudulent and dishonest, let them pursue their own course, but let us look for truth and integrity.

ADDRESS 9

Address given by John Taylor, President of the Quorum of the Twelve Apostles, at the 50th Annual General Conference of The Church of Jesus Christ of Latter-day Saints convened April 7, 1880, in the Tabernacle, Salt Lake City.

1. As I stated on the opening of the Conference, there were some things of considerable importance that we wished to lay before the Saints, and especially before the authorities of the Church today. We have had in operation for quite a length of time, what is known as the "Perpetual Emigration Fund Company," and a great many of you that are present have contributed to that Fund. And as it is a jubilee year to you—although I suppose the forty-ninth year would be the proper jubilee—it is really the fiftieth anniversary of the Church of Jesus Christ of Latter-day Saints. It occurred to me that we ought to do something, as they did in former times, to relieve those that are oppressed with debt, to assist those that are needy, to break the yoke off those that may feel themselves crowded upon, and to make it a time of general rejoicing. And as it is a matter in which you are all interested, it is thought proper to lay the matter before you, because we have contemplated to release one-half of the indebtedness of those who are indebted to the P. E. Fund Company. That is one subject.

2. There is a variety of other things, which I mentioned to my brethren of the Twelve, and they all join in the feeling with a hearty cooperation, all being desirous of seeing something of this kind done which will tend to produce happiness, joy and comfort, and a feeling of relief among many of our brethren.

3. We wish the brethren who have contributed to this fund, and all the officers of this Church, to have a voice in it, because it is our act; and we want to make it the act of the whole people, that all may have a voice, which we consider they ought to have in all these leading prominent actions wherein they are concerned.

4. The proposition is to release one-half of the people's indebtedness to the Perpetual Emigration Fund Company. I may say, I have also spoken to Brother Carrington on this matter, who is the president of this company, and learn that it meets his views. I would further state that to the best of my knowledge nobody has hitherto been oppressed or crowded on account of this indebtedness at all; they have been called upon and requested to meet their engagements, which is certainly just; because others were interested in these matters besides ourselves, who had a right to expect a return of means appropriated, that they also might be relieved, and partake of the benefits of this fund, which was properly named perpetual; that is, many of the poor for which the means were subscribed formerly, under the direction of President Young, who was the originator of the Perpetual Emigrating Fund Company.

5. I have some figures which I will read to you; they will show what has not been returned again by those who have been benefited by it. The amount of the original indebtedness is $704,000. The interest, extending along for many years at 10 per cent per annum, is some $900,000, which interest, in many instances, has had to be paid by us. The whole of the amount is $1,604,000. That is the amount of the whole indebtedness, principal and interest.

6. Now, we propose to forgive those who are poor and that are struggling with difficulties in life, who have not been able to meet their engagements in this matter; not half the amount that they are due, but the whole; and to those who are forgiven the debt it will be blotted out; not partly, but entirely; and the remainder will be left to those to pay who are able to and have not done it. And we shall expect that those who have not met their engagements to meet them; that is, when half has been forgiven to the poor. For in former times they did not release the rich, it was the poor. The rich can always take care of themselves—that is, so far as this world is concerned, I do not know how it will be about the next. [Laughter.] I wish it distinctly understood that it is one-half of the whole amount, which we wish to relieve the poor from. It will be a little start on the year of jubilee. This is one item. All of you who are in favor of this release signify it by holding up your right hand. [The congregation voted

unanimously in favor of the motion.] I will state that, as to the manner in which this will be done; it will be provided for hereafter; and a circular will be issued by the Twelve to the authorities, instructing them how to act in relation to this matter.

7. There is another thing we want to do at the same time; that is, there is a large amount of indebtedness on tithing account. You heard something about that yesterday; it was then averred that all the indebtedness was not reported; that is, if we had it all down it would be a great deal more than is here stated. We as a people believe in paying our tithes and offerings to the Lord—and when I get through I want Brother Hardy to get up and talk on tithing; he is quite a hand to talk on this subject. We believe it is proper for us to pay one-tenth of our increase, or one-tenth of our time, as the case may be, to the Lord regularly. And a great many men do this, and do it very promptly; but a great many more do not do it, only a very little—about that much sometimes [measuring the end of the finger. Laughter.] I think it will be a tight squeeze for some of them to dig through.

8. I am not talking about this because I care anything about it personally; but because of the interest of those who ought to do it, but do not. There are a great many who have neglected the payment of these things partly through carelessness, partly through poverty and a variety of circumstances, and it begins to feel oppressive to them. Now, we want to break off this yoke too, that is, off those who are worthy; the others we do not care much about—that is unless they turn about and reform and take another course, live their religion and act as Latter-day Saints. But we wish that there shall be a release of the poor and those who are unable to meet it. The amount that is behind, according to the bishops' records—which many of the people owing it signify their willingness to pay but are not able to—is $151,798. We propose releasing half of the amount to the deserving poor, and that will be $75,899. This of course will have to be managed by the proper authorities, the same as the others; that is, first on the recommendation of the bishop of the ward, approved by the president of the stake; and then to receive the sanction of the Presiding Bishop. The P. E. Fund matter will be subject to the recommendation of the bishops, the sanction of the presidents of stakes and also the President of the P.E.F. Company, sanctioned by the Council of the Twelve; so that those that are really worthy may be released, and those that are not, ought to pay it. And then, we who have got a little behind in our tithing, will try and pay it up and thus keep the record right between us and the Lord; and then we may look for blessings from his hands. I will call a vote on this subject that I have mentioned. All who are in favor of releasing the obligations amounting to $75,899, on tithing, signify it by holding up the right hand. [Unanimous vote in favor.] All right, we knew that would be the feeling of the brethren.

9. Another thing. We have had a great scarcity of water the last year, and consequently short crops. It is proposed that inasmuch as there may be suffering more or less in some places—we hope, however, that our brethren will not allow our poor unfortunate brethren to suffer, I have not heard of anything of the kind; but still a little help will not do any harm. And where people have been in straitened circumstances through the loss of crops and of stock—and some people have lost, perhaps, their last cow, and some have lost many of their stock, and yet have a good many left; but there has been quite a general loss. Now, we propose to raise 1000 head of cows—not old cows that do not give any milk; nor any one-teated cows, but good milk cows, and have them distributed among those that may be destitute in the different stakes, under the direction of the authorities thereof. And the Church will put in 300 of this 1000. I spoke to Brother Sheets and told him that we did not want any one-teated cows. The balance of this number, namely, 700, we would like the Stakes to make up. We have been informed by the presidents that this can be easily done. It would have been quite hard a while ago, before we lost so many of our animals; but now it seems we can do it quite easy. [Laughter.] It is much better to give them to the poor than to have them die, and they have not all died yet, so we may as well begin to dispose of them.

10. I want to call upon the presidents of stakes and the bishops to know if you are prepared to furnish the balance—you that are in favor of doing it, signify by holding up the right hand. [The presidents and bishops voted

unanimously in the affirmative.] To the congregation—all you Saints who approve of this motion, signify it by holding up the right hand. [The vote was unanimous in the affirmative.]

11. Now, we are going to come to our sisters. Some people think that the sisters cannot do anything; I will show you what they can do. President Young reorganized the Relief Society—it having been organized by the Prophet Joseph Smith in Nauvoo—and inasmuch as the brethren had been careless and slow to heed the counsel of President Young in relation to storing away wheat, he requested the sisters to do it, and some of we "lords of creation" thought it was a very little thing for our sisters to be engaged in. But we find now they are of some use, and that the "ladies of creation" can do something as well as the "lords."

12. I spoke to Sister Eliza R. Snow, who is the president of the Relief Society, and asked what her feelings would be, and that of her sisters, in relation to the distribution of their wheat, for those who are in need of seed, letting the people have it as a loan, for which the bishops should become responsible and see that it is returned after harvest. She replied that it would meet her entire approbation. The sisters have not had the opportunity to meet yet to get an expression of their minds in relation to it; but I will guarantee that they will do what they are requested to do, for they have already been doing something in that line, as I understand it. Is not that so Brother Hunter? [Bishop Hunter: "Yes, sir."]

13. Now, we want to show you, what the sisters can do. I will guarantee that they will do it, and that we will have a report from them before we get through. They have 34,761 bushels of wheat. Who of you men can raise that much? Where's your wheat? [Laughter.] Now, those 34,761 bushels of wheat will be of considerable importance judiciously managed, and loaned out to some of our poor brethren. It will furnish seed wheat, and after harvest they can return it again. We do not want any more harsh talk about the woman question after this. [A voice: "May they vote now?"] O yes, they may vote now if they choose to; everybody is willing that they should vote now. [Laughter.] That is, they are willing the sisters shall vote on the wheat question. [Renewed laughter.] We may as well call a vote on this question now, our sisters are present whom we will ask to vote. All you sisters who are in favor of carrying out this request, hold up your right hand. [A forest of hands went up.] There they go, you see. [Laughter.] I think that is the most hearty vote yet. I knew they would do it. [A voice: "Is it to be loaned without interest?"] Somebody asks if it is to be loaned without interest. Why, of course it is; we do not want any nonsense of that kind; it is the time of jubilee.

14. There is another thing. We have got through with many public matters, I will say something else. It is no more harm for private people to forgive one another than for public ones. If you find people owing you who are distressed, if you will go to work and try to relieve them as much as you can, under the circumstances, God will relieve you when you get into difficulties. I will tell you that in the name of the Lord. Let us act on a kind, generous, brotherly principle, doing good one to another and carrying out the principles of the everlasting gospel in our lives.

15. We talk sometimes about the United Order. There is a little of that spirit manifested in our operations today, is there not? Operating together for the welfare of all; that is what we ought to do; that is what the gospel teaches us.

16. I speak of these things for your reflection, and they are matters we will leave in your own bosom. And I would like to see ZCMI and our bankers, merchants and other creditors scratch off a few names of their debtors; and I think they feel disposed to do it; I have spoken to some of the directors of ZCMI, and find that they feel about as we do. We expect to hear a report from them before long. While God is blessing us, let us bless one another; although we are not suffering, neither do we intend to suffer; God will not let us if we will not let one another suffer. We will go along as if we had no drouth or dead cattle, or any other stop, and everything will be prosperous. There is now every prospect of a good harvest; the grain is not all in yet, but we have snow in the mountains, and things look quite prosperous. And if we take good care of one another, God will take care of us; and he will deliver us and stretch out his hand in our behalf, and we will be his people, and he shall be our God; and we will treat one another as we wish to be treated by one another, and then we are prepared to receive blessings from his hands. Amen.

ADDRESS 10

Closing remarks made by John Taylor, President of the Quorum of the Twelve Apostles, at the morning session of the 50th Annual General Conference of The Church of Jesus Christ of Latter-day Saints convened April 7, 1880, in the Tabernacle, Salt Lake City.

1. I do not know whether we fully understand what is meant by holding up our hands to testify that we will sustain these missionaries. I will tell you how I understand it. In the first place we select the very best men we can find, and we do not want anybody to go but those who have the spirit of their mission upon them, and who feel a desire to magnify their calling and priesthood. And when they go, we wish them to go as honorable men, and we also want their wives to be treated as honorable women while their husbands are gone, and inasmuch as they or their families need assistance or looking after—although it is not all who do—we expect the Presidents of Stakes and the Bishops will attend to such matters; that the wives of our missionaries may not feel as though they were outcasts; but as honorable women, the wives of honorable men, and more so than those who are not doing their duty. We want the missionaries' wives and children made comfortable and taken care of. The sisters have voted to let us have some of their wheat for the relief of the poor. Then on the other hand, let us do something for them.

2. It does not matter how much we pray for them, for this is in accordance with our covenants or voting. Some people would rather pray for them than relieve them. Prayers are all well enough; but a little flour, a little pork, a little beef, sugar, store goods, and temporal comforts are a great deal better than all our prayers without this material assistance. Let us look after their welfare as we do after our own families, while their husbands are making a sacrifice in leaving their families and homes, and God will bless us. "Every one," says the Lord, "that hath forsaken houses, or brethren, or sisters, or father, or mother, or wife, or children, or lands, for my name's sake, shall receive an hundred fold, and shall inherit everlasting life." Let us make the words of the Lord true. Amen.

ADDRESS 11

Address given by John Taylor, President of the Quorum of the Twelve Apostles, at the afternoon session of the 50th Annual General Conference of The Church of Jesus Christ of Latter-day Saints convened April 7, 1880, in the Tabernacle, Salt Lake City.

1. In relation to the subject that I referred to this morning pertaining to the Co-op, I am informed that they are very busy with their affairs and have not had time to make any specific statement pertaining to this matter; but they feel disposed to unite with us in relieving the necessitous and worthy, as far as they would be justified in the premises, and in accordance with correct principles, to do their part. I would here remark that the same kind of feeling would be very commendable on the part of other store-keepers, bankers, or any one of us to relieve each other.

2. I would make a statement in relation to the Co-op. I have had reports from the north, that some parties who ought to know better, had said that the Co-op. was no longer a Church institution, and that it was managed, directed and controlled by a few monopolists, and that we were asking the people to sustain them in their operations, which I consider very infamous talk, and especially coming from men who profess to be men of honor. The Church, I will here say, holds an interest in that establishment to the amount of $360,000, and then there are 580 stockholders, who are Latter-day Saints, in it, besides the interest which the Church holds. And when men make such statements I consider it infamous and contrary to correct principles; and I should recommend their bishops and the authorities of the Church where they live to bring them up for slander and treat them accordingly.

3. That enterprise was started as is properly implied by the initials of its name. What is it? "Zion's Cooperative Mercantile Institution." They had for sometime difficulties to cope with; perhaps things might not have been managed as well as they could have been. There may have been errors in judgment. For sometime they did not pay dividends; but latterly they have paid what might be considered a fair dividend, and the Institution never was in a better condition than it is today. I speak of this that you who are stockholders in that institution may not be imposed upon by speculators who would seek by false representations to get from you your stock at less figures than it is really worth, I think it is our duty, as Latter-day Saints, to sustain that institution; and then, on the other hand, I think it is the duty of that institution to sustain the Saints, and let us get closer together in our relationship, and act honorably and uprightly in everything we engage in, then we can secure the blessing of the Almighty. I thought I would say so much in relation to this matter.

4. In regard to the work we are engaged in, it is one of very great importance; it is one on which God and angels, apostles, prophets, patriarchs and men of God who have lived in the different ages of the world, have felt interested about; and do today. And about these little matters of dollars and cents we do not care so much about them or ought not to; although we have to attend to all these matters—matters temporal, matters spiritual, things pertaining to time and things pertaining to eternity. It is expected of us that we act wisely, prudently and understandingly in all of our doings.

5. And in speaking of the Perpetual Emigrating Fund Company's operations, we expect that all decent men will meet their obligations, and those who are not of that class will not. We will forgive the poor and let them go, and the others may go if they want to. But we will not release them from their indebtedness if they are able to pay it. Is not that just? I think it is. We will relieve the poor and needy; but as to those people who have called upon you—and you have sent out your teams and have loaded those teams with provisions of all kinds, and you have either gone yourselves or sent your sons to drive them, to help them in, if those men do not feel like acting just and right, let them be considered among the unjust who

have used your means which was appropriated by you to relieve the necessitous and have not had the honesty to return it, but as to the poor, the needy and distressed, we will come to their relief and help them, the same as we are obliged to go to God our Heavenly Father and ask him to help us, for we are all dependent upon the mercy of God, we live in him, we move in him, and to him we are indebted for our existence as well as for every blessing that we enjoy pertaining to time or eternity.

6. He has revealed unto us the fullness of the blessings of the gospel of peace, he has taken our feet from the mire and clay and has planted us upon the rock of eternal truth, he has imparted unto us the light, intelligence and revelation of heaven, he has made us to sit together in heavenly places in Jesus Christ, he has taught us how to save ourselves and our families, how to save our progenitors and how to save our posterity. And we have this labor to perform. And if we have gone forth and assisted our brethren we have only done our duty, and what was there so much after all? Not much, we have simply performed a duty—a duty we owed to God and our brethren. If we had not had the means we could not have given it, and having given it, we will continue to do the best we can and we will keep on doing, helping all, comforting all, relieving all, teaching all and seeking to promote the well being of the human family and to carry out the designs of God in the best manner that we can.

7. One duty we owe to the world is to preach to them the gospel, and for that the priesthood is organized in part. The Elders are sent forth from time to time—many that are around me on my right and left and also before me have gone forth "weeping, bearing precious seed," they have gone in the midst of persecution and affliction, to an unthankful world, to proclaim to the people the glad tidings of salvation, and they have "returned again rejoicing bringing their sheaves with them." And we are still doing the same, the Lord has laid it upon us and it must be done.

8. And when we send out missionaries—I was told that some did not hear what I said this morning upon this subject, I will try to make you all hear now—when we send out missionaries we want you to see that their families are provided for in their absence, if they have not the means to do it themselves, stand by them and treat them kindly and provide them with the necessaries of life that they require, that they may be comfortable and made happy and be one with us, and while our brethren are engaged laboring abroad, not able to provide for their families, let us provide for them. And we call upon the presidents of Stakes, and upon the bishops and upon the people where they reside to see that these things are attended too, that the families of our missionary brethren are made comfortable and happy. Our brethren under these circumstances can feel contented and can go forth with satisfaction and joy. "Why," they will say, "we are going forth in the name of the Lord trusting in the God of Israel, and while we are gone we have left our families among our friends who will take care of them, and all is well and all will be well." When you do that they will bless you and you will be blessed in time and in eternity. It is a great privilege to be able to do good. Did you ever think of it? Jesus said, "Make to yourselves friends of the mammon of unrighteousness, that when ye fail they may receive you into everlasting habitations."

9. Then let us feel after the welfare of our brethren, and we will not dwell much upon one another's weaknesses, for God knows that all of us have enough of them, at least, I feel I have, and I think my brethren feel that they have, and I do not think that many of you are very much better than we are.

10.But I tell you what we desire to do and to see carried out. We wish correct principles to be carried out, and while we are sending the gospel to the nations afar off, we want to see the pure principles of the gospel lived up to at home. We do not want to be influenced by the corruptions that float upon us here. While we respect proper authority and pay proper deference to all honorable men in all positions in our country, we do not want to copy after the devices of this corrupt generation, we want them to keep them to themselves if they admire them. We neither want drunkenness nor whoredom nor infanticide nor foeticide nor any of the corruptions that abound throughout the world, or of this nation, of which every honorable man ought to and does feel ashamed.

11. We want to train up our youth in the fear of God, and hence we have our Young Men's and Young Ladies' Mutual Improvement Associations, which are doing a great deal of good throughout the land in teaching and being taught correct principles. It is our youth that are growing up that we shall have to look to, by and by, to bear off this kingdom, and we wish the fathers and mothers to set their children a good and proper example, to be patterns of purity, of honesty, truth, integrity and uprightness, that they may be able to meet and look every man in the face with a clear conscience and open countenance, and not be obliged to dodge around corners for fear of some one seeing them and finding them out. There are no people under the heavens that make greater pretensions than we, there are no people under the heavens that have been more favored of God than we have been.

12. We feel inclined sometimes to murmur and complain about the nation to which we belong. It is true they have not treated us very generously or very kindly in many respects, but the Lord seems to take care of us, and we do not suffer much do we? We enjoy more liberty today than millions of the inhabitants of the world do. And I do not know of any nation under the heavens where we would be better protected than we are here, thanks to many honorable men and thanks to the God of Israel who has delivered us and who has told us that he would watch over us and take care of us and provide for us, which he has done, and I feel grateful to him. For this, however, we are not under any obligations to our enemies, but no matter, if they can stand it we can. When I see men violating the sacred principles of liberty and trampling under foot the institutions of our nation, I feel to realize that they are the enemies of mankind and of the nation. I do not care what position they occupy. God will hold them to an account, as breakers of their own covenants. We will try, however, to maintain our own, and treat everybody right, and pray for all honorable men, and let the devil take care of the balance. (Laughter). This is how I feel in relation to these matters.

13. We want among ourselves to learn strictly the principles of honesty, to have and maintain honest dealing one with another

and be true to our word, and to let our word be our bond. And never mind so much about litigation. I do not know that I ever sued a man in my life, and I do not think that I ever shall. I am not fond enough of law, or money either, to do it. And God will help us and protect us in our rights, if we will only do right. And then we Latter-day Saints, we elders of Israel and we sisters of Israel, we ought to be ladies and gentlemen, we ought to treat one another with courtesy and kindness, and true politeness. Lord Chesterfield and others have written long treatises on politeness. I will tell you, in a few words, what it is to be polite: try to make everybody as comfortable and happy as you can, in all your words and in all your acts, and then you will be polite. Study the feelings of those with whom you are associated and those with whom you come in contact. And when a man meets an elder, why, says he, that is an honorable man, that man is anointed of the Lord, I will respect him, I expect to be associated with him in time and in eternity, and shall I degrade myself by speaking harshly or acting harshly towards him? No, but we will treat one another with kindness and courtesy.

14. And we will treat our sisters in the same way, and act the part of gentlemen towards them, and protect them in all their rights and in all their privileges, and never be afraid that they are going to run away with some of our rights. When I hear people talk that way I think they are a little in doubt of themselves. Why, we expect our sisters—our wives—to be with us not only in time, but in eternity; and let us treat them accordingly, with kindness, with affection, with love and with esteem. And then let the sisters turn round and treat their husbands and brothers and fathers in the same way; and let us all cultivate those principles that are calculated to promote one another's happiness and peace, that it may reign in our own bosoms, and dwell in our habitations, and prevail throughout the land, that the peace of God and the blessing of God may rest upon us.

15. And while we feel a disposition to do right and to keep the commandments of God, God will bless us and sustain us in all of our operations; and every plot and every contrivance devised against us will fall to the ground, for God will be our deliverer and our

protector. Let us train up our children in the fear of God too, and watch over their morals, and especially the morals of our daughters, and see that they do not get led astray in the paths of iniquity; but watch over them and pray with them and for them; and pray for one another, and sustain one another, and help one another, and bless one another, and God will bless us.

16. We are sending out persons to go and extend the borders of Zion, to make new settlements. I was very much pleased to hear some remarks made by Brother Woodruff in relation to these things, and the acts and doings of the brethren in Arizona, and of some of the new settlements south and southeast. There is a number of those settlements referred to by Brother Woodruff, the members of which we advised when they went, to come as near to the United Order as they could—that is, to be united. Brother Woodruff says that in those new settlements he did not see a man drunk, he did not hear a man swear, neither did he see any person use tea or coffee. In this respect they are setting an example that it would be well for us to follow.

17. And, then, do not pursue that licentious course exhibited around us here. It is this d— d infernal "civilization" that has introduced these infamies into our midst. Let us purge ourselves from them, and not mix up with their ungodly doings. Excuse me for the remarks, but they are true before God; they are both damned and infernal, for those who practice them will be damned, and they are infernal, because they proceed from the infernal regions. I do not care who sustains them, whether governors, judges, priests, or whatever they may be; they are of their father, the devil, who sustains those things and maintains them. Those crimes are not original with us; they are brought here to try to corrupt and enslave and debase and pollute us. Keep yourselves pure from these corruptions, and walk worthily of the high vocation whereunto you are called.

18. I heard the other day from one of our speakers that there were Elders, High Priests and Seventies who got drunk. What are the Bishops doing? What are the Presidents of Stakes doing? Why do you not bring them up and cut them off from the Church—any such Elder, any such High Priest, or any such Seventy, or any of the Saints who may be found guilty of such thing? For they are hypocrites, and want dealing with and severing from the Church. Furthermore, I have heard of some Bishops who have been seeking to cover up the iniquities of men; I tell them, in the name of God, they will have to bear them themselves, and meet that judgment; and I tell you that any man who tampers with iniquity, he will have to bear that iniquity, and if any of you want to partake of the sins of men, or uphold them, you will have to bear them. Do you hear it, you Bishops and you Presidents? God will require it at your hands. You are not placed in position to tamper with the principles of righteousness, nor to cover up the infamies and corruptions of men. Now, do not say you did not know anything about it; I have given you fair warning, and I clear my skirts of your blood; and their infamies will cleave to you unless you attend to it.

19. God expects us to do right; he has given unto us the priesthood for that purpose, and he requires us to magnify it and honor it and carry it out. And it is the place of those men, and the place of the teachers to see that there is no iniquity in the Church; and if they do not do their duty, it then becomes the duty of the Bishops to see to it; and if the Bishops do not see to it, it is the place of the Presidents of Stakes to see to it; and if they do not see to it, and it comes to our ears, it will then become our duty to see to it, and also to see to them who do not magnify their calling. God will not be mocked. "Whatsoever a man soweth, that shall he also reap; if he sows to the flesh, he shall of the flesh reap corruption; if he sows to the spirit, he shall of the spirit reap life everlasting."

20. We are gathered here to serve God; we are gathered here to be taught in the ways of the Lord; we are gathered here to build up temples, and then to administer in them; we are gathered here to send the Gospel to the nations of the earth, and to fulfill those various requirements which God has placed upon us to attend to; and if we are faithful in all our duties, God will bless us.

21. I find that the time has expired. Shall we continue the Conference another day? All who desire to do so say aye. (The vast congregation responded "aye.")

ADDRESS 12

Closing Address given by John Taylor, President of the Quorum of the Twelve Apostles, at the 50th Annual General Conference of The Church of Jesus Christ of Latter-day Saints convened April 8, 1880, in the Tabernacle, Salt Lake City.

1. Shall we keep on a little longer, or shall we quit? I think we have a little time. We adjourned the first day of our meeting because it was rather cold, and now it is not quite so cold, and we will stay a little longer. I have felt a desire to hear the testimony of my brethren of the Twelve, and that of our Counselor who is here. All of the Twelve are present except one; he is at his post, attending to the interests of Zion. And we will pray for him, that God may be with him and sustain and preserve him, and through him preserve this people.

2. There are a few things I want to speak upon, and I realize that while I and my brethren are speaking, we are not only speaking to this congregation, but to others—to the Saints throughout this and adjoining Territories; to the inhabitants of the United States and to the world; because our testimony will go forth to them.

3. There are many things which I wish to draw the attention of the brethren to, that they may not lose sight of them. One is Cooperation. We have a number of Cooperative institutions; we have one here, which may properly be denominated the parent institution; we have also many others, and we wish to sustain them, and to do it not nominally, but really in our hearts, and with honesty of purpose; and do everything we do on that principle, without hypocrisy of any kind, in truthfulness before God, and operating together for the welfare of Israel. But Cooperation is not a system only for importing goods and selling them; we want to cooperate in home manufactures. We have done considerable of that, and we desire to do more of it. The Cooperative Store here has, I presume, as much as two hundred men at work in all—about 140 to 150 making shoes, and about 50 or 60 making certain kinds of clothing; and we want to see these things increased, until we can make all our own clothing right here at home; and instead of having to employ tailors abroad to make it for us, we want, as quickly as practicable—and I think it is practicable now—to make it ourselves. I mean the clothing which is imported here; and then, instead of employing comparatively only a few men, use all of our own labor; let our factories be run on double time and use our own wool at home, instead of exporting it, and thus increase the means of employment and be self-sustaining. And then if we could get some of the best machinery for the manufacture of hats, that would be another commendable enterprise, because we use a large number. I see there are a great many heads here, and there are a great many more in the Territory, all needing hats—and if we should supply them ourselves it would be much better than to take the other course.

4. Then there are some that are trying to engage in the United Order, up and down in different parts, especially far off in the South. They have our blessing and our prayers. I say God bless them in all their attempts to approach that order which is instituted of God. We have not got at it yet, by and by we will come to it; but in the meantime we will approach it as near as we can. God is pleased with the action of this people in their liberality towards the poor. Now be liberal one towards another, and help and relieve one another, and God will relieve and bless you.

5. Speaking again of Cooperation we have what are called Boards of Trade, and it is expected that they will operate and cooperate with our central institution. A meeting of that kind will be held this afternoon, therefore I do not wish at this time to say much upon that subject.

6. There is a subject I wish to speak a little upon to High Councils, to Bishops, to Bishops' Counselors and to the Presidents of Stakes particularly; but as we shall hold a priesthood meeting, what I am about to refer to can be more fully talked of then; but I will

allude to it briefly here. Reference was made by one of the speakers to a revelation contained in the Doctrine and Covenants, in which we are given to understand that the priesthood is given unto us, not for our own aggrandizement, nor to advance our own interests, but to build up the Church and Kingdom of God upon the earth, acting upon the principles of justice, equity and righteousness, as you are yourselves willing to be judged—and will be judged, before the Great I AM, when the time comes that we shall have to give an account of our stewardship. We want no favoritism shown to any man, or to any woman, or to any set of men, but in the administration of justice to do it as in the sight of God, with integrity of heart and uprightness; anything different from this cannot receive the approbation of God. And furthermore, this priesthood is not conferred upon men to exercise any degree of unrighteousness or tyranny, or to in any way oppress or injure anybody; but if any man use his priesthood to subserve any such purpose, God will take hold of him, as the Priesthood above him will take hold of him, and he will be removed out of his place except he repent.

7. Another thing. The Lord has given unto us our various Courts—Bishops' Courts, High Councils, etc., and it is expected that the Saints will adjust any matters of difficulty or dispute that may arise among them, before those courts, and that they do not go to law before the ungodly; and if any do so, I will promise them, in the name of the Lord God of Israel, that they will be destroyed by the ungodly. Hear it, you Elders of Israel, and you Saints of Latter days! Let us seek in the first place among ourselves to execute judgment in righteousness, and then let every man and every woman submit to them. That is God's law, and any man that acts contrary to this law cannot go into the temples of the Lord to receive the ordinances of God's house. For if we cannot submit to the law of God on the one hand, we cannot receive the blessings through his ordinances, on the other hand. Is that right? [The congregation answered, Yes.]

8. Again. I have been very much interested in our Sabbath School operations, and should have been pleased to have been present at the general meeting of the Sunday School Union, last evening, but having so much labor on hand, I thought it better to rest. But I am interested in the cause of our Sunday Schools, and so are my brethren of the Twelve. God has given unto us the most precious of gifts—children, and has placed us over them as the fathers and mothers of lives. They are eternal beings, and it should be our constant care to train them up in the fear of God. And we want the Bishops and the Presidents to sustain them, which I believe they do, and all good brethren and all good sisters should take an interest in the welfare of the rising generation, and do all they can to train the children in the fear of God. And God will bless you in your labors and desires, and the youth of Zion will rise up and call you blessed. And let no man or woman shirk the responsibility of teaching the children when it is put upon him or her.

9. And then, our Young Men's and Young Women's Mutual Improvement Associations are very good institutions, and the Lord is blessing them, and he will continue to bless them; and we desire to see them encouraged in their operations throughout the land, that the principles of righteousness, truth and purity may be promulgated and sustained; and that vice, evil, corruption, and infamy may be frowned upon, and the right honored and maintained; and that our youth may grow up as plants of renown and become mighty men and women in Israel, filled with the gift of the Holy Ghost and the power of God.

10. Again, in regard to the Relief Societies. They are doing a great deal of good, and I say, God bless the sisters, and let all the congregation say Amen. [The vast congregation said, Amen.] Sisters, continue your labors of love, and continue to propagate good, virtuous and holy principles; teach your daughters, and also your sons, principles of holiness and purity; and seek out the poor and distressed and minister to them, and God will bless you in your labors. We thank you, and I thank you in behalf of the Twelve, and in behalf of the people, for the liberal vote you gave us yesterday in regard to supplying the poor and the necessitous with the grain that you have stored—something which we, who profess to be so much more intelligent, have not been able to do. God bless you; continue your good works and adhere to the principles

of right and truth, and God will bless you, and he will bless your sons and daughters, and your names will be honored in Israel, and you will be honored by God and the holy angels.

11. Again, in regard to the building of temples, we are engaged in doing a good work. Our Salt Lake Temple is progressing very nicely, and we expect it will go forward as usual, only a little more so, next season. I would say in regard to this temple—there were some remarks made about no reports having been made. This is true; the people here have been careless and indifferent, at the same time a large amount of means has been used on it, and why the report has been omitted, I do not know. And the building known as the Salt Lake Assembly Hall has been erected within a short time, at a cost, I suppose, of not less than $100,000; besides attending to other things. I have no complaint to make, only we will try and do a little better; and when you are called upon to furnish quarry hands, be a little more prompt about it, and do not be backward; and when you are called upon to furnish men to assist us here, do not be backward about it. And we will try and improve, one and all, upon our past labors in relation to these things. In Logan and Manti we have two temples under construction, and when finished they will be a credit to the people. We are trying at least to carry out the word and will of God in this direction, and he is helping us to do it. We will build our temples and administer in them, and stand forth as the priests of the Most High God, administering salvation to the living and for the dead.

12. And then, we will continue to send forth, as we are doing, our missionaries to the nations of the earth. Although they do not, very frequently, receive us very kindly, but no matter; they did not receive Jesus, nor the prophets in ancient times, very kindly. The laws of God, nor the servants of God, never were received very kindly upon the earth, except for about two hundred years upon this continent; but the time is coming when the Saints of the Most High God will take the kingdom and possess it, and reign for ever and ever; and he whose right it is will come and take the possession.

13. I will speak a little in regard to our government. We complain a good deal about the way we have been treated. Well, we have been treated very scurvily, it is true—everybody will admit that—but we must consider the circumstances: they are not of our faith, they do not believe as we do, they have their ideas, and theories, and notions, and so have other nations as well as this. Well, what shall we do? We will do the very best we can. Do you think you could improve your condition in any other nation or under any other government, or receive any better treatment than you do in this? I tell you no, you could not. We here, at least, have the form and—I was going to say, the guarantee of liberty; that is, the promise of the guarantee. We have the form, but it is like a religion without the power. What shall we do? Consign everybody to damnation and destruction? No. Who are they? They are God's children. Would he like to see them reform? He would; and he has told us to try to do it. If we had children that had gone astray, would we not like to see them reform? Yes, we would, and if our children do anything wrong we tell them of it, and we try to reform them. We will therefore continue to go to this nation as we have done, as saviors, with the message of life and salvation, and we will pray for the honest, the upright and virtuous, and those who love righteousness, and those who are willing to accord to men equal rights, and a great many who are not; and we will do them all the good we can. We will sustain the government in its administration, and be true to it, and maintain this position right along. And when division, strife, trouble and contention arise, we will try to still the troubled waters, and act in all honesty as true friends to the government; and when war shall exist among them, and there is no one found to sustain the remnants of liberty that may be left, the Elders of Israel will rally round the standard of freedom and proclaim liberty to all the world. These things will assuredly take place, and when they do our motto will be as it now is, "Peace on earth and good will to men." These are our sentiments and feelings in relation to these matters. But while we feel liberal, generous and kind to all men of all nations, classes and creeds, we have no fellowship with unrighteousness; we do not

believe in the actions of many men, nor in their corruptions and evils; we want to purge ourselves from them and stand forth aloof as servants of God in the midst of a crooked and perverse generation, and try in all fidelity, in the interests of our common humanity, to bear off the government of God triumphantly.

14. I would also say a little about the P. E. Fund. While we have relieved a great many, to the amount of $800,000, of their indebtedness, which is right before God and all honorable men; there are a great many poor Saints among the nations yet. And we want those who are not forgiven—for we shall not forgive those that are able to pay and do not do it—to come forward and meet their obligations. And then, if there are those that are desirous of assisting any in this direction, who have it in their hearts to do so, and to impart a blessing to their friends in foreign lands, let them come forward and present their means to Brother Carrington, who is President of the Perpetual Emigration Fund Company, and he will see that the means are properly applied. We do not want to close up this avenue of relief to the scattered poor, but we will continue our efforts to gather Israel. And further; we will continue to build temples, and to administer in them, and we will also continue to preach the Gospel, until the word of the Lord be fulfilled pertaining to this and other nations, and then he will say, "Turn to the Jews, go to the House of Israel, the cup of the Gentiles is full. This time has not come yet."

15. Now, in regard to these matters, God is our God in whom we put our trust; we have nothing ourselves to boast of. Have we wealth? Who gave it to us? The Lord. Have we property? Who put us in possession of it? The Lord. Our horses, cattle and sheep, our flocks, herds and possessions, are his gifts. The gold and the silver and the precious things of earth, and also the cattle upon a thousand hills, are his, and we are his, and in his hands, and all nations are in his hands, and he will do with us and with them as seemeth him good. And as a kind, wise Father, he will watch over their interests; and when the time of judgment comes, it will not be withheld. We ought always to remember that our strength is in God; we have nothing to boast of ourselves, we have no intelligence that God has not given unto us; we have nothing in life, or property, but what has been given unto us of the Lord. Everything we possess pertaining to time and eternity has been imparted to us by him. Let us then act as Saints of God in all humility, without rebuke, in the midst of a crooked and perverse generation.

16. I say God bless you, and God bless my brethren of the Twelve, and God bless my brethren of the Seventies, and God bless my brethren of the High Priesthood, and God bless the Presidents of Stakes and their Counselors, and God bless the Bishops and their Counselors, and the Elders, Priests, Teachers and Deacons, our missionaries laboring in foreign lands, and all the Holy Priesthood, and God bless all the Saints. And let us all seek to do our duty and honor and magnify our calling.

17. Fear God and keep His commandments, and the peace and blessing of God will abide with us from this time henceforth and forever. And I now testify, as my brethren have done, that this is the work of God that has been revealed by the Almighty, and I know it. And God will sustain Israel, and no power can injure us if we will do what is right; and this kingdom will roll on, and the purposes of God will progress, and Zion will arise and shine, and the glory of God will rest upon her. And we will continue to grow and increase until the kingdoms of this world shall become the kingdoms of our God and his Christ, and he will reign for ever and ever. Amen.

ADDRESS 13

Address delivered by President John Taylor at the 50th Semiannual General Conference of The Church of Jesus Christ of Latter-day Saints convened October 10, 1880, in the Tabernacle, Salt Lake City.

1. I will make a few remarks while the Sacrament is being administered. It is gratifying to me to be able to state that now all the various organizations of the Church are provided for. For some time the Twelve have been operating in the capacity of a First Presidency, and it was very proper that they should have acted in that capacity. As you heard Brother Pratt state this morning, in referring to this subject, this was the course adopted at the time when the Prophet Joseph Smith left us. The Twelve then stepped forward into the position of the First Presidency, and operated for about three years in that capacity. And when President Young left us it was thought proper that the same course should be pursued. The Twelve, I believe, have in this respect magnified their calling and taken a course that is approved by the Lord, and I think also by the brethren, judging from the vote given here today.

2. Had it not been our duty to have the Church organized fully and completely in all its departments, I should have much preferred to have continued with the brethren of the Twelve, speaking of it merely as a matter of personal feeling. But there are questions arising in regard to these matters that are not for us to say how they shall be, or what course shall be pursued. When God has given us an order and has appointed an organization in his Church, with the various quorums of Priesthood as presented to us by revelation through the Prophet Joseph Smith, I do not think that either the First Presidency, the Twelve, the High Priests, the Seventies, the Bishops, or anybody else, have a right to change or alter that plan which the Lord has introduced and established. And as you heard Brother Pratt state this morning, one duty devolving upon the Twelve is to see that the churches are organized correctly. And I think they are now thus organized throughout the land of Zion. The Churches generally are organized with Presidents of Stakes and their Counselors, with High Councils, with Bishops and their Counselors, and with the Lesser Priesthood, according to the order that is given us.

3. Then we have the High Priests, Seventies and Elders occupying their places according to their Priesthood, position and standing in the Church. And the First Presidency seemed to be the only quorum that was deficient. And it is impossible for men acquainted with the order of the Holy Priesthood to ignore this quorum, as it is one of the principal councils of the Church. While the Twelve stand as a bulwark ready to protect, defend and maintain, to step forward and carry out the order of God's Kingdom in times of necessity, such as above referred to, yet when everything is adjusted and matters assume their normal condition, then it is proper that the Quorum of the First Presidency, as well as all other quorums, should occupy the place assigned it by the Almighty.

4. These were the suggestions of the Spirit of the Lord to me. I expressed my feelings to the Twelve, who coincided with me, and, indeed, several of them had had the same feelings as those with which I was actuated. It is not with us, or ought not to be, a matter of place, position, or honor, although it is a great honor to be a servant of God; it is a great honor to hold the Priesthood of God; but while it is an honor to be God's servants, holding His Priesthood, it is not honorable for any man or any set of men to seek for position in the Holy Priesthood. Jesus said, "Ye have not called me, but I have called you." And as I said before, had I consulted my own personal feelings, I would have said, things are going on very pleasantly, smoothly and agreeably; and I have a number of good associates whom I respect and esteem, as my brethren, and I rejoice in their counsels. Let things remain as they are. But it is not for me to say, it is not for you to say, what we would individually prefer, but it is for us holding the Holy Priesthood; to see that all the organizations of that Priesthood are preserved intact, and that

everything in the Church and kingdom of God is organized according to the plan which He has revealed; therefore we have taken the course which you have been called upon to sanction by your votes today.

5. I would further remark that I have examined very carefully for some time past some of those principles you heard read over in the Priesthood meeting, and which were referred to in part, by Brother Pratt, this morning. And there are other principles associated with the Priesthood that we wish and hope to have thoroughly defined; so that every man will know his true position and the nature of the calling and responsibility and Priesthood with which he is endowed. It is very proper and very important that we should comprehend these things; every man in his place, and every woman in her place; but I more particularly refer to the Holy Priesthood, that every man may feel and realize the duties and responsibilities which rest upon him.

6. It is gratifying to me, and it is no doubt satisfactory to you, to see the unanimity and oneness of feeling and the united sentiment which have been manifested in our votes. Those votes being taken first in their quorum capacity, each quorum having voted affirmatively, then by the vote of the Presidents of the several quorums united, and afterwards by the vote of the quorums and people combined, men and women, among the many thousands assembled who have participated in this vote, having a full and free opportunity, uncontrolled by any influence other than the Spirit of God, to express their wishes and desires, there has not been, from all that we could discover, one dissenting vote.

7. You could not find the same unanimity anywhere upon the earth. Union is a principle that exists in the heavens, and so far as we manifest this feeling in all sincerity, so far do we exhibit our faith in God, in His Priesthood, and in His law as revealed to us. For our religion, our Priesthood and all the blessings and ordinances that we possess were not given us by any man or any combination of men; it was the Lord who revealed all of these things or we could not have been in possession of them. We have had an example here today of the unanimity which characterizes those possessed of the Spirit of the Gospel, and it ought to be a pattern for us in all of our affairs.

8. And now let me refer with pride to my brethren of the Twelve here, which I do by saying that while they as a quorum held the right by the vote of the people to act in the capacity of the First Presidency, yet when they found, as Brother Pratt expressed it this morning, that they had performed their work, they were willing to withdraw from that Presidency, and put it in the position that God had directed, and fall back into the place that they have always held, as the Twelve Apostles of the Church of Jesus Christ of Latter-day Saints. I say it is with pride that I refer to this action and the feeling that prompted it. I very much question whether you could find the same personal exhibition of disinterested motives and self-abnegation, and the like readiness to renounce place and position in deference to principle, among the same number of men in any other place. They saw the necessity of this action; a motion was made in that Council; and the vote was unanimously adopted that the First Presidency be re-organized, and afterwards the brethren to fill this quorum were selected.

9. The next step was to present the matter to the Church, and it was laid before the Priesthood at a meeting, when there were present a representation of all the important authorities of the Church in the different Stakes in Zion. After having done that, lest some difficulty might exist some where, it was thought proper to pursue the course taken today—that each organization of the Priesthood, embracing all the quorums, should be seated in a quorum capacity by themselves, and separately have the opportunity of voting freely and fully without control of any kind, and of expressing their feelings, and finally, that the whole congregation should have the same opportunity.

10. This is emphatically the voice of God, and the voice of the people; and this is the order that the Lord has instituted in Zion, as it was in former times among Israel. God gave his commandments; they were delivered by His Prophet to the people and submitted to them, and all Israel said, Amen. You have all done this by your votes; which vote, so far as we can learn, has been without a dissenting voice either among the separate quorums, or in the vote of the combined quorums and people. Now, continue to be united in everything

as you are in this thing, and God will stand by you from this time henceforth and for ever. And any man who opposes principles of this kind is an enemy of God, an enemy of the Church and kingdom of God upon the earth, an enemy to the people of God, and an enemy to the freedom and rights of man.

11. The Lord has selected a Priesthood that He might among all Israel make known His mind and will through them, and that they might be His representatives upon the earth. And while He does this He does not wish men to be coerced or forced to do things contrary to their will. But where the Spirit of God is, there is union, harmony and liberty, and where it is not there is strife, confusion and bondage. Let us then seek to be one, honor our God, honor our religion, and keep the commandments of God, and seek to know his will, and then to do it.

12. I do not know but that I have spoken as long as I ought to. God bless you; God bless the Twelve; and God bless the Presidents of Stakes and their associates, and the Seventies and the High Priests, and the Elders, and the Bishops, and the Lesser Priesthood. And God bless the Relief Societies, and the Young People's Mutual Improvement Associations, and all who love and fear God and keep his commandments. And may God bless the Sunday Schools and the Primary Associations and the educational interests, and all interested in the welfare of Zion, as well as all the good and virtuous, the honorable and high-minded everywhere, who are seeking to promote purity, holiness, and virtue on the earth. And God bless our singers and all who make music for us; and may the peace and blessing of God rest upon all Israel. And when you go to your homes, carry out the principles you have voted for, and God will bless you and your generations after you; and you shall be blessed in time, and through all eternity. And I bless you by virtue of the holy Priesthood, in the name of Jesus Christ. Amen.

ADDRESS 14

Opening remarks made by President John Taylor at the 51st Annual General Conference of The Church of Jesus Christ of Latter-day Saints convened April 3, 1881, in the Tabernacle, Salt Lake City.

1. We have met this morning to attend to the duties and the responsibilities which devolve upon us at our Annual Conference. We thought that we would change the program a little as regards time; and as it is the spring season of the year, when men are generally engaged with their labor, we thought by commencing our Conference today, it would give men an opportunity of being present without losing a day's labor in their fields. We have this morning a delightful time, very pleasant weather, and everything favorable for our assembling together. And whilst we are thus assembled, it is proper that we, as Saints of the Most High God, ought to have our hearts and feelings under the direction and inspiration of the Almighty, that we may seek for the good Spirit of the Lord to be with us, to guide us and to direct us in all of our teachings, in all of our business transactions, in all of our counseling, and in the various duties and responsibilities which devolve upon us to attend to on this occasion.

2. This is the 51st anniversary of the organization of the Church of Jesus Christ of Latter-day Saints—or it will be next Wednesday morning—and when we reflect upon the circumstances with which we have been surrounded from that time until the present, we certainly must feel that we have cause to rejoice and to be grateful to the God of Israel for the many mercies and blessings which He has manifested toward us, and for His protecting care which has been over us in the midst of opposition, in the midst of calumny, and in the midst of reproach, having been assailed all the time by enemies to God and to His truth, the Lord has preserved us, and we will give to God the glory. And irrespective of the feelings and ideas and theories of men, we feel to rejoice and praise God our Heavenly Father from the bottom of our hearts for the kindness and mercy which He has vouchsafed unto us; and whatever may be the feelings of man toward us, our feelings are—glory to God in the highest, and on earth peace and goodwill to men, even to all who love the truth everywhere, among all peoples in all the world. And whatever may be the feelings of others toward us, our feelings are nothing but kindness and mercy and salvation to the human family.

3. We are here to carry out the word and will and designs of God. We are here to help to build up His kingdom, to combat error, to advance principles of truth, to establish Zion, and to bring to pass things that have been spoken of by all the holy prophets since the world was. And in our teachings, in our administrations, in our selecting missionaries to go forth to the nations of the earth to proclaim the unsearchable riches of Christ, and in all the relations that we may have to do with, in our assembling together, we ask for the guidance of the good Spirit of God to be with us. And I say to Israel, God bless you and lead you in the paths of life, in the name of Jesus. Amen.

ADDRESS 15

Remarks made by President John Taylor at the 51st Annual General Conference of The Church of Jesus Christ of Latter-day Saints convened April 4, 1881, in the Tabernacle, Salt Lake City.

1. With regard to the principles that have been advanced here this morning, they are things that demand our most serious consideration. We, as Latter-day Saints, profess to have come out of the world, gathered together to the land of Zion for the purpose of fulfilling the word, the will and the law of God. We are living in an eventful age, at a time when God has decreed to have a controversy with the nations, wherein he has determined to gather his people together, and wherein he has made manifest to them his will, his law, his Gospel, as it existed in other ages when God revealed himself to the human family.

2. And living as we are in this day and age of the world, having been gathered into the fold of God, having received the holy priesthood, and being placed in communication with the Lord, it behooves us as Saints to study and ponder well the path of our feet, to comprehend the position we occupy and our relationship to God, to each other, to our families, to the Church and the kingdom of God and to the world, that we may act wisely, intelligently, and understandingly, and that in all our doings we may be under the guidance and influence of the Spirit of the living God, that we may walk in the paths of life and under the guidance and direction of the Almighty, carrying out the great and sacred principles he has committed to our care.

3. When men do this they will not apostatize as has been referred to; when men fear God and humble themselves before him and place themselves under His influence and control, and seek the guidance of the Holy Spirit of God, they will not apostatize; but when men, under the cloak of the Gospel, introduce pernicious practices and permit themselves to be governed by wrong influences, then they place themselves in a position to be led captive by the devil at his own will. Hence the necessity of the Saints being humble and prayerful and diligent in the performance of their duties, and in seeking to magnify their callings and to honor their God. Especially are those duties more incumbent upon men in authority than upon others, and so far from men being puffed up in pride or with any ostentatious feelings because of any position they may occupy in the Church and kingdom of God, all that a good man will seek to do will be to know the mind of his Heavenly Father and to do it, and to seek to prove himself worthy to be accepted of God and the holy angels, and be esteemed by all good, and honorable and upright men. We have a reason given us here (Book of Doctrine and Covenants) why men apostatize. I will read it:

4. "Behold there are many called, but few are chosen. And why are they not chosen?" Here is the reason. "Because their hearts are set so much upon the things of this world, and aspire to the honors of men, that they do not learn this one lesson—That the rights of the priesthood are inseparably connected with the powers of heaven, and that the powers of heaven cannot be controlled nor handled only upon the principles of righteousness. That they may be conferred upon us it is true; but when we undertake to cover our sins, or to gratify our pride, or vain ambition, or to exercise control, or dominion, or compulsion, upon the souls of the children of men, in any degree of unrightousness, behold the heavens will withdraw themselves; the spirit of the Lord is grieved; and when it is withdrawn, amen to the priesthood, or the authority of that man. Behold! ere he is aware, he is left unto himself, to kick against the pricks; to persecute the Saints and to fight against God. We have learned by sad experience, that it is the nature and disposition of nearly all men, as soon as they get a little authority, as they suppose, they will immediately begin to exercise unrighteous dominion."

5. Hear it you Elders of Israel, you Presidents of Stakes, you Bishops and you men in authority, and you Elders everywhere! This is the reason why men have departed from the truth and have apostatized.

6. "Hence many are called but few are chosen. No power or influence can or ought to be maintained by virtue of the priesthood, only by persuasion, by long suffering, by gentleness and meekness, and by love unfeigned; by kindness and pure knowledge, which shall greatly enlarge the soul without hypocrisy and without guile."

7. This is the reason why so many have stumbled, and I will say still further that unless the elders of Israel realize their position, whether they be presidents of stakes, or whether they be the Twelve, or the First Presidency, or whether they be Bishops, or whether they hold any office of authority in the Church and kingdom of God—no matter what position they may occupy, if they go to work to seek to aggrandize themselves at the expense of the Church and kingdom of God, the Spirit of God will be withdrawn from them and they will be left as others have been left to "kick against the pricks" and to fight against God, and they will find their way to perdition instead of to the celestial kingdom of God. When we have great rights, great intelligence and great blessings conferred upon us, the more need we have of being watchful and prayerful and diligent in the observance of our duties, and to feel that we are the representatives of God on the earth, the mouthpieces of Jehovah, to proclaim the will of God to men and to act as shepherds in Israel, and feel interested in the welfare of the people and the building up Zion of our God. When we entertain feelings of another nature our minds become beclouded, we get led astray, as others have been led astray in former ages and other circumstances.

8. This is not a new thing. We can trace it back to eternity, and we can follow it also with the times to come. The Scriptures tell us that the angels who kept not their first estate, but rebelled against God and violated His law were cast out. How many of them? One-third of them we are told. Who were they? The children of our Father as we are. Were they cast out? Yes, we are told they were, and we believe it. Why were they cast out? Well, I will go a little further on this point and show the reason.

9. When the plans of God in relation to this earth on which we live were presented before the intelligences of heaven, there were many there who thought, as some men frequently think now, that they knew the proper course to pursue better than God our Heavenly Father knew; and hence we read of Satan presenting himself before the Lord and saying, "Father I will be thy Son." And what will you do?" I will redeem every soul of man, that there shall not one be lost"—just as people are trying to do now-a-days, as Brother Joseph F., has been telling us, and they would like to redeem your children, and redeem you, yes, and corrupt you and lead you astray—for we are told the devil was a liar from the beginning; and he keeps it up pretty well yet. The Lord then turned to his well beloved Son and said, "Father, thy will be done." "You have presented before us your plans, your ideas and views which are calculated to exalt and ennoble mankind; and believing in your intelligence and in your good motives, and in the instruction that comes from you, I shall be subject to you and your law. Father, thy will be done," while Satan said that he would go and save every soul, and then asked the Father to give him his honor. That is, in effect, "O Lord, thou art all powerful and great and magnanimous, bestow upon me thy power that I then, in thy name, may bring about the destruction of thy people.

10. Just as people now want to get in many instances the honor of the people and of the Priesthood to bring about their own purposes and to lead us down into the path that leads to death. What did the Lord do? He knew the designs of the enemy and the course which he would pursue. He wanted to do away with the free agency of men—like men do today in this broad republic, to deprive men of their liberty and their rights. God, being our helper, we will try to sustain from this time henceforth. [Amen by the congregation.] And because he sought to take away their liberty, their free agency, going contrary to the law of God, he was cast out, and those also who clung to him, even one-third of the angels of heaven, before they had their bodies.

11. What followed after? There is a big field before me and I have not time to enter into the question; but I will briefly touch upon a few principles.

12. Man came to the earth, and when man came, Satan came also. You know the history

in regard to this. God gave man a law, and Satan began to try to pervert that law; this was one of the first things he did. In process of time there were two men born—Cain and Abel, and many others besides; but these were representative men. One placed himself under the influence of God; the other under the influences of the devil, and he became the father of liars and deceivers, and was instructed by the enemy of all righteous to introduce murder and bloodshed and confusion, which we read of as having descended from Cain, passing through the different ages, and to many people of this age and continent; and it is now spreading among the nations of the earth in every form of terrorism and secret organizations; and murder, bloodshed and destruction are in their hearts. They hatch cocatrice eggs, and weave the spider's web; and those that eat of the eggs die; and the eggs that are hatched break forth into vipers.

13. We see this spirit in the earth; and that spirit would like to find a footing among us; and nothing but our adherence to God and His laws, our fidelity to truth and our integrity to correct principles, will preserve us from these infamies that are spreading themselves abroad in the world. And if we would secure to ourselves eternal lives and possess thrones and principalities and powers in the eternal worlds, it is for us to obey the Lord our God, to keep his commandments and square our lives according to the principles that God has revealed, be in communion with each other and with the holy priesthood on the earth, with God and the holy priesthood in the heavens, that we may be one with the Saints of God, one with the apostles and prophets and presidency, one with the ancient apostles and prophets and men of God, one with God our Heavenly Father and with Jesus the Mediator.

14. I would like to talk an hour or two on this subject if I had the time and strength to do it, but the time has expired.

15. Brethren, let us be for God, for truth, for righteousness, and watch over ourselves and our families that God has placed within our power and under our direction, and do not let us throw them into the hands of the destroyer as has been referred to, but let us cleave to the truth and honor our God and God will bless us and sustain us and exalt us in time and throughout all the eternities to come. And about the plans and contrivances of men, they may rage and imagine vain things, yet God has them and us in his charge and he will say to all as he did to the waters of the mighty ocean, "Hitherto shalt thou come and no further, and here shall thy proud waves be stayed." And the principles of eternal truth shall roll forward and continue to progress, until loud anthems will be proclaimed upon the earth, and glory and honor and might and majesty and dominion be ascribed to God that sitteth upon the throne and unto the Lamb forever. Amen.

ADDRESS 16

Remarks made by President John Taylor at the 51st Annual General Conference of The Church of Jesus Christ of Latter-day Saints convened April 5, 1881, in the Tabernacle, Salt Lake City.

1. In reading over these statements, there are some things it may be necessary to mention. It would take too much time to give before this conference a detailed account of all the receipts and disbursements of the Trustee-in-Trust. We have, however, an Auditing Committee, which was duly appointed by the conference for the purpose of examining all the income and expenditure, and comparing and investigating all these matters. We have to look to them for their action in regard to these details, and a vote has already been taken on the subject. However, it is proper you should know these things. And I would state that although I act as Trustee-in-Trust, still the Auditing Committee, I presume, know more of the details of these things than I do, because they come more especially under their supervision.

2. In regard to the operations of the Perpetual Emigration Fund Company, we remitted, as you know, at the jubilee, quite a large amount, leaving a debt, also, of a very large amount. I find the statement is not here. However, I suppose it amounts, in general terms, to some $700,000 or $800,000 yet due to that fund, and having remitted a like amount, we do expect the brethren who are owing this fund will try now to meet their obligations in order that we may have a better showing than we have today. We certainly ought to be ashamed, as a people, of our negligence in regard to this thing. Out of this $800,000, we have only received about $8,000 within the last six months—that is, about the one-hundredth part. It is rather a poor showing for Latter-day Saints who profess to be honest, and I think we ought to attend to these matters. This money has been laid out to assist people in coming to this land, and their promises to pay have been received. We have authorized the Bishops and Presidents of the several Stakes to remit a certain amount of this indebtedness, and we do expect that those who are owing a balance will he honorable enough to attend to it,

otherwise it places it out of our power, without calling upon those who have hitherto subscribed, to help us to meet obligations and, that would hardly be an act of justice. We therefore call upon those brethren who are owing the Emigration Fund to attend to it, in order that the funds of the company may be relieved, and that we may be able to give assistance to those who desire to emigrate to this country, for there are others, besides you, who ought to receive the benefit of this fund, and those who do not pay their indebtedness are depriving them of this privilege. Excuse me if I talk plainly upon this subject. It is a subject of importance, and men ought to meet their indebtedness; but when men do not attempt to meet obligations that are due to the poor, they become delinquent before their brethren and before their God. We do not have jubilees, you know, every year, they only come once in fifty years, therefore these things ought to be attended to. I speak thus in behalf of the poor in Europe. Their cries come to me from time to time, and to the Perpetual Emigration Fund Company, saying, "Cannot you assist us?" Why yes, we could help you bountifully if your brethren who have received assistance would only be honest and meet their obligations, and we would do it very gladly, with a willing heart, and with good feelings.

3. In regard to the labors of the Relief Society, they are certainly very creditable and very praiseworthy, and I felt unwilling that these sisters should not be made mention of, for they are doing a very creditable labor in Israel. It seems to be the peculiar province of the sisters to act in this capacity, and I do not know but they put to blush a little even some of us brethren. We act, it is true, pretty liberally in many instances, and in some not very; but the sisters have been very liberal and generous, and have accomplished the object they have had in view, which has been to look after the poor, the needy, the destitute, the sick and the afflicted, and to administer to

their wants. And I suppose they are about the best kind of teachers that our bishops have to assist them in their several wards. I think the bishops would give that testimony. They are very efficient in assisting them in their various wards, and they make splendid teachers in going round and looking after the welfare especially of their sisters, for they can sympathize and know their requirements better than men do sometimes. And than, these sisters are producing a very good moral influence in their teachings. We have many pure, high minded ladies who go forth among the people, and travel from place to place as missionaries, teaching, instructing, guiding, blessing and benefiting the people; and I say, God bless the sisters for their labors, and I say to them, continue in your good work, and God will continue to bless you and your children after you, and many thousands will yet rise and call you blessed.

4. Seek to instill into your daughters, as you are doing, and into your sons, the principles of chastity and virtue and honor, that while men without principle and without honor, and contrary to truth are maligning you, you may stand forth, and your children with you, as the protectors and maintainers of virtue, and keep your daughters from the contaminating influence of those abominable wretches, characters who are seeking to introduce iniquity in our midst, and to destroy your virtue. There are numbers of these men, and they publish unblushingly in their papers that they would rather your sons and your daughters were drunkards and prostitutes and debauchees, than be subject to the "tyranny" we exercise over you. Do you want their tender mercies? Do you want to wallow in their corruption? Do you want to be besmeared with their infamy? God forbid! (Amen by the congregation.) God forbid! I say "my soul enter not thou into their secret, and with them mine honor be not thou united." They are too low, too degraded for honorable men and women to have anything to do with.

5. I call upon the elders and upon the fathers of this people, and upon the sisters and mothers of this people, to protect their sons and daughters from those loathsome lepers that have come among you who profess to be the advocates of freedom, forsooth,

and equal rights—just as much as the devil is. "The devil is a pretended advocate of "freedom and of the rights of men," but we don't want to place ourselves under his tender mercies nor theirs.

6. I am pleased to listen to the statements that have been made in regard to out Sunday Schools, and I would say that there is not a more honorable employment in which our elders, our sisters and our brethren can be engaged than in training up our children in the ways of life, and I am happy to find that there are nearly 33,000 of our children that are under their influence, who are teaching them the Bible, the Book of Mormon, the Doctrine and Covenants, and the revelations of God; who are teaching them morality and purity and virtue, and training them up in the fear of God. Continue to do it, and you will have a generation that will rise up and bless you, and bless mankind in spite of themselves, and in spite of the corruption with which we are surrounded. God bless all men and all women who seek to promote good and pure, virtuous, holy and honorable principles, and the curse of God will rest upon those who take a contrary course. These things do not always appear at once, but these things will follow as sure as God reigns in the heavens.

7. Then in regard to the views, ideas and notions of those outside, many of whom are consistent and thoughtful, but a great many of whom are corrupt and led by improper and corrupt principles—in regard to their ideas, we ask very little odds of them.

8. We will try to pursue the even tenor of our way; we will cleave to God, to truth, to righteousness; we will stand as saviors upon Mount Zion, and bless all who will receive the truth, will maintain the principles of liberty, equality and brotherhood among all peoples, and we will oppose fraud, and corruption and illiberality and degradation in every form, and bondage in every shape, and we will pray to the Almighty to help us carry out these principles, which are in the interests of humanity, so far as he gives us strength and power to do it. But to barter away the principles that God has committed us—never, no never, no never! And let all the congregation say "Amen." [The vast assemblage responded as with one voice, "Amen."] God bless you, and lead you in the paths of truth. Amen.

ADDRESS 17

Opening remarks made by President John Taylor at the 51st Semiannual General Conference of The Church of Jesus Christ of Latter-day Saints convened October 6, 1881, in the Tabernacle, Salt Lake City.

1. We have met this morning in accordance with our adjournment six months ago, to attend to the affairs of our Conference; and on these occasions, as we are assembled from the different Stakes throughout the land of Zion, for the purpose of attending to all matters in which we as a people are interested, it is proper that we should comprehend the position that we occupy, and be prepared with prayerful hearts and with our spirits and feelings drawn out unto our Heavenly Father, to attend to all things that shall come before us in a manner that shall be just and right and proper, that we may have the Spirit of the Lord to rest down upon us, that in our teachings, in our business, and in all affairs that shall come before us in a Conference capacity, we may be under the guidance and direction of the Lord, as we ought always to be in all of the assemblies of the Saints.

2. We are placed today under rather peculiar circumstances. While we attend to our Conference, we at the same time are called to perform the obsequies connected with the death of our beloved brother and Apostle Orson Pratt. This is rather a peculiur phase to be entertained in a Conference capacity, yet he, though dead, yet lives, and while he lives in the heavens, he lives also in the hearts of the Saints and of the holy Priesthood, and we could not have a more fitting opportunity to attend to the obsequies of our beloved brother. And when we shall have finished paying the last tribute of respect to this our beloved brother, there is also another occurrence which has taken place, and we wish to hold memorial services pertaining thereto—that is in connection with the death of Elder Feramorz L. Young, son of President Brigham Young, who in returning from a mission to Mexico, in company with Moses Thatcher, one of the Twelve, died at sea, between Havana and New York. We thought that while attending to the funeral services of Brother Orson Pratt, it would be a fitting occasion to hold memorial services also pertaining to him, for he was accounted a faithful, intelligent, and an honorable young man, and a good Latter-day Saint, and as he has died in the harness, although his body is not present, we wish to show to him that respect which all honorable Elders of Israel ought to have. Therefore the ceremonies pertaining to his funeral will be attended to in connection with those of Brother Pratt this afternoon. And as the time seems to be progressing, and we wish to have everything done without confusion, that all may have an opportunity of viewing the corpse, we will not this morning prolong our remarks, for it would be irrelevant with so short a time, and under existing circumstances, to introduce any other subject at present.

ADDRESS 18

Remarks made by President John Taylor at the 51st Semiannual General Conference of The Church of Jesus Christ of Latter-day Saints convened October 7, 1881, in the Tabernacle, Salt Lake City.

1. It is interesting to some to read and hear read our statistical reports, and then to others it is what they call dry reading. Many seem not to be much interested in relation to these matters; still there are things exhibited therein which are or should be really interesting to all of us. There is one very remarkable feature associated with our statistical reports, and that is, that we find generally throughout the Territory about one-fourth of our population under eight years of age. I am told that this does not cover the whole, that it is nearer one-third than one-fourth. However, it is always better to keep within the figures. There are some other ideas associated with these things in my mind. We sometimes talk about the great many deaths that have occurred. Well, yes, that is true. Then we may as well talk, on the other hand, about the great many births we have, and put one fact to offset the other.

2. But there is a grand principle connected with this thing which many have not thought of. I will briefly refer to it. It is supposed by some statisticians who have written on this subject, that about one-half of the human family die before they arrive at five years of age. As to the truth of that I am not prepared to say, but will give it a little more latitude, and allow them eight years instead of five, to make their calculations from. That I do not vouch for myself, as some of these statements are a little exaggerated, and sometimes it is very difficult for statisticians to get an accurate account of the births and deaths in the various nations of the earth. But there is a principle associated with this, as I said before, that I wish here to introduce.

3. There has been, as there is today, a war between God and the devil—between the powers of light and the powers of darkness. The rebellion was first started in the heavens by Satan, and in consequence of that rebellion, he and a third part of the hosts of heaven, we are told, were cast out. That rebellion was thus transferred from the heavens to the earth. Cain was influenced by that same spirit, and became the representative of the enemy of mankind, and was called in that day the great Master Mahan. He loved Satan, we are told, more than he loved God, and consequently the wrath of God was kindled against him. But Satan and his followers— for he has had a large following—have been, as they are today, in opposition to God and to his people and to his law. And he has planted hatred to God in the minds of the human family who have yielded themselves submissive to his will, and he has desired to destroy the human family. He so led them in early days that every imagination and thought of the heart was evil, and that continually.

4. The wickedness and corruption of the people increased. We are told, "it repented the Lord that he made man." That is a slight mistake. It should read that, "It repented Noah that God had made man." In order to stop the propagation of this iniquitous race, they were cut off from the face of the earth by the flood. The power to propagate their species was not taken from them, they had that agency and that power, and I suppose it is very likely that the devil laughed heartily when he saw that those people were destroyed. But there comes another feature in the scene, namely, Jesus, who was "the Lamb slain before the foundation of the world." Satan thought that when he had got the people who were in the world destroyed he had accomplished his object. In this, however, he was very much mistaken, for we read that the Son of God "being put to death in the flesh was quickened by the spirit, by which also he went and preached unto the spirits in prison, which sometime were disobedient when once the long-suffering of God waited in the days of Noah." And what did he preach? The Gospel. Hence Satan did not secure the whole of the people that were then destroyed.

5. Then again, taking the statement of the statisticians which I before referred to, there

is another class that Satan has no power nor dominion over, and that is over children under eight years of age. He has nothing to do with them. They are redeemed through the atonement of our Lord and Savior Jesus Christ; and Jesus, when he was upon the earth, said, "Suffer little children to come unto me, and forbid them not, for of such is the kingdom of heaven."

6. There is another slight mistake he has made in relation to these matters, and that is, that there is one half of the whole human family of every nation, of every people of every tongue of the myriads born upon the earth, that are saved through the atoning blood of Jesus Christ, or that proportion of them at least that die in their infancy. When we look at these things and are troubled about our children leaving us we will not mourn as those who have no hope. If our brethren who hold the holy Priesthood leave us we will not mourn much for them. God dictates these things and takes care of them; they go to their places, to their quorums, and to their associations in the eternal worlds. Therefore we have no cause to lament.

7. There is another class of people with regard to whom Satan will miss his mark and his calculations. We are told that all those who have lived in the different ages of the world who have not had the Gospel preach to them, shall yet have the opportunity of receiving it if they choose. And that is one reason why we are building Temples, that we may administer for those who are worthy behind the veil, who have lived among the various nations that have existed in the different ages. These will all have the opportunity.

8. And thus the Priesthood that administers in time and in eternity will operate both on the earth and in the heavens. We are operating now for ourselves, for our friends and relatives, tracing out these things as well as we can and acting as saviors upon Mount Zion. And while we are operating here, there are thousands also who are operating in the heavens. The Priesthood that have lived in the different ages who have died, are operating there in the interests of humanity. And it is for them, by and by, when we get through the affairs pertaining to our own little matters here among ourselves, to look after them—for them to communicate with us, for

we need their assistance here upon the earth, and the assistance of God our Heavenly Father, and they need our assistance here. Hence saviors shall come upon Mount Zion; and saviors are not saviors unless they save somebody. This is the labor we have to do connected with the earth and with the heavens. And when men are on the earth they operate in the Priesthood, and by the power and authority of God, our Heavenly Father, in the name of Jesus Christ; and we are told that whatsoever they shall seal on the earth, shall be sealed in the heavens; and whatsoever they bind on the earth shall be bound in the heavens. And the two Priesthoods are united for the accomplishment of those purposes that God has designed from before the foundation of the world.

9. And will Satan be disappointed? I guess he will, notwithstanding the course that he has taken and the influence he has used, and the power he has exercised among men. There will be a great war by and by that will culminate in his overthrow, it will be between Michael or Adam, and Satan, and his forces will be over come and cast into the bottomless pit, that he can deceive the nations no more until God shall give him some other little opportunity, for the perfecting and benefit and exaltation of man. However, this is an extensive subject to talk upon. I thought I would say so much on it; and if men live in the fear of God, and keep his commandments, they live unto God; and if they die they die unto God, and God will take of them, inasmuch as they are faithful in keeping the commandments of God. And I will say that the liars and the calumniators, and the wicked and the irreligious—I do not care what name or profession—and those fighting against the Lord, God will be after them, and He that sits in the heavens will laugh and hold them in derision; and so will we. And Zion will arise and shine, and the glory of God will rest upon her.

10. There is one little piece of advice I want to give you. There have been what some people would call pretty good times; we have been blessed with very good harvests and an abundance of the good things of the earth, for which I feel grateful in my heart, and for which we ought to render praise and thanksgiving to God; and all of

you who feel like this, say Amen. (The congregation unitedly responded Amen.) Now, let us be careful of the means which God has provided and blessed us with; and do not squander them. And you that have jeopardized yourselves by encumbrances, make use of the means you get to release yourselves from your embarrassments, and get out of debt: and then do not get into debt again. Let us be free, free in our feelings to carry out correct principles; and trust in God, and he will take care of the rest.

11. One thing more. There will be, by and by, a reaction in the times. While you enjoy the opportunity improve it for your advantage, and do not be caught in an embarrassing position again.

12. God bless you. Amen.

ADDRESS 19

Discourse delivered by President John Taylor at the 51st Semiannual General Conference of The Church of Jesus Christ of Latter-day Saints convened October 9, 1881, in the Tabernacle, Salt Lake City.

1. We have now been in session for some time. We have listened to a great many interesting things associated with the Church and kingdom of God. We have had also, during the Conference, matters to reflect upon, pertaining to the departure of some of our brethren, whom we loved and esteemed. They have been taken away from us, and have gone into another state of existence, which is all perfectly right. We have nothing to say particularly in relation to these matters.

2. The Lord has revealed unto us his holy will. He has by his own voice, by the ministering of holy angels, restored to us the everlasting Gospel, that plan which was ordained by Jehovah, before the world rolled into existence, or the morning stars sang together for joy. Associated with the Gospel he has restored the Priesthood, which is simply, in a few words, the rule and government of God, whether in the heavens or on the earth. This Priesthood, this law, this government and these principles have been communicated from the heavens. They originated not with man upon the earth. They did not originate with any church upon the earth, or any people, or any authority. This is the gift of God to man. This Gospel places man in communication with God, his Heavenly Father; this Gospel brings life and immortality to light; this Gospel is proclaimed in the interest of all men in all parts of the earth; the Priesthood in connection with the Gospel has a commission to proclaim to all the world, to every nation, kindred, tongue and people. It is a message of salvation to the nations of the earth, and it is very different from that which many call the Gospel, whose followers would seek to destroy, to defame, to overturn and to injure all humanity who are opposed to them, and to their views and feelings.

3. God feels interested in the welfare of the whole human family, and for this purpose he has established principles upon the earth which exist in the heavens—a Gospel that has prevailed among the Gods in the eternal worlds, containing principles which are calculated to elevate, ennoble and exalt the human family. The principles are eternal as the Gospel itself is eternal; and as the love of God was manifested in former times by the giving of His son for the redemption of the world, so the goodness of God is extended in the last days to save, to bless, to elevate and to dignify the human family. And those who are in possession of these principles are in possession not only of the love of God, but of the love of man, and will seek, by every means in their power, aided by the Spirit of God, and that light, love and intelligence which dwell in his bosom, to spread these sacred principles and to save men, if possible almost contrary to their own will.

4. It is a mistaken notion, let me say here, that some people entertain, that because men persecute us, we must persecute them: that because men would proscribe us in our religious faith, we must persecute them in theirs. There is no such principle associated with God, or with those who dwell in the love of God, or who are actuated by the Spirit of God. Everything of that kind proceeds from beneath and not from above. God is interested in the welfare of all people, all nations, all kindreds, and all tongues. He is the Father of the spirits of all flesh, and however narrow and contracted men may be in their ideas, he can afford to let his rain descend on the evil and the good, and cause his sun to shine on the just and on the unjust.

5. For this purpose he has introduced the Gospel; for this purpose he is gathering together a people under the influence of the Gospel, which Gospel, when received and obeyed, imparts the Holy Ghost, and which Holy Ghost takes of the things of God, and shows them unto us. He has gathered us together here in this place and in this land, in order that we may be more fully instructed in His law, for men are not acquainted with God by revelation anywhere else to my knowledge.

6. Very few men upon the face of the earth believe in revelation from God. They believe in their own theories, and notions and ideas and principles, but they know nothing about "Thus saith the Lord," as men used to do when they had the Gospel; and wherever the Gospel exists, there exists with it a knowledge of God, and of the laws of life.

7. God has committed to us the Gospel and the High Priesthood, which is not intended, as some suppose, to bring men into bondage or to tyrannize over the consciences of men, but to make all men free as God is free; that they may drink of the streams "whereof shall make glad the city of God;" that they may be elevated and not debased; that they may be purified and not corrupted; that they may learn the laws of life and walk in them, and not walk in the ways of corruption and go down to death. Jeremiah tells us that the Lord says, "I will take you one of a city and two of a family and I will bring you to Zion; and I will give you pastors according to mine heart, which shall feed you with knowledge and understanding."

8. We have learned this, that God lives; we have learned that when we call upon him he hears our prayers; we have learned that it is the height of human happiness to fear God and observe his laws and keep his commandments; we have learned that it is a duty devolving upon us to try and make all men happy and intelligent, which happiness and intelligence can only be obtained through obedience to the laws of God. It is in him that we trust. We are not so much concerned about the destiny of this kingdom as some people think we are. God is interested in it, the holy angels are interested in it, the ancient Patriarchs and Prophets and men of God who have lived in other ages are interested in it, and in the councils of heaven it was agreed that this kingdom should be established; it is according to the word and will and eternal designs of Jehovah. And as he called men in other days he has called them in these days, and this Priesthood administers in the earth and in the heavens.

9. And when Brother Moses Thatcher talks about a man being called, having finished his course here, to go into another state of existence, he talks understandingly on that point. This Priesthood is an everlasting Priesthood, as was the Priesthood of Jesus, after the order of Melchizedek, and it administers in time and eternity. This Gospel brings us into communion with God our Heavenly Father, with Jesus the Mediator of the New Covenant, with the general assembly and church of the First Born; and while they are operating there, we are operating here. For this reason we are building our Temples and administering in them, and these are things that I wish to speak a little upon to you Latter-day Saints who are assembled here from the various parts of the Territory.

10. It is not an idle phantom that has been presented to us in this matter. There is nothing vague or visionary about it, we are dealing with sober, serious, solemn facts. Elijah it was prophesied should come and turn the hearts of the fathers to the children and the hearts of the children to the fathers. That prophesy has been fulfilled, and while millions and myriads of the human family have died without a knowledge of the Gospel, we are instructed what our duty is towards them; and while we are engaged in building Temples and administering therein both for the living and the dead, the everlasting Priesthood in the heavens are engaged in operating in the same way in the interests of all humanity, not only of those who now live but those who have lived. We need, it is true, the assistance and guidance of the Almighty, and the Holy Priesthood behind the veil also requires our assistance and our help. Paul, who understood these things, said, "that they without us should not be made perfect," and we without them cannot be made perfect. They in their day had obtained a knowledge of God and his law, and we are permitted to obtain the same. God has been pleased to restore the same principles and to place us in communion with him and them. Hence, while they are operating in the heavens we are operating here upon the earth. We build Temples and administer in them. They are attending to those who have died without a knowledge of the Gospel, and who will communicate from time to time with us to show us our duty.

11. It is written that saviors shall come upon Mount Zion. How can a man be a savior if he saves nobody? And how can they save unless God shows them how? How can they build Temples unless they have a

knowledge of the work in which they are engaged? And how can they administer in these Temples, unless God instructs them? They cannot do it; we cannot do it; nobody can do it; and therefore it is necessary that we should all the time be under the guidance and direction of the Almighty, for without Him we can do nothing.

12. The reports that we hear concerning the Temples that are being built are very interesting. We hear they have placed the roof on the one in Cache Valley; in Manti, they are progressing with another very favorably, and the people all around in those districts are contributing and aiding all they can for the advancement of the work, and then with the one already built there will soon be two and three and then four Temples in operation for the labor in which we are engaged. Some people I know will say it is a very poor speculation, a very singular kind of religion. Yet we are carrying out the counsel of God, for all these things are designed by the Almighty, and emanate from Him. And if we die what then? We shall live and reign throughout eternity, worlds without end, and we know it. Therefore we are satisfied as to the work in which we are engaged. It is all right.

13. I say to the brethren and all who are engaged in this labor, I say God bless you, and if you could hear the voices above, you would hear loud cries of "Amen" for all heaven is interested in the work in which we are engaged; and whatever other men may think about these things, we know what we are doing, and we shall try, in the name of the Lord, and under His guidance and direction, to build up his Zion upon the earth; that there may be a phalanx of people that God will acknowledge—a phalanx of people that will bow to the behests of Jehovah; a phalanx of people in whom the heavens are interested; a people who are engaged in rolling forth the work of God, and establishing not only the Church of Christ, but His Zion and the kingdom of God upon the earth.

14. This is a work that is not popular among men. They want their ideas, their theories, and their notions; we want the ideas and theories, the word and will, and the guidance and direction of the Almighty; and if we are connected with his kingdom, if there is such a thing as the kingdom of God upon the earth,

it means the rule and government of God.

15. Peradventure some will say, "We won't let you do it." Now, don't stop the Lord, will you? No matter about the theories, ideas and notions of men. God has committed to us certain principles, and by the help of God we mean to carry them out. In doing this it devolves upon us to send the Gospel to every creature under heaven, and for this we have a First Presidency; for this we have the Twelve Apostles; for this we have some seventy times seventy of Seventies; for this we have several thousand High Priests; for this we have some eight or ten thousand Elders, and God has called us to do his work, and by the help of Israel's God we will do it in the name of the Lord, and let all Israel say, Amen. (The vast congregation responded, "Amen.") These are our feelings on that subject. And let the Twelve, let the Seventies, let the High Priests, and let the Elders work up to the dignity and importance of their calling, and feel that they are under command, as the servants of God, to do his will in spreading the Gospel of life and salvation to the nations of the earth. The world will hate you. No matter— they hated your master before you. They persecuted Him before they persecuted you. He endured it; we will try to.

16. What then? We will go on building our Temples, and when we have built them we will administer in them according to the word of God. And who else knows this order but us? Let the Latter-day Saints build these Temples and hand them over to the divines of the world, and what would they do? Why, all they would do would be to quarrel about theology. What do they know about the ordinances of the Gospel? Nothing. What do they know about salvation for the living and the dead? Nothing. They would not know how to administer in a Temple if they had one, and further, we should not know if God had not shown us how. We are dependent upon the Lord; but we have our friends, as I have said, behind the veil. They have the same Priesthood which we have, and they are operating in our interests and it is that which frequently operates among men now, silently working when they know nothing about it. They rage in many instances, and foam and get up resolutions; generally very religious people. Well, it was that class of people that

persecuted Jesus and his disciples; they thought they were unfit to live.

17. What of it? Do you hate them? No. Would I injure any of them? No, they are injuring themselves, God knows, ten thousands times more than I could. Any man who departs from the principles of right; any man who tramples upon human rights and human liberty; men who cannot allow other men to worship God according to the dictates of their own conscience, are in a deplorable condition; they are fast going back to barbarism; and it is necessary that God should introduce principles to lift man above these groveling ideas. We can look upon all mankind as our brothers, and can try to benefit and elevate the human race. This is the mission which God has given us to attend to—first, in regard to religious matters, and afterwards to political matters, that all men may enjoy perfect freedom in every respect, not in name, not in theory only, but in reality.

18. I find that time is passing. We scarcely have time in our assemblages to attend to things and talk about principles that we would like to. There are ten thousand things present themselves before my mind, which I would like to lay before this congregation; but we have not time. We shall have to take these things by degrees, little by little, line upon line, precept upon precept.

19. There is one thing I wish to speak about here politically. "What do you think about the government of the United States," some people say. "What are your opinions?" I will tell you what I think about the Constitution. I have just the same opinion of it that Joseph Smith had, and he said it was given by inspiration of God. The men did not know this who wrote it; the men did not know it who adopted it; nevertheless it is true. There is an embodiment of principles contained therein that are calculated to bless and benefit mankind. "What do you think about the government of the United States as a government?" I think it is a good deal ahead of most governments, but I think the administrators are apostatizing very fast from the principles that the fathers of this nation instituted. It has become quite a question now-a-days, whether men can be preserved in their rights or not, whether men can worship God according to the dictates of their conscience

or not, or whether we are living in a land of freedom or not. What is the matter? Why, they are like the religionists. How is it with them? They profess to believe in the Bible. They do believe it shut, but when you open it they deny it. The people of this nation profess to believe in the Constitution. They do until it comes to be applied to the people and then they do not. That is perhaps too broad a saying; but I will say there are many who feel like this—not all by a long way. There are thousands and tens of thousands who are imbued with the same principles as were the framers of the Constitution and who desire to see human freedom perpetuated. The principles of freedom and the love of human liberty have not quite died out of the hearts of all men in these United States.

20. There is a respectable balance in favor of liberty and freedom and equal rights. But there are others—why they talk sometimes about our polygamy until you would think from what these open-mouthed people say, that we were the most corrupt people on the face of the earth. I could say something about them if I wanted to talk, I would say here that we respect family virtue, and we protect virtue among us. We associate with our families upon principles that have been ordained of God, and sanctioned by Him, in the different ages of the world. And then we are true to our covenants, while they profess to be true to theirs, and violate them and disgrace and corrupt themselves. God save us from their infamies! Do not follow after their example. What have we seen of men here right in our city sent to evangelize us— seducing females when they could, and then go into courts, churches, etc., and talk about the impurities of the "Mormons?" This is not a very good way to evangelize people nor to exalt them; it does not produce a love of those ennobling principles which all honorable men ought to be governed by.

21. We would say then in regard to religionists—if you profess a religion be true to it; if you profess to believe in the Bible when shut, believe it when open, and practice its principles.

22. We would say to men who profess so much loyalty and patriotism to the government, be true to your institutions, be true to the Constitution of the United States, as we

say to all our people to be true to the same. We expect the Latter-day Saints to be so, and to be subject to law, to avoid lawlessness of every kind and the interference with men's rights in any shape. Let all men worship as they please. That is a matter for their own consciences, it is not for us to dictate. Let all men be free in their business relations, that in all things we may feel that we are performing our part as citizens of the United States and citizens of the Church and kingdom of God upon the earth; and if other people can afford to traduce us, we can scarcely afford to tell the truth about them. I might talk about thousands of things that I am acquainted with that I know as well as I am standing here; but we will leave them to their master. If they choose evil let them choose it.

23.We talk sometimes about the influence of saloons, of whisky and beer, and all these kinds of things. Cannot you Latter-day Saints let them alone? If you cannot you are not fit to be Latter-day Saints and you will not be so long. If the world choose to wallow in these things, let them wallow. But would an Elder in Israel and a saint of God disgrace himself by being found in such dens? Yes, many have, but they have got to repent and turn round a short corner and purge themselves from these things, or they will be severed from the Church and kingdom of God, and they will have no association among us. We are after truth and after righteousness, and let us, as we have been exhorted, maintain our purity and our virtue, and if others introduce corruption among us, let them alone, let them take their own course, but "O my soul, come not thou into their secret; unto their assembly, mine honor, be not thou united." Ye Latter-day Saints purge yourselves from iniquity and speak the truth, act honestly, be pure and virtuous, and honor God and your calling, and God will honor you, but if you do not, you will be speedily rooted out. There is a day of reckoning fast coming. God is beginning to trouble the nations of the

earth, and these things will grow and increase, and it is time for you Elders of Israel to be on the side of right, to depart from evil, to cleave to the truth, to work righteousness, and to honor God. God expects it of you, the holy angels expect it of you, and if you do not leave your evils you can have no place with the Saints of God on the earth or in the heavens.

24.As I before said, we have not time to enter into all these matters. You have had a good deal of needful instruction. Let us profit by it and honor our God. And I say God bless all men who love the truth, whether here or anywhere else; God bless all men who maintain human rights and freedom; and God confound the opposers of these principles everywhere. These are my principles and feelings. We want nothing like communism, or nihilism, or any of the outrageous infamies that are beginning to vex and perplex the nations. Yet these things will roll on until it will be a vexation to hear the reports thereof, and unless this nation speedily turns round God's hand will be upon them; unless they speedily adhere to the principles of equal rights and freedom, He will be after them. Now, you can set that down if you like and see whether it will come to pass or not.

25.I say, then God bless every lover of right, whether among this people or anywhere else, and God bless the rulers of this land who rule in righteousness, and God remove those who do not. (Amen). And let us honor our God and our religion and adhere to the principles of truth. God will stand by us, and the glory of God will rest upon us, and no power this side of hell can hurt us if we be followers of that which is good.

26.I ask the blessing of my Heavenly Father to be upon this congregation, upon all Israel who love the truth, and all men everywhere who are desirous to do right and keep the commandments of God, in the name of Jesus. Amen.

ADDRESS 20

Opening remarks made by President John Taylor at the 52nd Annual General Conference of The Church of Jesus Christ of Latter-day Saints convened April 6, 1882, in the Tabernacle, Salt Lake City.

1. We are now commencing the Fifty-second Annual Conference which has been held by the Church of Jesus Christ of Latter-day Saints. Since the commencement of this work the Church has had to pass through a great variety of changes. We have had revealed unto us the ever lasting Gospel as it has existed in the various ages of the world, and no matter how we have been situated, the same spirit, power, light and revelation have been with Israel. We have been deprived of our rights, and have been robbed and pillaged and plundered time and time again, but we have always felt and still feel to put our trust in the living God and the principles revealed for the exaltation of the human family. A message of life and salvation has been revealed by God through his servant Joseph, and the keys of the Holy Priesthood have been conferred through Joseph upon many men, and they have gone forth to the nations of the earth telling of the unspeakable riches of the Kingdom of God. It is a message of peace on earth and goodwill toward man. We have gone forth without purse or scrip, and the Lord has so abundantly blessed us that we have gathered thousands and tens of thousands from the nations, and we expect still to do it, without any fear, without any trembling, asking no odds of any man, only being careful to put our trust in the word of Him who made the earth and those who people it. The antagonism and opposition we have had to meet has always existed, for warfare always existed against God and his principles. Everything is right and will come out right.

2. My feelings are peaceful to the world, and to this people I would say, be calm, be peaceful. I feel like shouting, "Hallelujah, the Lord God Omnipotent reigneth and will take care of His Saints!"

ADDRESS 21

Remarks made by President John Taylor at the 52nd Annual General Conference of The Church of Jesus Christ of Latter-day Saints convened April 7, 1882, in the Tabernacle, Salt Lake City.

1. When we make motions of this kind we should mean to carry them out, and in the instances of voting to sustain the missionaries, we should do it not only in our faith and prayers, but by helping the families of these missionaries, making them comfortable and happy, and scattering smiles around their homes. Some folks are very religious, and will center the whole of their actions in their prayers, but I tell you that a little beef and pork and flour are necessary to be added to the prayers, or they are not of much good to the poor and the needy. I have been a missionary myself several times, and know all about the feelings of men while on missions.

2. In relation to the storm now hanging over us, all we have to do is just the same as we had to do this morning when out in the snowstorm, just round up our shoulder's, turn up our coat collars and let the wind blow and the storm exhaust itself, and when the howling surrounds us who cares. After the storm subsides the sun shines and everything is pleasant and joyful. In Far West we had a rough experience, and a few had some little fears and creepy feelings, but we lived through it and the kingdom survived and grew. We were loyal to the government under all our persecutions, and there is no other place in the United States where the people are as loyal and revere the Constitution as right here in this Territory. We are trying to do good and keep on doing right, and be patriotic and sustain the Constitution and the country. We sometimes do too much good, I think, when taking into consideration the circumstances that surround us.

3. We have had come into our midst some professedly very pious people, but they encourage whoredom, they encourage the social evil, they fight against sobriety, and make it very difficult for the city councils to keep down the liquor business; yet they say we are loathsome. These pious people claim to be virtuous people and truthful people.

Now I would not pollute the stores of these people with my presence, I might injure their goods, and I would say that we had better keep among our own people and trade among ourselves. There are persons who send carriages and wagons here, and we pay for them thousands and thousands of dollars, yet these persons cannot raise a finger in our behalf. I wouldn't ride in their carriages.

4. We have lots of fair weather friends, but they are not of much use; still there are some outspoken friends. I was pleased with the Senators and Representatives in the late discussion of the Edmunds Bill, who were possessed of manhood enough to stand by their oaths and say they could not sanction such a measure; there is a little salt in the United States yet, and though they may want to cast us off, we will not cast them off. Many are jealous of our organization, and think we have a different organization to anybody else; So we have, but we did not get it from the United States, nor from England, nor from any man, but from God and it is good and true. I feel like saying again, as I said yesterday, Hallelujah! The Lord God Omnipotent reigneth, and will continue to reign until he has put his enemies under his feet. So we can do right, and a part of that right is to keep from polluting these traders here.

5. In the meantime we will keep our coat collars up and wait until the storm passes over. Some of our kind friends have suggested that we cast our wives off, but our feelings are different to that. We are bound to them for time and eternity; we have covenanted before high heaven to do it, and I feel like saying in the name of Israel's God we will keep them, and let all say Amen. (A loud and hearty Amen was given by the congregation.) We may have to nestle behind a hedge while the storm is passing over, but let us be true to ourselves, to our wives, our families and our God, and all will be well.

ADDRESS 22

Comments made by President John Taylor at the 52nd Annual General Conference of The Church of Jesus Christ of Latter-day Saints convened April 9, 1882, in the Tabernacle, Salt Lake City.

1. Said there is one thing I wish to make a remark or two upon. I want us all to be liberal and deal with people on liberal and just principles, but when any man or set of men manifest a hostile spirit against us it is wise and proper for us to take care of ourselves a little. We have talked about the united order and about cooperation, as being something preparatory to a better and higher state of things. There has been a feeling among many of our brethren to branch out into mercantile affairs and go off on their own hook. My idea is that if people will deal honestly, justly and conscientiously, one with the other, it is better for our brethren to do this than our enemies. It is better to put means into the hands of our friends than our enemies, for some of the latter are not slow to use the means we pay them to injure us.

Self-preservation is the first law of nature. Our cooperative institutions have done very well; and if there are institutions that can be introduced by our brethren, let them be sustained. But we want them to be honest, to put away chicanery and evil doings; sustaining the Church and its principles, paying their tithing and upholding the hands of good men. If they will not do this we will find somebody that will. We want to sustain no hypocritical men, either Mormon or Gentile. We want to go right along in the path of duty and fear no Canaanites or any other ites; They can do no more than the Lord will let them. I feel all the time like saying, Hallelujah! Hallelujah! Hallelujah! The Lord God Omnipotent reigneth, and he will reign until he hath put his enemies under his feet.

ADDRESS 23

Discourse delivered by President John Taylor at the 52nd Annual General Conference of The Church of Jesus Christ of Latter-day Saints convened April 9, 1882, in the Tabernacle, Salt Lake City.

1. In attempting to address the congregation this afternoon, I trust that all will be as quiet as possible. It is extremely difficult to make the congregation hear in this place, especially in so large an assembly, when there is the least confusion. While I address you, I wish to speak such words as shall be interesting, edifying and instructive, and I desire an interest in the prayers of the faithful, that I may be able to do so intelligently, that we may be the better for our coming together.

2. I am aware of the position that we occupy today. I feel that I am surrounded by a large number of intelligent men and women, and while I am addressing you, I am also addressing the world, for the remarks I make will be reported and published to the world. Therefore, I am desirous to advance such sentiments as will be in accord with the enlightenment of the Latter-day Saints, with the intelligence of the 19th century, and with the principles that have emanated from God.

3. Any intelligence which we may possess and which we may be able to impart, is not of ourselves, but of God. It did not originate with us; it did not originate with Joseph Smith, with Brigham Young, with the Twelve Apostles, nor was it received from any institution of learning, nor of science, either religious, political, or social. Our philosophy is not the philosophy of the world; but of the earth and the heavens, of time and eternity, and proceeds from God.

4. A message was announced to us by Joseph Smith the Prophet, as a revelation from God, wherein he stated that holy angels had appeared to him and revealed the everlasting Gospel as it existed in former ages; and that God the Father and God the Son had also appeared to him: the Father pointing to the Son, said, "This is my beloved Son, hear ye him." Moroni, a prophet that had lived on this continent, revealed unto Joseph the plates containing the Book of Mormon, and by the gift and power of God he was enabled to translate them into what is known as the Book of Mormon. That book contains a record of the ancient inhabitants who dwelt upon this continent, a part of whom came from the tower of Babel at the time of the confounding of tongues, and another part came from Jerusalem in the time of Zedekiah, king of Judah, 600 years before the advent of our Lord and Savior Jesus Christ. This book contains a record of the dealings of God with those people; it contains a record of their worship, of their wars and commotions, of their righteousness and iniquity, and of the coming of the Lord Jesus Christ unto them, and of His preaching unto them the same Gospel that was taught on the continent of Asia, attended by the same ordinances, the same organization and the same principles.

5. I shall not attempt to bring any proof with regard to these matters today; I am simply making statements, the truth of which you Latter-day Saints know, as it would be impossible to enter into all the details in a short discourse. Suffice it to say, that the Father having presented His Son to Joseph Smith, and commanded him to hear Him, Joseph was obedient to the heavenly call, and listened to the various communications made by men holding the Holy Priesthood in the various ages under the direction of the Only Begotten. He and Oliver Cowdery were commanded to baptize each other, which they did. John the Baptist came and conferred upon them the Aaronic Priesthood. Then Peter, James and John, upon whom was conferred, in the Savior's day, the keys of the Melchizedek Priesthood came, and conferred that Priesthood upon them. Then Adam, Noah, Abraham, Moses, Elijah, Elias, and many other leading characters mentioned in the Scriptures, who had operated in the various dispensations, came and conferred upon Joseph the various keys, powers, rights, privileges and immunities which they enjoyed in their times.

6. Again, Joseph was commanded to preach this Gospel and to bear this testimony

to the world. He was taught the same principles that were taught to Adam, the same principles that were taught to Noah, to Enoch, to Abraham, to Moses, to Elijah and other Prophets, the same principles that were taught by Jesus Christ and the Apostles in former times on the continent of Asia, accompanied with the same Priesthood and the same organization, only more fully, because the present dispensation is a combination of the various dispensations that have existed in the different ages of the world, and which is designated in the Scriptures as the dispensation of the fullness of times, in which God would gather together all things in one, whether they be things in heaven or things on earth. Therefore, whatever of knowledge, of intelligence, of priesthood, of powers, of revelations was conferred upon those men in the different ages, was again restored to the earth by the ministration and through the medium of those who held the holy Priesthood of God in the different dispensations in which they lived.

7. Under the direction of the Almighty, Joseph organized a church; and when people were called upon to believe on the Lord Jesus Christ, to repent of their sins, to be baptized in the name of Jesus Christ for the remission of sins and to have hands laid upon them for the reception of the Holy Ghost, those who did believe and obey received the attendant blessings. Then the various offices of the Priesthood began to be conferred upon men who believed, and in due time the quorum of the Twelve was organized, whose commission was to proclaim this Gospel to every people, to every nation, to every kindred, to every tongue. Then a quorum of seventy Elders was selected, known by the name of Seventies; and we now have some 76 times 70 of those Elders.

8. A First Presidency was also organized to preside over the whole Church in all the world. Then there were High Priests ordained whose office was principally to preside as well as to preach the Gospel. Then there were Elders, Priests, Teachers and Deacons; and this organization was given by direct revelation, by which the Church has been governed from that time until the present. Bishops were also appointed whose position in the Church was clearly defined by the word of the Lord. Then High Councils were organized for the adjustment of all matters of difficulty, for the correction of incorrect doctrine, for the maintenance of purity and correct principles among the Saints, and for the adjudication of all general matters pertaining to Israel.

9. This was the testimony and this is our testimony today to the nations of the earth. The Lord stood at the head as instructor, guide and director; and the Elders were told to go forth and to preach the Gospel to every creature, because confusion, disorder, sectarianism and the theories of men had been substituted for the word and will, and the revelation, law and power of God. These Elders were told that we approached the latter times, when God would have a controversy with the nations, and the message which they had to proclaim was that which was described by John when wrapped in prophetic vision upon the Isle of Patmos. Among other great and important events he said, "I saw another angel fly in the midst of heaven, having the everlasting Gospel to preach unto them that dwell on the earth, and to every nation and kindred, and tongue, and people, saying with a loud voice, Fear God and give glory to Him, for the hour of His judgment is come." This was the commission given by the Lord to the Latter-day Saints. This is the mission we have been trying to carry out from that time to the present; and I myself have traveled tens of thousands of miles without purse or scrip, trusting in God, to teach these holy principles, and so have many of my brethren by whom I am surrounded.

10. When we started we were told that we were not sent to be taught, but to teach. Why? Because the world was not in possession of the principles of life, and therefore could not teach them. We went in obedience to the direct command of God to us through his servant Joseph, and we have spread forth the Gospel among the nations. And is there anything unreasonable about it? No. Is it true? Yes. Is it scriptural? Yes. Is it philosophical? Yes. And I say today, not by way of boasting, because we have nothing to boast of (I have no intelligence but what I am indebted to God, my heavenly Father and my brethren for,) that while I have traveled through various parts of the United States

and the Canadas, also in England, Ireland, Scotland, Wales, France, Germany, and different parts of the earth, among the wise and intelligent as well as the poor and ignorant, among all classes of men—I have stood in their halls and talked with their professors, ministers, legislators, rulers, divines, judges and wise men of every class, grade and position in life—but I have never met with a man who could gainsay one principle of the Gospel of the Son of God, and I never expect to; because truth, eternal truth, as it emanates from God, cannot be controverted.

11. And what is the nature of the Gospel? It is the same as that taught on the day of Pentecost by the Apostles, when they cried out to the multitude, "Repent and be baptized every one of you in the name of Jesus Christ for the remission of sins, and ye shall receive the gift of the Holy Ghost." That was the testimony which they bore to the people. That is the testimony which the Elders of this Church bear. There is something about this that is reasonable, that is intelligent, and that is susceptible of proof. It was a very fair proposition for the Apostle to make, promising the people who would obey the requirements which the Gospel imposes upon its adherents, that they should receive the Holy Ghost. And what should this do for them? It was to cause their old men to dream dreams and their young men to see visions, it was to make their sons and daughters prophecy, it was to bring things past to their remembrance, to lead them into all truth, and to show them things to come.

12. This proposition was not alone of a religious nature, but it was also strictly philosophical. The farmer sows oats or wheat, or plants corn, and what does he expect? He expects oats, wheat or corn, as the case may be, and nothing else. There are laws and principles in nature, in the vegetable, the animal and the mineral kingdoms, as well as in all the works of God, that are true in themselves and they are eternal. There are such metals as gold, silver, copper or iron, each possessing certain distinctive elements which they always did possess; and the different bodies in their chemical relations possess principles that are always true to unchangeable laws. It is so also in regard to all the elements by which we are surrounded, and also in regard to the heavenly bodies. Because of these unchanging laws, we know precisely when the sun will rise and when it will set. We know when certain planets or comets will appear and disappear. All their movements are undeviating, exact and true according to the laws of nature.

13. Now here is a principle of the Gospel that will admit of as strong evidence as anything in nature. What is it? "Repent, and be baptized every one of you in the name of Jesus Christ for the remission of sins, and ye shall receive the gift of the Holy Ghost." Or in other words, sow wheat and you reap wheat; plant corn and you gather corn. It was a bold position to take.

14. I remember that on these points I questioned the Elder who brought the Gospel to me. I asked, What do you mean by this Holy Ghost? Will it cause your old men to dream dreams and your young men to see visions; will it bring to pass the scripture which saith: And on my servants and on my handmaidens I will pour out in those days of my Spirit, and they shall prophecy? Yes. Will it give you the permeating influence of the Spirit of the living God, and give you a certain knowledge of the principles that you believe in? "Yes," he answered, "and if it will not, then I am an impostor." Said I, That is a very fair proposition. Finding the doctrine to be correct, I obeyed, and I received that Spirit through obedience to the Gospel which gave me a knowledge of those principles which I simply believed before, because they were scriptural, reasonable and intelligent, according to that scripture which saith, "If any man will do His will, he shall know of the doctrine, whether it be of God, or whether I speak of myself." I was ordained an Elder by the proper authorities, and I went forth to preach this Gospel.

15. Other Elders went forth as I did to the civilized nations, preaching the same doctrine and holding out the same promises. Some of them were not very learned; some were not very profoundly educated. We send a singular class of people in our Elders. Sometimes a missionary is a merchant, sometimes a legislator, a blacksmith, an adobe maker, a plasterer, a farmer, or common laborer, as the case may be. But all under the same influence and spirit, all going

forth as missionaries to preach the Gospel of light, of life and of salvation. They have received the treasures of eternal life, and they are enabled to communicate them to others; and they hold out the same promises.

16. You who hear me this afternoon, as well as thousands upon thousands of others, have listened to those principles, you have had held out unto you those promises; and when you obeyed the Gospel, you received this same spirit; and you are my witnesses of the truth of the things that I now proclaim in your hearing, and of the Spirit and power of God attending the obedience to the Gospel, and you will not deny it. This congregation will not deny it. When you yielded obedience to the laws of God, obeyed His commandments, were baptized for the remission of your sins and had hands laid upon you for the reception of the Holy Ghost, you did receive it; and you are living witnesses before God.

17. This is a secret that the world does not comprehend. Its people have not obeyed it and they do not know it; and the things of God, say the scriptures, no man knoweth but by the Spirit of God; and this Spirit has imparted to us that intelligence and that knowledge. This people have in their possession a hope that enters within the veil, whither Christ, our forerunner, has gone. They are living and acting and operating for eternity. God is their Father, and they know it. Some people think we are a set of ignorant boobies, who do not know what we are talking about, and they try to overrun the faith of the Latter-day Saints by sophistry, falsehood and folly. Whilst the fact is, we are in possession of the principles of eternal life, and are operating for eternity; and then we are operating to build up the Zion of God, where righteousness can be taught, and where men can be protected, and where liberty can be proclaimed to all men of every color, of every creed and of every nation.

18. Being placed in communication with God, the sophistry, nonsense and dogmas of men have no influence upon us. We are built upon the rock of revelation, as Peter was, and on the same principle. Said Jesus to him, "Whom do men say that I, the Son of Man, am?" The answer was: "Some say thou art one of the Prophets; some say thou art the Elias who was to come," etc. "But whom say

you that I am?" Peter answered and said: "Thou art the Christ, the Son of the living God." Jesus replied, "Blessed art thou, Simon Barjona, for flesh and blood hath not revealed this unto thee, but my Father which is in heaven; and I say also unto thee, that thou art Peter, and upon this rock will I build my Church, and the gates of hell shall not prevail against it." What rock? The rock of revelation—upon the intelligence communicated by the Holy Ghost to those who obey the Gospel of the Son of God; by this, men shall know for themselves, and stand as the rock of ages, invulnerable, immovable and unchangeable. That is the position which we the Latter-day Saints occupy.

19. This, then, is the religious part of the question. What do we believe in? We believe in purity, in virtue, in honesty, in integrity, in truthfulness and in not giving way to falsehood; we believe in treating all men justly, uprightly and honorably; we believe in fearing God, observing His laws and keeping His commandments. Do we all do it? No, not quite. I wish we did. But a great majority of the Latter-day Saints are doing this; and if there are those that are not, let them look well to their path, for God will be after them, and their brethren will be after them, for God cannot look upon sin with any degree of allowance. And as we are here for the purpose of building up Zion, He expects that we will be upright and honorable in all our dealings with one another and with all men.

20. One part of the Gospel is that we should be gathered together to a land that should be called Zion. Have we been doing this? Yes. Some people are very much opposed to it. Have we injured anybody by gathering in this way? Is this indeed the land of the free, the home of the brave, and the asylum for the oppressed? Cannot the people of this nation afford to listen to the principles of truth, and allow men who are fearing God to assemble together to worship Him according to the dictates of their own consciences? Have we violated any law of the United States in thus gathering together and in thus worshipping our God? Not that I know of. Have we been opposed to the United States? No! no! no! we never have, and we are at the defiance of all men to prove anything of the kind. There are falsehoods set afoot by low, degraded, unprincipled men.

21. We believe that the Constitution of the United States was given by inspiration of God. And why? Because it is one of those instruments which proclaims liberty throughout the land, and to all the inhabitants thereof. And it was because of those noble sentiments, and the promulgation of those principles which were given by God to man, we believe that it was given by the inspiration of the Almighty. We have always esteemed it in this light, and it was so declared by Joseph Smith.

22. Did we do any wrong in coming here in the way we did? I think not. Did we transgress any of the laws of the United States? I think not. Did we transgress any of the laws of the nations we left? I think not. We gathered together simply because we were told there was a Zion to be built up. And what was that Zion? The term means the pure in heart.

23. In connection with our gathering, I would remark, that a short time ago, at one of our public celebrations, there were twenty-seven nationalities represented. This is in accordance with the scripture which says: I will take them one of a city and two of a family, and bring them to Zion. And I will give them pastors after mine own heart, that shall feed them with knowledge and understanding. This is what we find in the Christian Bible, and there is certainly no harm in believing the Bible. The Christians send their Bible missionaries among us to circulate it, and we are always glad to receive the Bible and be governed by it.

24. Now, then, being gathered together, we necessarily required some kind of social relations with each other, for when we came here we brought our bodies with us as well as our religion, and we brought our wives and families with us as well as our religion; and we needed to cultivate the earth and build houses, and plant orchards, and vineyards, and gardens, and attend to the common affairs of life. And then as we began to increase we began to open and build farms, hamlets, villages and cities. Is there anything wrong in this? No.

25. Finally, when we came here we petitioned for a State government, the people held a convention and a constitution was framed, and forwarded to Washington. Congress refused our application for a State, but they gave us a Territorial form of government and named the Territory Utah; and strange to say, how men and nations change, they are trying to interfere with us because of our polygamy, and at that time the government appointed a polygamous governor, Brigham Young. People change in their sentiments and views; I suppose they call it progress. Apostle Orson Pratt, whom you all knew, as soon as that revelation was made public, went down to the city of Washington, and there published the doctrine of plural marriage and also lectured upon it. The paper he published was called The Seer, which many of you brethren remember very well. They were not in ignorance in relation to these matters. It was then well understood by the nation that these were our sentiments, and that President Young was a polygamist.

26. But passing on. Sometime after that, we had some United States officials sent out here, who were not polygamists, but one of them went so far as to show us what beautiful civilization they had where he came from, and he left his wife at home and brought with him a strumpet and took her on to the bench with him, to let the people see how intelligent and enlightened the people were in the United States. However, fortunately for him, there was no Edmunds Bill then. Still, we were not much edified. It might be according to some people's system of ethics; it may be considered beautiful or aesthetic by the admirers of this fast and progressive civilization; but we could not appreciate it, and the consequence was, that the people felt indignant, they looked upon him as a profligate, and that he had defiled and disgraced the ermine. These were the sentiments of the people then, and they are yours today, for you have never been taught anything else. He and some others went back to Washington, and reported that the "Mormons" were in a state of rebellion; that they were a very wicked people, very corrupt and very depraved, almost as bad as some of our truth-telling ministers make us out to be, for some of them are not very notorious for telling the truth, nobody believes them here; but then they have reverend put before their names and that, of

course, covers—what is it? a multitude of sins. And therefore, the mendacious stories that they tell and circulate are received as actual truth by thousands of blind, ignorant, bigoted people, who, doubtless, are far more sincere and far more honest and pure in their lives than these specimens of fallen humanity who, in the garb of sanctity, manufacture falsehoods and prepare them specially for the vitiated taste of the age.

27.But to return; judges and other officials were sent here, and suffice it to say, we did not like their civilization; and, then, they were not much enamored with ours, because whatever we may be in the estimation of the world generally, we are utterly averse to anything like licentiousness and debauchery; and, if there is any among us, we are indebted to our Christian friends for it, and to our Christian judges for maintaining and protecting it in our midst. We have no affiliation with such things; they cannot exist among us as a people, only by the force, the power and influence of this federal Christianity that has been introduced among us. Until these people came into our midst we had no house of ill-fame; and a lady could travel as safely in our streets at any time of night as in the day; we had no occasion to lock our doors to prevent thieves from preying upon us; we had no drunkenness, ribaldry or blasphemy in our streets; all these things have been introduced among us by our good, kind, pure, pious Christian friends, and in scores of our remote settlements where this civilization has not penetrated, they are free from these vices today.

28.Now we will go back to the statement of these men. They were believed in Washington. What did they state? Among other things they said that we had burned the United States library, and the court records, and that a dreadful state of anarchy was in existence; and instead of the United States sending out a commission to inquire into these matters they took the statement of a Lothario and his associates, and sent out an army to destroy us. And these troops were reduced to gnawing mules' legs about the vicinity of Bridger, refusing salt when we sent it to them—for we would have done them good, notwithstanding they came as our enemies.

29.I remember writing a letter to one of the officers who had a letter of introduction to me, and forwarded it by a messenger; I told him that I was very sorry, that as a United States' officer, as an honorable man, he should be placed in the situation he was then in; because he could not help it, as an officer, any more than we could, as he was operating as a servant of the government under military rule and had, therefore, to obey orders. And that while we esteemed him and other officers as patriots and high-minded, honorable men, who had exhibited their patriotism and bravery in Mexico and other places, and while we heard of their excellent military equipments, we did not like the idea of their trying the temper of their steel upon us. I told him that republics which reflected the voice of the people were in many instances excitable and erratic, and that I looked for a reaction in public opinion, and that when that change came I expected the difficulties that the government had placed us in would be done away, and that then I would be glad to extend to him that courtesy in our city that one gentleman should extend to another, and would then be happy to see him. But we could not meet then of course; they could not come to us, and we could not very well go out to them.

30.So that the Latter-day Saints may know the truth or falsity of the allegations made by Judge Drummond, I will have the official statement of Governor Cumming, who came out with the army, read to this congregation.

31.It would be unfair and disingenuous to blame one administration for the acts of another, yet when we see a disposition to listen to the same kind of popular clamor that then existed, we cannot but notice a great similarity of circumstances.

32.[Elder L. John Nuttall then read the following extracts from the official statement of Governor Cumming, which was dated Great Salt Lake City, April 15th, 1858:]

33."Since my arrival I have been employed in examining the records of the Supreme and District Courts, which I am now prepared to report as being perfect and unimpaired. This will, doubtless, be acceptable information to those who have entertained an impression to the contrary.

34.I have also examined the Legislative Records and other books belonging to the office of Secretary of State, which are in perfect preservation.

* * *

35.The condition of the large and valuable Territorial Library has also commanded my attention: and I am pleased in being able to report that Mr. W. C. Staines, the librarian, has kept the books and records in most excellent condition. I will, at an early day, transmit a catalogue of this library, and schedules of the other public property, with certified copies of the records of the Supreme and District Courts, exhibiting the character and amount of the public business last transacted in them."

36.Thus it appears that the allegations made by our enemies were false, and the army was sent out under false representations, and their own Governor furnishes the evidence for their own refutation. Yet we were subjected to the indignity and outrage of having an army sent among us, predicated upon these false statements.

37.From the above and other similar actions manifested towards us as a people we have learned in the sad school of experience, and by the things that we have suffered, the excitability of the populace, and the unreasonable, savage and relentless feelings that frequently possess the people in their antagonism towards us, to be very careful, in all our acts among men, not to excite that feeling of hate which seems to be implanted in the human bosom against the principles taught by the servants of the Lord in all ages of the world.

38.Our mission is and always has been peace on earth and goodwill to man, to all men. We have in our midst Baptists, Methodists, Presbyterians, Roman Catholics and all kinds of "ites." Does anybody interfere with them? Not that I know of. Yet there was a man, a professed minister in Sanpete County—[addressing President Canute Peterson of Sanpete Stake] Brother Peterson, did you not have a man in your Stake who got up a sensation by publishing far and wide that he had to preach the Gospel in Sanpete with a revolver on his desk, to prevent the "Mormons" from interfering with him—was not that the purport of his statement?

[President Peterson: Yes, sir.] Do you know the man? [Ans.: Yes, sir.] Is he there yet? [Ans.: No, sir.] [Laughter.]

39.Others have stated lately that we were in a state of sedition, and that in our different counties there were armed bodies of men prepared to fight the United States. The person that made and published this last statement was, as I understand, also a minister, one of these reverend gentlemen. Do any of you know his name? [A voice: Sheldon Jackson.] I am told it was one Sheldon Jackson; a reverend gentleman with a big R, a pious man, of course, and therefore what he says must be true. [Laughter.]

40.We have a set of people that seem to be prowling about; I suppose, however, they are as necessary as anything else; I do not know but what they are. We have a species of birds called buzzards, whose natural tastes are for any kind of nauseous food; nothing suits them better than to gorge on carrion. Like them, these defamers are fond of trying to root up something against our people here. They themselves fabricate all kinds of notions and opinions, similar to the above that I have mentioned, that everybody here knows to be false, and they circulate them, and they have fanned the United States almost into a furor. People generally are ignorant of what these men and women are engaged in. They think these persons are honorable men and women; and they get up a lot of stories about some poor woman or some poor girl who has been crowded upon by her husband, and that in this state of polygamy there is the most abject misery, and the greatest distress that can be found anywhere. Are they true? Some individual cases may be true. Some of our men do not treat their wives right, and then some wives do not treat their husbands right. We do not all do right by a great deal. I wish we all did right. But supposing we were to go down to the places where these people hail from, to the slums of Chicago, St. Louis, Cincinnati, Philadelphia, New York, and other cities, beginning, say, in New York, with the gilded palaces of 4th and 5th Avenues, and trace the thing down to Five Points, and then go through other cities in the same way, and what would we find there? Do you not think one could get up something as dirty and filthy as the most foul-minded person can get up about us? A thousand times more so.

41. They say we are an ignorant people. We admit that we are not so very intelligent, and we never boast of our learning or intelligence; but then, they should not boast of theirs either. However, we can compare favorably with them any day; and while they have had millions of the public funds to sustain their educational establishments, we have been despoiled, plundered and robbed over and over again, yet we are prepared to compare notes with them on education, and also on virtue, honesty and morals, any way they can fix it. And I would be ready to say, as one said of old, Thou fool, first take the beam out of thine own eye, that thou mayest see the more clearly to take the mote out of thy brother's eye.

42. We will have read some figures for the information of the brethren who come from a distance, who may not be acquainted with these matters....

43. From statistics contained in the Report of the Commissioners of Education for 1877, it is shown that in the percentage of enrollment of her School population, Utah is in advance of the general average of the United States, while in the percentage in actual daily attendance at school, she still further exceeds the average of the whole Union.

44. In 1877, when the school population of Utah numbered 30,792, there was invested in the Territory in school property the creditable sum of $568,984, being about eighteen and one-half dollars per capita of the school population.

45. In contrast with this, take the amount per capita of their school population, which some of the States have invested in school property: North Carolina, less than $0 60; Louisiana, $3 00; Virginia, about $2 00; Oregon, less than $9 00; Wisconsin, less than $11 00; Tennessee, less than $2 50; Delaware, less than $13 00.

46. In respect to the amount, per capita, of her school population, which Utah has invested in school property, she exceeds several other Southern and Western States, is in advance of the great States of Indiana and Illinois, and I believe in advance of the general average of the entire Union.

47. Thus, in the matter of education, Utah stands ahead of many old and wealthy States, and of the general average of the United States in three very important respects, namely, the enrollment of her school population, the percentage of their daily attendance at school, and the amount per capita invested in school property.

48. From the census of 1880 I have compiled the following:

COMPARISON OF ILLITERACY
The United States & Utah Territory:

	United States	Utah
Total population	50,155,783	143,963
Total over 10 years of age who cannot read	4,923,451	4,851
Percentage who cannot read, 10 yrs. & over	9.82	3.37
Total over 10 yrs. of age who cannot write	6,239,958	8,826
Percentage who cannot write, 10 yrs. & over	12.14	6.13
Total white population	43,402,970	142,423
Total white population over 10 years of age who cannot write	3,019,080	8,137
Percentage of white population who cannot write, 10 yrs. & over	6.96	5.71

49. Of all the States and Territories in the Union there are but thirteen showing a lower percentage of total population who cannot read, Connecticut having the same 3.37. The rest range all the way up 32.32. percentage of total population in South Carolina.

50. We will now produce some evidence with regard to crime, etc., drawn from official sources: The population of Utah by the census of 1880 is about 144,000, divided as follows:

Mormons		120,283
Gentiles	14,155	
Apostate Mormons	6,988	
Josephites	820	
Doubtful	1,717	
	———	23,680
Total		143,963

51. It will be seen that the "Gentiles" constitute only ten percent of the population, yet from this small minority are taken the incumbents of nearly every position of influence and emolument. They have the Governor, with absolute veto power, Secretary, Judges, Marshals, Prosecuting Attorneys, Land Register, Recorder, Surveyor-General, Clerks of the Courts, Commissioners, principal Post-office Mail Contractors, Postal Agents, Revenue Assessors and Collectors, Superintendent of Indian Affairs, Indian Agencies, Indian Supplies, Army Contractors, express, railroad and telegraph lines, the associated press agency, half the jurors in law, but at least three-fourths and always the foreman in practice, in fact, every position not elective.

52. Last winter there was a census taken of the Utah penitentiary and the Salt Lake City and County prisons, with the following result: In Salt Lake City there are about seventy-five Mormons to twenty-five non-Mormons. In Salt Lake County there are about eighty Mormons to twenty non-Mormons. In the city prison there were twenty-nine convicts, all non-Mormons; in the county prison there were six convicts, all non-Mormons. The jailer stated that the county convicts for the five years past were all anti-Mormons except three.

53. In Utah we have seen that by the United States Census the proportion of orthodox Mormons to all others is as eighty-three to seventeen. In the Utah penitentiary there were fifty-one prisoners, only five of whom were Mormons, and two of the five were in prison for imitating Father Abraham in their domestic menage, so that the seventeen per cent "outsiders" had forty-six convicts in the penitentiary, while the eighty-three per cent Mormons had but five! The total number of Utah lockups, including the penitentiary, is fourteen; these aggregated one hundred and twenty-five inmates. Of these one hundred and twenty-five, not over eleven were Mormons, several of whom were incarcerated for minor offenses and polygamy; while if all the anti-Mormon thieves, adulterers, blacklegs, perjurers, murderers and other criminals who are at large, were sent to prison, the Mormons claim that their prisons could not hold them.

54. In 1878 a Mormon publication made the following boastful statement:

55. Out of the twenty counties of the Territory, most of which are populous, thirteen are, today, without a dram-shop, brewery, gambling or brothel-house, bowling or billiard-saloon, lawyer, doctor, parson, beggar, politician or place-hunter, and almost entirely free from social troubles of every kind; yet these counties are exclusively 'Mormon;' and with the exception of a now and then domestic doctor or lawyer, the entire Territory was free from these adjuncts of civilization (?) till after the advent of the professing Christian element, boastingly here to 'regenerate the Mormons,' and today every single disreputable concern in Utah is run and fostered by the very same Christian (?) element. Oaths, imprecations, blasphemies, invectives, expletives, blackguardism, the ordinary dialect of the "anti-Mormon," were not heard in Utah till after his advent, nor till then, did we have litigation, drunkenness, harlotry, political and judicial deviltries, gambling and kindred enormities.

56. This is what the Mormons assert. Let us see how the case stands today, and what the facts attest.

57. Out of the two hundred saloon, billiard, bowling alley and pool table keepers, not over a dozen even profess to be Mormons. All of the bagnios and other disreputable concerns in the Territory are run and sustained by anti-Mormons. Ninety-eight per cent of the gamblers of Utah are of the same element. Ninety-five per cent of the Utah lawyers are Gentiles, and eighty per cent of all the litigation there is of outside growth and promotion.

58. Of the two hundred and fifty towns and villages in Utah, over two hundred have no "gaudy sepulcher of departed virtue," and these two hundred and odd towns are almost exclusively Mormon in population. Of the suicides committed in Utah, ninety odd per cent are non-Mormon; and of the Utah homicides and infanticides, over eighty per cent are perpetrated by the seventeen per cent "outsiders."

59. The arrests made in Salt Lake City from January 1, 1881, to December 8, 1881, are classified, as follows:

Men	782
Women	200
Boys	38
	———
Total	1,020

Mormons, Men & Boys	163	
Women	6	169
Anti-Mormons, Men & Boys	657	
Women	194	851
		———
Total		1,020

60. A number of the Mormon arrests were for chicken, cow and water trespass, petty larceny, etc. The arrests of anti-Mormons were in most cases for prostitution, gambling, exposing of person, drunkenness, unlawful dram selling, assault and battery, attempt to kill, etc.

61. If the seventy-five per cent Mormon population of Salt Lake City were as lawless and corrupt as the record shows the twenty-five per cent anti-Mormons to be, there would have been 2,443 arrests made from their ranks during the year 1881 instead of the comparatively trifling number of 169 shown on the record; while if the twenty-five per cent anti-Mormon population had as law-abiding and upright a record as the seventy-five per cent Mormons, instead of the startling number of 851 anti-Mormon arrests during the year, there would have been but 56 made."

62. I give these statements of facts for the information of the brethren who are here from a distance; but, then, they know them as facts; that is, they know how these soi disant regenerators act, but many of them do not know what their civilization is here, and what is sought to be introduced among us, and the infamous statements circulated concerning us. We are ready, as I said before, to compare notes with them or the people of this or any nation at any time. And then again, we ought to be more pure and virtuous than they, for we do profess to be the Saints of the Most High God.

63. With this view, when this Edmunds Bill was being canvassed, and there was a prospect of its passing—although we thought at first it was impossible that such a concern could pass through Congress; but when we saw the falsehoods that were being circulated, the furor that was being raised and fanned by religious fanatics and political demagogues, petitions were gotten up by the people here, one of them representing the male class, another our Relief Societies, another our young men, and another our young ladies' Improvement Societies. All of them represented that we were a virtuous people— that polygamy was a religious institution; and the young people asserted that it had been taught to them by their parents from their youth up, and that the principles of purity, virtue, integrity and loyalty to the government of the United States had been instilled into their minds and hearts since their earliest childhood; and further, that they had been taught and understood that chastity was their greatest boon, far above jewels or wealth, and more precious than life itself. In a few days we had 165,000 signatures, and they were forwarded to Washington. The request was that Congress would not act as the government had before—first send out an army and then send commissioners to inquire, but that they would send commissioners first to inquire into the facts of the case. But they did not choose to listen. In fact, there has been a great furor in the United States in relation to these matters, and that has originated to an extent through our Governor.

64. Now I am very much averse to talking about official men; I do not like to do such things. They ought to be honorable men; the most charitable construction I could put upon his acts would be to say that his education had been sadly neglected, and that he was not acquainted with figures. He might have learned to read and write perhaps, but I would question his having gone so far as arithmetic; because he did not apparently know the difference between 1,300 votes and 18,500 votes. It does denote a lamentable absence of a knowledge of the rudiments of a common education; but then, a man should not, perhaps, be blamed for that which he does not know. And, indeed, it would seem that some of our lawmakers in Washington are not educated. With all due respect to them, with these facts before them and condemned throughout the United States, they did not think it was any crime for a man to be thus ignorant, or they would not have sent

him back again. We hope the Commissioners will be better educated, that they will be men who can tell the difference between 1,300 and 18,500. Now we may be very ignorant—and we do not boast much of our intelligence, but when such people perpetrate such palpable, flagrant outrages, we have to resort to a political phrase in order to express our disgust towards them by saying, "There is something rotten in Denmark." I have to be a politician as well as everything else.

65. Still, in the midst of these things, what are you going to do? Do the very best we can. Are you going to rebel? That would please our enemies, but we do not have much of that spirit in us. We feel to sympathize with people who have not better judgment than to adopt so suicidal and dishonorable a course as that which has been pursued towards us. Yet notwithstanding this, we are unshaken towards the principles of our government and believe that we have got the best on the earth, these evils arising from the corruptions of men and maladministration. It is said that error and falsehood will run a thousand miles while truth is putting on its boots, but truth ultimately will triumph, as according to the old adage, "Truth, crushed to earth, will rise again." And what will you do? Contend for constitutional principles, or lie down and let the vicious, the mendacious and unprincipled run over and overslaugh you?

66. We have peacefully, legally and honorably possessed our lands in these valleys of the mountains, and we have purchased and paid for them; we do not revel in any ill-gotten gain. They are ours. We have complied with all the requisitions of law pertaining thereto, and we expect to possess and inhabit them. We covet no man's silver or gold, or apparel, or wife, or servants, or flocks, or herds, or horses, or carriages, or lands, or possessions. But we expect to maintain our own rights.

67. If we are crowded upon by unprincipled men or inimical legislation, we shall not take the course pursued by the lawless, the dissolute and the unprincipled; we shall not have recourse to the dynamite of the Russian Nihilists, the secret plans and machinations of the communists, the boycotting and threats of the Fenians, the force and disorder of the Jayhawkeers, the regulators or the Molly Maguires, nor any other secret or illegal combination; but we still expect to possess and maintain our rights; but to obtain them in a legal, peaceful and constitutional manner.

68. As American citizens, we shall contend for all our liberties, rights and immunities, guaranteed to us by the Constitution; and no matter what action may be taken by mobocratic influence, by excited and unreasonable men, or by inimical legislation, we shall contend inch by inch for our freedom and rights, as well as the freedom and rights of all American citizens and of all mankind. As a people or community, we can abide our time, but I will say to you Latter-day Saints, that there is nothing of which you have been despoiled by oppressive acts or mobocratic rule, but that you will again possess, or your children after you. Your rights in Ohio, your rights in Jackson, Clay, Caldwell and Davis counties in Missouri, will yet be restored to you. Your possessions, of which you have been fraudulently despoiled in Missouri and Illinois, you will again possess, and that without force, or fraud or violence. The Lord has a way of His own in regulating such matters. We are told the wicked shall slay the wicked. He has a way of His own of "emptying the earth of the inhabitants thereof."

69. A terrible day of reckoning is approaching the nations of the earth; the Lord is coming out of His hiding place to vex the inhabitants thereof; and the destroyer of the Gentiles, as prophesied of, is already on his way. Already the monarchs of the earth are trembling from conspiracies among their own people; already has one Czar of Russia been destroyed and another holds his life by a very uncertain tenure through the perpetual threats and machinations of an infuriated populace; already have the Emperor of Germany, the King of Italy, the Queen of England, the King of Spain, the Sultan of Turkey, and many others of the honorable and noble rulers of the earth had their lives jeopardized by the attacks of regicides; already have two of the Presidents of this Republic been laid low by the hands of the assassin; and the spirit of insubordination, misrule, lynching, and mobocracy of every kind is beginning to ride rampant through the land; already combinations are being entered into which are very ominous for the future

prosperity, welfare and happiness of this great Republic. The volcanic fires of disordered and anarchical elements are beginning to manifest themselves and exhibit the internal forces that are at work among the turbulent and unthinking masses of the people.

70. Congress will soon have something else to do than to proscribe and persecute an innocent, law-abiding and patriotic people. Of all bodies in the world, they can least afford to remove the bulwarks that bind society together in this nation, to recklessly trample upon human freedom and rights, and to rend and destroy that great Palladium of human rights—the Constitution of the United States. Ere long they will need all its protecting influence to save this nation from misrule, anarchy and mobocratic influence. They can ill afford to be the foremost in tampering with human rights and human freedom, or in tearing down the bulwarks of safety and protection which that sacred instrument has guaranteed. It is lamentable to see the various disordered and disorganized elements seeking to overthrow the greatest and best government in existence on the earth. Congress can ill afford to set a pattern of violation of that Constitution which it has sworn to support.

71. The internal fires of revolution are already smoldering in this nation, and they need but a spark to set them in a flame. Already are agencies at work in the land calculated to subvert and overthrow every principle of rule and government; already is corruption of every kind prevailing in high places and permeating all society; already are we, as a nation, departing from our God, and corrupting ourselves with malfeasance, dishonor, and a lack of public integrity and good faith; already are licentiousness and debauchery corrupting, undermining and destroying society; already are we interfering with the laws of nature and stopping the functions of life, and have become the slayers of our own offspring, and employ human butchers in the shape of physicians to assist in this diabolical and murderous work.

72. The sins of this nation, the licentiousness, the debauchery, the murders are entering into the ears of the Lord of Sabbaoth, and I tell you now, from the tops of these mountains, as a humble servant of the living God,

that unless these crimes and infamies are stopped, this nation will be overthrown, and its glory, power, dominion and wealth will fade away like the dews of a summer morning. I also say to other nations of the earth, that unless they repent of their crimes, their iniquities and abominations, their thrones will be overturned, their kingdoms and governments overthrown, and their lands made desolate. This is not only my saying, but it is the saying of those ancient prophets which they themselves profess to believe; for God will speedily have a controversy with the nations of the earth, and, as I stated before, the destroyer of the Gentiles is on his way to overthrow governments, to destroy dynasties, to lay waste thrones, kingdoms and empires, to spread abroad anarchy and desolation, and to cause war, famine and bloodshed to overspread the earth.

73. Besides the preaching of the Gospel, we have another mission, namely, the perpetuation of the free agency of man and the maintenance of liberty, freedom, and the rights of man. There are certain principles that belong to humanity outside of the Constitution, outside of the laws, outside of all the enactments and plans of man, among which is the right to live; God gave us the right and not man; no government gave it to us, and no government has a right to take it away from us. We have a right to liberty—that was a right that God gave to all men; and if there has been oppression, fraud or tyranny in the earth, it has been the result of the wickedness and corruptions of men and has always been opposed to God and the principles of truth, righteousness, virtue, and all principles that are calculated to elevate mankind. The Declaration of Independence states that men are in possession of certain inalienable rights, among which are life, liberty and the pursuit of happiness. This belongs to us; it belongs to all humanity.

74. I wish, and the worst wish I have for the United States, is, that they could have liberality enough to give to all men equal rights, and, while they profess to have delivered the black slaves, that they strike off the fetters of the white men of the South, who have been ground under the heel of sectional injustice, and let them feel that we are all brothers in one great nation, and deliver all people from

tyranny and oppression of every kind, and proclaim, as they did at the first, liberty throughout the land and to all people. That is the worst wish I have for them. And when I see them take another course I feel sorry for it.

75. I would like if I had time to talk a little upon constitutional rights; I would like a little to discuss the unconstitutionality of that Edmund's Bill; but it was ably done by many senators of the United States, and by others in the House of Representatives. Very ably done; and I honor the men who maintain such sentiments. It is true that most of them apologized and said that they were as much opposed to polygamy as anybody. Well, that is a matter of their own; they have a right to their opinions as much as I have a right to my opinion. Would I deprive them of that right? No, I would not.

76. I preach the Gospel to the world. What is it? Force, tyranny and oppression? No: it is all free grace and it is all free will. Is anybody coerced? Did anybody coerce you, Latter-day Saints? Are any of you forced to continue Latter-day Saints if you do not want to? If you think you are, you are all absolved today. We know of no such principle as coercion; it is a matter of choice. The principle that I spoke of before—that is, men receive the Holy Ghost within themselves, is the cementing, binding, uniting power that exists among the Latter-day Saints.

77. What right have I to expect that members of the House of Representatives or the people of the United States should advocate polygamy? They would not understand it. Nor would it be reasonable for us to expect it at their hands; but what I admired in those Senators and Members was their fealty to the government, to the Constitution and the maintenance of the freedom and the inalienable rights of man, of every color, creed and profession.

78. I will relate a little conversation that I had with President Hayes, when he was here, on the subject of polygamy. I said to him, we are not generally understood by the people of the world, by the outsiders; and I can look with very great leniency upon the action of members of the House of Representatives and the Senate, the governors, and others who have expressed strong indignation against this principle. From your standpoint, you think we are a corrupt people; you think it is a part or portion of the thing you call the social evil, that permeates all classes of society, and is sapping the foundation of the life of so many throughout the land. You think that we are trying to introduce something that is encouraging licentiousness and other kindred evils among the people, and to legalize these things by legislative enactment and otherwise, and trying to popularize and make legal those infamies. I continued, that is a false view to take of the subject. Mr. President, I have always abhorred such practices from the time I was quite young; when I have seen men act the part of Lotharios, deceiving the fair sex and despoiling them of their virtue, and then seeing those men received into society and their victims disgraced, ostracized and esteemed as pariahs and outcasts, I could not help sympathizing with a woman that was seduced. I looked upon the man who seduced her as a villain; I do so today. Said I, when Joseph Smith first made known the revelation concerning plural marriage and of having more wives than one, it made my flesh crawl; but, Mr. President, I received such evidence and testimony pertaining to this matter, scriptural and otherwise, which it was impossible for me as an honest man to resist, and believing it to be right I obeyed it and practiced it.

79. I have not time now to enter into all the details; but in regard to those honorable gentlemen in the Senate who maintained the principle of constitutional rights and who declare, as I declare today, that that instrument which was then gotten up was unconstitutional in several particulars, I could not expect them to advocate my religion; it is not their business, but is mine and yours. They can take what religion they please; we do not wish to force our religion nor our marital relations upon them, nor have we ever done it, nor could we do it if we wished, for this principle is connected with the Saints alone, and pertains to eternity as well as time, and is known to us by the appellation of "celestial marriage." It does not belong to them, nor does it pertain to all of our own people.

80. None but the more pure, virtuous, honorable and upright are permitted to enter into these associations. Now I speak to the Latter-day Saints, who are acquainted with what I

say. If I state untruths, tell me, and I will consider you my friends, and the friends of this community. Should we preach the doctrine of plurality of wives to the people of the United States? No; you know very well that it is only for honorable men and women, virtuous men and women, honest men and women who can be vouched for by those who preside over them, and whom they recognize as their Presidents; it is only such people as these that can be admitted to participate in this ordinance. You know it. I know it, you Presidents of Stakes know it and the people know it. There are any number of people in this Territory who are good people in many respects, but who cannot come up to that standard. That is the position we occupy in relation to this principle.

81. If the United States were to ask us if we could give to them the same ordinance, we would say, No; no, we cannot. Why can you not? Because it is a religious ordinance, as I have stated; because it connects men and women together for time and for eternity; because it associates people of this world in the next; because it makes provision for our marital associations in the other world, and that while we have our wives here we expect to have them in eternity; and we believe in that doctrine that reaches beyond time into eternity. Others make their marital relations to end in death; their covenants last only till death does them part. Ours take hold of eternity, they enter into the eternal state of existence, and contemplate an eternal union of the sexes worlds without end.

82. We believe in the resurrection of the dead and the life in the world to come; and not only in the resurrection of the male, but also of the female. We believe also in eternal unions, union on earth and in heaven. And as the heavens declare the glory of God, and the stellar universes roll on according to eternal laws implanted in them by the Deity, and perform their revolutions through successive ages, so will man progress and increase—himself, his wives, his children—through the eternities to come. Who is injured by this faith? Cannot a great and magnanimous nation afford the privilege to enjoy these principles without passing bills of pains and penalties for the belief and enunciation of such divine, ennobling and Godlike principles?

83. Man is a dual being, possessed of body and spirit, made in the image of God, and connected with Him and with eternity. He is a God in embryo and will live and progress throughout the eternal ages, if obedient to the laws of the Godhead, as the Gods progress throughout the eternal ages. Is it a thing incredible in this generation that God shall raise the dead? Is it a thing incredible that the finest and most exalted ties and sympathies of humanity, sanctified by family relations— pure undefiled love, should continue in the resurrection?

84. We have no fault to find with our government. We deem it the best in the world. But we have reason to deplore its maladministration, and I call upon our legislators, our governors and president to pause in their career and not to tamper with the rights and liberties of American citizens, nor wantonly tear down the bulwarks of American and human liberty. God has given to us glorious institutions; let us preserve them intact and not pander to the vices, passions and fanaticism of a depraved public opinion.

85. Cannot the enlightenment, civilization and statesmanship of the nineteenth century in this great American nation find a more worthy object than to fetter human thought, to enslave its own citizens, to forge chains for the suppression of human progress, to bind in Cimmerian darkness the noblest aspirations of the human soul, to tear down the pillars of the temple of liberty, to inaugurate a system of serfdom and oppression, and to copy after Egypt, Russia, and the late practices of this nation in enslaving and brutalizing humanity, tearing to pieces that great palladium of human rights, the Constitution of the United States? Can they afford to do this? If there are supposed wrongs, can they not find a legal and constitutional way of correcting these wrongs? Surely the tearing down of the bulwarks, the very temple of freedom, will not aid them in the solution of this, to them, vexed question, for if they tear away the strongholds of society, they themselves will perish in the ruins.

86. But with regard to those not of us, I will tell you what I believe about the matter. I believe it would be much better for them to have even polygamy in their state of existence than this corroding, corrupting, demor-

alizing and damning evil that prevails in their midst. We look upon it that polygamy is the normal condition of man; but that has nothing to do with Mormon plurality of wives, or what is termed "celestial marriage." I would state also, that when we speak of its being the normal condition, it has so existed throughout all ages.

87. And when we talk about polygamy, I have read the speeches of men in Congress when speaking about the Mormon position, telling us that the British in India put down suttee, which is the burning of widows on the funeral pile of their husbands; casting children into the Ganges, etc.—that the British put that down by force of law. But the British, if my memory serves me right, have about two hundred millions of polygamists under their jurisdiction, and they can afford to treat them right and to give them the protection of law; but our free government cannot. And when we talk about the suttee, that is the destruction of life, while polygamy means the propagation of human life. One tends to destruction and death, the other to the propagation of life. I will guarantee today, without fear of contradiction, that there is more of the suttee in the United States today pertaining to infants than there ever was in India among the same number of population.

88. It has become unfashionable in the east for women to have large families. I have heard remarks like this: one lady was asked, How many children have you? One or two. Is that all? What do you take me for, do you think I am a cow? Why no, you are not a cow, for cows do not murder their offspring. What a terrible tale is here told! What a horrible state of affairs is here exhibited. And I am told that some of these iniquities are being introduced here. I tell you, in the name of God, if you do we will be after you. I am told of physicians who are acting as they do in the east—as the butchers of infants. Let us look after these things, you Bishops, and if you do find it out, bring them up. As God lives we will not permit such infamies in our midst; you will not commence your fashionable murders here. And I will say now, Wo to this nation and to the nations of Europe, or any people among any nation, that sanctions these things. Have you not read that no "murderer hath eternal life abiding in him?"

What shall be thought of those unnatural monsters, the slayers of their own offspring? This revolting, unnatural, damnable vice may be fashionable, but God will require this crime at their hands. Wo to men and to women that are licentious and corrupt, depraved and debauched, and especially wo, tenfold wo, to the murderers of helpless innocence. I tell you this in the name of the Lord. If these things are not stopped, God will arise and shake the nations of the earth and root out their infamies.

89. Now then what shall we do? We do not wish to place ourselves in a state of antagonism, nor to act defiantly, towards this government. We will fulfill the letter, so far as practicable, of that unjust, inhuman, oppressive and unconstitutional law, so far as we can without violating principle; but we cannot sacrifice every principle of human right at the behest of corrupt, unreasoning and unprincipled men; we cannot violate the highest and noblest principles of human nature and make pariahs and outcasts of high-minded, virtuous and honorable women, nor sacrifice at the shrine of popular clamor the highest and noblest principles of humanity!

90. We shall abide all constitutional law, as we always have done; but while we are Godfearing and law-abiding, and respect all honorable men and officers, we are no craven serfs, and have not learned to lick the feet of oppressors, nor to bow in base submission to unreasoning clamor. We will contend, inch by inch, legally and constitutionally, for our rights as American citizens, and for the universal rights of universal man. We stand proudly erect in the consciousness of our rights as American citizens, and plant ourselves firmly on the sacred guarantees of the Constitution; and that instrument, while it defines the powers and privileges of the President, Congress and the judiciary, also directly provides that "the powers not delegated to the United States by the Constitution, nor prohibited by it to the States, are reserved to the States respectively or to the people."

91. I have heard it boasted by British statesmen, that as soon as a slave planted his foot on British soil, his fetters were broken and he was a free man. It is the proud boast of

Americans that her flag floats for all; and while Congress claims the right of dominion and legislation over territories, with that same right is associated the right of manhood, freedom and American citizenship.

92. We need have no fears, no trembling in our knees, about these attempts to deprive us of our God given and constitutional liberties. God will take care of His people, if we will only do right. I am thankful to say that you are doing pretty nearly as well as you know how. There are many things among us that are wrong, many things that are foolish, but generally you are seeking to fear God and keep His commandments.

93. Now, treat your wives right, but do not subject yourselves to the infamous provisions of the Edmund's' Act more than you can help, avoid all harsh expressions and improper actions, act carefully and prudently in all your social relations. Be wise as serpents and harmless as doves. A gentleman in Washington told another, who related it to me, in answer to the question, What will the "Mormons" do with their wives and children when this bill passes? he was told: Turn them out in the streets as we do our harlots. I say in the name of God we will not do any such thing, and let all Israel say Amen. [The vast congregation, amounting to from 12,000 to 14,000 persons, responded Amen.] We will stand by our covenants, and the Constitution will bear us out in it. Among other things, that instrument says that Congress shall make no law impairing the validity of contracts. You have contracted to be united with your wives in time and in eternity, and it would not do for us to break a constitutional law, would it? [Laughter.] Others may do it, but we cannot. We cannot lay aside our honor, we cannot lay aside our

principles; and if people cannot allow us freedom, we can allow freedom to them and to all men. We will be true to our wives and cherish them and maintain them, and stand by them in time, and we will reign with them in eternity, when thousands of others are weltering under the wrath of God. Any man that abuses his wife, or takes advantage of this law to oppress her, is not worthy of a standing in the Church of Jesus Christ of Latter-day Saints; and let the congregation say Amen. [The immense congregation responded by a loud Amen.]

94. Now, what will we do in our relations with the United States? We will observe the law as we have done, and be as faithful as we have been. We will maintain our principles and live our religion and keep the commandments of God, and obey every constitutional law, pursuing that course that shall direct us in all things.

95. Brethren and sisters, God bless you and lead you in the paths of life, and give you wisdom; be calm and quiet; all is well in Zion. You need not be under any fears about anything that may transpire, as though some strange thing had happened. We have met such things before; we can meet them again. God has delivered us before. He will deliver us again, if we put our trust in Him and remain true to the covenants we have made with Him. Our trust is in God. You have heard me say before, Hosanna, the Lord God Omnipotent reigneth; and if this congregation feels as I do we will join together in the same acclaim. Follow me.

96. [The speaker then repeated and was followed by the congregation: Hosanna! Hosanna! Hosanna! to God and the Lamb, for ever and ever worlds without end, Amen, Amen and Amen.]

ADDRESS 24

Discourse delivered by President John Taylor at the 52nd Semiannual General Conference of The Church of Jesus Christ of Latter-day Saints convened October 8, 1882, in the Tabernacle, Salt Lake City.

1. We have had a very interesting Conference, and a great many thoughts, ideas and reflections have been presented to the people in a clear and pointed manner, and I have been pleased to see the unanimity and harmony that have existed in our midst. And while I attempt to speak to you I shall ask an interest in your prayers that I may be strengthened to perform the labor.

2. It is difficult for a people to understand and to retain everything that may be said in a Conference like this, where there are so many subjects dwelt upon and so many principles enunciated; but it is a great blessing for us that we are situated as we are, and that we possess the intelligence which has been communicated from time to time. Many great and precious principles having been revealed unto us, it becomes necessary for us to try to comprehend them, that we may understand the position we occupy before God, before the world in which we live, and before the intelligences that exist behind the veil in the eternal worlds. We have a great and important mission committed unto us, and it is for us to seek to comprehend that mission and fulfill the various duties and responsibilities devolving upon us. The Lord has given unto us a form of government, an organization, priesthood and authority to enable us to perform these several duties, and he has certain plans, purposes and designs to accomplish pertaining to us, pertaining to this nation, to other nations, and to the world in which we live,—pertaining to those who have lived and are now in another state of existence, and also pertaining to those who shall yet live.

3. The time in which we live is denominated in Scripture "the dispensation of the fullness of times," wherein it is said God will gather together all things in one, whether they be things in the earth or things in the heavens. This dispensation embraces all other dispensations, all principles and powers, rights, privileges, immunities and developments that have existed among men in the various ages that are past.

4. This globe did not originate with man, nor was it constructed, designed or manipulated by him, nor were any of its organisms, sentient or inanimate; for we are told that in the beginning God created the heavens and the earth and all that in them is: nor did this dispensation with which we are associated, nor have any of the dispensations associated with the works, plans or designs of the Almighty originated with man. After man had fallen, and it became necessary that he be driven from the garden, it needed the interposition of the Almighty, for as is said in the Book of Job, it was necessary to "deliver his soul from the pit; I have found a ransom." That ransom was the Only Begotten Son of God who offered himself in the beginning to meet the demands of justice, to carry out the purposes of the Almighty, and to be a Savior and Redeemer to man. Adam was perfectly helpless in this respect, and it needed the direct interposition of the Almighty for the accomplishment of this object.

5. In the patriarchal, or antediluvian age, when men were put in possession of any hope, any intelligence, any knowledge, or any revelation pertaining to God, these things did not originate with man, they came from the Lord and were given by inspiration; and when on account of the wickedness and corruption of mankind the old world had to be destroyed, a way was provided for a small remnant to be spared, By whom? By man? No. God dictated it. The Prophets prophesied about it. They taught the antediluvians as the people of this day are being taught, they warned them of the impending ruin that would overwhelm them, of the prison house to which they would go, and of the wrath and indignation of Heaven which would be poured out upon the peoples of the earth. It came to pass as they had declared. But God provided a way for the perpetuation of the human family. It was foretold to Methuselah

that his seed should be preserved to perpetuate the human family upon the earth, and it was so, Noah, who was one of his descendants, fulfilled that decree.

6. Again, in later ages when the children of Israel were in bondage in Egypt, they did not originate the method of their own deliverance, or point out the way for its accomplishment. They were in a state of bondage and vassalage. God raised them up a Moses, revealed His will to him, set him apart for this mission, told him what to do, and after some little difficulties arising from human weakness were removed, Moses was accepted, and the Lord became his instructor, and pointed out in all instances the course that he should pursue, and in what manner the children of Israel were to be delivered, and He, the Holy One of Israel, gave them His law and ordinances, and revealed unto them His will, and stood by and sustained, guided and directed them. This salvation did not come from the people, it did not originate with them, they owed it all to God, the source of all truth, all light, all intelligence, all power and blessings.

7. The time at length arrived that the Son of God was to come. Neither the Scribes and Pharisees, the High Priests and Saducees, nor any of the sects and parties of the day comprehended the things that were about to transpire, and had nothing to do with bringing them to pass. His advent was announced to His mother by an angel, and His birth was heralded to shepherds by an angelic host, and the wise men of the East were led by his star to Bethlehem of Judea, where they found the infant Savior, whom they recognized as the Messiah, and to whom they brought presents of gold, frankincense and myrrh; and whom they worshipped.

8. It is said in speaking of the Son of God, that he did not come to do His own will, nor to carry out His own purposes, nor to fulfill any particular plan of his own, but he came to do the will of his Father who sent him. Jesus in selecting his disciples, took one man here and another there—a tax gatherer, a fisherman, and others who it was thought were the most unlikely of any men to carry out the purposes of God. He left the great men out of the question, that is the High Priests and the popular and pious of all classes, and he selected his own laborers to perform his own work;

and he subsequently told them, You have not chosen me, but I have chosen you and set you apart unto this mission.

9. When a message had to be proclaimed to the world in these last days the agents were chosen on the same principle. There was any amount of teachers of divinity, any amount of professors of theology, any amount of reverend, and right reverend fathers and all classes of religious men and religious teachers; but God did not recognize them. He chose a young uneducated man and inspired him with the spirit of revelation, and placed upon him a mission and required him to perform it; and he was obedient to that requirement. I speak of this to show that we none of us had anything to do with the introduction of this work, but that, as in all other dispensations in the various ages of the world, God was the originator of everything that tended to develop a knowledge of Himself and of his plans and purposes; to unfold the past, to develop the present, and to make manifest the future.

10. To whom are we indebted for this book, called the Bible. We are told that holy men of old spake as they were moved upon by the Holy Ghost. And from whence did they receive that Holy Ghost? Not of man, nor by man, but by the revelations of God, through our Lord and Savior Jesus Christ.

11. We sometimes feel to exalt ourselves a little in the position that we occupy pertaining to the Priesthood, pertaining to our organization, and pertaining to ordinances, etc. What have we to glory in? Nothing. None of us knew anything until it was revealed. None of us could comprehend any of these principles only as they have been made manifest. But by obedience to the Gospel we have received the Holy Ghost, and that Spirit takes of the things of God, and shows them to us. We have received this and hence have been baptized into one baptism, and all partaken of the self-same Spirit, as Paul expressed it, "dividing to every man severally as he will."

12. The question arises, what is the object of this? It is that the world should be visited from time to time and communications made to the human family. Because light cleaves to light, truth cleaves to truth, intelligence cleaves to intelligence; and as we are all

made in the image of God, and as God is the God and Father of the spirits of all flesh, it is His right, it is His prerogative to communicate with the human family. We are told that there is a spirit in man and the inspiration of the Almighty giveth it understanding. God having made the earth, made the people to inhabit it, and made all things that exist therein, has a right to dictate, has a right to make known His will, has a right to communicate with whom he will and control matters as he sees proper: it belongs to him by right; and he has seen proper in these last days to restore His Gospel to the earth, and, as I said before, intelligence cleaves to intelligence.

13. We read in the Scriptures concerning man being a son of God. We read in the Scriptures about men becoming the adopted sons of God through obedience to the Gospel. Hence it is said: "Now are we the sons of God, and it doth not yet appear what we shall be; but we know that when he shall appear, we shall be like him; for we shall see him as he is." By what means? Through the atonement of Jesus Christ and by the medium of the Gospel, which has been introduced in different ages for that purpose. God having felt disposed to reveal the Gospel in these last days, has given the same principles and powers, the same light, revelation and intelligence that he did in former ages, for the accomplishment of the same work, and for the fulfillment of his purposes relating to the human family who are his children. Hence we occupy a very peculiar position in relation to God, in relation to the earth in which we live and the people thereof—in relation to both—to the living and to the dead.

14. It is proper for us to comprehend the position that we occupy. We sometimes arrive at curious conclusions pertaining to the wickedness of the world, and a variety of other things associated therewith. And permit me to say here, that we had no more to do with the peoples of the world, or the placing of them in the position they occupy, than we had in restoring the Gospel. We find ourselves a few people mixed up with the world. We find too that when the word of God is made manifest and the revelations of God are developed, that many things as they exist amongst mankind are out of order. There is a great amount of priestcraft, idolatry, corrup-

tion, oppression, tyranny, murder, bloodshed, covetousness, licentiousness, and every kind of iniquity that can be conceived of; and that is more clearly made manifest to us because the Lord has been teaching us through the Prophets, and inspiring us with other feelings, and given unto us to comprehend things more clearly than others do.

15. But what have we to do with the people of the world? We complain sometimes that they do not treat us exactly right. Well, they do not in all respects, and I do not think this is very difficult to understand. But there is nothing new about that, God has revealed unto us His law, and they do not comprehend it, neither do they want to; nor did the antediluvians. They were very wicked, very corrupt and very depraved, very immoral and very dishonest; but that was a matter between them and the Lord, and he dealt with them; and it is his business to deal with the nations of the earth at the present time and not ours further than we are directed by him.

16. What is the mission that we have to perform to this nation? It is to preach the Gospel. That is one thing. That was the mission given to the disciples of Jesus in his day: Go ye into all the world and preach the Gospel; he that believeth and is baptized shall be saved; and he that believeth not shall be damned. This mission is being carried out in the fact of our sending representatives of this latter-day work to all the civilized nations that will receive our missionaries.

17. But we are not placed here to control people; we are not placed here to use any improper influence over the minds or consciences of men. It is not for us to attempt to do what Mohammed did—to say that there was but one God, and Mohammed was his prophet, and by force compel all others to acknowledge it. To attempt to do that would be to attempt to interfere with the agency of man; and anything of that kind is altogether foreign to the character and spirit of our mission. We preach the Gospel to the people, and it is for them to receive or reject as they may choose. We have done this to a great extent. Many of you Elders who are before and around me—and there are some thousands—have been engaged preaching this Gospel, but none of you ever used coercion, none of you ever attempted to force any man

to obey the message you had to declare. If you did, you did not understand your calling. And when you have been among the different nations preaching this Gospel, have you sought to interfere with their governments or with their laws, or endeavored to stir up commotion or rebellion or trouble of any kind? No. I am at the defiance of the world to prove any such statement. That does not belong to our faith. When the Elders are sent forth, they go as servants of God with a message from the Lord, to unfold the Scriptures, and to bear testimony of the things that they themselves are witnesses of; and to administer the ordinances of the Gospel to all those who believe on their words. This is the position that we occupy in these matters.

18. And what else do we do? We gather the people together; and they no sooner receive this Gospel than they are anxious to gather with the people of God. Why? Because the Scriptures say that they would? Because the Scriptures say, "gather my people, those that have made covenant with me by sacrifice?" No, but because they have obeyed the Gospel and received the Holy Ghost, and that Holy Ghost has instructed them pertaining to these matters, as it instructed the prophets in former times that such an event would transpire. The people have gathered together, and you could not keep them back if you were to try to. They have been trying.

19. You know that Mr. Evarts wrote communications to the European ministers requesting them to use their influence by way of putting a stop to the "Mormon" emigration. It is rather a sorry comment upon the government of this nation, that boasts of being "the land of the free, the home of the brave, and the asylum for the oppressed," and that a little over a hundred years ago the chief complaint against the nation from whence the colonists came, was the lack of religious toleration; to think that they should so far forget their original condition as to call upon what they term the effete monarchies of Europe to assist them in suppressing religious liberty and controlling human freedom. And when this subject was brought before Mr. Gladstone, the Prime Minister of Great Britain, a short time ago by some pragmatical zealot in the British Parliament, calling his attention to the request of the

American Secretary, he very distinctly told him that "he was unable to interfere with the operations of the Mormons in England, as he presumed their converts went with them willingly." Thus while the American government is trying to exert force and to interfere with religious matters and bind the consciences of men, the British government pleads for and guarantees to its subjects religious and social liberty. I am told that Mr. Evarts is a great-grandson of Roger Sherman, one of the signers of the Declaration of Independence. I should not have thought that that gentleman would have so soon forgotten the position occupied by his ancestor. But it seems that such is the fact, nevertheless.

20. I repeat, our mission is to preach the Gospel, and then to gather the people who embrace it. And why? That there might be a nucleus formed, a people gathered who would be under the inspiration of the Almighty, and who would be willing to listen to the voice of God, a people who would receive and obey His word when it was made known to them. And this people in their gathered condition are called Zion, or the pure in heart. I wish we were pure in heart; that is, I wish we were more so than we are. And this is something that we all need to reflect upon, to consider the pit from whence we were dug, and the rock from whence we were hewn. I have heard people say, they were born in sin, and cradled in iniquity. It is probably very true. Many of us have been rocked in these cradles, and we have been nurtured amidst infamies, and we have been surrounded by and enveloped in evils of all kinds. We talk sometimes about Babylon—"Come out of her O my people, that ye partake not of her sins, nor receive of her plagues." We need not say too much about those people, for we came out from them ourselves; and it would not be becoming on our part to speak badly about our former status.

21. That reminds me of a conversation I had some years ago with some Protestants who were abusing the Catholics. I reminded them of the fact that they descended from them. They were calling the Catholic Church the Mother of Harlots. Well, said I, if that be true, she has brought forth a scurvy offspring. History certainly informs us that the

Protestants came out from the Catholics, and therefore, if the Catholic Church is the mother, they certainly must be the daughters, and one would think there should be some affinity between them. It is not considered proper for persons to rail against their mother.

22. It is well for us to comprehend our position with regard to the nation. Being gathered together, as a people, we have assumed a political status, for we not only brought our religion and our spirits with us, but our bodies also; and by thus being gathered in this land we become naturally an integral part of the United States. We have received by the act of the government of the United States a territorial from of government, in which we are authorized to perform certain functions of a political nature, and to enjoy, as do all other Territories, the free and full rights of American citizens therein, and thus have become a part of the body politic of these United States, with all the rights, privileges and immunities pertaining thereto, as exercised and enjoyed by all American citizens throughout this broad land; and these are guaranteed unto us in the Constitution of the United States and by the Congress of the United States, in an instrument denominated the Organic Act. And I will say this much for the United States; with all her faults and infirmities, I do not believe there is a nation upon the face of the earth today, where we could have as much liberty as we here enjoy, and that is precious little, God knows.

23. We are told sometimes that we live under popular government, and that the voice of the people rules. It used to, but who rules now? Well, no matter, we have got to make the best we can of it. We have a territorial form of government, with a governor appointed by the administration. I was going to say, God save the mark. We have judges and other officers; and we have a nominal legislature that makes our laws, but those laws can be vetoed by one man. There is a great deal of absolutism about it. But these are the circumstances in which we are placed; and I suppose it is thought by a great many that we ought to consider it a great privilege to be allowed to live. We do think so, but we are not indebted to any officials for it; they did not give us our life, neither did this government.

24. There are certain principles that are inherent in man, that belong to man, and that were enunciated in an early day, before the United States government was formed, and they are principles that rightfully belong to all men everywhere. They are described in the Declaration of Independence as inalienable rights, one of which is that men have a right to live; another is that they have a right to pursue happiness; and another is that they have a right to be free and no man has authority to deprive them of those God-given rights, and none but tyrants would do it. These principles I say, are inalienable in man; they belong to him; they existed before any constitutions were framed or any laws made. Men have in various ages striven to strip their fellow-men of these rights, and dispossess them of them. And hence the wars, the bloodshed and carnage that have spread over the earth. We therefore are not indebted to the United States for these rights; we were free as men born into the world, having the right to do as we please, to act as we please, as long as we do not transgress constitutional law nor violate the rights of others.

25. Being organized, then, into a government such as it is—that is, the name of a government, the name of a legislature, the name of a free people—being organized as we are, what next? We are necessarily obliged to look after our affairs as men, our political affairs. Our mission to the world is a mission of peace, the Gospel proclaims peace on earth and good will to man. Then, being organized in a governmental capacity, we have certain rights. They profess to give them to us, but they don't. They try to deprive us of them while professing to impart them. I might enter into a long line of argument here; no matter, I am merely speaking upon some general principles. What then is our duty here, say as a people—leaving religion out of the question altogether? As men and as American citizens, we have the right to all the privileges, and immunities, protection and rights of every kind that any men in these United States have, and no honorable man or men would seek to deprive us of them. When we talk about rights, these are the rights, as I understand them, that we possess in this nation.

26.Is it proper, therefore, for us, as men and as citizens of the United States to look after our rights? I think it is. Do we want to violate law? No, we do not, although we know many of these laws are wrong, corrupt and unconstitutional. We have no right to find fault with others about their religion. We preach the Gospel; they receive or reject it as they please. If we have found the benefit of embracing it, let us be thankful; but we will not interfere with them in their religion. Are they Methodists? They can worship as they please—Presbyterians, Catholics, Baptists, or any other "ists" can worship as they please, that is none of our business, that is a matter between them and their God. But when they interfere with our rights as citizens of the United States, it becomes our business to look after our liberties.

27.As religionists we call upon them, as a duty committed to us, as we aver, by the Almighty. Our mission is to call upon this nation and all nations to repent of their sins, of their lasciviousness, adulteries, fornications, murders, blasphemies and of all dishonest and corrupt practices. But in this we use no force; having laid these matters before them, they have their free will to receive or reject. As religionists they may proclaim us bigamists or polygamists or what they please, that is their business, and they must answer for their own acts; as politicians or statesmen they must at least give us the benefit of the Constitution and laws; these, as a portion of the body politic, we contend for as part of our political rights. We do not claim, nor profess, nor desire to interfere with any man's religion or conscience. We have nothing to do with their religion, nor they with ours. Religious faith or belief is not a political factor. The Constitution has debarred its introduction into the arena of politics; and every officer of the United States has pledged himself under a solemn oath to abide by and sustain that Instrument, and not one of them can interfere with it without a violation of his oath.

28.What have we done in defense of our liberties? I have heard several people say that we are inclined to be aggressive. I think we are not aggressive, but some of the laws are very aggressive. We have a grand jury organized of some fifteen men. How many of them are Latter-day Saints? Two, I think.

So I suppose there is one-tenth of the citizens of this Territory loyal, patriotic and honorable, and the rest are considered to be unpatriotic, disloyal, etc. But we ought at least to be tried before we are condemned; that is the law as I understand it. Now this one-tenth of loyal, good and virtuous people get thirteen men impaneled, and the nine-tenths get but two to represent them. But unfortunately for these loyal and patriotic people carefully prepared statistics show that this ten percent of population supplies eighty percent of the criminals.

29.How is it in other things? There is considerable said about offices and officers. Where is there a man appointed from among the people to hold any office in the gift of the national government? To use the words of a thoughtful non-"Mormon" observer, though the 'Gentiles' constitute only ten percent of the population, yet from this small minority are taken the incumbents of nearly every position of influence and emolument. They have the governor, with absolute veto power, secretary, judges, marshals, prosecuting attorney, land register, recorder, surveyor-general, clerks of the courts, commissioners, principal post-office mail contractors, postal agents, revenue assessors and collectors, superintendent of Indian affairs, Indian agencies, Indian supplies, army contractors, etc."

30.According to the common usage's of men, we have at least a reasonable right to our proper proportion, but it is evident we do not have it. And then our educational interests are interfered with by these very men who state how ignorant we are. For instance, the Legislature of Utah appropriated the means of the people to help build a university. Who was to furnish the means? The people of this territory. Who said they should not do it? The Governor, and through his action the appropriation was vetoed. These are some of the things we have to contend with. On the other hand, laws are enacted inimical to the interests of this people. And then His Excellency goes to work and appoints a set of officers contrary to the law of the land; goes beyond the act of Congress and appoints officers to fill nearly every office in the Territory, vacant or not, as the case may be. I am not going to enter into the details of it, but we have generally found that there were people in those offices; that they had a right there, and that the law provided that they should hold over until their successors were elected and qualified. I believe the law so reads; indeed, I am told that the law not only reads so, but that the Governor's commissions to many of these officers also reads so, and hence his present action is violative of his own commission.

31. These are some of the things we have to contend with. Do we wish to fight the government of the United States? No. What shall we do? Stand up for the rights granted to us by the laws and constitution of the United States as American citizens. We have ex post facto laws, religious inquisitorial laws, we have laws which smack strongly of bills of attainder, and we have test oaths presented, all of which and many others are unconstitutional and are violative of our constitutional rights. I have the opinion of some of the best jurists of the nation to the effect that all these things are a violation of law, and that men have no business to be subjected to such infamies, nor become their own accusers. An eminent jurist speaking of this queried how this kind of thing would apply in Washington, where miscegenation has prevailed to so great an extent. Suppose some of those who practiced this thing were placed under such a law, how would it operate with them? Why several members of Congress have said that if the Edmunds law had been made applicable to adulterers, and men had to become their own accusers, it would unseat three-fourths of the members of Congress. Ex post facto laws, have been passed, which are clearly unconstitutional, and it is for us to test them in the courts, and we mean to do it; for although as religionists we go as messengers of peace to the nations, yet as American citizens we mean to contend for our rights, inch by inch, legally and constitutionally, God being our helper.

32. Another thing God expects us to do, and that is to maintain the principle of human rights. I have felt sorrowful in watching the action of Congress towards us — sorrowful, not only on our own account, but on theirs. We fear no evil arising from those things, for we are anxiously performing our duty before God. But we owe it to ourselves as men, we owe it to our families, our chil-

dren, and to posterity; we owe it to the lovers of freedom in this land, of which there are thousands, yea, millions, who despise acts of oppression and tyranny; we owe it to all liberty-loving men, to stand up for human rights and protect human freedom, and in the name of God we will do it, and let all the congregation say Amen. (The immense congregation responded, Amen.)

33. Joseph, the despised of his father's house became their deliverer. Moses, the foundling and outcast of Egypt, became the deliverer and lawgiver of Israel. Jesus, the despised Nazarene, introduced principles that revolutionized the moral ideas and ethics of the world. And it may not be among the improbabilities, that the prophecies of Joseph Smith may be fulfilled and that the calumniated and despised Mormons may yet become the protectors of the Constitution and the guardians of religious liberty and human freedom in these United States.

34. Now these are some of my feelings upon some of these points. And I will proceed a little further and say that I do not blame many men for entertaining the sentiments which they do towards us. There is a feeling and desire to see fair play and honesty deep down in the hearts of millions of the people of these United States, who ardently desire to see justice equally and honorably administered to all people within the nation. That was manifested very clearly during the passage of the Edmunds Bill, and while many of those venerable Senators and honorable members of the House could not conscientiously with their limited information and the false statements made by our enemies sustain Polygamy, yet, to their honor be it spoken, they endeavored to maintain human rights, free toleration and religious liberty, and the rights of man without distinction of party throughout the realm. We honor, appreciate and respect such men as honorable representatives of the founders of this nation, and of the thousands who today embrace similar opinions. It is the debauched, the corrupt, the violators of principles and law and desecrators of the sacred principles of liberty, it is their pernicious practices which are striking at the foundation of the institutions of this country and which are demoralizing and destroying

the nation, and there are thousands of high-minded and honorable men today who, on account of trickery, hypocrisy, dishonesty and crime stand aloof from the filthy pool of politics. They have seen honor, truth, integrity and virtue trampled under foot, they have seen corruption and crime like a repulsive octopus pushing its Briarean arms into every department of State; they have seen corruption and crime like a deadly simoom permeating every department of the body politic, and debauching and corrupting the nation, and they have shrunk from the disgusting contact; how far they can reconcile this with their ideas of patriotism it is for these aggressors to say. It is not the honorable and upright, the men of virtue and integrity that we would proclaim against; it is the vicious, the untruthful, the calumniators, the corrupt and debauched, the stirrers up of sedition and strife, and the enemies of law, order, virtue, righteousness, justice, human liberty and the rights of man to whom our remarks would apply.

35. Again, Presbyterians, Baptists, Methodists, Catholics, and all classes have come among us, and who has interfered with them? Has anybody interfered with their worship? No. Has any violence of any kind been offered them? No, you cannot find it. We are at their defiance to show any such thing here. What have we done? We have fostered them, as has been referred to; we have treated them courteously and kindly and gentlemanly as honorable people ought to do. What have they done? Combined together to publish some of the most abominable falsehoods that were ever circulated with regard to any community. Now, this becomes rather a serious matter. Talk about love for these people! I would do them good. If they were hungry I would feed them; if they were naked I would clothe them; if they were sick I would administer to them; but if they lied about me and about this people I would tell them they were liars and defamers; I do not care how pious they are, or how much religion they have got, I would tell them the naked truth in relation to these matters.

36. They are the avowed advocates of moral reform, profess to be shocked at our moral obliquity and complain of us as being licentious and corrupt. Even every prominent Christian minister in this city joined in a protest against customs inculcated in the Scriptures by the Almighty, and practiced by Abraham, Jacob, David, and hosts of the most venerated and honorable men that ever lived, practices which they aver are lascivious and corrupt; and these same ministers issued a circular calling upon their fellow-ministers and brother Christians throughout the United States to petition Congress for legislation which should stop, as they claim, the "foul system of polygamy," and hypocritically inserted, to blind the eyes of those not familiar with Utah matters, a request for legislation for the suppression of "adultery, seduction, lewd and lascivious cohabitation and kindred offenses," that they might "be punishable as in the States and other Territories of the Union;" and political demagogues joined with them in the crusade.

37. Predicated upon these solicitations scores of petitions were forwarded to Congress to this effect. They obtained their legislation and in their frantic Christian zeal to stamp out polygamy, a Bible institution, Congress, under this priestly influence so far forgot the inalienable rights of man, constitutional guarantees and forms of jurisprudence, as to disfranchise nine-tenths of this community for the alleged crime of the one-tenth, and that too, without trial; thus making the innocent suffer for the alleged acts of the guilty. And today an infamous, expurgatory test oath is introduced, at variance with all precedents in this nation, which as stated by Judge Black, is altogether "odious, unjust and unconstitutional," which "reverses those rules of evidence which lie at the foundation of civil liberty," and is a flagrant, violent and direct attack upon the inherent rights of man. Thus in their intemperate, religious zeal making a direct onslaught upon the bulwarks of republican institutions, jeopardizing the safety of the state, and thoughtlessly, recklessly and inconsiderately ignoring every just principle; assailing the fundamental doctrines of political and religious freedom; and exerting all their energies in attacking a phantom to tear down the pillars of state and to destroy the Temple of Liberty, though they themselves, as a Samson, perish in the ruins.

38. What is the moral effect? This same test-oath, while it assails a scriptural usage practiced by the most renowned, revered and honorable men of antiquity, who are denominated men of righteousness and the friends of God, protects and sustains the degraded, corrupt and licentious who are supposed to be good Christians and not polygamists.

39. A very honorable, upright and virtuous gentleman, whom no one will accuse of immorality or vice—the respected ex-mayor of this city, who has filled that office with dignity and honor for the last six years, has a son who was appointed registrar for the Fifth Precinct in this city; this son had the painful and humiliating duty to perform of refusing to register his father's name, because many years ago he had had more than one wife, but who, through death, was for some time without a wife at all, and has lately married one wife; and yet this young man had to perform the disgusting task, according to the provisions of said test-oath, of registering a notorious keeper of a bagnio, and many of her harlot associates. Another circumstance occurred of a gentleman who came to be registered, but thought it would be impracticable for him to take the test-oath. More honorable than many of his pious associates, he suggested that he did not know that he could take the prescribed oath, for he not only had a wife, but kept a mistress, but on examination he found the oath exempted all those who might engage in illicit intercourse, provided the association was not, as expressed in the oath, "in the marriage relation." On discovering this, he observed, "I can take that oath, for I am only married to one;" and he was accepted. Another young man in this city, whilst having the test oath read to him, said he could not take it, as he could not swear that he had not cohabited with more than one woman; but when the reading was continued and the words "in the marriage relation" sounded in his ears, he said, "I can go that," and was duly sworn.

40. Thus these moral and religious reformers and teachers, these professors of high moral ideas, these inveighers against a scriptural practice professedly because it is immoral, have introduced safeguards to protect the libertine, the voluptuary and the harlot, whilst they have made criminals of those who have been observing a law instituted by the Almighty. Perhaps it would be considered too severe to call these "reverend gentlemen" and those "venerable seigneurs" who occupy honorable positions in Congress by the harsh name of hypocrites, yet it is very humiliating to the sensitive and virtuous to contemplate the result of their ill-timed and intemperate acts, for they have thus made themselves, while professing purity, the advocates and abettors of vice, licentiousness, immorality and crime.

41. I wish here to apologize a little for the people of the United States, for I think sometimes we carry the thing too far in relation to them. Here are men supposed— would be in any other community—to be honorable men, reverend men that are teachers of religion, combining against us. And because they are considered honorable men, people say, why there is the Reverend Mr. So and So and So and So, they have requested us to send petitions to Congress, to do this and that because of the wickedness and abominations of this people, and their misrepresentations and falsehoods have been circulated in the religious magazines and in the political papers, until the people abroad hardly know what to think. Many of them think we are a very infamous people; they think we are a great deal more corrupt than they are, and that we need not be. And they go to work to legislate to correct our morals. Now, with thousands of papers circulating these falsehoods, and these falsehoods coming from supposed religious and honorable men, is it any wonder that the people should be deceived with regard to us. I read today an account of an attempt to drive our Elders from some of their fields of labor? What for? Because they are "Mormons." They are so wicked and so corrupt, and all because the papers and reverend ministers said so and so; and thus thousands of honorable men are deceived; but many of them, when they come to a knowledge of the truth, will rejoice in it. I want, then, to stand in defense of many of the people of the United States who are thus deceived.

42. It is said in the scriptures that the serpent cast out of his mouth water as a flood. We have certainly had floods of falsehoods, originating, many of them, with these pious people. Do we want

much association with these people? I think not. If they circulate falsehoods about us, can we respect them very much? I think not. We cannot hold communion with people who are corrupt, low and degraded. We were down in the sloughs a little while ago ourselves; we have come out from among them and know what they are. We know the infamies which exist there, the licentiousness, the corruption, the social evil, adulteries, fornication, sodomy, child murder, and every kind of infamy. And they come here and want to teach our children these things. We have got to be careful how we guard our homes, our firesides, our wives, our sons and our daughters, from their association. We don't want these practices insidiously introduced among us. We want to preserve our purity, our virtue, our honor, and our integrity.

43.The time is hastening on, and I shall have to stop. I wish to make some further remarks, and would have liked to have talked some time longer. But what shall we do? I will tell you what I will try to do. I will try and humble myself before the Lord and seek for his blessing, and say as one of old said: "Search me, Oh God, and know my heart; try me and know my thoughts; and see if there be any wicked way in me, and lead me in the way everlasting." I have talked with my counselors in the same way, and they are of the same mind. We have talked with the Twelve about these things, and they are of the same mind. Now, we call upon all you Seventies, High Priests and Elders, you Bishops, Priests, Teachers and Deacons individually and your quorum capacity, upon the heads of families, upon the various organizations in the Church, upon all the Saints who profess to revere His name, to humble yourselves before God, to lay aside your covetousness and your evils of every kind. And when you have done so, you that meet together for prayers in your holy places, call upon God for guidance, direction and deliverance, and he will hear your prayers and deliver you, and your enemies shall have no power over you, for God is on the side of Israel, and he will preserve his people. No power can stay

the progress of this work, for it is onward, onward, onward, and will be, until the kingdoms of this world become the kingdoms of our God and His Christ, and until every creature in heaven and in the earth and under the earth shall be heard to exclaim, Blessings and glory and honor and power and might and majesty and dominion be ascribed to Him that sitteth upon the throne and unto the Lamb for ever.

44.We will leave the wicked in the hands of God: He will deal with them in his own way. We are told that the wicked shall slay the wicked; and one thing that I am sorry over in this nation is this: that they are striking at the tree of liberty and trying to fetter humanity and bring men into bondage, they are laying the ax at the root of this government, and unless they speedily turn round and repent and follow the principles they have sworn to sustain—the principles contained in the Constitution of the United States—they will be overthrown, they will be split up and divided, be disintegrated and become weak as water; for the Lord will handle them in his own way. I say these things in sorrow; but as sure as God lives unless there is a change of policy these things will most assuredly take place.

45.Let us be pure, let us be virtuous, let us be honorable, let us maintain our integrity, let us do good to all men, and tell the truth always, and treat everybody right, no matter their profession or creed, and love our religion and keep the commandments of God, and it shall be well with Zion in time and throughout eternity.

46.God bless you. God bless all the Latter-day Saints. God bless all rulers and all men everywhere in responsible situations who seek to do right and to preserve law and justice and equity, and to maintain the rights of all men, and let his wrath and indignation rest upon the perverters of justice and those who seek to bind down the human conscience and enslave their fellowmen. God bless you and lead you in the paths of life, in the name of Jesus. Amen.

ADDRESS 25

Discourse delivered by President John Taylor at the 53rd Annual General Conference of The Church of Jesus Christ of Latter-day Saints convened April 8, 1883, in the Tabernacle, Salt Lake City.

1. We have had a very interesting Conference, and a great many very excellent principles have been presented to the people. As I told the Priesthood last evening we are occupying a very peculiar position in the earth, a position that has not been of our own seeking. God has set His hand to accomplish His purposes upon the earth, and for this purpose He has revealed Himself from the heavens, as we have heard since this Conference commenced. In pursuance of this He has manifested Himself and His Son Jesus Christ, and has restored the Holy Priesthood by and through the medium of a Priesthood, or various parts of a Priesthood that existed in former ages—those holding that everlasting Priesthood, which administers in time and in eternity, have been commissioned from the heavens to come to the earth to bring to pass the very things of which they themselves had prophesied.

2. Although we are, comparatively speaking, a small people, few in number, yet as it was in the days of Jesus so it is today. The Gospel is like a little leaven put into a certain portion of meal, and it is working and operating, and the ultimate result will be that the whole lump will be leavened. Not that everybody that is in the world will obey the Gospel; but the Lord will have His own way in manipulating His affairs, and great tribulation will overtake the inhabitants of the earth. As you have heard, many of the wicked will slay the wicked; but after these things have taken place the good, the honorable, the virtuous, the pure, those that are desirous to serve God will all have their position, and that thing will be fulfilled which was spoken of by Jesus—"Blessed are the meek for they shall inherit the earth." The time will yet come when the Saints of the Most High will take the kingdom and hold dominion under the whole heavens. These are principles that are familiar to us all.

3. In the meantime, however, many important events have to take place, and a great labor has to be performed, and will be performed by the agencies which have been introduced by the Lord, and which will be hereafter introduced by Him for the accomplishment of His purposes, and the bringing to pass of His righteous will. For this purpose the Holy Priesthood has been restored; for this purpose the message of life and salvation has been proclaimed to the nations of the earth; for this purpose after the reception of the Gospel, the people have been gathered together in order that the Lord might have a people who would be under the influence of His Holy Spirit.

4. We have all been baptized by one baptism, and have all partaken of the same Spirit, and wherever these ordinances have been administered according to the order of God, and have been received by the faithful among the nations of the earth, these effects have always followed. I have been among the nations myself, and I have baptized people and confirmed them at least in three different languages, and the same spirit rested upon all of those different people, and so it is throughout all nations.

5. The Lord has said he would gather together His elect from the four quarters of the earth. And how does He do it? By operating upon the minds of those who obey the Gospel. Jesus said in His day and it is true today—"My sheep hear my voice and know it, and follow me and a stranger they will not follow because they know not the voice of a stranger." It is under the influence of this Spirit that we have been gathered together. We used to sing:

Whither shall we follow, follow, follow;
Whither shall we follow, follow thee?
All the way to Zion, all the way to Zion,
All the way to Zion,
We will follow thee.

What made you gather here? The impulse of the Spirit of the living God, and you could not keep away. We have representatives here from very many nations today. Here are

Elders who have preached the Gospel in many nations. A few years ago we had some twenty-five nationalities represented at one of our public demonstrations. And thus our work is to go on and spread and increase.

6. The Apostles, the Seventies, the Elders, and men who have received the light of truth, will spread forth that light to others of the family of God throughout the world. This is a labor resting upon the Elders of Israel, and until it is accomplished we shall not have fulfilled our mission here upon the earth. Then, again, we have other works to perform associated with the Church, with the Kingdom and with the Zion of God.

7. I think sometimes that we as a people are a good deal sectarian in our feelings, and it is necessary for us occasionally to look at the pit from whence we were dug, and the rock from whence we were hewn. We are all too ready to cry out, as the sectarians do in their different orders, "The temple of the Lord, the temple of the Lord, the temple of the Lord are we." And we are apt to forget sometimes the mission that God has placed upon us, which is a mission of mercy, a mission of light, a mission of intelligence, a mission that is calculated to elevate the world of mankind even all those who will receive and obey it. It is not intended for us alone; it is intended for all men. Who are the world, and who are we?

8. We say we are the children of God our Heavenly Father. That is true; we are the children of God our Heavenly Father. And is God our Father? The Scriptures say so. But what of the rest of the world—say of this nation, and all other nations—what of them? Whose children are they? They are also the children of our Heavenly Father, and He is interested in their welfare as He is in ours; and as a kind and beneficent father towards His children, He has been seeking from generation to generation to promote the welfare, the happiness, and the exaltation of the human family. And let me say here, that He is the fountain of life, the fountain of light, and the fountain of intelligence, as we used to say in the Church of England when I was a little boy, and I suppose they say so now; it is He that hath made us, and not we ourselves; we are His people and the sheep of His pasture," He provides for us. We some-

times talk about the hand of God being over us. Of course it is, and will be over us forever, if we will only serve Him, for He is always true. But His hand is over the nations of the earth also. He is interested in the welfare of this nation and all other nations and all other peoples as well as in our welfare.

9. What was the greatest blessing conferred upon Abraham? One was that his seed should be numerous as the stars of heaven, and as the sand upon the sea shore. I do not know that he would have got along very well in this land now a days; they would have been after him for polygamy. People do not believe so much in these things now as they did formerly. Nevertheless, the Lord told him to take another wife; but, then, perhaps the Lord made a mistake, He had not studied modern Christianity. He was, to use the language of the advanced Christian, behind the times. But whatever may be thought or said about it, according to the record that has come down to us, He used to talk to people in that day.

10. But let me refer you to another blessing connected with Abraham, namely, that in him and his seed should all the nations of the earth be blessed. Or, in other words, that God would honor him by making of him and his seed agents through whom He would communicate truth, intelligence and salvation to the world. It is said "the glory of God is intelligence," and He is desirous to impart this intelligence to the human family, that through it they may be exalted to the Godhead. Abraham's posterity were to stand as messengers of God, as legates of the skies, commissioned of the great Jehovah to proclaim His word to fallen man, even to His children; for God has made, we are told, of one blood all the families of the earth, and has given unto them a portion of His Spirit, if haply they would feel after Him, although He is not far from any one of us.

11. For in Him we live, and move, and have our being. And under the influence of His Spirit man has accomplished very much good; and today there are hosts of honorable, upright men who in their hearts fear God, but they have not yet found the right way. But in the providences of His mercy He has gathered a people from the nations that they may be taught and instructed in regard to the laws

of life and salvation. And this has been brought about in fulfillment of ancient prophecy. Jeremiah, for instance, in referring to it said, that he would take them one of a city and two of a family, and bring them to Zion. And what was He to do with them when He should get them there? He would give them pastors after His own heart who should feed them with knowledge and understanding. And the same great event is referred to by other Prophets.

12. I was very much pleased with the remarks made by Brother Erastus Snow, with regard to our own nation, in which he said that it had been by and through the power of Almighty God, and in accordance with the words of the Lord as contained in the Book of Mormon, that the people were, in the first place, impelled to come here, and after coming here, to contend for human freedom upon this land; and it was by and through the power of God, that the fathers of this country framed the Declaration of Independence, and also that great palladium of human rights, the Constitution of the United States. There is nothing of the bigoted, narrow, contracted feeling about that instrument; it is broad and comprehensive. And they had a bell in Philadelphia, which I, and perhaps many of you have seen, upon which was written, "Proclaim liberty throughout the land, and to all the inhabitants thereof;" but I was sorry to see that the bell was cracked. I suppose it got cracked after the grand effort that was made to proclaim liberty throughout the land; and I have thought since that it has not been soldered up yet.

13. But with all the weaknesses and imperfections associated with men, the government of this nation has been a great bulwark for human freedom, and I felt proud at the time when Mr. Edmunds, with his colleagues, introduced his bill, known as the Edmunds Bill, that there was such a number of gentlemen who had the manhood and the moral courage to oppose it in the bold and manly way in which they did, showing plainly that they cherished in their bosoms the principles contained in the Constitution. I respect such men, and they command the respect and esteem of all honorable, right-thinking people. They could afford to render themselves unpopular in the eyes of religious bigots and fanatical politicians, but they could not afford to be amongst those that are ready to tear down the bulwarks of human freedom, and trail in the dust the flag of our country. They did not believe in our religion. Of course, that is a matter of their own, it is none of our business, neither is our religion any of their business, which they understand and appreciate.

14. There are two things that I have felt very decided upon ever since I could comprehend anything; one was that I would worship God as I pleased without anybody's dictation; and that I would dictate to no man his faith, neither should any man dictate to me my faith; and the other was that I would vote as I pleased. And I entertain the same sentiments today. When the Commissioners, operating under the Edmunds' Law, made their extraordinary rulings and authorized the administering of the test oath, declaring who should vote and who should not, I could not help remarking that people were acting very foolishly, that they did not know what they were doing; but whether they knew it or not their attempts to wrest from this people their rights and liberties, were no more or less than indirect attempts to tear down the bulwarks of American liberty. But in this inexcusable attack upon human rights and the principles of liberty we can take no part.

15. What then will we do? They have no right, it is true, to interfere with us in the way they have done; they have no right, it is true, to prohibit us from voting without a hearing and without a trial; they have no right, it is true, to present to us a test oath, it being illegal and contrary to our rights as American citizens. But we will submit gracefully for the time being, withdraw from the polls, rather than act in the capacity of obstructionists; and when the time comes we will test these proceedings according to the laws of the land, and the principles of liberty guaranteed by the Constitution of the United States, which we recognize and respect. Have we yielded up our franchises? No, we have not. Will we ever do it? No, never; no, never. Have we in the least backed down from the principles by which we have been guided from the beginning? No; we still mean to live by them and to maintain them, and to contend for our rights, not by dynamite or nitroglycerin, but

to do so legally and constitutionally, not only in defense of our own rights, but the rights and liberties of our children and those of every free man throughout the land. This is the course we propose taking.

16. As I before stated we have been called from the nations of the earth by Him who is our Father, we being His children. And He has told us to ask, and we shall receive. He has told us to seek and we shall find; to knock and it shall be opened to us. Very well. What shall we do? We will use the best means we can to defend our rights; and after we have done this we will then go to our Heavenly Father and ask Him to help us. Will He do it? Yes. Has He done it? Yes, and we acknowledge His hand in regard to these things. He has heard our prayers without noise, without tumult. He has told us thus far that if we will continue to obey Him and to observe His laws, He will deliver us and direct us even to the end. And we need have no fears whatever about the result. He has promised us that inasmuch as we do His will and keep His commandments, He will fight our battles. And I feel confident and perfectly easy, and I felt just as easy during the furor and commotion that raged through the land a few months ago as I do today; knowing, as I do, that if we will perform our part, the Lord will not fail to do His. Because others act foolishly we cannot afford to imitate them. We profess to be the Zion of God, the pure in heart. We profess to be men and women of integrity, of truth and virtue, and to have faith in God. This must not only be our profession, but our practice; we must carry out and fulfill the word and will and law of God.

17. Jesus taught His disciples how to pray. Said He: "Our Father who art in heaven." That is, your Father and my Father, the God and Father of the spirits of all flesh. "Our Father who art in heaven, hallowed be thy name," O, God, we reverence thee; we observe thy law, and we wish to keep thy commandments, and purge ourselves from all evil, that we may be acceptable to thee. "Hallowed be thy name; thy kingdom come." We reverence thee, O, God, and attribute to thee all that we have in this world, and all that we expect to have in the eternities to come. "Hallowed be thy name. Thy kingdom come." Thy what? Thy king-

dom come. That is the rule of God, the government of God, the dominion of God, the time when men will not be ashamed to acknowledge God as their Father, their friend and benefactor. "Thy kingdom come." When all will submit to thy rule, to thy law, to thy jurisdiction, to thy dominion; that thy will may be done on earth as it is done in heaven.

18. How was it done in heaven? God spake, chaos heard, and this world rolled into existence; and so did other worlds under the same divine impulse and power. And all those systems that revolve around us were made and are upheld by the mighty power of God, who governs in the heavens above, and upon the earth beneath, and among the worlds. Whether men acknowledge that or not, the time will come on this earth when every knee shall bow to Him, and every tongue shall confess that Jesus is the Christ, to the glory of God the Father. That time will come. It is not here now; but as I have said He has introduced this Gospel as the entering wedge, as the little leaven by which he can operate, that He may have a people under the influence of the Holy Ghost, a people that can hold communion with him, like so many thousand strings penetrating the eternal worlds and drawing down blessings from the Almighty, drawing fire, and life, and intelligence from Him; for we ourselves are sparks struck from the blaze of His eternal fire, emanating from God our Father, and we wish to operate with Him and for Him and under His guidance, for the accomplishment of His purposes here upon the earth. This is what we are here for.

19. Now I come to another point. We pray "Thy will be done on earth as it is done in heaven." How is it done there? As I said, God spake, chaos heard, and the world rolled into existence, and it is supported by the mighty power of God, and who can stay His hand. Do you think that if all the Legislatures, all the Congresses, all the Parliaments, and all the Reichstags, all the Chambers of Deputies and Senates of the earth were to get together and pass a decree that the sun should rise five or ten minutes or half an hour later or earlier than it does—do you think it would have any effect upon it? I do not think it would—I think it would still go on in its usual course, and they

would feel that they were dependent upon God. Do the world know that in Him we live and move and have our being? Does this congregation know that there is not one of them could leave this house unless God permitted it and sustained them in so doing? Do the nations of the earth comprehend that they are in His hands, and that he puts down one nation and raises up another according to the counsels of His will, and none can say, "Why doest thou thus."

20. What have we to do? To begin with, we should deal justly and honorably with all men, and should seek to protect all men in their rights so far as we have the power to do so, and then to maintain our own on the same principle. And what then? Fear God and observe His laws, and we ought every one of us to place ourselves in communication with the Lord, and He has tried to make us understand this, but it seems very difficult for us to do so. It was in former times, and it is now. He says, "ask and ye shall receive." Is it not a very simple thing? "Seek and ye shall find." Is it not very easy. "Knock and it shall be opened unto you." But says He, you do not understand it aright.

21. Now, let me mention a thing to you. If a child ask of you bread, would you give it a stone—you fathers and you mothers? I think not. If the child asked a fish would you give it a scorpion." Why, no. The mother would say, "Sammy, or Mary," as the case might be, "you want some bread—well I will give you some with butter and molasses." The mother would try to meet the wishes of the children, and sometimes give them a little candy to boot. Now, then, says the Lord, "If ye then, being evil, know how to give good gifts unto your children, how much more shall your Father which is in heaven give His Holy Spirit to them that ask Him."

22. It is very plain when you get at it, and it is very simple, and people wonder sometimes, they think it an astonishing thing that God should hear people's prayers. Why, bless your souls, that is the strongest fort we have, and when we get into any difficulty in the nation or anywhere else, we humble ourselves before the Lord—and we all need to do this, for we all have our weaknesses and imperfections; and it is necessary that He should be very merciful to us. And He is, and knows how to bear with us. We need also to know how to bear with one another, and to place ourselves in communion with God, and in doing this to purge ourselves from everything that is wrong and evil.

23. And I tell you—you Elders of Israel, you brethren and you sisters, that if you will begin to do the will of God on the earth as it is done in heaven, the power and blessing of God will rest upon you and upon this people, and no power will be able to injure you from this time forth. God expects us to do His will, to carry out his purposes, and if His will is ever done on the earth as it is done in heaven, where in creation will it start, if it does not start here? Let every man put himself right, and every woman and every family do the same, and all the Priesthood in all its various departments and ramifications, and let every one walk up to the line and perform his duty, and in the name of Israel's God, Zion shall arise and shine, and the glory of God shall rest upon her. Our progress is onward and upward, until the kingdoms of this world become the kingdoms of our God and His Christ, and loud anthems be sounded from among the nations—glory and honor and power and might and majesty and dominion be ascribed unto Him that sitteth upon the throne and unto the Lamb forever and forever. Amen.

ADDRESS 26

Discourse delivered by President John Taylor in the Priesthood Session of the 53rd Semiannual General Conference of The Church of Jesus Christ of Latter-day Saints convened October 6, 1883, in the Assembly Hall, Salt Lake City.

1. It is quite a privilege for us to meet together in such assemblies as this—to associate with the Priesthood of the Son of God, which Priesthood is also after the order of Melchizedek, and after the power of an endless life. It is a great privilege for us to meet together, to talk over the things pertaining to the Kingdom of God, and to reason and reflect upon those things that God has revealed for our salvation in time and throughout the eternities that are to come. It is proper that we should comprehend the various positions of men in relation to this Holy Priesthood, and further that we should understand the various orders, callings, ordinances and organizations associated with the Church and Kingdom of God upon the earth; that we each of us may be prepared to magnify our calling, to honor our God, and to pursue that course always which shall be acceptable in the sight of our Heavenly Father.

2. We are here as Jesus was here, not to do our own will, but the will of our Father who sent us. He has placed us here; we have a work to do in our day and generation; and there is nothing of importance connected with any of us only as we are associated with God and His work, whether it be the President of the Church, the Twelve Apostles, the Presidents of Stakes, the Bishops, or anybody else, and we can only thus be of any service by placing ourselves in a position to act as God dictates us; as He regulates and manipulates the affairs of His Church in the interests of humanity, in behalf of the living and of the dead, in behalf of the world in which we live, and in behalf of those who have lived before us, and who will live after us. We can none of us do anything only as we are assisted, guided and directed by the Lord. No man ever lived that could. Adam could not. Noah could not. Even Jesus could not. Nor could the Apostles. They were all of them dependent upon the God of Israel to sustain them in all of their acts.

3. And in regard to Adam himself, as we are, so was he very ignorant of many principles until they were revealed to him. And if they were revealed to him they did not originate with him; and so it was with others. We find that Adam was directed of the Lord to do a certain thing—that is, to offer up sacrifices—and when the angel of the Lord came to him and said: "Adam why do you offer up sacrifices?" Adam replied, "I do not know; but the Lord commanded me to do it, and therefore I do it." He did not know what those sacrifices were for until the Lord revealed unto him the doctrine of the atonement and the necessity of the fall of man, and pointed out to him the way and manner to obtain an exaltation. Then he and Eve his wife rejoiced exceedingly at the mercy and kindness of the Almighty, and realized that even in their fall they were placed in a position to obtain a higher glory, and a greater exaltation than they could have done without it. Now, who revealed this to them? The Lord, through the ministering of an holy angel; and in relation to the dealings of God with all of the human family it has been precisely the same.

4. We are told, for instance, that when Adam had lived to a great age—that three years before his death he called together his family—that is, some of the leading branches thereof who held the Holy Priesthood, mentioning the names of many of the more prominent that had received certain peculiar blessings from the hand of God—and there was manifested to him all things that should transpire to his posterity throughout all the future generations of time, and he prophesied of these things; and also upon those who were with him rested the spirit of prophecy, and he blessed them, and they turned around and blessed him and called him Michael the Archangel, the Prince of Peace, etc.

5. By what spirit then did Adam prophesy, and under what influence was he operating at that time? We are told in Scripture that the

testimony of Jesus is the spirit of prophecy, and he in common with his sons who were then associated with him were in possession of that spirit which enlightened their minds, unfolded unto them the principles of truth, and revealed unto them the things that would transpire throughout every subsequent period of time. Who manifested these things? The Lord. Who organized the world? The Lord. Who placed man upon it? The Lord. Who placed upon it the fowls of the air, the beasts of the field, and the fish of the sea? The Lord. Who sustains all things by his power? The Lord. Who controls the affairs of the world? The Lord. To whom are we indebted for life, for health, and for every blessing that we enjoy? To the Lord. He is the God of the earth, and the giver of every good and perfect gift which we enjoy, and He desires to gather together a people that will observe His laws, that will keep His commandments, that will render obedience to His will, that will submit to His authority, and for this purpose, in different ages of the world, He has introduced the Gospel and has placed man in possession thereof.

6. Now, what about the positions of men? Why, it is a good deal as spoken of in the Scriptures and in the revelations which have been given to us pertaining to these matters— that many have been called and chosen, and that many were elected and selected to fulfill certain offices. It was so revealed to Abraham. He was told that there were a great many spirits, many of whom were noble, who were destined to hold particular positions among the children of men, and it was said to him, "And thou Abraham wast one of these."

7. Now, there are events to transpire in this day as there have been in other days; and we, the Elders of Israel of the Church of the living God, have to build up the Church of God, the Zion of God, and the Kingdom of God, and the Church has to be purified according to the law, order, rule and dominion which God has appointed. It is not for us—as the brethren have expressed it—to receive certain portions of light and intelligence, and with regard to other portions follow the desires of our own hearts, thus laying aside God, His rule, His dominion and His authority. "Having begun in the spirit,"

as Paul said, "are ye now made perfect by the flesh?" No, that is the wrong way about; but on the contrary we ought to add to our faith virtue, to virtue brotherly kindness, to brotherly kindness charity, to charity godliness, that we may be full of the light and life, and of the spirit and power of God, and approach more closely to the law of God, and be governed thereby.

8. Why are we gathered here to the land of Zion? This is called the land of Zion. We are called the people of Zion. What does Zion mean? The pure in heart. Why are we gathered here? One of the Prophets in talking about it, says: "I will take you one of a city, and two of a family, and I will bring you to Zion." What then? "I will give them Pastors according to mine own heart, which shall feed you with knowledge and understanding." That is what we are here for. That we may be fed with knowledge and understanding, that we may learn the law of the Gospel, the law of the Zion of God, the laws of the Kingdom of God, and that we may be instructed in all things tending to promote the welfare, exaltation and happiness of ourselves, our wives, our children, the people with whom we are associated, and the world in which we live and act; and that we may operate for the benefit of those who have lived, and stand as "saviors upon Mount Zion."

9. In all this, as has been said, there is an order. We are all dependent the one upon the other. The head can not say to the foot I have no need of thee, nor the foot to the head I have no need of thee, nor the hand, the arm, the leg to the body, I have no need of thee. We are formed into a compact body according to the law of God in the organization of His Church, and it is for us to magnify the callings unto which we are called, and unless we all of us are placed under the guidance and direction of the Almighty, we cannot do so—that is, those who do not yield themselves subject to the law of God, cannot do that thing. But those who yield themselves subject to the law of God, can do it and do it quite easily, for Jesus says: "Take my yoke upon you, and learn of me; for I am meek and lowly in heart; and ye shall find rest unto your souls. For my yoke is easy, and my burden is light."

10. Now, if we yield obedience to God and to the spirits that dwell within us, then will

our light become like that of the just that shineth brighter and brighter unto the perfect day; but if we do not yield an obedience to the law and word and order of the Church and Kingdom of God upon the earth, the light that is within us will become darkness, and then, as it is said, how great is that darkness! We see sometimes men of that character. They are occasionally referred to as cranks, or, as the Germans use that term, sick. They lose the light, spirit and power of God, and they do not comprehend the order of the Church and Kingdom of God, nor do they place themselves in the way to obtain a knowledge of these things. The first thing they begin to do is to try to pervert the order of God, and to find fault with their brethren in the Holy Priesthood—with their Bishops, with their Bishop's Counselors, with the High Council, perhaps with the Presidents of Stakes, as the case may be, or with the Apostles, or with the First Presidency; no matter which, or how, or when, or where. Now, if these men were walking in the light as God is in the light they would have fellowship one, with another, and the blood of Christ would cleanse them from all sin; but when they begin to murmur and complain, to find fault and to give way to improper influences, they give place to the devil, and he takes possession just as fast and as far as he can, and forces upon them feelings, ideas and principles that are at variance with the law and order, and word and will of God.

11. What, then, are we here for? What did Jesus come to do? He tells us that He "came not to do His own will, but the will of His Father who sent Him." How are we to obtain a knowledge of that will? I will tell you what Joseph Smith told me. I have frequently mentioned it. Between forty and fifty years ago he said to me this: "Elder Taylor, you have received the Holy Ghost. Follow its teachings. Sometimes it will seem to you as though it was hardly the right way. No matter, follow its teachings, and it will always lead you right, and if you do so it will, by and by, become to you a principle of revelation, so that you will know all things that are necessary for you to become acquainted with." Now, I know that is true. I know that he spoke the truth. And I would say that it is the privilege of every Elder in Israel who has

received the gift of the Holy Ghost, to follow its teachings. What was said by one of the old Apostles? "As many as are led by the Spirit of God are the sons of God." Follow its teachings, therefore, and do not give way to your own feelings, nor to covetousness, to pride, nor to vain glory; for we none of us have anything to boast of. We have none of us received anything but what God has given us. If we possess light, or intelligence, or a knowledge of the things of God—which we do—from whence did it emanate? From God our Heavenly Father, through the medium that He has appointed. I do not wish to dictate to Him the way these things shall be done. I never did.

12. While Joseph Smith was on the earth I looked to him as a Prophet of God, and I do not believe I ever disobeyed Him in one solitary thing that he ever required at my hands, and I have been put in some pretty tight places. But that was my feeling, that was the idea I entertained towards the Priesthood of the Son of God.

13. I have also lived in wards. I do not know that I have ever disobeyed the requests of a Bishop. Why? Because he presided over me in a ward capacity, and if he had a right to respect me as an Apostle, I had a right to respect him as a Bishop, and I always felt a desire to comply with all the requirements that were made of me by any of the proper authorities.

14. I feel and always have felt the same towards Teachers. If a Teacher came to my house—or Teachers, they generally come two at a time—if I happened to be there I have told them that I felt happy to meet with them, and I called together the members of my family that were within my reach, and told them that the Teachers had come to instruct us. Permit me here to ask, have not I a right—say as the President of the Church, or as an Apostle, which I was for many years—have not I a right, or my family a right to possess the same privileges that others possess, and to have the Teachers come to inquire after my welfare and that of my family, and to see that there is no wrong existing—have not I that right? I think I have. If they are the servants of God, have not I a right to listen to them? Yes, I have, and I feel it my duty to receive them kindly,

treat them properly and listen to their teaching. On the other hand, when the Teachers got through, I might give them a little instruction, say as an Apostle, or as a brother—put it any way you like; that while I and my family were receiving benefits from them, it was my duty, on the other hand, to teach and instruct them in some things that I thought might benefit them.

15. Now, these are correct principles in the Church and Kingdom of God. The Teacher occupies his place; the Priest and Deacon occupy their places; the Elder occupies his place; the High Councils their places; the Presidents of Stakes their places, and every one in his position ought to be honored—the Twelve in their place, the First Presidency in their place—each one yielding proper respect and courtesy and kindness to the other. And when we talk about great big personages, there is no such thing. We are none of us anything only as God confers blessings upon us, and if He has conferred anything upon us, we will give Him the glory. Having been called to these positions, God expects that we will honor them; that we will esteem it an honor to be the messengers of salvation, the legates of the skies, to the nations of the earth.

16. We have a great work to perform both at home and abroad. We are preaching the Gospel to the inhabitants of the earth. Israel is being gathered home to Zion. And in Zion we are rearing temples to the name of the Most High God. And I will tell you how I feel—that as these temples are advancing, while we are preparing holy places in which to administer the ordinances of God pertaining to the living and the dead—I feel that we ought to begin to prepare ourselves to enter into these holy places, and to feel that we are the sons of God without rebuke in the midst of a crooked and perverse generation. We ought to wake up and put our houses in order, and our hearts in order; we ought to conform to the word, the will, and the law of God; we ought to let God rule in Zion, to let His law be written upon our hearts, and to feel the responsibility of the great work we are called upon to perform. We should see that our bodies and our spirits are pure, and that they are free from contamination of every kind. We are here to build up the Zion

of God, and to this end we must subject our bodies and our spirits to the law, to the word, and to the will of God. Being here in Zion we want to see that thing that Jesus told His disciples to pray for take place. "Thy Kingdom come, thy will be done on earth as it is in heaven." How was it done in heaven? God spake and the worlds were formed according to His word. God said let us do this, and that and the other, and it was so. Was there anybody in heaven to object and say, "don't you think you had better put it off a little. Would not this be a better way?" Yes, the devil said so, and he says so yet, and he is listened to sometimes by sinners and sometimes by Saints; for we become the servants of those whom we list to obey.

17. There are besides these other considerations in connection with these matters.

18. The brethren who have preceded me this evening have referred to the celestial, terrestrial and telestial kingdoms, and the laws pertaining thereunto. We are told that if we cannot abide the law of the celestial kingdom we cannot inherit a celestial glory. Is not that doctrine? Yes. "But," says one, "Are not we all going into the celestial kingdom?" I think not, unless we turn round and mend our ways very materially. It is only those who can abide a celestial glory and obey a celestial law that will be prepared to enter a celestial kingdom. "Well," says another, "are the others going to be burned up, etc.?" No. Do you expect everybody to walk according to this higher law? No, I do not. And do I expect those that do not, are going into the celestial kingdom? No, I do not. Well, where will they go? If they are tolerably good men and do not do anything very bad, they will get into a terrestrial kingdom, and if there are some that cannot abide a terrestrial law, they may get into a telestial kingdom, or otherwise, as the case may be, etc., etc. Did you ever read in your Bibles that "Strait is the gate, and narrow is the way, which leadeth unto life, and few there be that find it." Did you ever read of the parable of Jesus, where He speaks of the sower going forth to sow, and some seed fell by the wayside, some among thorns, and some on stoney ground, etc.? "But," says one, "we thought we had got it all." Yes: but the thorns have grown up in many places and choked the good seed.

Sometimes you keep down your weeds in the field, but do they come up again? Yes; fresh crops keep coming all the time; and I think, too, that the wheat and the tares were to grow together for a certain length of time.

19.Well, what shall we do? Shall we go to work and get angry against people that do not do exactly right? No. They can only do right as God helps them to do it. They can only do right as they seek to God for His help to enable them to do so; they can only do right as they are sustained by the power of God; and if we allow covetousness, pride, envy, jealousy, hatred, malice, lasciviousness, drunkenness, Sabbath-breaking, or any other influence to corrupt and lead us astray from the light of truth and the sweet consoling influences of the Spirit of God, we shall get into darkness, and then, as I said before, if the light that is within us becomes darkness, how great is that darkness!

20.It is for us to do right—to observe the law and to keep the commandments of God. It is right also for the Presidents of Stakes and for the Bishops to see that none of these things that I have referred to be permitted among the people over whom they preside. What! Shall we not let the drunkard wallow in his drunkenness? No; deal with him according to the law of God. Shall we not let the lascivious man wallow in his corruption? No. According to certain principles that are laid down in the book of Doctrine and Covenants in regard to those things, those who have entered into the new and everlasting covenant, and have taken upon themselves certain obligations, if they commit adultery it is positively said they shall be destroyed. Now, can you change that, or can I change it? No, I cannot, and you cannot; and you have no right to permit men to break the Sabbath, nor to do many of those acts that many of the Saints are doing. What are Apostles, Prophets, Pastors, Teachers, Evangelists, etc., placed in the Church for? What were they for in former days? For the perfecting of the Saints, for the work of the ministry, for the edifying of the body of Jesus Christ. What are the High Councils and Bishops' Counsels for but to adjudge all these things? What are the Teachers and the Priests for? To assist the Bishops in their endeavors to promote purity and virtue,

holiness and righteousness among the people. That is their office, and if they do not fulfill that office they are not magnifying their calling. They have no right to condone the sins of men. The law of God is perfect converting the soul, and we must be governed by that law and carry it out, or be made amenable unto the Lord our God for the course we pursue, or for neglecting to perform our duties. That is the way I look at these things, and if that is not the case, why are these laws given to us. Are they the laws of God? We so understand them. Then let us perform our duties and seek to magnify our callings that we may stand approved and acknowledged of the Lord.

21.When I speak of these things, I do not believe in any kind of tyranny. I believe in long-suffering, in mercy, in kindness, in gentleness, and in the love and fear of God. I do not believe that the Priesthood was given to man to exercise dominion and authority over the souls of other men. Everything ought to be done with kindness and long-suffering, yet with fidelity to God. The Church must be purified from iniquity of every kind, that we may stand before God "a glorious Church, not having spot or wrinkle, or any such thing;" that when we get our temples finished we may enter therein, approach the living God, and call upon Him for blessings, for life and salvation for ourselves and others, for deliverance from our enemies, and God will hear our prayers if we will only be obedient and observe His law. God is on our side. All heaven is on our side. The ancient Prophets and Patriarchs, and the Son of God and God the Father, are enlisted in the cause of Zion. It is for us to be true to ourselves, and I ask no odds of this world or of its powers. ("Amen") God will take care of His Saints, but we must be careful to be Saints.

22."Arise therefore, ye Elders of Israel—ye Priests, Teachers and Deacons, ye Presidents of Stakes, Bishops and High Counselors, ye Apostles and First Presidency, and all of us— Arise and let us go to work with a will to do the will of God on earth as it is done in heaven! For if ever that is done, where is it to start, do you think, if it does not begin here among us? God expects it at our hands. We are full of weaknesses and imperfections, every one of us; but we want to learn the word, the will, and the law of God, and to conform to that word and will and law. Let that law be written upon our hearts. Let us seek to magnify our callings and honor our God, and the Lord will take care of the balance.

23. We need not trouble ourselves much about our enemies. They have their ideas, we have ours. We will do as we have done. We will do the best we can with them, put our trust in the living God, and pursue a course that is wise, prudent and intelligent. We will glory not in ourselves, but in the Lord of Hosts. We will dedicate ourselves, our wives, our families, our houses and our lands, and all that we possess to the Lord, and feel that we are His children. If we do this, He will bless us with life, health and prosperity. He will control the efforts of our enemies in the future as He has done in the past. And here I feel to call upon every soul to bless and magnify the God of Israel for His mercies extended to us in the past; for putting a hook into the jaws of our enemies that they have not had power to harm us, and He will continue to do it, if we will continue to be faithful, only much more so; and woe unto them that fight against Zion, for the Lord God of Hosts will fight against them. Amen.

ADDRESS 27

Discourse delivered by President John Taylor at the 53rd Semiannual General Conference of The Church of Jesus Christ of Latter-day Saints convened Sunday afternoon October 7, 1883, in the Tabernacle, Salt Lake City.

1. Permit me to say that in consequence of the immense multitude that has assembled on this occasion, it will be absolutely necessary that the strictest order and quietude should be maintained, in order that all may hear; for it is a great labor to address so many thousands of people. As I feel a little weak in body I hope, therefore, you will give me your quiet and considerate attention.

2. We have listened to a great many interesting principles since the commencement of this conference.

3. We occupy today a very peculiar position, and it is proper that we, as Latter-day Saints, should comprehend that position and our various responsibilities in relation to the world in which we live, the nation with which we are associated, and the duties and responsibilities which devolve upon us as messengers of salvation to proclaim the Gospel to mankind. It is further necessary that we should comprehend the past, that we should comprehend the present, and that we should also—under the influence and by the direction of the Spirit of the living God—comprehend the things of the future; for we, as Latter-day Saints, have to do with the past we have to do with the present, and we have to do with the future.

4. In relation to the inhabitants of the world generally, I sometimes think that we entertain very erroneous notions concerning them—that our ideas are too narrow and too contracted, that we do not comprehend the relationship in which they stand to God our Heavenly Father—and we are apt to fall into an error which was indulged in by the Jews in former ages, and to cry out, "The temple of the Lord, the temple of the Lord, the temple of the Lord are we." Because God has conferred upon us light and intelligence, and revealed His will unto us, we are too apt to look down upon the rest of mankind as aliens and undeserving of Divine regard; but we are told that God has made of one blood all the families of the earth, and that He has given

unto them a portion of His Spirit to profit withal. We are also informed, that God is the God and Father of the spirits of all flesh. We are given to understand that He feels interested in the welfare of all the human family, for it is written that they are all His offspring.

5. Therefore, we as Latter-day Saints, ought to feel towards the world and the inhabitants thereof, as God our Heavenly Father feels towards them; for we are told that God so loved the world, that He gave His only begotten Son to atone for their sins, that whosoever believeth on Him might not perish, but have everlasting life, and if this is the feeling of our Heavenly Father towards the inhabitants of the earth, we ought to entertain the same sentiment. When Jesus was on the earth, when He established the Gospel upon it, as it has been established in these last days, He said: "God sent not His Son into the world to condemn the world; but that the world through him might be saved." And when He commissioned His Apostles, His command was: "Go ye into all the world, and preach the Gospel to every creature. He that believeth and is baptized shall be saved; but he that believeth not shall be damned." The damnation or condemnation of the people who rejected the Gospel He could not help; He offered unto them the words of life, and according to eternal laws that exist in the heavens, men must be governed by certain principles, if they desire to associate with the Gods, and if when the Gospel was preached they did not receive it, the condemnation rested with them. And the condemnation grows out of this: that light had come into the world, but men loved darkness rather than light, because their deeds were evil.

6. The Lord Jesus has given us a commission of the same kind to the world of mankind, and you have heard during this Conference of the manner in which these things were introduced, so that it is unnecessary for me to repeat them. Suffice it to say, that they were introduced by the opening of

the heavens, by the appearance of God our heavenly Father and His Son Jesus Christ, by the administering of holy angels, by the restoration of the Priesthood, and by the revelation of His will to man. You comprehend very well the nature of the organization, and the duties devolving upon certain individuals and quorums in this Church. The Twelve are set apart as special witnesses to the nations of the earth, and are empowered and authorized to open up the Gospel, to introduce it, and to turn the keys thereof to all people, and the word to the Apostles—and to others associated with them—to the Elders of Israel generally is, "Go ye into all the world, and preach the Gospel to every creature. He that believeth and is baptized shall be saved; and he that believeth not shall be damned." This is just as it was in former ages. To assist the Twelve in the labors in which they are engaged, are the Seventies, who are called as special witnesses to the nations of the earth. What for? Who organized these Seventies, and these Twelve, and who dictated their duties and responsibilities? The Lord.

7. Why did He do it? Because, as in former ages, He felt interested in the welfare of the human family, and it is not and never was the will of God, that mankind should perish, but that they all might be brought to a knowledge of the truth, and to an obedience thereof, if they saw proper, and if not, when the Twelve, the Seventies, the Elders, and the various officers who have been ordained and set apart to preach the Gospel, have fulfilled their missions to the nations of the earth; they have done just what the Lord has required at their hands, and no more.

8. I further wish to state to the Twelve and to the Seventies, and to the Elders, that they are not responsible for the reception or the rejection by the world of that word which God has given to them to communicate. It is proper for them to use all necessary diligence and fidelity, and to plainly and intelligently, and with prayer and faith, go forth as messengers to the nations, as the legates of the skies, clothed upon with authority from the God of Heaven, even the authority of the Holy Priesthood, which is after the order of the Son of God, which is after the order of Melchizedek, which is after the power of an endless life. He has endowed them, as you

have heard, with authority to call upon men to repent of their sins, and to be baptized in the name of Jesus for the remission of sins, and then He has told them to lay hands on the people thus believing, and thus being baptized, and to confer upon them the gift of the Holy Ghost, and when they have performed their labors, and fulfilled their duties, their garments are free from the blood of this generation, and the people are then left in the hands of God their Heavenly Father. For the people, as before stated, will be held responsible to God for their rejection of the Gospel, and not to us.

9. I will talk a little further about the people of the earth, who have in their midst Christianity, and other religious professions. I have quoted what is stated in the Scriptures—that God has given to every man a portion of His Spirit to profit withal. But that has nothing to do with the Gospel particularly. It is a principle which is implanted in the heart of every human being outside of the Gospel; and under its influence there are and have been many great and good principles in existence on the earth and among the peoples thereof.

10. All men almost everywhere, possessing any degree of intelligence, feel that it is right to be honest; and all civilized nations, influenced by that feeling, pass laws to punish the thief, the rogue, and the man who possesses himself of other people's property in any unjust manner, and these feelings and principles are generally sustained by the honorable of all countries, and operate more or less among all nations. Chicanery, deception and fraud are looked upon as evils in the moral world; and men influenced by that principle—which, as I stated, is planted in the bosom of every individual—feel to abhor acts of deception and fraud of any kind, although some people practice them to a very great extent. Men under the influence of this spirit in the mercantile world, for instance, consider it a disgrace not to keep their engagements, not to pay their honest debts, and laws are made to reach offenders in those cases. So strong is the feeling of honor among many,—in this nation, in England, in France, in Germany, and in other European nations,—that very many of those people who would be esteemed honorable in their

feelings and instincts, if calamity overtake them and they are unable to meet their liabilities, very frequently commit suicide, wrong though it be; they would rather die than be dishonored. Now, these sentiments of honor are good so far as they go; but this is outside of the Gospel.

11. There are, of course, many dishonest merchants and men of large means, who use their talent and wealth for the purpose of taking advantage of the unwary, and oppressing the poor; and in this and in other countries, annually filch thousands of millions of wealth from the unsuspecting and poor by their questionable acts and insatiable greed; carrying poverty, sorrow, misery and distress to millions of the honest laboring classes. As God has planted a portion of His Spirit within them, He will hold them, and not us, responsible for their acts; and instead of possessing riches and honor their names will become infamous on earth and hereafter. And instead of wallowing in their ill-gotten gains, they will find themselves with Dives, calling upon their victims for a drop of water to cool their parched tongues. Gospel or no Gospel, honorable men cannot condescend to chicanery and deception; and while following the lead of that inward monitor, they could not yield themselves to those heartless and cold-blooded practices. Again, there is a horror in the minds of men generally, about shedding innocent blood, and laws are passed to prevent crimes of that kind and to punish the offender.

12. Where do all these things come from? From that spirit which God has planted in the bosom of all men. You may take the lowest and most degraded of men, some of the greatest criminals perhaps, and they will say, if they see an honorable man, a virtuous man, a kind hearted and generous man, a man who acts uprightly—"We respect that man, we honor him, we respect him for his virtues; we cannot imitate him, we are sorry to say," and in this way they will acknowledge that which is good and feel that they themselves are doing wrong. These are some of the principles that exist in human nature. They are so far good.

13. At the same time there is another sentiment prevails—that is, to protect virtue and chastity. It is not practiced as extensively as it ought to be; a great amount of hypocrisy exists on this subject. But nevertheless it is implanted in the hearts of millions of the human family; and they look upon the seducer of woman and the defiler of himself, and upon those who practice crimes associated with these matters, with disgust. The nations today, however, are wallowing in rottenness and corruption in regard to these matters, yet there are thousands and millions of men and women who abhor impurity and vice, and cannot sanction licentiousness in any of its disgusting forms. All these things are good in their place; but this alone is not the Gospel.

14. Now, in former times, in the days of the flood, for instance, the people became very corrupt, so much so we are told, that the imaginations of the hearts of men were only evil and that continually, and the Scriptures say it repented the Lord that He had made man because of his corruptions and wickedness; but some tell us that it repented Noah that man had been made because of the abominations and evils that he witnessed in his day. God destroyed the wicked of that generation with a flood. Why did He destroy them? He destroyed them for their benefit, if you can comprehend it, but I very much question whether all of you can or not. Let me explain a little. We are told, as I have already said, that God is the God and Father of the spirits of all flesh. We are further told that Jesus the Son of God, existed before the worlds were. It is also stated that He is our elder brother, and that we pre-existed also—that is, our spirits did. When Satan had gained an ascendancy over the inhabitants of the earth so far that they had departed from God, and violated His laws, what would be the feelings of those spirits in the eternal worlds? Let me ask all intelligent people, would they not be apt to turn to their Heavenly Father and say: "Father, look down upon those corrupt inhabitants. Do you see them?" "Yes, I see them and I know them." "Is it just that we, thy children, should be doomed to inhabit those filthy, corrupt bodies, and thus be subjected to Thy wrath and indignation, and it may be thousands of years before we can come back again into thy presence?" "No, it is not just," and on this principle the Father destroyed them with a flood, and recommenced peopling the earth with the seed of a righteous man.

15.But, let me ask, what did the Lord do before He sent the flood? He sent Noah among them as a preacher of righteousness; He sent Enoch; He sent many Elders among the people, and they prophesied to them that unless they repented, judgment would overtake them; that God would overwhelm the earth with a flood and destroy the inhabitants thereof—that is, those who would not listen to the Gospel of the Son of God; for the Son of God was in existence then, not personally on earth, but existed in the spirit, and the promise to them was that He should come and atone for the sins of the world. They were taught these things, but they rejected them, that is the great majority of them did so.

16.We are also told that Enoch walked with God, and that he had a city which they called Zion, and people gathered to Zion then, as we gather the people to Zion in this day. Enoch walked with God, and was instructed by Him, and he instructed the people of Zion. There is a very short account of it in the Bible. There we are simply told that "Enoch walked with God and was not; for God took him." It was not thought necessary to say more upon this subject; but the facts were that Enoch and the people of his city, having been taught for upwards of 300 years in the principles of the Gospel before the judgment overtook the world, were translated. Thus the people in that day, had had fair warning, but only a very few paid any attention to it. We are told concerning the Book of Enoch that it is to be testified of in due time, and then we shall know more about these things than we do now.

17.But what of those who were disobedient? They were thrown into prison. How long did they continue there? Until Jesus came. What then did He do? He went and preached to the spirits in prison. He was "put to death in the flesh," we are told in the Bible, "but quickened by the spirit: by which also He went and preached unto the spirits in prison, which sometime were disobedient, when once the long suffering of God waited in the days of Noah." Is that in the Bible inquire the Christians? Yes, that is in your Bible.

18.Thus we see the dealings of God with those people. Noah had nothing to do but to preach the Gospel, and obey the word of the Lord. We have nothing to do but attend to the same things. We then leave the inhabitants of the earth in the hands of God. It is not for us to judge them; for the Lord says: "judgment is mine and I will repay." When men have offered unto them the words of life, and they reject these words, they then become amenable to their God, and the condemnation is, as I stated before, that light came into the world; but men love darkness rather than light, because their deeds are evil.

19.Men persecute the Elders when they go forth to preach. They persecuted Jesus. They persecuted His disciples. Men, in many instances, even in this nation—a nation that is emphatically called the land of the free, the home of the brave, and the asylum for the oppressed—have put to death some of our Elders, because of the testimony they have borne to them. This, however, is all in accordance with the predictions of Jesus. He told His disciples that, "if the world hate you, ye know that it hated me before it hated you." In other words, the Savior said, "If they love me, they will love you; if they receive me, they will receive you; if they reject me, they will reject you; if they persecute me they will persecute you." And He further said—and it is singular that He should have to say it to His disciples, men who were good, virtuous, pure, upright, and desirous to promote the welfare of humanity—it is singular that He should have to say: "Blessed are ye, when men shall revile you, and persecute you, and shall say all manner of evil against you falsely, for my sake. Rejoice and be exceeding glad; for great is your reward in heaven: for so persecuted they the Prophets which were before you." Were these men the enemies of mankind because they told them the truth? All intelligent men would say, No. Are those Elders who go forth to proclaim the Gospel today, the enemies of mankind? All intelligent men will say, No.

20.Well, would you try to coerce men? No. Why? Because God does not do it, and He does not want us to do it. I would not use any influence but that of truth to lead any man to a knowledge of the truth. Any other influence, any other power, any other spirit is not of God. There is a species of false Christianity that thinks it is right to persecute people because of their religion, but those possessed of that spirit, whoever they are, are of their father the devil, because his works they do. God believes in the freedom of mankind, and Satan was cast out of heaven because he sought to take away the free agency of man. In various ages of the world, under various guises, the same thing has been attempted. Sometimes political, sometimes religious, and sometimes other pretexts are introduced to oppress mankind, and to deprive them of that liberty which it is their birth right, and which all men have a right, under God's law, to enjoy.

21. Now I come to talk of our relationship to this nation in a political point of view. We are here in this Territory of Utah. We were told to gather here by the Lord, and we have obeyed His command, just as they did, as I before stated, in the Zion of Enoch in his day. When we came here we brought our bodies with us. It is not a spiritual thing, for we are all of us very literal and very temporal. We have arms and legs, eyes and ears, like other people—we are the children of our Heavenly Father as others are. He has introduced the Gospel, as I have before said, and one of the principles thereof is that of gathering, and we have gathered together. I need not quote to you the Scriptures in the Bible on this subject, for you know them, and I need not occupy time in quoting them today. We are here. Who came in the first place? A number of people from the eastern, western and southern States, who believed the Gospel and obeyed it. It is not necessary to go into our history, and dwell on events as they transpired in Ohio, in Missouri, or in Illinois. Let all those things pass. You can read them in our history. But as I have said we are here. Under what auspices? According to the laws and usages of the United States we settled cities, towns and villages; we settled on farms, etc., which we had a right to do. We purchased and paid for the property that we possess as other citizens do.

22. At this point, President Taylor, feeling weak, requested President Geo. Q. Cannon to talk a little on the subject.

23. President Cannon said: President Taylor is suffering from fatigue and will take a little rest. We have gathered here, as he has said, and have built up a common-wealth in these mountains—a commonwealth which, if it were not for the prejudice that we have to contend with, would be the admiration of mankind. The despised "Mormons" stripped of their properties, driven out into the wilderness as outcasts, as unfit for the society of their fellow citizens; having been treated in this manner because of alleged crimes—that at least was the justification that was offered for the treatment of the Latter-day Saints—because they were such a wicked people that they deserved to be treated by mob violence, and the whole world, it may be said, acquiesced in the verdict that had been pronounced upon us, or at least there was not sufficient manhood and courage in the nation to raise the voice against it, though thousands of people felt that it was an outrage. Driven into the mountains in this manner, stripped of our possessions; some of us coming into these valleys barefooted, with scarcely enough clothing to cover us for the succeeding winter, God has blessed the people, and through the wisdom and the power and influence that He has given to this people, they have built, as I have said, a commonwealth in these mountains, that is the admiration of every unprejudiced man. These so-called "Mormon thieves," these "Mormon outlaws," these people who were considered unworthy to live in Illinois and in Missouri have come here, and we behold today hundreds of settlements, hundreds of cities, built in the most admirable manner. A government exists here for the protection of the poor as well as the rich; and I have often said, that when we take into consideration the fact of the poverty of the people, that we have had an influx every year of about 3,000, on an average, of foreign immigrants, unacquainted with our methods of living, not familiar with our climate, coming here stripped—that is, coming here with very little to aid them—it is one of the most wonderful things that a community like this can absorb so many people annually, and show no evidences of pauperism. We have no paupers.

24. Now, my brethren and sisters, these results—and I think them under the circumstances significant—are due to the blessing, wisdom, power and guidance of our God. We have been sustained here by His arm.

Yet at the same time we have been treated like a stepchild by our parent government. Loyal as we are to the core; believing as we do that the constitution of our country is inspired of God; looking upon this form of government as God-given, and as the best possible form of human government; notwithstanding we entertain these views, we have been treated from the beginning as though we were aliens, and as though we were a stepchild, instead of one born legally, and entitled to the blessings that the rest of our brothers and sisters in the compact of the Union are entitled to. We have had this sort of treatment from the beginning. Every act of ours has been viewed with jealousy. Nevertheless, we have prospered. God has been with us. His blessing has been upon us. We have maintained good order in these mountains, not because governors have been sent here not of our choosing; not because federal officials have been sent here in whose selection we have had no voice; not because for several years back, it has almost been deemed a qualification for officers to hate the "Mormon" people among whom the federal officials were going to serve; but because there has been a union in the midst of the people, there has been a wisdom, there has been a power in the government which God has given.

25. God has developed true statesmanship in the midst of these Latter-day Saints. There are hundreds of men in this community who can take a body of people and go into these desert wilds and build up a city, or a number of cities, and govern and control them in a manner that if the whole world were governed in that way would produce the grandest and happiest results. We have demonstrated our capacity for self-government, and it is inherent, it may be said in the people, springing, as I believe, from the wisdom and blessing that God has bestowed upon men. There is no community today, within the confines of these United States, that can furnish so many practical men of this character as can the Latter-day Saints, and the evidences of it are to be seen in the good order that prevails throughout these mountains from north to south, and from east to west, wherever the Latter-day Saints live and have influence. I praise God for it. I claim no cred-

it for man in this matter. It is the divine blessing, and it is in accordance with the plan that has been pre-arranged in the heavens.

26. Why, the very fact that we were permitted to be driven to these mountains, shows us the hand of God in it. There was no room for expansion in our old position. We could not have grown; we could not have developed. But our enemies were determined to make us great, and they thrust us out, and sent us into a land which God evidently had designed to be settled by just such a people as ourselves. There is no such land under the sun today. It is the habitat, the true habitat of the Latter-day Saints, admirably adapted in every feature of its climate, of its conditions, of its mountains, of its valleys, of its crystal streams, and the scarcity of water making it admirable for settlement by a sparse people, a people such as we are. No dense populations could live here.

27. President Taylor, at this point, again took the stand and said: I have felt the exertion almost too much for me. I am not very strong in body at present, but I will continue.

28. We consider as Latter-day Saints, that we have rights here, and although we have been dealt with, as we would call it, rather scurvily by the government that ought to foster us, yet at the same time we have strictly adhered to the letter of the law, even in the face of the assumed purity those people (our enemies) profess to attach to themselves. We have not resisted any of these things, but have treated those men who came as our oppressors, if you please, with kindness and due respect, notwithstanding they have introduced many things in our midst, at variance with the laws and constitution of the United States, and with our rights as American citizens. We have yielded for the time being, but we purpose in behalf of ourselves, of our children, in behalf of the institutions of this nation, and of thousands of honorable men in it, to test these things to "the last bat's end," and see, legally and constitutionally, whether this nation will sustain these acts or not, and then if they do we will leave them in the hands of God, and pursue our course, trusting in Him. But one thing I will say, and that is that this cause is onward; and as my brethren have said, so say I, that God has commenced it, and He will take

care of it. I know what I am saying. I know when I am speaking that I am speaking not only to you, but to the whole world; for it will be published to the world. And I tell you Latter-day Saints not to fear, not to have any trembling in the knees, for the God of Israel is on the side of Israel, and hosts of angels also. There are more for us than there can be against us; and God will sustain the right and take care of, and preserve His people, if they will only do right.

29. We have embraced the Gospel. We have placed ourselves in another position from that of the world. We have entered into sacred covenants with the Lord, and He expects us to fulfill our covenants, and those who do not fulfill them will be condemned. There are certain rules and regulations that exist in the heavens, as well as on the earth. We are told that before we can enter into the celestial kingdom of God, we shall have to pass by the angels, and the Gods, and if the Latter-day Saints aim at a celestial exaltation, they must live and abide by the celestial law, or they will not get it, any more than the Gentiles will. Hear it, ye Latter-day Saints! God expects you to be pure, virtuous, holy, upright, prayerful, honest, obedient to His law, and not to follow the devices and desires of your own hearts. God has revealed many things to you, and He will reveal many more. He expects you to abide His law, and those who do not want to abide it, had better quit today, the sooner the better, for God expects us to do His will in all things.

30. If we are Seventies we have to go to the nations of the earth. If we are members of the Twelve, we have also to go to the nations and preach the Gospel, or see that this work is done. If we are Presidents of Stakes, we must do our duty, draw nigh to God, and seek for the revelation of His will, that we may know the things we do, and the things whereof we testify. If we are Bishops, we must perform our duties, or we will be moved out of our place. I do not care who it is these words may effect; for God is building up a Zion, and that Zion means pure in heart, the honorable, the upright, the virtuous, and those whose sympathies extend to the promotion of the welfare of the human family. He expects us to operate in behalf of the interests of a fallen world, and to bring all to a knowledge of the truth that will listen to it and obey it. He then expects us to build temples as we have been and are doing.

31. And here permit me to say that I commend the Latter-day Saints for the energy they have displayed in these things. And it is for us to honor our God, and to obey all just and constitutional laws, and to be quiet and peaceable, and operate for and be the friends of mankind, but do not condescend to their pernicious, corrupt, and damnable practices, or God will judge you as He will judge them. It is for us to do right, and work righteousness, and God will bless us.

32. We need have no fear pertaining to the future; and when we have completed these temples, we will go and administer therein the sacred ordinances of God's house, and the Spirit and blessing of God will rest upon us, and we will stand, as the Scriptures say, as saviors upon Mount Zion, and the Kingdom shall be the Lord's; and woe to them that fight against Zion! Amen.

ADDRESS 28

Opening statement made by President John Taylor at the 54th Annual General Conference of The Church of Jesus Christ of Latter-day Saints convened April 4, 1884, in the Tabernacle, Salt Lake City.

1. I am thankful for the many favorable circumstances surrounding us, and for the beautiful weather we are having for conference. These conferences are fraught with much good to the people, affording them an opportunity to meet old friends, to listen to good instruction, and to imbibe the spirit of the times.

2. The work in which we are engaged is not a work originated by man, but is one established by Jehovah. It was contemplated by ancient prophets. God our Heavenly Father is interested in it, as is His Son Jesus Christ. It was planned before the world was created, and men of God, in every age, have contemplated it with pleasure. It is called the dispensation of the fullness of times, in which God will gather together all things both in the heavens and the earth. Unaided by the powers of heaven, no man or set of men could establish a work like that in which we are engaged and we are indebted to God for the inception, continuance and support of it. Therefore it behooves us to understand where our strength lies. In the organization of the Church, revelation was indispensibly necessary and revelation has continued to be a necessity in it. As Saints we must learn that it is by the power of God that we exist. That it is in Him that we live, move and have our being, and I care not what position any man may hold, he can do nothing without the aid of God. All the human race past, present and future, are interested in our work and upon our acts, not as individuals but as a people, depends the fate of nations. It is necessary that every member of the priesthood should comprehend our position as a people, that all may aid in rolling forth the great work in which we are engaged.

3. We shall have a variety of business to present to the Saints during conference. We hail you as brethren and sisters and pray God to bless you. (The congregation said Amen.) I pray God to bless all who seek the welfare of Zion, and to let His wrath and indignation rest upon her enemies: in the name of Jesus, Amen.

ADDRESS 29

Remarks made by President John Taylor at the 54th Annual General Conference of The Church of Jesus Christ of Latter-day Saints convened April 6, 1884, in the Tabernacle, Salt Lake City.

1. I have been very much interested in the remarks which have been made on this subject—the subject of home industries—and I would ask this congregation if I may have the privilege of aiding them as Trustee-in-Trust. We have some iron works started in the south, and I want to know if this congregation will authorize me to assist those iron works? If you do, make it manifest by raising the right hand (a forest of hands went up). I believed that you would feel just so, and I have already assisted them (laughter). There is another thing I want to ask associated with this affair. You have given me the privilege of assisting this industry, now I want to ask if you yourselves will assist in this matter; and all who are in favor of doing so hold up the right hand [all hands went up]. Now, we will say Yankee Doodle do it.

2. There are a great many other things associated with our temporal interests—some of which have been referred to—which we must look after. There has been a good deal said in regard to the United Order. We have had this talked about a long time. We shall have a United Order by and by. As one of the brethren mentioned—I think it was Brother Young—there is a feeling of the kind growing among the people. But we have not yet had the order that we shall have. By and by people will not have to be asked to go into the United Order, for they will beg for the privilege of coming in. If we will only do right—which we are seeking to do—and keep the commandments of God—which I am very much pleased to hear, with all our infirmities and weaknesses, and we have a great many of them, we are trying to do—the time is not far distant when Zion, as the Scriptures say, will be the richest of all people. And when it comes to pass you will know it.

3. Let me make a remark or two upon this subject. What do the Scriptures say upon it. They say: "For brass I will bring silver, for silver gold, and for stones iron." Well, that is rather a singular exchange. What else? "I will make thine officers peace and thine exactors righteousness." Justice, righteousness, truth and integrity, and not covetousness, deceitfulness and self-interest, must be associated with the law of God, the work of God, the order of God, and the kingdom of God. When we can prepare ourselves to observe His laws and keep His commandments, God is prepared to cause the riches of the Gentiles to flow unto us, as the Scriptures say. But we have to learn to observe the law of God, and to keep the commandments of God.

4. I feel sometimes a little unpleasant on one subject. I am appointed here as Trustee-in-Trust, and I have a great responsibility devolving upon me in regard to the financial affairs of the Church. I have associated with me my brethren of the First Presidency and my brethren of the Twelve and the Presiding Bishop to counsel in regard to those matters. It has been stated here that there is a great outside pressure, and a great desire to become acquainted with our affairs and our monetary matters. I have been applied to time and time again in this respect, and I cannot conceive of any other idea associated with it than that they would like to do with our finances as they would with our wives—take them from us (laughter). Now, we have a financial report here. My idea would be to have it presented in all its details to this congregation, but it is thought not wise to do so. This is the thing that does not suit me exactly—that is, it does not suit me not to be able to put this report before the people, so that everybody may hear and see and know and comprehend for themselves, for I think it is our right to understand these things, and what is done with our financial matters. But, as I have said, it is thought wisdom not to have the report presented to the general public—not to put them in possession of information in regard to our matters. Let them find

them out. Some one suggests that the conduct of our enemies would be exhibited in the utterance of a prayer, "Let us arise and rob somebody in the name of the Lord"—or rather in the name of the law (laughter). Well, we do not propose to put them in possession of this information. But we have got our record which tells what every man has done and what they have not done in relation to these matters. We have faithful records pertaining to all these thing, and anybody that is interested, and that has a right to inquire, can come and obtain the information pertaining to their affairs individually, or to Stakes or to Wards, as the case may be; but it is none of the business of outsiders to know about our financial matters; it don't belong to them; it didn't come from them; we never received anything at their hands. It is simply our own, and they may as well ask to examine our letters as to be made acquainted with our financial affairs. All who favor this idea of not reading the report, signify it by holding up the right hand. [Unanimous vote. On motion the financial report was referred to the auditing committee.]

5. I have not yet been furnished with the report of the auditing committee on the last financial report submitted to them, but as soon as received I will communicate it. I will state, however, for the satisfaction of the brethren and sisters—and I see them from all parts, from the far south, from the far north—that our financial affairs are in a very good position, that our tithing, instead of being on the decrease, is on the increase, and that there is a general feeling to meet the requirements of the law of God pertaining to all these matter; and we think that all of us— or say the major part of us—we do not expect everybody to do exactly right—are striving to carry out the law of God, and if we will continue to observe His requirements and keep His commandments, the blessings of the God of Israel will rest upon Israel. Men may plot and contrive, and calculate and try to manipulate the affairs of Israel, but our affairs are in the hands of God, and He will take care of us if we will obey His law, and our progress is onward and upward; God will stand by Israel if we only stand by Him. Amen.

ADDRESS 30

Opening remarks made by President John Taylor at the 54th Semiannual General Conference of The Church of Jesus Christ of Latter-day Saints convened October 4, 1884, in the Tabernacle, Salt Lake City.

1. We are met this morning to attend our Semi-Annual Conference, and to attend to the various kinds of business that may be presented to us, associated with the interests of the kingdom of God on the earth. We have met for this purpose for a great many years, and have enjoyed ourselves generally very much on such occasions. Being gathered to hear and to speak, and to present doctrines, principles and business, it is proper for us to thank God the eternal Father, and seek for his guidance and blessing in all things we may engage in. We occupy a peculiar position among the nations, and associated with this nation. It is proper for us to seek to comprehend our relationship to our Heavenly Father and Jesus, the Mediator of the new covenant and heavenly intelligences, and the relationship we sustain to each other, and the kingdom of God on the earth, and understand the various duties devolving upon us in connection with the Church, this nation and all other nations, to whom we have a message to deliver. We must also seek to understand all the duties of life. People are gathered here from all the Stakes. The representatives of the people should always be present on these occasions, especially the Presidents of Stakes, Bishops and Counselors, High Counselors and the officers of the Church generally, that they, and through them the people of Zion, may be instructed in regard to all the leading principles developed on these occasions.

2. On account of the weather being inclement, not many are present. The old people, however, are well represented, and it is to be presumed the younger ones are stopping at home to take care of themselves. When they got older they will probably learn better.

3. We are living in peculiar times, and the position of the Latter-day Saints is a singular one. This is the dispensation of the fullness of times, when all things in heaven and on earth are to be gathered together in one. The principles of salvation in this dispensation are and will continue to be more clearly taught in this than in any former dispensation. The Lord has initiated it by opening the heavens. He is gathering to Himself a people to whom He has revealed things that have been hidden from the beginning. All His promises will be fulfilled both in regard to the living and the dead. Our duties embrace all conditions connected with human life, past, present and future. God has greatly blessed us in our settlements, and continues to increase us year after year, and we feel to rejoice in the God of Israel.

4. There is in the world and this nation strong hatred to us as a people, and we have to endure persecution, reproach and falsehood, set on foot to injure us. Yet these things make but little difference to us. We know in whom we believe, and that God has set His hand to accomplish His purposes in the last days; no power can stay His work. As regards other people and their ideas, it matters but little to us. Although they show a disposition to break the Constitution and bring us into vassalage, God has maintained our freedom, and if we do right He will continue to do so.

5. We are commanded to preach the Gospel. This has been done, and thousands, inspired by the fear of God, have gathered here in consequence. And the Lord has blessed us in our gathering together; in our houses, orchards, gardens, fields, flocks, and the labor of our hands. Although we have some settlements which have suffered from floods, the crops throughout are generally good, and the granaries are full to running over. God's mercy has been manifested unto us. There is generally manifested among the people a desire to act as become Saints of the Most High God. We feel grateful unto the God of heaven for His mercy. There is occasionally a complaint that the brethren have a large amount of grain and it fetches a low price, and embarrassments arise from this situation. But we may have worse things than plenty of wheat, cattle, sheep and other sub-

stances. There are thousands of happy homes and families, with as good prospects as are before any other people in existence. Jesus said His disciples are known by the love they bear each other. It applies to the Saints now. While contentions exist elsewhere, we do not have them, for the Lord is teaching us a better way. There have been times when we did not have much substance to trouble us to take care of. I recently paid a visit, with others, to the northern settlements, on which occasion a distance of a thousand miles was traversed, and a most satisfactory condition found to exist. A similar report comes from the south. It is desired that the people preserve themselves in all purity, and that all may operate together in the building up of Zion, teaching our children the principles of life, continuing our labors until the will of God is done on the earth as it is done in heaven.

6. President Taylor concluded by expressing his pleasure at meeting with the people, and desiring the blessing of God upon the Conference.

ADDRESS 31

Discourse delivered by President John Taylor at the 54th Semiannual General Conference of The Church of Jesus Christ of Latter-day Saints convened October 6 and 7, 1884, in the Tabernacle, Salt Lake City.

1. If the congregation will endeavor to preserve as much order as possible, and prevent the crying and disturbance of children, I will try and address you for a short time. Last evening I made quite a lengthy address in this hall; but we had very good order. There was no whispering, no talking, nor disturbance of any kind. It requires, in a large congregation like this, quite an exertion to speak so as to make the people hear. I am told that the people could not hear half of what was said by several of the brethren yesterday. It is wrong for us to have disorder in the house of God, a place where we meet for instruction.

2. Last evening I talked of some matters of considerable importance to the Priesthood, of which there was an immense number present; they nearly filled this hall. I wish to continue some of these remarks; for it is necessary that all of us should be instructed in the great principles which God has revealed for the guidance, salvation and exaltation of the Saints of God, and also for the benefit of the world wherein we live. There were very many promises made to eminent men in generations long since past; but these generally had reference more particularly to the benefit of the world of mankind than to individuals.

3. There were certain great principles involved in the organization of this earth, and one was that there might be a place provided whereon the children of our Heavenly Father could live and propagate their species, and have bodies formed for the spirits to inhabit who were the children of God; for we are told that He is the God and Father of the spirits of all flesh. It was requisite, therefore, that an earth should be organized; it was requisite that man should be placed upon it; it was requisite that bodies should be prepared for those spirits to inhabit, in order that the purposes of God pertaining to His progeny might be accomplished, and that those spirits might be enabled, through the medium of the everlasting Gospel, to return unto the presence of their Heavenly Father, as Gods among the Gods.

4. There have been different agencies at work throughout this world's history. Lucifer has been and is one of these agencies. There was a garden planted, and Adam and Eve were placed in it, and there they had communion with God. There was another being whose name was Lucifer, who is called in some places, "the son of the morning." Job speaks of a time at the creation of this earth when "the morning stars sang together, and all the sons of God shouted for joy," (Job xxxviii, 7). As it was necessary that there should be a God, a man, an earth and a heaven, it was also necessary that there should be a devil, that man might be tried, and by trial be instructed. Indeed, in the economy of God, it was not only necessary that man, but the Savior also should be perfected by suffering. It is written: "For it became him, for whom are all things, and by whom are all things, in bringing many sons unto glory, to make the captain of their salvation perfect through sufferings." (Hebrews, ii, 10.) It was further necessary that there should be a Redeemer according to the plan which was devised from before the foundation of the world, and also that man might be a free agent to act and operate for himself, to receive the good and reject the evil, or reject the good and be governed by the evil. And there were certain rewards promised to those who would obey the laws of God, and keep his commandments, and certain punishments inflicted upon those who would not.

5. Satan has made very great ravages among the human family in trying to accomplish his purposes; for he has been the enemy of God, and the enemy of man, and in ages past he wrought upon mankind until after a certain period he had contrived to get the great majority of them on his side.

6. Nevertheless, they had the Priesthood among them in those early days as we have among us today. After Adam there were Seth, Enos, Mahalaleel, Methuselah, Lamech, and a great many others until we arrive at Enoch

and Noah, who operated especially in behalf of the interest of the human family. They preached the Gospel as we preach it, and taught the same principles that we teach. They gathered the people to a Zion as we gather them, and when they had been gathered together, they had enemies as we have, who arrayed themselves against them. But Enoch was clothed upon with the power of God. He walked with God for 365 years, and, we are told, "he was not, for God took him." That is about all that is said about him in the Bible; but we have other information. Many others walked with God, and there was a city that the people were gathered to—a Zion. They walked with God and they were instructed of the Lord; but it took at any rate, 365 years to accomplish this object.

7. Furthermore, in the latter days there is to be a Zion built up: but in these days we are told that the Lord will cut His work short in righteousness. Enoch, in his day, had his messengers go forth among the people, and when they gathered, it induced the rage of man, and great armies assembled against the Saints, but Enoch prophesied by the power of God, and the earth shook and the mountains trembled, and the enemies of the Saints in fear fled afar off. By and by when the time came for the accomplishment of the purposes of God, and before the destruction of the wicked, Enoch was caught up to heaven and his Zion with him. And we are told in latter revelation in relation to these matters that a Zion will be built up in our day; that great trouble will overtake the inhabitants of the earth; and that when the time arrives, the Zion that was caught up will descend, and the Zion that will be organized here will ascend, both possessed of the same spirit, their peoples having been preserved by the power of God according to His purposes and as His children, to take part in the events of the latter days. We are told that when the people of these two Zions meet, they will fall on each other's necks, and embrace and kiss each other.

8. As they in that day were placed under the guidance of the Almighty, so are we. As they had a work to perform associated with the welfare of the human family, so have we. As they had the Gospel to preach, so have we. As they had a Zion to build up, so have

we. As they needed the support of the Great Jehovah, so do we. As they were dependent upon Him in all their movements, whether in relation to earth or heaven, so are we. The work in which we are engaged is one that has been introduced by the Great Eloheim, the God and Father of the human family, in the interests of His children. And wherever and whenever these principles have existed, this same being that was in the garden with our first parents still goes forth and has gone forth as a raging lion, seeking whom he may deceive, seeking whom he may devour, seeking whom he may lead down to death. And in these latter days God has introduced these same principles with the same object in view. He has revealed the same principles of heaven, and as heretofore, in the interest of humanity. Who was Enoch? Was he a man of God? Yes. Who were the Elders with him, were they men of God? Yes; and they received their instructions in that Zion that was then built up, and more or less directly from God; for Enoch walked with God. Whom was Enoch operating for? For God his heavenly Father. He was there, as Jesus was on the earth in his time, as he said, not to do His own will, but the will of his Father who sent him. And whom did those people operate for? They operated for the welfare of the human family who would receive the truth and be governed by it.

9. And whom did Jesus and His Apostles in their day operate for? For the benefit of all the world. Jesus Himself appeared as the Redeemer of the world, and He commissioned His Apostles to preach the Gospel to every creature, saying: "He that believeth and is baptized shall be saved, and he that believeth not shall be damned."

10. What is this salvation and condemnation? That would take a long time to tell. Suffice it to say that there are bodies celestial, bodies terrestrial, and bodies telestial; one glory of the sun, another of the moon, and another of the stars; but straight was the gate and narrow was the way that led unto the lives, and few there were at that time and few there have always been who have gone in thereat. And what was it that they sought? It was the Celestial Kingdom of our God, that they might come forth in the first resurrection and be one with the Father and one

with Jesus, and belong to the Church of the First Born whose names are written in heaven, and become Gods among the Gods, and participate in all the glory of the Celestial Kingdom. But few there were who found the narrow path. It is so today.

11. Were the Apostles of Jesus commanded to preach the Gospel? Yes. Are we commanded as they were? Yes. What was the position of the Apostles? They were simply messengers of life and salvation to a fallen world. What are the First Presidency, the Twelve, the High Priests, the Seventies, and the Elders to day? What are they? Bearers of life and salvation to a fallen world, the messengers of God to men, the legatees of the skies commissioned by the Great Jehovah to introduce the principles of eternal life, and gather in his elect from the four quarters of the earth, and to prepare them for an exaltation in the celestial kingdom of God.

12. And what becomes of those who choose the other path? They are still God's children, and He feels interested in them. What will He do with them? They will be judged according to the deeds done in the body, and according to the light and intelligence which God communicates to them. Then there is another glory a telestial glory. Those who enter into that glory will also be judged according to their deeds and be rewarded according to their acts.

13. We are told of others who will suffer the wrath of God, and in the revelations given to us we learn that eternal punishment is God's punishment, that everlasting punishment is God's punishment, for He is eternal, and He is everlasting. We are informed the cities of Sodom and Gomorrah suffered the vengeance of eternal fire. We are told, too, that the inhabitants of the antediluvian world who were destroyed because of their wickedness, were shut up in prison and they remained there for a long, long time. How long? We read that Jesus, who was put to death in the flesh, but quickened by the Spirit, went and preached to the Spirits in prison which were sometime disobedient when once the long-suffering of God waited in the days of Noah. How long had these people been there? At a rough guess about 2,400 years. It was quite a painful ordeal to go through. It is one that none of us would

like very much. It is a fearful thing to fall into the hands of the living God—a fearful thing to violate His laws.

14. We have gathered here that we may learn those laws, the laws of God, the laws of life, and prepare ourselves under His guidance for an inheritance in the Celestial Kingdom of God. But are all the Latter-day Saints going into that kingdom? No. How is that? It is just as Jesus declared. "It is not every one that sayeth Lord, Lord, that will enter into the Kingdom of God, but he that doeth the will of the Father who is in heaven." Did Jesus come to do the will of His Father in heaven? He did, and He expects all who aim at Celestial glory to do the same, and if they do not they will not get there. He says, "Many will say to me in that day, Lord, Lord, have we not prophesied in Thy name? and in Thy name have cast out devils? and in Thy name done many wonderful works?" And He will say unto them, "Depart from me, ye workers of iniquity, I know you not, you have not lived as becometh Saints."

15. Oh, say some, that don't mean the Saints. No, it don't, but it means many who profess to be Saints. Do the world profess to cast out devils, to heal the sick and to do many mighty works? They do not. Do the world prophesy in His name? No. Do the world preach in the name of God? They preach in His name, many of them, without having the authority, as we have heard at this conference; but they do not propose to do many mighty works in His name, but many of our Elders do—Elders who magnify their calling and honor their God. On the other hand there are Elders who are careless, wayward and rebellious against God and His laws—who seek to trample under foot the principles that He has revealed—who seek to set themselves up to guide, direct, and manipulate the affairs of the Church and Kingdom of God, and yet these same persons know nothing but what they know naturally, as do the brute beasts, made to be taken and destroyed; and we none of us know anything only as God instructs us.

16. We are indebted to Him for the introduction of this work, and for all the information pertaining thereto. It has been from no man nor set of men, nor organizations of a professed spiritual or temporal nature, that

we have received intelligence pertaining to the things of God, the Church of God, or the Kingdom of God. It has come directly from the Lord, through the Gospel of the Son of God, which brings life and immortality to light; and if men think—and we every once in a while meet with such characters—they know better than the Lord how to manipulate affairs they will find out their mistake. The Lord will say to them, "Depart from me, I never knew you;" for it is not every one that sayeth Lord, Lord, that shall enter into the Kingdom of God, but He that doeth the will of our Father in Heaven.

17. Hence there is a great work for us to do. There is something comprehensive in it. It is indeed the dispensation of the fullness of times spoken of by all the holy prophets since the world was. It relates to the interests of men that now live: it relates to the interests of men who have lived, and it relates to things that are yet in the future. It is a thing in which the Gods in the eternal worlds are interested, and all the ancient Patriarch and Prophets that have lived upon the earth are all interested in the work in which we are engaged. There is a Priesthood in the heavens, and we have the same Priesthood on the earth, but there should be a closer communion between the Priesthood on the earth and the Priesthood in the heavens; it is desirable that we should be brought into closer proximity, we want to be advancing as Enoch advanced.

18. After the appearance of Jesus upon the earth, there was to be a certain power who would make war with the Saints and prevail against them; and it is said, "they shall be given into His hands until a time and times and the dividing of time:" (Daniel vii, 25:) but in this day we are told that "the Saints of the Most High shall take the kingdom, and possess the kingdom for ever, even for ever and ever," (18 verse).

19. You and I may violate our covenants; you and I may trample upon the principles of the Gospel, and violate the order of the Priesthood and the commands of God; but among the hosts of Israel there will be thousands and tens of thousands who will be true to the principles of truth, and God in the heavens, the holy angels and the ancient Priesthood that now live where God lives are

all united together, for the accomplishment of this purpose. The Lord will roll forth His purposes in His own way and in His own time. And having thus organized, as I before stated, it is not for us to act as we may think individually, but as God shall dictate.

20. We have a regular order in the Church. You brethren, who hold the holy Priesthood, understand these things. Has God not given to every man a portion of His Spirit to profit withal? Yes. Has He not done more than this to the saints who are true and faithful? Has He not given to them the gift of the Holy Ghost? He has, and they know it and realize it. They are brought into communion with each other, and into communion with God and the heavenly hosts. But having this Spirit do we need others to guide us? Yes, all the time. Why? Because of the powers of darkness, the influence of Satan and the weakness of human nature. We need watchmen upon the towers of Zion, who are on the alert to look after the interests of Israel, and see that God's people do not go astray. Hence it becomes the duty of the Teachers to look after the people, to see that there is no hard feeling, no covetousness, no fraud, no adultery, no iniquity of any kind; but that purity, holiness and righteousness prevail among those that they preside over. And how far does this extend? To every place where there is a ward or a portion of a ward—to the utmost extremity. It may be compared unto the body—from the head to the feet, from the toes to the fingers, and to every other part.

21. All the officers necessary for the work of the ministry are to be found in the Church, and everything has been organized according to the order of God. Are any of these men who are called to presiding positions autocrats—men who exercise undue authority over the feelings and associations of their fellow man? No. Have any of them the right to disregard the feelings of their brethren, trample them under foot, and act as tyrants? No. Have the Apostles, or High Priests, or Seventies, or Elders, any such right? No. Brother Cannon will read an extract from the Book of Doctrine and Covenants, on this question.

22. President George Q. Cannon then read as follows from Section 121, of the Book of Doctrine and Covenants—

23. "Behold, there are many called, but few are chosen. And why are they not chosen?

24. "Because their hearts are set so much upon the things of this world, and aspire to the honors of men, that they do not learn this one lesson—

25. "That the rights of the Priesthood are inseparably connected with the powers of heaven, and that the powers of heaven cannot be controlled nor handled only upon the principle of righteousness.

26. "That they may be conferred upon us, it is true; but when we undertake to cover our sins, or to gratify our pride, our vain ambition, or to exercise control, or dominion, or compulsion, upon the souls of the children of men, in any degree of unrighteousness, behold, the heavens withdraw themselves; the Spirit of the Lord is grieved; and when it is withdrawn, Amen to the Priesthood, or the authority of that man.

27. "Behold! ere he is aware, he is left unto himself, to kick against the pricks; to persecute the Saints, and to fight against God.

28. "We have learned, by sad experience, that it is the nature and disposition of almost all men, as soon as they get a little authority, as they suppose, they will immediately begin to exercise unrighteous dominion.

29. "Hence many are called, but few are chosen.

30. "No power or influence can or ought to be maintained by virtue of the Priesthood, only by persuasion, by long suffering, by gentleness, and meekness, and by love unfeigned.

31. "By kindness, and pure knowledge, which shall greatly enlarge the soul without hypocrisy, and without guile.

32. "Reproving betimes with sharpness, when moved upon by the Holy Ghost, and then showing forth afterwards an increase of love toward him whom thou hast reproved, lest he esteem thee to be his enemy.

33. "That he may know that thy faithfulness is stronger than the cords of death.

34. "Let thy bowels also be full of charity towards all men, and to the household of faith, and let virtue garnish thy thoughts unceasingly, then shall thy confidence wax strong in the presence of God, and the doctrine of the Priesthood shall distill upon thy soul as the dews from heaven.

35. "The Holy Ghost shall be thy constant companion, and thy scepter an unchanging scepter of righteousness and truth, and thy dominion shall be an everlasting dominion, and without compulsory means it shall flow unto thee for ever and ever."

36. President Taylor continuing his remarks said: We have many specimens of the characters referred to in this revelation read by Brother Cannon. These things continue to exist more or less. Some people are very desirous sometimes to instruct me about how I ought to manipulate and manage affairs. Well, if they were set as my instructors I should be much pleased to get all the information I could from them, and I would be pleased to get information from the humblest person in existence—if it was information. Among other things I find that a good many begin to think that we are very much persecuted and proscribed in our marital relations, according to the revelations which God has given us, and there is sometimes a little trembling in the knees. I am pleased there is not much of it, but there is a little once in a while. Sometimes I get advice from outsiders, from the newspapers, etc., and sometimes from some of our brethren, (but from very few of our brethren) in relation to these matters.

37. God has given us a revelation in regard to celestial marriage. I did not make it. He has told us certain things pertaining to this matter, and they would like us to tone that principle down and change it and make it applicable to the views of the day. This we cannot do; nor can we interfere with any of the commands of God to meet the persuasions or behests of men. I cannot do it, and will not do it.

38. I find some men try to twist round the principle in any way and every way they can. They want to sneak out of it in some way. Now God don't want any kind of sycophancy like that. He expects that we will be true to Him, and to the principles He has developed, and to feel as Job did—"Though He slay me, yet will I trust in Him." Though other folks would slay us, yet we will trust in the living God and be true to our covenants and to our God. These are my feelings in relation to that matter. We have also been told that "it is not mete that men who will not abide my law shall preside over my

Priesthood," and yet some people would like very much to do it. Well, they cannot do it; because if we are here, as I said before, to do the will of our Father who sent us, and He has told us what to do, we will do it, in the name of Israel's God—and all who sanction it say Amen—[the vast congregation responded with a loud "Amen."]—and those that don't may say what they please. [Laughter.] If God has introduced something for our glory and exaltation, we are not going to have that kicked over by any improper influence, either inside or outside of the Church of the living God. We will stand by the principles of eternal truth; living we will proclaim them, and dying we will be true to them, and after death will live again in their enjoyment in the eternal worlds. That is my feeling; so I don't feel very trembly in the knees, and I do not think you do, generally.

39. I see sometimes a disposition to try to ignore some of the laws which God has introduced, and this is one of them. People want to slip round a corner, or creep out in some way. There is something very creepy about it. There was a man in former times we are told, came to Jesus by night. His name was Nicodemus. He was one of those persons who did not like the daylight. I have known some people who would want to be baptized in the evening, or get into some corner that they might not be seen. Well, there is not much to such folks. Jesus was very unpopular, quite as unpopular as we are, in His day. Nicodemus was a prominent man among the Jews, and he thought it might injure his reputation if he was seen visiting that Nazarene, to get instruction from Him, so he crawled in at night. Jesus talked quite plainly to him, as you can read for yourselves; but we find some folks of a similar kind now creeping around. They have not the manhood to stand true to their colors and to their God.

40. Some folks think that we polygamists are very much indebted to our brethren who are monogamists to help to steady the ark, (God save the mark!)—(Laughter.)—to help to save us, and that we need such men in the Legislature, etc., and to fill our various offices. Well, I won't tell you all I think about some of these things, but I do think we are all of us dependent upon God our

Heavenly Father, and if He don't take care of us we shall not be taken care of; if His arm is not extended in our behalf we shall have a poor showing; but if God is with us, we ask no odds of the world, for He governs the destinies of the human family. He puts down one man and exalts another. He dethrones one king or president as the case may be, and sets up another, and He rules as He pleases among the nations of the earth and all the children of men, although they don't know it. We live in Him, we move in Him, we have our being from Him. We are not dependent very much upon the monogamists about any of these things. You need not plume yourselves very much in these matters; and I will tell you, if you want to get along smoothly, you had better find among your various neighbors, when you have some matter of difficulty to settle, some of these polygamists and ask a little counsel at their hands. They will be able to advise you about many things, especially if they are men of God, humble men, living their religion and keeping the commandments of God.

41. There are some few things I have been reflecting about, and have noted them down, and I think I shall read them now.

42. The distinction being made between Polygamy and Prostitution:

43. 1st. Congress made a law which would affect both; and cohabitation with more than one woman was made a crime whether in polygamy or out of polygamy.

44. 2nd. The Governor turned legislator, added to this law, and inserted in a test oath to officials, the following words regarding cohabitation, "in the marriage relation;" thus plainly and definitely sanctioning prostitution, without any law of the United States, or any authority.

45. 3rd. The United States Commissioners, also, without legislation, adopted the action of the Governor, and still insisted on this interpolation, in the test oath in election matters, and placed all polygamists under this unconstitutional oath, and released prostitutes and their paramours from the obligations placed upon others.

46. 4th. The Prosecuting Attorney has sanctioned these things, and pursued a similar course; and while he has asked all the "Mormon" jurors certain questions pertain-

ing to their religious faith in the doctrines of the "Mormon" Church, and challenged them if they answered affirmatively as to their belief in polygamy, he has declined to ask other jurors whether they believed in prostitution, or whether they believed in cohabiting with more than one woman or not.

47. 5th. Chief Justice Zane when appealed to on this question refused to interfere, or give any other ruling, and thus aided in packing the jury.

48. Thus a law was first passed by Congress, which has been perverted by the administration, by all its officers who have officiated in this Territory, and made to subserve the interests of a party who have placed in their political platform an Anti-Mormon plank; and have clearly proven that there is a combination in all the officers of State, officiating in this Territory, to back up this political intrigue in the interest of party, and at the sacrifice of law, equity, jurisprudence and all the safeguards that are provided by the Constitution for the protection of human rights.

49. These are some points that are of considerable importance. Similar things have been exhibited in former times—an animus, a united operation against justice, equity and law, and, in our case, against the Constitution of the United States, and the rights and privileges and immunities of the Latter-day Saints. A law was framed professedly in the interest of purity and virtue. When it got here it was perverted and made to subserve the interest of prostitution and prostitutes; and the lowest class of men, who violate their marital relations, and trample under foot all principles of virtue and integrity, can go on our juries, can vote at the polls, through the intrigues of corrupt men; and they thus try to shackle a free people, bring them into bondage, and make slaves of them, unless they will bow to their infernal behests, and in the name of Israel's God we will not do it. [The congregation responded with a loud Amen.] We are not going to elevate prostitutes and men who violate their marital relations above men and women who are virtuous, honorable and upright. These are my feelings, and I am not afraid to proclaim them to the world. So much for these things.

50. Do we want a class of men along with us that will submit to these kind of things, and are we to share in this hypocrisy, this infamy and degradation? What mean these dens in our city that are introduced by our Christian friends—dens of infamy, dens of prostitution, gambling holes, houses of assignation, dram-shops, etc.? They are to cater to the virtuous (?) feelings of these honorable, high-minded, pure reformers that have come among us—(Laughter)—or what are they for? They are sanctioned, I am ashamed to say by the officers of government, and protected in their libidinous and degrading pursuits.

51. How was it some time ago when the Edmunds Law was first introduced? A son of Mayor Little was one of the election registrars. His father some years ago had had two wives—I am sorry to say he has not got them now, they are dead—and because some years before any law of this kind was in operation in the United States he had practiced plural marriage, his son was obliged to tell his father that he could not register. Shortly afterwards a notorious courtesan known as Kate Flint, with some of the inmates of her bagnio, drove up and requested to be registered. "Why, of course." And this same gentleman that could not register his honorable father, who had never violated any law of the United States, had to endure the mortification of taking the names of these others and placing them on the list as respectable voters in our midst! About this time another non-Mormon came along to one of the other registration officers, and on partly reading the oath—this test oath that had been prescribed—said, "I am afraid I can't take that?" "Why can't you take it?" Well, he was an honest man among the Gentiles; he did not like to forswear himself; so he said, "I have a wife, and then I keep a mistress." "Oh, well," says the man, "read on a little further." He read on until he came to the words, "in the marriage relation." "Oh, well, yes, I can take that," he said, and registered. These are facts that are stuck before our noses here in the City of Salt Lake by the officials sent among us, and who are instructed particularly to look after our morals.

52. So much, then, for such affairs. Now, do we want affiliation or association with such practices and principles as these? God forbid. And we want no falterers in our

ranks. What shall we do? Live our religion, be true to our covenants, and keep the commandments of God. What shall the Presidents of Stakes do? Look after our Stakes, and if you find adulterers or adulteresses among you, don't permit them to go into the temples of God; for we won't have such people; they cannot be sanctioned by us, nor have our fellowship. We will not have them; the world may take the strumpets; they may wallow in their filth, but we will not have our holy places polluted by people calling themselves Latter-day Saints, who indulge in these abominable practices; we will not have them; and anybody who permits them to go into these holy places will have to be responsible for it. Many Bishops do it, they will be held responsible. Therefore, be careful, you Presidents of Stakes and you Bishops, how you act, and look well after your people, for be it understood that before our Lord Jesus Christ shall come, "righteousness shall go before Him and shall set us in the way of his steps." (Psalms lxxxv, 13.) We are preparing ourselves to build up a Zion of God, and these people, whoremasters and whores, liars and hypocrites, will never get into the city of the living God, they will be found outside the gates.

53. Now, have I any ill feelings towards these people that persecute and proscribe us? No. I would do them good for evil, give blessings for curses; I would treat them well, treat them honorably. Let us be men of truth, honor and integrity; men that will swear to our own hurt and change not; men whose word will be our everlasting bond. If you see men hungry, feed them, no matter who they are: white, black, or red, Jew, Gentile or Mormon, or anybody else—feed them. If you see men naked, clothe them. If you see men sick, administer to them, and learn to be kind to all men; but partake not of their evil practices. "O my soul, come not thou into their secret; unto their assembly, mine honor, be not thou united." We are trying to raise up a people that shall be men of God, men of truth, men of integrity, men of virtue, men who will be fit to associate with the Gods in the eternal worlds.

54. We are accused on being corrupt, degraded, low and debauched. Who by? By people, as I will show who are ten times as degraded, ten times as debauched, ten times as low and guilty of ten-fold more crime than we are. These are our professed reformers. I speak of these things therefore in our defense, and were we not accused by men void of honor and principle, I never would broach such a subject; for, I do not delight to dwell on the infamies, the corruptions and abominations of the world. I would rather speak of their good qualities and honorable principles, and I am thankful to say that there are thousands and tens of thousands and millions in these United States and in other nations who look with contempt upon all the chicanery, deception and fraud, whether of a moral, social, political, legislative, or judicial character; thousands and millions of men; I see many of them, very many of them, who pass through here, men of note, of position in society from the United States, and from the different nations who call upon me from time to time, and express their sentiments pertaining to these matters. In order to sustain what I say, I will have Brother Cannon read over some statistics in regard to crime. We are, as I have said, represented as a very bad people, and I want to show a comparison between us and our reformers, or those that profess to be our reformers in relation to these matters.

55. President Cannon then read the following, being the criminal statistics for the year 1883.

56. "The population of Utah may be estimated at 160,000 in 1883.

57. "Of these say 130,000 were Mormons, and 30,000 Gentiles, a very liberal estimate of the latter.

58. "In this year there were 46 persons sent to the Penitentiary convicted of crime. Of these 33 were non-Mormons, and 13 reputed Mormons.

59. "At the above estimate of population the ratio or percentage would be one prisoner to every 10,000 Mormons, or one hundredth of one per cent, and of the Gentiles one convict in every 909, or about one ninth of one per cent. So that the actual proportion of criminals is more than ten times greater among the Gentiles of Utah, with the above very liberal estimate, than among the Mormons.

60. "It is urged that these non-Mormon prisoners are not a fair representation of the

average of crime throughout the country, but are the result of the flow of the desperate classes westward to the borders of civilization; with greater truth we reply that the Mormon prisoners are not representatives of Mormonism, nor the results of Mormonism, but of the consequences of a departure from Mormon principles; and of the 13 prisoners classed as "Mormons," the greater portion were only so by family connection or association:

Arrests in Salt Lake City, 1883:

| Mormons | 150 |
| Non-Mormons | 1,559 |

or more than ten times the number of Mormon arrests.

61. "Again, it is estimated that there are 6,000 non-Mormons, and 19,000 Mormons in Salt Lake City, which shows of Mormon one arrest in 126 2-3.

62. "Non-Mormons one arrest in a fraction less than every four, or rather more than twenty-five per cent."

63. As I have said before, (continued President Taylor,) if we were not on the defensive in this case, I would say nothing about these things; but it ill becomes men who have got ten criminals to our one to come here as our reformers, and try to disfranchise men who are ten times as good as they are. These are facts that are not of my getting up. They come from the public records and can be verified by the prison and other statistics. And the question is, how much of that rule do we want here?

64. The questionable honor is reserved to these advocates of "advanced high moral ideas" to trample upon all judicial precedents. It was not enough that an insignificant minority should have more than an equal showing with the majority, being equal in numbers in the drawing to make up a venire. It was not enough that every Mormon was questioned as to his religious faith, and that no Gentile was. It was not enough that all "Mormons" were excluded from this so-called "impartial grand jury," and that their avowed enemies were to be their judges. It is not enough that our people must be tried by men whose average record shows them to be ten times their inferiors as law abiding citizens; but not having enough men to pack this "impartial grand jury" according to the provisions of law, under the guise of virtue, and in the name of morality and justice, edicts are issued to the officers to go into the purlieus of the city and gather up ad libitum from among the gutter snipes creatures to form "a jury of the peers" of the accused with which to persecute and prosecute honorable men and women.

65. These are things we object to, and I wish our brethren and sisters to be informed in regard to these matters, that they may have a correct estimate of the position that we occupy pertaining thereto. We cannot respect and esteem such operations, and while we are desirous to place ourselves in conformity with all law, all order and all correct principle, yet we despise in our hearts this chicanery, hypocrisy, fraud and deception. But do we expect to see such things? Yes. Are we surprised at it? No. Why? Because we have been told over and over again, and the Elders have preached over and over again, and the Prophets have prophesied of it over and over again, that the world will grow worse and worse, deceiving and being deceived.

66. Who is it that embarks in these things? It is the corrupt, the ungodly, the debauchee, the adulterer, the liar, the men who violate every principle of honor, truth and integrity, and who are enemies to this nation, and the same class of people are enemies to any nation. They are laying the ax at the root of the tree of liberty, and trying to overturn the freedom of man, and to place free men in bondage, a thing no honorable man would condescend to for a moment. And there are many in this city who despise these things as they do the gates of hell, who are not associated with us in a religious capacity, many honorable men who have feelings of this kind, and then there are tens of thousands in the United States who possess the same feelings and the same abhorrence of this corruption, degradation and infamy that is sought to be palmed upon us. But while we can estimate these things at their worth, we can also estimate the actions of honorable men who are not of us at their true worth.

67. Because a man is not a believer in our doctrines, that is no reason why he should not be an honorable man, for there are thou-

sands and millions of them: it would be a pity if they were in the same condition as the others. But we as a people have to defend ourselves against the aggressions of an unscrupulous enemy who is instigated by the power of the adversary to overturn and destroy the truth today as he has done in other ages, in other nations and among other peoples. Therefore it becomes us to look well after our affairs, and protect ourselves as best we may from the calumnies, the reproach, and the infamies that are sought to be foisted upon us by an ungodly, hypocritical and corrupt people.

68.Now, having got through with this, I want to refer to something else. It has been stated that the reason why we have so many of these criminals is because that the scum of society from the eastern States floats out here, and that therefore a rough, uncouth, lawless class finds its way into this community. Now, I want something read to you about some of these so called virtuous people in the east.

69.President Cannon again read as follows:

70."Dr. Nathan Allen, of Lowell, has declared in a paper read before a late meeting of the American Social Science Association, that "nowhere in the history of the world was the practice of abortion so common as in this country; and he gave expression to the opinion that, in New England alone, many thousands of abortions are procured annually."

71."Dr. Reamy, of the Ohio State Medical Society, says: "From a very large verbal and written correspondence in this and other States, together with personal investigation and facts accumulated * * that we have become a nation of murderers."

72.The Rev. Dr. Eddy writes to the Christian Advocate regarding one little village of 1,000 inhabitants: "Yet here, and elsewhere, 15 per cent of wives have the criminal hardihood to practice this black art, there is a still large and additional per cent who endorse and defend it. * * Among married persons, so extensive has this practice become, that people of high repute not only commit this crime, but do not shun to speak boastingly among their intimates of the deed and the means of accomplishing it."

73."Dr. Allen further states: "Examining the number of deaths, we find that there are absolutely more deaths than births among the strictly American children, so that aside from immigration and births of children of foreign parentage, the population of Massachusetts is rapidly decreasing. * * The birth rate in the State of New York, shows the same fact, that American families do not increase at all, and inspection of the registration in other States shows the same remark applies to all."

74."Bishop Coxe, of the Protestant Episcopal Church of New York, in a pastoral letter to his people, writes: "I have heretofore warned my flock against the blood guiltiness of ante natal infanticide. If any doubts existed heretofore as to the propriety of my warnings on this subject, they must now disappear before the fact that the world itself is beginning to be horrified by the practical results of the sacrifices to Moloch which defile our land. Again I warn you that they who do such things cannot inherit eternal life. If there be a special damnation for those who shed innocent blood, what must be the portion of those who have no mercy upon their own flesh."

75."Dr. Cowan, M. D., writing on what he styles "The Murder of the Unborn," says: "That this crime is not only wide spread on this great continent, but is rapidly on the increase, we have the testimony of physicians, whose investigations have been thorough, and whose social standing and sincerity cannot be questioned."

76.President Taylor continuing said: These are the people that are coming here to reform us, and are so disgusted with our corruptions. Yet I am pleased to find that there are, once in a while, men who have the courage to speak against these damning evils. Bishop Coxe, of the Episcopal Church, is one of these men, and I honor such men whenever I hear of them, and should be glad at all times to extend to them all courtesies possible. Dr. Allen and Dr. Ready are inspired, it seems, by the same detestation of these hellish, these fiendish, these outrageous acts. Yet from these people come our reformers, who are so horrified at the evils they see in Utah. But fortunately, the bed is too short, they cannot stretch themselves on it; and the covering is too narrow and too contracted, it will not cover them, and their evils and abominations crop out on every side, and they become their own accusers.

77. It is their own statements that I have had read to you this morning. I am sorry to know that these things are as they are; but these are facts, and we do not feel very much honored with the association of such people. We do feel honored always to associate with honorable men and women; but with the seducer, with harlots, with thieves, with murderers of the innocents, no! never! no never! We want no association with them. As it is stated here by one of these reverend gentlemen in the East, speaking of these things, no murderer hath eternal life in him, nor no murderesses have eternal life in them.

78. I have had these things read to you for two reasons: First, to show the corruption that exists among these so-called virtuous people, honorable people, pure people, who are so shocked at the atrocities that take place in Utah. Another reason is that I want to warn our brethren and sisters against these infamies, and against permitting these filthy wretches to come into their houses. They are too low, too debased, too corrupt; and I speak of it because I know what I am talking about; there are some of these people crawling around us like so many vipers, and insinuating their hellish, murderous practices into the families of some who call themselves Latter-day Saints.

79. Woe! to such Saints. You cannot have a place among us. No woman murderer, no man murderer can have a place among the Latter-day Saints, and I speak of it that the Presidents of Stakes and the Bishops may be apprised of these things. And some of these people would try to pass by the Bishops, and then by the Presidents of Stakes, and then by the President of the Church, and crawl with all their slime and damnable hypocrisy into the Temples of the living God. They may pass by these, but they will have to pass by the angels and the Gods, before they get through, and they will never inherit the Kingdom of God. Hear it you sisters! Hear it you brethren! Hear it you Bishops, and you Presidents of Stakes? Watch well and know well what you are doing, when you sign recommends for doubtful characters to go into these holy places. We do not want them there. It is not their place, and you will have to account for your acts if you permit these things knowingly. It is necessary that you should be particular about these matters, for you will have to answer for your doings as I have for mine. We cannot, because of relationship, because somebody is a cousin, or an uncle, or an aunt, or a brother, or a sister, or a son or a daughter, or a father or a mother—we cannot admit and will not admit them to any of these holy places unless they are worthy. I call upon you if you know of adulterers or adulteresses, or people that practice these unnatural infamies, to sever them from the Church; they shall not have a place in the Church and Kingdom of God.

80. Mr. Murray here, and others, may make laws and test oaths, with provisions in them to screen the adulterer, the whoremonger, and the seducer; but we will tear that away from our people, and all such shall have no place with Israel, and all who are in favor of it, signify it by saying "Aye." (The congregation responded with a loud "Aye.") These are our feelings, and it is some of these things which has led me to talk as plainly as I have done in regard to some of these other matters. I wanted to present the contrast so plainly before you that he that runneth might read. Enough of this, however, for the present:

Handle it carefully.
Deal with it gently,
Speak of it tenderly,
Poor Justice is blind.

ADDRESS 32

Due to the question over the legality of polygamy and the desire of certain Federal officials to imprison, prosecute, and/or otherwise hound church leaders into compliance with questionable civil law, many of the Brethren, notably members of the First Presidency (Joseph F. Smith fled to Hawaii) were forced to go underground to avoid any public appearance. Unable to attend the 55th Annual General Conference of The Church of Jesus Christ of Latter-day Saints, President John Taylor issued the following epistle which was read on the opening day of General Conference by Elder B. F. Cummings, Jr. on April 4, 1885. As a number of the Brethren were having the same difficulty with the law, it was thought advisable to hold conference in Logan, Utah, rather than in Salt Lake City.

EPISTLE of The First Presidency to the Officers and Members of the Church of Jesus Christ of Latter-day Saints in Conference assembled:

BELOVED BRETHREN AND SISTERS:

1. It is eminently proper, under the circumstances, not being able to be with you in person at our Annual Conference, that we should address you a few lines and express to you our faith, feelings and hopes concerning the great work of our God in which we are all mutually interested. Never at any time in our lives have we had more joy and satisfaction in the Gospel, and in the labors thereof, than we have at the present time. Profoundly grateful to our God for His kindness to us in permitting us to have a name and a place among His people, and to be the bearers of His everlasting Priesthood, we are determined with His help to press forward with increased diligence and zeal in doing our part towards the carrying on of His purposes and work. We see His hand marvelously manifested in behalf of His people. We know that His power is with us, that His angels have charge concerning us, and that no affliction can fall upon any one, however humble, without it being fully known to Him. This knowledge that God is near to us, and hears and answers our prayers, is an unceasing cause of thankfulness and praise.

2. For a wise purpose in His providence He permits the wicked, in the exercise of their agency, from time to time to afflict His followers. Since the days of our father Adam this has always been the case, and it will continue to be, so long as Satan has any power over the hearts of the children of men. We are all children of the same Great Parent, and each one has the opportunity and privilege granted to him or her to exercise his or her agency. We have chosen to serve the God of Israel. We have submitted to His laws, have obeyed His Gospel, and have chosen the path which He assures us will bring us into His presence. Others of His children prefer a different course. They yield to a different influence, and, under its power, they seek to destroy the work of God and all who are connected with it. This they can do in the exercise of the agency which the Father has given unto them. Not only in times past, but in our own day, the wicked have persecuted, tormented and murdered the Saints of God. But, while in so doing, they bring upon themselves everlasting condemnation, their acts are overruled for the glory and exaltation of His faithful people, and the accomplishment of His purposes in the redemption of the earth.

3. For a few months past we have seen in these valleys an exhibition of this deadly hostility against the Latter-day Saints. We need not enumerate to you all these acts of oppression and wrong. You are familiar with them. But the best men in the community, men of pure lives, men who have set an example to the people ever since they came to these mountains, and in all their days, who have led in works of righteousness, who have been citizens of the highest type of character, have been selected as victims of a vile persecution, and been assailed and denounced as criminals of the lowest grade. Juries have been selected for the express purpose of convicting men who are prominent in the Church; and their partisan bias has become

so thoroughly known in the community, that
the common expression is, that an accusation in
the courts, as now constituted, is equivalent to
a conviction. The rule of jurisprudence which
has come down for ages past has been, that the
accused shall be deemed innocent until proved
guilty. In our courts, we are sorry to say, this
has been reversed. The burden of proof has
rested upon the accused in almost every
instance—the judge, the jury, equally with the
prosecution, appearing to view him as guilty,
and that it was his duty to furnish all the proof
necessary to exculpate him from the accusation
of guilt. Among all the English-speaking people, and for ages past, the jury has been looked
upon as the palladium of human liberty. It has
been the richest fruit of our civilization. No
greater guarantee of fairness could be imagined
by our ancestors than that a man accused of
crime should have his case submitted to the
judgment of his peers—his neighbors living in
the vicinage and presumably acquainted with
his life, and with the motives which may have
prompted him to commit the crime of which he
was accused. The wisdom of man has failed to
devise fairer or more just means than this of
deciding upon their fellowman's guilt or innocence when accused. But in this Judicial
District, for a long period past, we do not know
of a jury that has been thus constituted. Jurors
have been selected for their known enmity to
the parties accused, or to the principle involved
in the trial.

4. The result has been that a Latter-day
Saint would almost be as safe in seeking for
justice in the infernal regions, or at the hands
of Algerian pirates, as in courts of this character. Indictments have been found against different parties upon the flimsiest evidence, and
in some instances upon evidence which would
have no weight with any fair-minded jury. The
result has been that a reign of judicial terror
has prevailed and still prevails in these valleys.
Seeing no prospect of fair trial, men have
deemed it better to avoid arrest for a season, or
until there was a prospect of receiving impartial treatment by the courts and juries.
Prosecution has degenerated into persecution.
A law which is in and of itself, as we believe,
unconstitutional, and aimed at the practice of
religion, and so viewed by a number of our
leading statesmen in Congress, is taken advantage of and carried to lengths probably never

dreamed of by many of the men who voted for
it. We have sometimes thought that it was
impossible for men to indulge in such vindictive feelings as have been manifested here; but
in searching for a cause we have been forced
to the conclusion that these violent prosecutions were only intended to provoke the people
to commit some overt act whereby the incom-
ing administration might be embarrassed.

5. Permit us to refer to our own cases.
President John Taylor, at the beginning of this
year, hearing of the persecution to which our
brethren were subjected in Arizona, determined
to visit that region, in company with a number
of the Elders. His object in going there was to
visit with and, as far as possible, comfort the
Saints. Five of our co-religionists had under-
gone a form of trial, a travesty of justice, and
three of them had been sent, under a sentence
of imprisonment of three and a half years and
$500 fine each, to what may be rightly termed
the American Siberia, upwards of 2,000 miles
distant from their own homes the House of
Correction at Detroit. The other two had been
sentenced to six months' imprisonment and
$500 fine in the Territorial Penitentiary at
Yuma. Every member of our Church was
shocked at these outrageous proceedings. For,
while all were prepared to endure the legal consequences of the violation of the Edmunds
Law, they were not prepared for such gross and
tyrannical perversions of the law as were
involved in these sentences. No man who could
by any possibility be accused, any longer dared
to submit his case to such treatment. Many of
them, therefore, left their homes, to seek in a
foreign land that freedom from persecution
which was denied them in their own.

6. It was under these circumstances that
President Taylor, and the company of Elders
referred to, visited Arizona. Upon his return,
and while at San Francisco, he received
telegrams informing him that it was unsafe for
him to come back to Salt Lake City.
Disregarding these, however, he did return,
and publicly attended to his business for some
time; in the meanwhile delivering a discourse
to the Saints in the Tabernacle. Seeing, however, how determined certain Federal officers
here were to embarrass, arrest and place under
bonds every prominent man, and being
informed of threats made against his own liberty, he deemed it wise, under the circum-

stances, to withdraw for awhile to attend to his business in a more private manner than he had been in the habit of doing in his public office. This he has continued to do up to the present writing, receiving and answering letters, giving counsel and instruction, and devoting himself assiduously to all the duties of his calling, except in delivering public addresses from the stand. Neither he, President George Q. Cannon nor President Joseph F. Smith, have had any official notification or reliable information from any officer of the court that process of any kind has been issued against them; at the same time their residences, especially that of Brother Joseph F. Smith, have been invaded and searched, and the Marshal, his deputies and their spotters and spies have displayed a zeal to ascertain the whereabouts of the First Presidency, that has led to the conclusion that they wished to get them into their power and place them under arrest. And not only this anxiety was manifested in their cases, but President Woodruff and several of the Twelve Apostles, besides numbers of other leading men, have been threatened and sought for with assiduity.

7. In England, upon one occasion, the eloquent Lord Chatham said, in speaking of the rights of the subject, that man's house was his castle; that though it might be so poor that the rains of heaven could penetrate it, and the winds beat through its crevices, yet the King of England himself could not cross its threshold without its owner's permission.

8. A recent illustration of the zeal of these officials and their creatures has come to light in the case of President George Q. Cannon, who has just returned from the East. The railroads and highways have been swarming with Deputy Marshals and their myrmidons to intercept and arrest him. We have yet to learn that it has become necessary for honorable gentlemen in America to report themselves to courts, Marshals, or any civil officer, when they leave home on business, or to ask for passports or to have them vised.

9. The question has been asked us, how long we intend to pursue this course. In answer we say, that at no time during our existence have we ever shrunk from the investigation of our conduct, our utterances or of our lives by any fair tribunal. We have lived under the gaze of the public, and where every act

and expression could be scrutinized. We are as ready today, as ever, to submit our cases to a properly organized court and jury of our peers to decide upon. So confident are we of our innocence of alleged wrong-doing, that we entertain no fears of the result of such a trial. We are willing to meet the issue at any moment. We are fully conscious of our innocence of all violation of the laws of God or of Constitutional laws enacted by man. But if there are laws made to entrap us, because of our belief in and practice of the revelations which God has given to His Church, which a court and jury shall decide we have violated, we desire at least that it shall be upon what all the world calls good evidence and substantial proof, and not upon religious prejudice, and through a determination to convict and punish, evidence or no evidence. We ought, at least, to have the same rights that burglars, thieves and murderers are accorded under the law. In that case, should conviction follow, we should submit to it as martyrs have submitted in every age when God has had a people upon the earth, as persecution inflicted upon us for our adherence to His laws.

10. Our faith and practice for which we are sought to be condemned and punished, is the faith and practice of the best and holiest of God's children. If we are sinners in this respect, then Abraham, who is distinguished by the Lord himself as the friend of God, was a sinner. If we are sinners, then Jacob and Moses and Elkanah, Solomon and David, and a host of others too numerous to mention, were also sinners. Even Jesus himself, the Being whom we adore as our Redeemer and the Author of our salvation, called the Eternal Father whom He worshipped, and whom we are commanded to worship, the God of Abraham, Isaac and Jacob, showing that the God of heaven himself attached no condemnation to these men for their practice of patriarchal marriage, but in many instances commanded it, provided laws for its arrangement, and called those who practiced it His friends and men after His own heart. And, what is still more worthy of remark, that in choosing a lineage from which His beloved Son Jesus should descend, He chose a lineage distinguished in the earth among all nations as polygamic. The most renowned ancestors of the Savior of the world, and to whom He most

frequently alluded, were polygamists. Can, therefore, our belief in and practice of this system of marriage be as wrong as our opponents would have it appear? When this noble array of God's favorite children are remembered, and when, in addition, we call to mind the fact that the Bible itself, which has given to the Christian world all the knowledge it has of God and godliness, has principally, under God, polygamists as its authors.

11. It is averred by some of our enemies that this is not religion. This is not the view, however, of the members of the Utah Commission, for they have said: "This article of faith is as much as essential and substantial part of their creed as their belief in baptism, repentance for the forgiveness of sins, and the like." And again: "All orthodox Mormons believe polygamy to be right, and that it is an essential part of their creed.

12. It has also been alleged to Congress, by those who take pleasure in denouncing our system of marriage, that the English government in India has put down the Suttee, and that, therefore, the United States ought to put down plural marriage. If those generable Solons had made themselves a little more acquainted with the action of the Imperial Government of Great Britain, they would have found that, while that government put down widow burning, it protects by law, in all their rights, privileges and franchises, 180,000,000 of polygamists, and places them on an equal footing with others.

13. The Lord has revealed to us by His special revelations, as clearly and positively as He ever did to any of the ancient Prophets, certain principles associated with the eternity of the marriage covenant, has given definite commands pertaining thereto, and made them obligatory upon us to carry out. He has made manifest to us those great and eternal principles which bind woman to man and man to woman, children to parents and parents to children, and has called upon us in the most emphatic and pointed manner to obey them. These glorious principles involve our dearest interests and associations in time and throughout the eternity's that are to come. We are told that this is His everlasting covenant, and that it has existed from eternity; and, furthermore, that all covenants that relate only to time shall be dissolved at death and he no longer binding upon the human family. He

has, moreover, told us that if we do not obey those principles we shall be damned. Believing these principles to be of God and from God, we have entered into eternal covenants with our wives under the most solemn promises and in the most sacred manner.

14. Among the rights guaranteed to us in the Constitution of the United States is not only that "Congress shall make no law respecting an establishment of religion or prohibiting the free exercise thereof," but that no State shall enact any "law impairing the obligation of contracts." Ours are contracts of a most sacred character, and of such vital importance for time and eternity, that all worldly obligations and contracts sink into insignificance in comparison with them.

15. Among many of the professors of modern Christianity this is looked upon as an error, and without inspiration or revelation on this subject, all the idea that is ever presented associated with the marital relations, is that they enter into these contracts "until death do them part." The beauties, the glories and perpetuity of those domestic ties, those endearing associations which cluster around the family organization, perish whenever the grim messenger Death approaches. It is now made a crime by uninspired men to possess those hopes and practice those principles which the most virtuous, upright, holy and eminent men of God have esteemed as treasures beyond price. Under an infatuated, mistaken and suicidal policy they seek to blast those hopes which are a solace to the life of the believer in the revelations of God, and to sever those connubial ties which bud in time and will blossom and bear fruit in the Celestial Kingdom of our God in the eternities to come.

16. The Christianity of today cannot offer us anything of an eternal character to compensate us for the abandonment of the truth which is demanded of us. The fact is, mankind, in their endeavor to correct God's system of marriage, have adopted a system which is entirely inadequate to save man from the dreadful evils by which he is surrounded. While there are thousands and millions of honorable, upright men in the world, who have devoted their entire lives to the promotion of mortality and virtue, and the extirpation of every sinful practice, the evils against which they battled have steadily increased

around them. The system which they taught was not God's system; it did not, therefore, meet man's wants. Those channels which God has provided for the lawful exercise of the appetites with which He has endowed man, under the system now in vogue, have been dammed up, and the history of Christendom informs us with what terrible results the degradation and prostitution of woman, and the spread of the most terrible scourge known to humanity, the social evil, with its attendant train of loathsome horrors. With our knowledge of God's laws we never can adopt such a system and call it civilization.

17. And we again take this opportunity of warning the Latter-day Saints against those murderous and damning practices of foeticide and infanticide, to introduce which in our midst attempts have been made. These practices are also the horrible fruits of a man-made system of marriage, and so terrible have they become, that many of the leading thinkers of the East have told their people, and brought statistics to prove, that unless these crimes are stopped, it will only be a short time until the primitive Puritanic stock will become extinct and foreigners take their place, their lands, their houses and their homes. These fiendish practices are becoming so common that one of the most reliable historians positively asserts that "millions do them, because they think they cannot afford to raise children."

18. As the male members of our Church who practice plural marriage are estimated as not exceeding but little, if any, two per cent, of the entire membership of the Church, we consider it an act of great injustice to the ninety-eight per cent to be abused and outraged, and have all their business relations disturbed, values of every kind, unsettled, neighborhoods agitated and alarmed, and the property of the people generally jeopardized, because of this "raid" upon these alleged breakers of the law. The statement of how small a portion of the males is engaged in this practice, exhibits in the clearest light now destitute of foundation are the charges made against us respecting this institution threatening the monogramic form of marriage, claimed to be the feature of the present civilization.

19. Need we ask you, Latter-day Saints here assembled: Do the lives and conduct of our present would-be reformers afford you examples that you would choose to adopt, or have your children follow? Again, need we ask you: Who have been the introducers of drinking saloons, gambling dens and brothels into our towns and cities? Or who have been their patrons and the aiders and promoters of every form of licentiousness which, when we came to these mountains, we hoped to have left forever behind us? We call upon you to guard and protect yourselves and families against their corrupt and insidious influences. Their ways are the ways of death, and their paths lead down to destruction. We exhort you, therefore, to preserve your bodies and spirits pure, to protect the virtue and honor of your wives and daughters, to live your religion, to deal honestly and honorably with all men, and to maintain inviolate those glorious principles which have been revealed unto you.

20. And, furthermore, do not permit any of these abuses with which we have to cope, to tempt you to retaliate in kind, or to violate any Constitutional law of the land. You will remember that Joseph Smith has said that that sacred instrument was given by inspiration of God, and it becomes our bounden duty to sustain it in all its provisions. And while men may in their blind zeal seek to oppress us and bring us into bondage, we must not be provoked to do as they do; but to maintain the rights, immunities, and seek for the happiness and well-being, as well as to maintain the freedom of all men of every name, color and creed.

21. In conclusion, we solemnly testify to the Latter-day Saints and to the world, as we have done so often in the past, that God has established His Zion, and His work will roll forth, and that all those who fight against it will perish. You have seen this fulfilled to the letter in the past.

22. We pray God, the Eternal Father, to bless you in your families, in your fields, and flocks and herds, and in your business and in all your righteous undertakings, and to preserve you from the hands of all your enemies, and to eventually save and exalt you in His Celestial Kingdom, in the name of Jesus Christ, our Savior and Redeemer. Amen.

Your Brethren,
JOHN TAYLOR,
GEORGE Q. CANNON
First Presidency of the Church of Jesus Christ of Latter-day Saints.

ADDRESS 33

As a result of the question over the legality of polygamy and the desire of certain federal officials to imprison, prosecute, and/or otherwise hound church leaders into compliance, many of the Brethren, notably members of the First Presidency, were forced to go underground to avoid any public appearance. Unable to attend the 55th Semiannual General Conference of The Church of Jesus Christ of Latter-day Saints, President John Taylor issued the following epistle which was read by Elder Moses Thatcher on the second day of the conference, October 7, 1885. As a number of the Brethren were having similar difficulties with the law, general conference was held in Logan, Utah rather than in Salt Lake City, the customary location.

AN EPISTLE from the First Presidency to the Officers and Members of the Church of Jesus Christ of Latter-day Saints:

BELOVED BRETHREN AND SISTERS:

1. As the time for holding our Semi-annual Conference has again come around, and we are still prevented from addressing the Saints in public, we deem it proper to take this method of communicating with you, that you may know the counsel we have to give, and that we are not neglectful of the duties which devolve upon us as the First Presidency of the Church.

2. As all the Saints doubtless understand, there has been no cessation since we last wrote in the work of persecution. It rages, if anything, more fiercely than ever. Under cover of what is called the Edmunds Law, the most outrageous acts of oppression are being perpetrated against the Latter-day Saints. The avowal has been openly made that this law was expressly designed for the destruction of a principle of our religion, and in this spirit all the prosecutions have been conducted. Thus far no criminal, however guilty, who has not been a "Mormon," has been punished under it. Acts of the most sickening depravity have been committed by non-"Mormons" within easy reach of its arm, but have scarcely had a passing notice. While it is also worthy of note that, up to the present writing, out of all who have been accused and brought before the District Court, only one "Mormon" has been acquitted. The man acquitted, we understand, was charged with being the husband of a woman, on the ground that he had camped in his wagon in a ten acre lot in which her residence stood, and

had carried some chickens for her to market!

3. One of the most remarkable features connected with the administration of this law, is the extraordinary rulings which are made in its enforcement. The Judge who presides in the Second Judicial District, in the recent trial of a case of unlawful cohabitation, gave instructions to the jury, at the request of the defense. Several accused persons would have been cleared in the Third Judicial District, had the juries which rendered verdicts in their cases been similarly instructed. They are as follows:

a. Prior to the act of March 22, 1882, cohabitation with more than one woman was not unlawful.

b. If you find from the evidence that the defendant, since the passage of the Edmunds Act, March 22, 1882, and within the dates named in the indictment, has not held out to the world, introduced, or announced more than one of the women named in the indictment as his wife, you should acquit the defendant.

c. It is not necessary that the parties to a polygamous marriage, or who have lived in the practice of cohabiting with two or more women should divorce themselves, in order to entitle them to the presumption of innocence of cohabitation after the passage of the law.

d. As all children of polygamous marriages, begotten before March 22, 1882, are legitimated, and no cohabitation before that date was unlawful, no criminating inference can be drawn by the jury from the defendant's later acknowledgments of his paternity of such children by the women mentioned in the indictment, nor from later recognition of such women as their mothers, and as women whom he had before said date, taken into the polygamous relation with him.

e. The law presumes innocence, and therefore, that all persons who were cohabiting when the Edmunds Act took effect, contrary to the provision of that act, then ceased to do so.

f. The law presumes all persons charged with a criminal offense to be innocent until the presumption is overcome by proof; therefore it presumes that all persons who were living with more than one woman as wives prior to March 22, 1882, have since that date ceased to so live and cohabit.

g. If you find from the evidence that defendant had children by the women named in the indictment prior to March 22, 1882, then the defendant had a right to visit his children, and support them, and make arrangements as to their welfare. He had a right also to assist their mothers in their support, and for such a purpose could visit the house where they and their mothers live. He could furnish them a home, he could visit the mother, the same as if they had been divorced, or as if no such previous relations had existed between them, but he should not associate with her as a husband associates with his wife.

4. Do we say too much if we state that there are those now undergoing punishment in the penitentiary in the society of thieves and murderers, who would be as free as the prosecuting officers themselves, had the law been construed by the legal canons applied to other laws, and according to the instructions given above?

5. The practice in these attacks upon us has not been to presume the accused innocent until proved guilty, but to view him as undoubtedly guilty because accused; and the rulings of the Court in several instances have been made to secure conviction where the evidence was open to question. The extraordinary ruling concerning "holding out," is one in point; notwithstanding the Edmunds Law specifies that the penalty for unlawful cohabitation shall not be more than six months' imprisonment, and three hundred dollars' fine, the notorious ruling from the same bench concerning the number of indictments which can be found against a person accused of unlawful cohabitation, states that he not only can be indicted once for the whole period since the passage of the law, but an indictment can be found for every week of that time; so that, if found guilty in this manner, a man's punishment would aggregate an imprisonment of 92 years, and fines to the amount of $55,200.

6. Still more extraordinary is the ruling of another Judge, who, not to be outdone in his zeal, says, that an indictment can be found for this charge against a man for every day, or other distinct interval of time since the enactment of the law! As about 1,292 days have passed since then, a man found guilty can be incarcerated in prison for 646 years, and made pay fines to the amount of $387,600. Comment upon this absurdity is unnecessary.

7. Before the Edmunds Bill became law, and while on its passage, it was claimed that its provisions were of general application and in the interests of morality, and not, as we asserted, a measure directly aimed at religious liberty and for purposes of persecution. But time has fully revealed its true character. Stripped of all disguise, it stands out now in all its hideousness. The most shocking immorality flourishes in its presence and thrives under the very eyes of its administrators. All forms of vice, if not directly encouraged by those who are charged with the duty of administering the Edmunds Law, are at least viewed by them with indifference. They appear to have no care as to the most flagrant sexual crimes, if they are only committed by non-"Mormons," or outside of the pale of matrimony. "Mormons" also, under the present administration of the law, may do what they please with women, be guilty of the foulest injustice to them and their offspring, if they will only disown them as wives. The war is openly and undisguisedly made upon our religion. To induce men to repudiate that, to violate its precepts and to break its solemn covenants, every encouragement is given. The man who agrees to discard his wife or wives, and to trample upon the most sacred obligations which human beings can enter

into, escapes imprisonment and is applauded; while the man who will not make this compact of dishonor, who will not admit that his past life has been a fraud and a lie, who will not say to the world, "I intended to deceive my God, my brethren and my wives by making covenants I did not expect to keep," is, besides being punished to the full extent of the law, compelled to endure the reproaches, taunts and insults of a brutal judge.

8. Notwithstanding all these cruelties are practiced against us, we do not feel that, as Latter-day Saints, we should mourn because of them. We should mourn because of our weaknesses, follies and sins, and repent of them. But to be persecuted, to be discriminated against, to be separated from the rest of the world, to be imprisoned and abused are not causes of sorrow to true Saints; they are causes of rejoicing. If, in the great hereafter, we expect to be admitted to the society of the Son of God, our Redeemer, to the society of Prophets and Apostles, and holy men and women, ought we not to be willing to endure the tribulations which they received so joyfully? Where is the Prophet or Apostle who did not endure persecution, whose liberty and life were not in almost constant jeopardy? They did not have an Edmunds Law, perhaps, enforced against them; but they had laws which emanated from the same source. With few exceptions they were all punished, deprived of liberty and of life, in the sacred name of law. Even the holiest Being that ever trod the earth, the great Redeemer of mankind Himself, was crucified between two thieves to satisfy Jewish law.

9. There has probably never been a time in the history of mankind when those whom we now revere as martyrs, and whose sacrifices adorn and glorify our humanity and lift it nearer to God, could not, by being recreant to the truth entrusted to them, have escaped the fate which made them so admirable to the generations which followed them. The Savior Himself had it in His power to compromise with His enemies and escape the cruel and ignominious death inflicted upon Him. Abraham might have bowed to the gods of his idolatrous father, and needed no angel to rescue him from his impending doom. Daniel and his three brethren, also, might have submitted to the decree and law of the ruling powers under which they lived, and escaped the fiery furnace and the den of lions. Their refusals to obey the decree and law doubtless appeared to those who had not the knowledge of God which they possessed, as acts of wicked obstinacy that should be summarily punished. But had they, to escape the threatened penalty, obeyed these edicts, posterity would have lost the benefit of their example, and the great God would not have been glorified before their contemporaries as He was by their acts. Instead of their names being, as now, radiant with light and resplendent with heroism, they would, had they reached us, been covered with odium, and been mentioned in the same category with the Jews, concerning whom the Prophet Jeremiah said: "They bend their tongues like their bow for lies; but they are not valiant for the truth upon the earth; for they proceed from evil to evil, and they know not me, saith the Lord."

10. Well-meaning friends of ours have said that our refusal to renounce the principle of celestial marriage invites destruction. They warn us and implore us to yield. They appeal to every human interest, and adjure us to bow to a law which is admitted on all hands to have been framed expressly for the destruction of the principle which we are called upon to reject. They say it is madness to resist the will of so overwhelming a majority. They say they see the gathering clouds, that they hear the premonitory mutterings of the resistless tempest which is about to break in destructive fury upon our heads, and they call upon us to avert its wrath by timely submission. But they perceive not the hand of that Being who controls all storms, whose voice the tempest obeys, at whose fiat thrones and empires are thrown down—the Almighty God, Lord of heaven and earth, who has made promises to us, and who has never failed to fulfill all His words.

11. We did not reveal celestial marriage. We cannot withdraw or renounce it. God revealed it, and He has promised to maintain it, and to bless those who obey it. Whatever fate, then, may threaten us, there is but one course for men of God to take, that is, to keep inviolate the holy covenants they have made in the presence of God and angels. For

the remainder, whether it be life or death, freedom or imprisonment, prosperity or adversity, we must trust in God.

12. We may say, however, if any man or woman expects to enter into the celestial kingdom of our God without making sacrifices and without being tested to the very uttermost, they have not understood the Gospel. If there is a weak spot in our nature, or if there is a fiber that can be made to quiver or to shrink, we may rest assured that it will be tested. Our own weaknesses will be brought fully to light, and in seeking for help, the strength of our God will also be made manifest to us. The Latter-day Saints have been taught this from the beginning. Such scenes as we now witness in these mountains, and hear about in lands where the Elders are preaching the Gospel, ought not to be a surprise to us. The Prophets and Apostles and Elders of this dispensation would be false Prophets and Apostles and Elders, if these events did not take place; for they have predicted them, and warned the people unceasingly concerning them.

13. Speaking concerning law, the Lord, in a revelation given through the Prophet Joseph, Aug. 6, 1833, says:

14. And now, verily, I say unto you concerning the laws of the land, it is my will that my people should observe to do all things whatsoever I command them;

15. And that law of the land which is constitutional, supporting that principle of freedom in maintaining rights and privileges, belongs to all mankind, and is justifiable before me;

16. Therefore I, the Lord, justify you, and your brethren of my church, in befriending that law which is the constitutional law of the land;

17. And as pertaining to law of man, whatsoever is more or less than these cometh of evil.

18. I, the Lord God, make you free, therefore ye are free indeed; and the law also maketh you free;

19. Nevertheless, when the wicked rule the people mourn.

20. Wherefore, honest men and wise men should be sought for diligently, and good men and wise men ye should observe to uphold; otherwise whatsoever is less than

these cometh of evil.

21. And I give unto you a commandment, that ye shall forsake all evil and cleave unto all good, that ye shall live by every word which proceedeth forth out of the mouth of God;

22. For he will give unto the faithful line upon line, precept upon precept; and I will try you and prove you herewith;

23. And whoso layeth down his life in my cause, for my name's sake, shall find it again, even life eternal:

24. Therefore be not afraid of your enemies, for I have decreed in my heart, saith the Lord, that I will prove you in all things, whether you will abide in my covenant even unto death that you may be found worthy;

25. For if ye will not abide in my covenant, ye are not worthy of me.

26. Fifty-two years have passed since this was given to the Church, and we are now witnessing its fulfillment. The Saints are required to do whatsoever the Lord commands them, to live by every word which proceedeth forth out of the mouth of God. They are also instructed to befriend every constitutional law of the land; for such laws support the principle of freedom; they maintain rights and privileges. This, as a people, we have striven to do from the beginning of our organization. We have ever been a law-abiding people. Times without number we have suffered the most grievous wrongs without resenting them. We have ever thought it better to suffer wrong than to do wrong.

27. Such was the case when we suffered expatriation from the State of Missouri. We were robbed and pillaged, despoiled and persecuted, yet we had no idea of retaliating on account of these wrongs upon the government and its institutions, which to us are sacred. The same loyal spirit animated us when we were beset by blood-thirsty mobs in Illinois, one of which murdered Joseph Smith, our Prophet, and Hyrum Smith, the Patriarch, while they were under the pledged protection of the State, given through the Governor. On the same occasion one of the signers of this address was also brought to the gate of death, by being shot by the same band of assassins. When driven from the homes we had established in Illinois, we had no disposition to hold the

nation at large, nor the government of our beloved country, responsible for those inhuman deeds, nor to allow the spirit of vengeance to rankle in our hearts. We took the first opportunity to exhibit the spirit of true patriotism. While undergoing great hardship on account of being subjected to a compulsory exodus, when called upon by the government to furnish a body of men to take part in the war with Mexico, 500 of the flower of our camp responded with alacrity, and in accordance with the call of our country, traversed the great American desert, penetrated to Mexico and completed an arduous and hazardous campaign and journey to California.

28. You have no doubt read, through the papers, an account of the terrible affair which recently occurred at Rock Springs, in Wyoming Territory. We could not help feeling a little anxiety lest some of our people should have been connected with that bloody riot, and immediately requested Brother Cluff, President of Summit Stake, to inquire into the matter. So far as we have obtained information to the present, however, we find that not more than one has been in any way mixed up with that matter, and he a person of doubtful standing. We are pleased to learn of this, because we cannot associate with any deeds so revolting and inhuman, and we take this opportunity to express our opinion on this subject to the Saints. A great number of secret societies are being formed with which we cannot affiliate. Such organizations are generally inimical to law, to good order, and in many instances subversive of the rights of man. We cannot amalgamate with them. They are very distinctly spoken against in the Book of Mormon, as among the calamities which should afflict the people.

29. We are expressly commanded, and it becomes our duty, to uphold and sustain every law of the land which is constitutional; we have always had a strong desire to obey such laws, and to place ourselves in harmony with all the institutions of the country.

30. We repeat, that we desire that all men should be aware of the fact that we have been the upholders of the Constitution and laws enacted in pursuance of that sacred instrument. We still entertain the same patri-

otic disposition, and propose to continue acting in conformity with it to the last. Neither have we any desire to come in active conflict even with statutes that we deem opposed to the Constitution both in letter and spirit. Whatever opposition has been offered in that line has been only of such a character as is justified by the usages and customs of this and all other civilized countries, and such as the laws and institutions of this nation provide. Nor have we the least desire to shun the consequences of our acts in their relationship to the laws to which we refer, providing there were any assurance that our cases would be submitted to a fair and just adjudication. Events of the past few months give no ground for hope that such treatment would be accorded. It must be contended, however, that, as stated elsewhere, connected with this disposition to have our conduct passed upon as provided by law administered in the genius of justice, there never can be any hope of our yielding up, under any circumstances, a principle of conscientious or religious conviction. Were we to make such a surrender, our conduct in that respect would not be in harmony with the guaranties of the Constitution, which we are in duty bound to uphold.

31. In order to place our people at a disadvantage, and to crush out their religious system, the Constitution has been violated in a number of ways. It does not require any depth of legal learning to understand what is meant by a religious test, which is forbidden by the "supreme law of the land." Yet laws have been passed applicable to a wide section of this northwestern country, disfranchising and inflicting total political disability upon our people, without regard to their acts. The offense for which this restriction has been prescribed is simply religious belief, and the means of application is religious test. It is consequently unconstitutional upon its fact. This and other laws—notably the Edmunds Act—inflict disabilities upon those of our people who are not in any way associated by their acts, with polygamy. Thus probably about nine-tenths of our community are punished for alleged offenses for which they are in no way responsible, and in which they have taken no part. Surely no person who is unbiased, that gives this subject even the

most casual attention, can characterize such treatment as other than flagrantly unjust.

32. It has been estimated that out of a community of about 200,000 people, more or less, from 10,000 to 12,000 are identified with polygamy. When the Edmunds Act was passed, this small minority who were deprived by it of the right to vote or hold office, voluntarily, without the application of coercion, withdrew from those privileges, notwithstanding the high estimate they placed upon them. It may well be asked wherein is the justice of placing the bulk of the people at a disadvantage as well, seeing they have done nothing to furnish an excuse for such treatment? Granting that the small minority connected with polygamy are criminals before the law, what justification is there, on that account, for punishing, as the Edmunds and other acts do, the overwhelming majority? If such doings were perpetrated in any other connection, they would be unsparingly denounced as oppressive and tyrannical in the most extreme degree. If one portion of a community are designated as criminal, to hold the other and much the greater portion responsible for such a condition is not only unjust, but decidedly absurd.

33. Statements upon this subject have been made to the Chief Executive of the nation, in the form of a protest and petition for redress of grievances. Knowing that misrepresentations have taken the place of impartial scrutiny of the question with which the Latter-day Saints are associated, the consequences being a general misapprehension of the community and their affairs, we presumed that Mr. Cleveland was not acquainted with the real situation. An opportunity was thus sought to acquaint him with the facts. The very reasonable desire was expressed in this connection that a commission of inquiry be appointed, that the truth might appear and be given to the nation. Was it too much to expect that this action, supported by a representation of 200,000 people, would meet with some favorable response, which thus far has not, however, been made? Yet it would be unfair to attribute the delay of the President either to indifference or a disposition to refuse to accord justice to a people whose liberties are being trampled

upon to an extent that is almost past human endurance. It is still hoped that he will take some consistent and humane action in the premises. In alluding to the delay in granting a response to the representations made to the President, we must not forget the extensive and arduous character of the duties devolving upon him as the head of the administration of a great government. We mention this that you may not be disposed to be too censorious in regard to the actions of men in high places who have the power to redress our grievances. And even when we feel that we are wronged, it is proper for us to follow the example of our Lord and Master, and say: "Father, forgive them, they know not what they do."

34. Referring once more to the situation in a more local sense, we are not oblivious to the anomalous position in which the Federal judicial officers are placed in dealing with a subject which appears to occupy a large share of popular attention. While it is impossible for them to escape pronounced exceptions being taken to their official course, on account of its harshness, undue rigor, and unjust discrimination in administering the laws, they are entitled to some consideration, justified by well understood circumstances. The Latter-day Saints are the objects of popular obloquy. Their institutions appear to be greatly disliked. The officers are doubtless influenced by the general clamor for the application of heroic treatment to the Saints. They themselves have doubtless been influenced to some degree by personal prejudices, and their official conduct, by these conditions, is thrown out of balance. While their course cannot be sustained in the light of fair play, some allowance should be made on account of the liability of the human mind to be warped by influences in conflict with the principles which should universally obtain in courts of law and presumed justice. Neither would it be justifiable on the part of the Saints to entertain toward them, on account of their departures from their proper line of duty, any rancorous or vengeful feeling. A spirit of that character is not in unity with the genius of the Gospel of peace. All men are in the hands of a just God, whose mighty, penetrating power is

capable of analyzing all the motives which prompt human action, and He can and will deal with us and them and all men according to the principles of eternal justice.

35. Upwards of forty years ago the Lord revealed to His Church the principle of celestial marriage. The idea of marrying more wives than one was as naturally abhorrent to the leading men and women of the Church at that day as it could be to any people. They shrank with dread from the bare thought of entering into such relationships. But the command of God was before them in language which no faithful soul dare disobey.

36. "For, behold, I reveal unto you a new and an everlasting covenant; and if ye abide not that covenant, then are ye damned; for no one can reject this covenant, and be permitted to enter into my glory." "And as pertaining to the new and everlasting covenant, it was instituted for the fullness of my glory; and he that receiveth a fullness thereof, must and shall abide the law, or he shall be damned, saith the Lord God."

37. Damnation was the awful penalty affixed to a refusal to obey this law. It became an acknowledged doctrine of the Church; it was indissolubly interwoven in the minds of its members with their hopes of eternal salvation and exaltation in the presence of God. For nearly twenty years this continued to be our faith and practice. Then a law was enacted against it. Another twenty years elapsed, and the Edmunds Law was passed. Nearly forty years had thus elapsed from the first revelation of this doctrine, during which period thousands had lived and died, firmly believing and solemnly testifying that it was divine. At great sacrifice they had obeyed it, and based their hopes of eternal felicity upon the promises which the revelation contained. They never dreamed that they had not a constitutional right to obey God, especially when in obeying Him they did not interfere with nor encroach upon the rights of any human being, either man or woman. It never entered into their minds to suppose for a moment that man had a right, after God had given a law to His Church for its salvation and exaltation, to enact a counter law forbidding, under severe penalties, man's obedience to God's law. Who could suppose

that any man, in this land of religious liberty, would presume to say to his fellow-man that he had no right to take such steps as he thought necessary to escape damnation! Or that Congress would enact a law which would present the alternative to religious believers of being consigned to a penitentiary if they should attempt to obey a law of God which would deliver them from damnation! Or that, under a plea of maintaining a certain form of civilization, God's authority to direct His people how to escape from the abominable corruptions and evils which are eating out the vitals of man's much vaunted civilization, should be disputed and utterly rejected!

38. What is this "Mormon" problem, so-called, and why should it disturb the people? It is an unpopular religion. But so was that of the ancient Prophets. Jesus told the Jews that they garnished the tombs of the dead Prophets, but killed the living ones. They crucified Jesus and were almost as unanimous in their cry to crucify Him, as the people and rulers of the United States are today to destroy the "Mormons." They killed all of His Apostles except one, and he was banished to work as a slave on the isle of Patmos. It is said they cast him into a caldron of boiling oil, but he was not killed; and if the Scriptures are true, he still lives; for he was to tarry till the coming of the Savior. We receive as the word of God, and so do millions of the human family, the writings and testimony of the Prophets who were killed. It is published by the millions of copies, and sent to the various nations of the earth, by the very people who would now seek to destroy us. Jesus, who was crucified between two thieves, is now worshipped by millions in Christendom as the Son of God, the Redeemer of the world. The Twelve Apostles, His disciples, who suffered such ignominious contumely and death, are now designated by the millions of Christendom as "The Apostles of the Lamb of God," and churches and cathedrals are called after them, as St. Peter, St. John, St. Mark, St. Luke, etc. It was then the "Christian problem;" it is now the "Mormon problem" the same problem though called by a different name. Was Jesus the enemy of the people in His day? Only as He told them the truth.

"What evil hath He done?" asked Pilot, the Gentile Judge. No matter what evil or what good, vociferated the Jews: "Crucify him, crucify him!" What evil hath the "Mormons" done? is asked, and the cry comes back: No matter, no matter, let them be destroyed.

39. By the circulation of endless slanders and falsehoods concerning us and our marriages, wrath and indignation have been aroused against us in our nation. The ignorance of the people concerning us and our doctrines and system have been taken advantage of. Constant attempts have been, and still are being made to induce the world to believe that our motive in espousing patriarchal marriage has been the gratification of gross sensuality—that our belief in and practice of the doctrine had its origin in licentiousness, and that the sanction of religion is merely invoked to furnish greater license for the indulgence of base passions and devouring lust. This, as you know, is the exact antipodes of the truth. But the world generally do not know it. Those of them who know how utterly false are these charges, are either so cowed down by a fierce public opinion that they dare not speak, or if they have the courage to speak, are almost unheard amid the noisy clamor against us. Thousands upon thousands of honest people in this and other nations, whose voices, did they know the truth, would be raised in our favor, are deceived by these lies and are arrayed against us. This persecution, if it serve no other purpose, will do good in this direction. It brings home to the hearts of the people, as no protestations or arguments of ours ever could do, that there is something more in this doctrine and practice than they have been led to believe. Reflecting people will see that there must be a great principle involved in this, or men and women would not be willing to suffer fines, bonds and imprisonment as they do.

40. Is there any necessity for lustful men and women in this age and nation to suffer martyrdom to gratify their passions? Whoever heard of a people preferring imprisonment and all manner of cruel treatment for the indulgence of appetites which they could gratify to the fullest extent in popular ways, especially when the judges upon the bench, the prosecuting attorneys at the bar, the juries who bring in verdicts, point out the way in which marriage obligations can be discarded and sensuality be gratified without risk or without punishment? The press and sectarian pulpits also echo the advice. The universal voice is: Put away your wives; cease to support them and their children; be as we are, and you need not be put under bonds, be fined or be incarcerated in prison.

41. Foul desire opens wide her arms and invites all to her lecherous embrace by easier paths than honorable marriage and the begetting of numerous children to be carefully trained and educated and made respectable and useful citizens.

42. Will the world see this? Every man who goes to prison for his religion, every woman who, for love of truth and the husband to whom she is bound for time and eternity, submits to bonds and imprisonment, bears a powerful testimony to the world concerning the falsity of the views they entertain respecting us and our religion. If such noble and heroic sacrifices as men and women are now called upon to make for their religion by Federal Courts do not teach the world the truth concerning us, then woe to the world, for nothing but the wrath of Almighty God will reach it.

43. We join with all Saints in invoking blessings upon the noble men and women who have exhibited their integrity to God and His cause, and their devotion to principle, by submitting to bonds and imprisonment rather than deny their faith or break their covenants. If anything were needed to show to the world that our marriages cannot be reduced to the level of the vile practices to which our defamers would drag them down, their heroic conduct has furnished it. Thank God that, so far in this persecution, at least as large a proportion have stood the test, without flinching or cowering, as Jesus in His parable of the ten virgins intimated would be ready to meet the Bridegroom at His coming. Their names will be held in everlasting honor in time and eternity, not only as martyrs for religious truth, but as patriots who suffered in defense of the principles of religious liberty.

44.Truths, such as God has revealed in these days, are not established without suffering and sacrifice on the part of those who espouse and advocate them. It was for these truths that we were driven time and again from our homes, and were finally compelled to seek refuge in this mountain country, then known as the American Desert. And now again we are menaced with ruin; and for what? Whom have we injured? Upon whose rights have we trespassed? It can be truthfully said we have not injured or trespassed upon any. Have we not, under the blessing of the Lord changed these barren valleys into fruitful fields and gardens? Have we not established and maintained good and cheap government in every place which we have settled? Has not every man who came into our borders and behaved himself been safe in his property, person and religion? Have not peace and good order been the fruits of our presence? To all these we can answer in the affirmative. Have we endeavored to force our doctrines or practices upon any one? Have we in any manner threatened the peace of our neighbors or of the nation? We certainly have not.

45.Respecting the doctrine of celestial marriage, we could not, however much we might be disposed to do so, teach it to or enforce it upon others not of our faith, without violating a command of God. We do not stand in the attitude of propagandists of polygamy. We never have believed or taught that the doctrine of celestial marriage was designed for universal practice. The Lord has made this clear, and recent events among us have also made it clear. "Strait is the gate," says Jesus, "and narrow the way that leadeth unto the exaltation and continuation of the lives, and few there be that find it."

46.There appears to be a fallacious idea abroad regarding this doctrine. It has been asserted that there was a design to propagate it outside of our community, and thus introduce into the United States an element opposed to the Christian views of this and other nations. On the contrary, our Elders have been instructed not to introduce the practice of that principle anywhere outside of the gathering place of the Saints; and they do not preach it abroad to any extent even in theory, except on occasions when it is called

for, or when they are assailed on account of it. At such times they respond by defending it as a doctrine of the Bible and not inconsistent with the laws of nature. It should also be understood that the practice is not generally admissible even among the Latter-day Saints. It is strictly guarded, the intention being to allow only those who are above reproach to enter into the relationship. The practice of the doctrine is not for extension beyond the Church, and is even limited within its pale. The idea, therefore, that plural practice is a menace to the general monogamous system is without foundation. This fallacy is further exhibited by the fact of the popular antipathy with which it is regarded, people outside of our Church exhibiting a disposition the reverse of favorable to its establishment in other communities, making the extension of its practice abroad impossible. Furthermore, being strict believers in free-will, you Latter-day Saints know that no man or woman has ever been coerced into obligations of that kind, much less would we desire to enforce it upon any other class of people.

47.But in all these events which are now taking place we recognize and acknowledge the hand of God. There is a wise purpose in it all, which He will yet more fully make plain to us. One thing is clear, the Saints are being tried in a manner never before known among us. The faithful rejoice and are steadfast; the unfaithful fear and tremble. Those who have oil in their lamps and have kept them trimmed and burning now have a light for their feet and they do not stumble or fall; those who have neither light nor oil are in perplexity and doubt; they known not what to do. Is not this the fulfillment of the word of God and the teachings of His servants? Have not the Latter-day Saints been taught all the day long that, if they would remain faithful and endure to the end, they must live their religion by keeping every commandment of God? Have they not been continually warned of the fate which awaited them if they committed sin? Can adulterers, fornicators, liars, thieves, drunkards, Sabbathbreakers, blasphemers, or sinners of any kind endure the trials which Saints must pass through and expect to stand? If there are any who entertain such a hope, they deceive themselves. Upon these sins God has pronounced judgment. No man or woman, who is guilty of any of these transgressions of God's law, can stand and retain His Spirit. They must repent of them and put them far from them, or they will be left in darkness, and misery will be their doom. The Lord will not be mocked. He will not bear with hypocrites; but they will be spewed out.

48. If all who call themselves Latter-day Saints were true and faithful to their God, to His holy covenants and laws, and were living as Saints should, persecution would roll off from us without disturbing us in the least. But it is painful to know that this is not their condition. There are secret abominations practiced by those who are called Saints, which the trials we are now passing through will reveal in a manner terrible to them. Open sins are also winked at and condoned by Presidents, Bishops, Teachers and parents in a manner offensive to God and grievous to man. Proper care and vigilance are not exercised to keep Wards and Stakes cleansed from iniquity and to have transgressors dealt with. The innocent are thus made to suffer with the guilty; for the Lord has commanded that the inhabitants of Zion must purge themselves from iniquity, folly, covetousness and vanity, and listen to and obey His laws, or they cannot have His protection.

49. He has also said that if His people will obey His laws and keep His commandments, to do them, not in name only, but in reality, He will be their shield and protector and strong tower, and no man will be able to hurt them, for He will be their defense. These trials of our faith and constancy which we are now passing through will be overruled for our good and future prosperity. In days to come we shall be able to look back and perceive with clearness how visibly God's providence is in all that we now witness. Let us do all in our power to so live before the Lord that if we are persecuted, it shall not be for wrong-doing, but for righteousness.

50. At the present time we may very pertinently inquire: Why are the people of these mountains treated as we now are? Where in this broad land is the virtue of women so amply guarded or so jealously protected as here? No cry of hungry, naked or outraged humanity has ever ascended to heaven from our borders against the men whom the courts are now so busy in sending to prison and treating as criminals. There was a time in these mountains when adultery, fornication, whoredom and illegitimacy were almost unknown. A woman was as safe from insult in traversing over our streets and highways as if she were under her husband's or father's roof. Marriage was encouraged, vice was repressed. Women were free to form connections with the opposite sex to suit themselves, so long as those connections were sanctified by marriage. But what a change we now behold! A tide of evil surges around us. It threatens to overwhelm us and to reduce us to ruin. The flood gates of vice are opened upon us, and not content with the rush of this filthy stream into our cities and settlements, those who hate us would do more. They would invade our dwellings; they would destroy our families; they would loosen every bond which has held society together; they would array wife against husband, child against parent, friend against friend; they would make every man, woman and child a spy, an informer and a betrayer; they would sap the foundation of faith, confidence and honor and make every one distrust his fellow. Satan never wrought greater ruin in Eden than these enemies of ours would work in our midst if we would listen to their blandishments or be frightened by their threats. And is all this havoc to be wrought because of our wickedness? No, ten thousand times, NO.

51. Let those who are so loud in denouncing us, so active in persecuting us, look around them. Are there no people but the "Mormons" to regenerate and purge from sin? Read the daily record of black crime which fills the journals of the land. If the correction of evil, the improvement of morals, the uprooting of vice, the repression of violence and crime were objects which animate those who seek to destroy society in these mountains, then we could say in the language of the Savior: "Thou thyself beholdest not the beam that is in thine own eye. Thou hypocrite, first cast out the beam out of thine own eye; and then shalt thou see clearly to cast out the mote out of thy brother's eye."

52. We speak to you, a people who have traveled and mingled much in society all

over the world. You are not ignorant of the world, its ways or its corruptions. You know, therefore, how great is the beam that is in the eyes of those who reprove us for the mote they imagine they perceive in our eye. We know that from the household of every faithful Latter-day Saint daily and fervent thanksgiving ascends to the God of heaven for having shown them how to escape from the frightful evils under which society groans in so-called civilized lands. Nevertheless, we will not indulge in recrimination. We sincerely mourn over the existence of the dreadful sins which are permitted to flourish and to spread with unblushing front through the land. As a people, we have lifted our voices in warning against these sins and against those who practice them. We shall still continue to do so. If in return for all this we are treated with violence and reproach, it is no more than our Lord and Master was before us. We may rest assured that the predictions concerning the calamities and judgments which are about the fall upon the wicked, the unbelieving and the unrepentant will all be fulfilled, as will every word and promise which the Lord has spoken to us. But while we warn others, let us not forget ourselves, or our families. Let us look well to our own lives and the conduct and lives of those who belong to our household. If we keep ourselves unspotted from sin, rest assured the Lord will never forget or forsake us.

53. Upon Presidents of Stakes, Bishops and other leading officers great responsibility rests. They are placed as shepherds over the flock of Christ. If through any neglect of theirs the flock is injured or destroyed, the blood of those souls will be found upon their garments. The Melchizedek and Aaronic Priesthoods confer great power and authority upon man; they lift man nearer to God and make him His representative. But woe to the men who use their Priesthood for base purposes, and fail to use it for God's glory and the salvation of His children. Far better for them if they had never received it.

54. We have been commanded of the Lord to set our households in order. Apostles, Presidents of Stakes and Bishops, have you done this with your own households? Have you also seen that the Saints have done the same? Have you impressed upon the people under your charge the absolute necessity of purity if they desire the blessing and protection of the Most High? Wolves never watched with greater cunning and more ravenous hunger a flock of sheep and lambs than the people of your Wards and Stakes are now being watched by those who are ready to devour them. Are you awake to this danger, and do you take every precaution against it?

55. Parents, are you full of fidelity yourselves to every principle of godliness, and do you surround your sons and daughters with every safeguard to shield them from the arts of the vile? Do you teach them that chastity in both man and woman should be more highly esteemed than life itself? Or do you leave them in their ignorance and inexperience to mix with any society they may choose, at any hour that may be convenient to them, and to be exposed to the wiles of the seducer and the corrupt? These are questions you will all have to answer either to your shame and condemnation or to your joy and eternal happiness. Know this, that God, in giving us the precious blessings we possess, demands from us a suitable return. By receiving them we are placed under obligations. If these are not discharged, condemnation inevitably follows.

56. We hear favorable accounts of the action of Primary Associations, Sunday Schools, Young Men's and Young Women's Mutual Improvement Associations, and Relief Societies. These organizations have unlimited opportunities of doing good. If those who have them in charge are faithful in attending to their duties, great will be their reward. If we desire the prosperity of Zion, we will carefully guard and train our young. They come to us pure from the Lord. By proper training we can make them mighty instruments for good. But, Superintendents and Teachers of Primary Associations and Sunday Schools, and Presidents of Young Men and Young Women's Associations and Relief Societies, remember this, that God will never bless an unvirtuous people, and while a flood tide of corruption, destructive of all true morality and virtue, is sweeping over the land, we must erect barriers to stop its contaminating influence. You have the young in your charge. Teach and impress

upon them by every means in your power how dreadful a sin is unchastity. They are taught to shrink in horror from murder; but they should be taught to shrink with abhorrence from the next great sin to shedding blood, and that is unchastity.

57. From the Elders who are abroad in our own and in other lands we hear generally favorable reports. They have much to contend with. The world is waxing worse and worse. Iniquity abounds. Men's hearts are hardened against the truth, and the nations are fast being prepared for the judgments which the Lord has said He will pour out in the last days. The Elders are required to carry the message which God has sent to mankind to every nation and to warn them, not in anger or in scorn, but in meekness and humility, that they may flee from the wrath to come. To them we say: Be pure in all your thoughts, words and acts. Keep yourselves unspotted from every evil. Avoid all vulgarity of act and expression. Put away all your light speeches, and be sober men of God, filled with the Holy Ghost and the power of your Priesthood.

58. To the Twelve Apostles and their Counselors we say: Remember the weight of your high calling in Christ Jesus. You are called to be His special witnesses in all the world, to bear testimony that He lives and reigns on high, to see that the Gospel is preached to all the inhabitants of the earth, and that the earth is prepared by suitable warning for the coming of the Son of Man. How great and all-important is your calling. It may be said that the souls of a world are entrusted to you. Through your labors and testimony, either in person or through other chosen messengers whose labors you direct, the inhabitants of the earth will be judged. Is there any law of God, then, which you should neglect; is there any degree of purity which you should not reach, is there any sac-rifice which you should not be willing to make? Can men with such a calling as yours be other than holy and yet please our God? Who among you can neglect the duties of your high calling to devote time and care to the world and its pursuits? We say to you in all truth and solemnity that no one of you can do this without displeasing your God and endangering your salvation.

59. To the Saints we say that President Woodruff, at our last accounts, was in good health and spirits notwithstanding his advanced age, and as full of zeal and faith as ever.

60. President Joseph F. Smith, our fellow laborer in the First Presidency, though not with us, is actively employed in the ministry and rejoicing greatly in the work of God. He is as ardent, as devoted and as persevering as ever. Were he here, his name, without doubt, would appear with ours to this epistle.

61. Notwithstanding all that we are now passing through, our hearts are filled with joy and peace. We can truly say, Hosanna to God in the highest. We know that Zion will not be overthrown or be made desolate. Every promise made concerning Zion by the Almighty will be fulfilled. The only thing which ever disturbs our serenity is the report of wrong-doing by those who are called Latter-day Saints.

62. Praying that God will bless and preserve you and lead you in the path of righteousness, and that you may all operate together in the accomplishment of the purpose of God and the purification of His Church and the establishment of His Kingdom, we remain, with much love,

63. Your friends and fellow-laborers in the New and Everlasting Covenant,

JOHN TAYLOR,

GEORGE Q. CANNON,

Of the First Presidency of the Church of Jesus Christ of Latter-day Saints.

Salt Lake City, October 6, 1885.

ADDRESS 34

Due to the question over the legality of polygamy and the desire of certain federal officials to imprison, prosecute, and/or otherwise hound church leaders into compliance, many of the Brethren, notably members of the First Presidency, were forced to go underground to avoid any public appearance. Unable to attend the 56th Annual General Conference of The Church of Jesus Christ of Latter-day Saints, and in lieu of what they might have said had they been able to attend, President John Taylor issued the following epistle which was read to the conference by Bishop Orson F. Whitney and Elder James E. Talmage on April 6, 1886. As a number of the Brethren were experiencing the same difficulty with the law, it was thought advisable to hold general conference in Provo, Utah, rather than in Salt Lake City as usual.

AN EPISTLE of the First Presidency to The Church of Jesus Christ of Latter-day Saints in General Conference Assembled.

BELOVED BRETHREN AND SISTERS:

1. In the plenitude of God's mercy the Saints are once again permitted in peace to assemble in General Conference to worship the Lord, to extol His goodness, to glorify His name, to hear His word, and to receive such instruction from His servants as the Holy Spirit shall dictate, as well as to transact such business pertaining to His Church as may be presented for their consideration. But as we, your brethren of the First Presidency, are, by the force of peculiar circumstances, deprived on this occasion of your society and you of ours, we deem it consistent with the duties of our calling to address you by letter, and in this way to lay before you that which under more favorable conditions we should have been pleased to have delivered orally.

2. In the first place, we extend our congratulations to you, as Latter-day Saints and members of the Church of Christ, that affairs with us are so favorable that so many can meet together as you do on this the fifty-sixth anniversary of the organization of the Church in General Conference. Persecution has raged, and hideous wrongs have been and are being perpetrated against us as a Church, but thus far our enemies have not been permitted to go to such length as the persecutors of the people of God did in the days of the first Alma, when they put tasks upon his people and put task-masters over them, and put to death those whom they found calling upon God. Though many of us are deprived of the privilege of meeting together in public, yet a goodly number of you can assemble, as you do this day, and worship your God and listen to His word; and we all—prisoners, exiles and free—can call upon our God without danger of punishment therefor.

3. Indeed, we need not go to the days of Alma for contrast between the condition of the people of God then and our present condition, to find causes for thanksgiving and praise to our God this day for His mercies unto us. We have only to refer to our own history, to scenes in which many of you have taken part, to find contrasts which should prompt us to bear our present afflictions with patient equanimity. Some of the Saints, perhaps, feel that their sufferings under the tyranny which is now exercised over us in the name of law are very severe, and they may ask how long shall these outrages be permitted to continue? But if they would understand how much worse our positions might be, let them recall the scenes enacted in the State of Missouri, when the Latter-day Saints were driven by mob violence out of Jackson County into Clay County, and thence into Caldwell County, and finally were compelled to flee in the depth of an inclement winter, out of the State, under an order of Lilburn W. Boggs, the Governor, which said "that the Mormons must be treated as enemies, and must be exterminated or driven from the State," and this, too, after many of their num-

ber had been killed, and the remainder had been robbed of nearly all the property they had in the world; or, recall the treatment the Latter-day Saints received in the State of Illinois, when, after murdering in the most savage and heartless manner, and while under the pledged honor of the State, the President and Patriarch of the Church, and wounding almost to death one of the Twelve Apostles, mobs organized themselves, burned the houses of the Saints in the outer settlements, destroyed their property and drove them for their lives to the City of Nauvoo; and then, not content with this, brought the whole power of the State to bear upon them to compel them to leave that city and the State, and to take refuge, stripped and destitute, in the wilderness, where their enemies hoped internal dissensions, starvation or wild Indians would complete the work of destruction which they were not permitted to accomplish.

4. However grievous the wrongs under which we suffer today, there is much yet to be thankful for. Our land is filled with plenty. No cry of man nor beast ascends from our borders to high heaven for the want of food; no beggars plead for alms in our streets, and no destitute soul has denied to him that sustenance necessary to supply his wants. And with these blessings of good food, comfortable raiment and sufficient shelter, we have the inestimable blessing of the peace of God, which He gives to every faithful Saint—peace in our hearts, peace in our habitations, peace in our settlements—a peace which the world cannot give, and which, thank the Lord, it cannot take away. Let your hearts, therefore, brethren and sisters, be filled with thanksgiving and praise to our God for His goodness and mercy unto us as a people. He has made promises concerning Zion; be assured He will not forget them. Zion may say, in the words of the Prophet Isaiah, "The Lord hath forsaken me, and my Lord hath forgotten me."

5. But the Lord replies:

6. "Can a woman forget her sucking child, that she should not have compassion on the son of her womb? Yea, they may forget, yet will I not forget thee. Behold, I have graven thee upon the palms of my hands; thy walls are continually before me."

7. At no time has the Lord led His people to expect that they would not have to endure trials, or not have their faith fully tested.

8. Soon after this Church was organized His people were told: "for I have decreed in my heart, saith the Lord, that I will prove you in all things whether you will abide in my covenant even unto death, that you may be found worthy; for if ye will not abide in my covenant, ye are not worthy of me." We scarcely need remind you that if you live godly in Christ Jesus, while Satan has power, you will suffer persecution.

9. In the providence of the Almighty persecution serves a most useful purpose. Every faithful Saint must perceive and acknowledge this. Each one feels its effect upon himself; he sees its effect upon his friends and neighbors. Persecution develops character. Under its influence we all know ourselves better than we did before we felt its pressure; and we discover traits in our brethren and sisters of the existence of which, perhaps, we were in entire ignorance. The persecution from which we have been suffering during these eighteen months past, though very painful, has not been without profit to the Latter-day Saints. It has strengthened and infused new zeal, courage and determination into the faithful. It has also caused many who were careless and indifferent to arouse themselves from their lethargy and to renew their diligence in the work of God. It has also brought to light the hypocrisy of many, and caused them to throw off the mask of friendship and fellowship which they wore, and to exhibit themselves in their true lineaments.

10. But it is upon the young of our community that the effect of this persecution has been most marked. Many of the young of both sexes, when all was peace and no war was made upon their parents and friends seemed to be of the opinion that they could, without any danger to themselves or their faith, be in full fellowship with the world. The names Latter-day Saints and Gentile were alike to them. They appeared to see no reason why they could not be on terms of perfect friendship with both classes. Every Latter-day Saint of experience knows how dangerous it is for children to stand upon this ground. But from this delusive dream they have been awakened by the rude shock of this persecution. The line of demarcation between the Latter-day Saints and the world

has been drawn so sharp and distinct that they find themselves (unless they become open apostates) compelled to take sides with their parents and friends, and the difference between their religion and that which is opposed to it is brought home to their hearts and consciences with a force never before known to them. This persecution is driving the rising generation together with surprising compactness. It is making impressions upon the youngest children of the community which the lapse of years can never obliterate. They are learning the truth of the words of the Savior by the painful experience which our enemies are now giving them. "If ye were of the world, the world would love his own; but because ye are not of the world, but I have chosen you out of the world, therefore the world hateth you."

11. The Lord has said that the wrath of man shall be made to praise Him, and in this attack which is being made upon us and our religion we see this verified. Our enemies have designed to destroy the work of God. For this they plot and toil and descend to the depths of infamy. So absorbed are they in their wicked schemes, and so bent upon carrying them into effect, that they fail to look beyond the immediate acts which they perform and perceive the consequences which follow. They harass, annoy and torment men, women and children; they compel men and women to conceal themselves to escape from their cruelties and injustice and tyrannical abuse of power; and they consign other men and women to prison; and from these proceedings they derive great satisfaction, as they look upon them as so many evidences of their success in sapping the foundation of the Church of God and in uprooting our religion. We need not say to you, who have so often witnessed the effects of persecution upon our religion and Church, how fallacious are these hopes of our present persecutors.

12. Instead of crushing the truth they are advertising it; instead of showing the world how unworthy and contemptible we are, they are, unwittingly, furnishing us with opportunities to exhibit the heroic qualities we possess; instead of weakening or unsettling the minds of true Latter-day Saints, they are stimulating their faith and supplying them with additional proofs of the divinity of their reli-

gion. They would have the world believe that we are low, sensual, ignorant, and degraded, that our religion is a system of lust; but the thinking people of the world know that there is no necessity to endure that which the Latter-day Saints are now enduring to gratify lustful appetites or desires. Licentious, depraved men and women would not suffer such treatment as Federal officials are now extending to us, and bear all manner of indignities and go unmurmuringly to prison, if they are assured, as we are, by courts and prosecuting officers that the war is against our marriages and not against sensuality if indulged in according to popular methods.

13. This persecution attracts the attention of the world. Its disgraceful features may be concealed for a while from public knowledge, through the lies so industriously propagated by those who are its promoters and instruments; but the truth concerning it is coming to light. For a while the feeling among those ignorant of our true character may have been one of indifference as to our fate, or to any treatment we might receive. As the persecution continues, the truth leaks out by degrees. Men and women hear that scores of men, rather than accept the alternative of renouncing their wives and children, pay heavy fines and costs and go cheerfully for long, weary months to prison; and that delicate women, too, rather than betray their husbands, and by their testimony involve them in the toils of their persecutors, go willingly to the penitentiary where the greatest criminals are confined. Thinking people read of these proceedings, and their former indifference gives place to interest.

14. But while we acknowledge the hand of the Lord in these wicked acts of our enemies, they are not relieved from the condemnation which will follow them. They would deny us our rights as citizens, and they talk about us and act towards us as though we were not entitled to any such rights; but this is mere impudent assumption and claptrap on their part. We have rights. We were born free men and women, and it is a duty we owe to ourselves and our posterity, and to all the people of this land, that we should contend for and maintain the principles of freedom and transmit them unimpaired and undiminished to those who follow us. We do not ask for this

freedom as a favor; we demand it as a right. We are as much entitled to the full rights of citizenship in these mountains as any other citizens who dwell under the flag of the Republic. Under any and all circumstances we are their peers.

15. Such trials as the Latter-day Saints now undergo in the courts in these Territories are not the trials of ordinary, vulgar criminals. However much those who figure as prosecutors, judges or jurors in these cases may scheme and plot and falsify to reduce them to this level, and to fix the brand of criminality or the stigma of infamy upon our conduct, they cannot deceive the world. This which we are now passing through is to all intents and purposes a religious persecution and nothing else. It will yet be recognized as such by the whole world. Its hideous features, its atrocious character, its travesties of justice, cannot be concealed by any amount of falsification or disguise. Already men are beginning to understand the motives and objects of those who are engaged in it, and history will set its seal of condemnation upon it and them, and it will yet stand as an ineffaceable blot upon the boasted civilization and liberty of our generation.

16. The scenes which we are now witnessing in this Territory are the results of a deep-laid and carefully planned conspiracy, which has been in process of formation for years. Its originators knew the elements they had to deal with, and by cunning contrivance they have effected a wonderful combination. Religious and irreligious, ministers in sacerdotal robes and atheistic scoffers, business men of integrity and blacklegs, temperance men and drunkards, men of strict morality and pimps and harlots, are crowded together on the platform they have constructed, and they find no inconvenience from each other's companionship. Each is made to believe that it is to his direct interest to combine to destroy "Mormonism." A more motley collection of human being was never witnessed. Differ as they may upon everything else, there has been one common thought and purpose running through the whole and holding them together, and that is hatred of the religion of the Latter-day Saints and a determination to destroy it and them. The conspirators have appealed to the prejudices of each one to induce him to work in concert for this common end. In the ministers they have found ready and willing allies; in fact, these have been the chief authors and promoters of the conspiracy. The Pharisees in the days of the Savior were no more ready to egg the multitude on to cry out, "Crucify him, crucify him," than many of the ministers of our time are to urge Congress to enact measures for our destruction. It is now some years since the sectarian ministers here (with the exception of the Catholic clergymen) combined in a document to Congress, urging that body to legislate against us.

17. This action they have often repeated since. Destitute of confidence in their own religious systems and their power to cope with the truth which we possess without aid from the secular power, they make the air resound with their clamors for Congress to pass laws to crush us and our religion. They enlist men of their cloth elsewhere in the same unchristian business. It is only a few months since, and at the time the whole machinery of the court here was being used most savagely in sending men, and women also, to prison on account of their religion, that a representation of these professed teachers of the doctrines of the crucified Redeemer called upon President Cleveland and presented a memorial signed by upwards of a thousand persons, and, it was signed, by some of the most prominent divines in the country, earnestly urging him to enforce the anti-polygamy act! Could the old Pharisees have done any more?

18. But while the ministers engaged in the conspiracy through zeal for their own craft and sectarian hate, the moralist and the politician, the debauchee and the drunkard, were drawn into support of the plot by appeals to their interests. The cry of polygamy has made a good battle cry; this has called the fanatical element into line; but underneath and above this question of polygamy, and completely enveloping it, has been the design to destroy our rights as citizens, to take away from us our liberties under the Constitution and the laws, and to obtain the political control of our country, so that, being as voiceless in the affairs of government as the Indians or Chinese, we could be taxed and plundered with impunity, and be lorded over by a set of political harpies who

would revel and fatten at our expense. This has been, and still is, the object of all the outcry raised against us, of the innumerable falsehoods with which the public journals have teemed, of the constant appeals to Congress to legislate against us, and of all the outrages in the name of law inflicted upon us by the courts. The same covetousness and envy that led mobs to band themselves together to drive us from our former homes, are the sentiments which prompt the present attack upon us and our liberties. Then mobs acted openly and defiantly, regardless of law: now the policy is a more subtle one; it is to reach the same ends under the shelter and pretense of law. It meant robbery and the deprivation of rights under the old system; under the new tactics it means the stealing of the political control of the country, to be followed by rapine and spoliation.

19. Trace up the acts of the conspirators from the treason of the Governor in setting aside the will of the people and his usurpation of the powers of the National House of Representatives, in pronouncing upon the qualifications of one of its members, and giving a certificate of election as Delegate to Congress to a man whom the people had rejected, down through the greater part of the proceedings of the courts, and especially the conduct of the Governor during the last two sessions of the Legislative Assembly, and irrefragable evidences of conspiracy against the liberties of the people are apparent at every step. Every act of the conspirators is consistent with every other act to make their plot a success. While engaged in this nefarious business, they throw dust in the eyes of the nation by making an outcry against polygamy—as if they cared anything about our marriages—in order to conceal and accomplish their deeper design.

20. The most active tools in this conspiracy have been some of the Federal officials. Their positions have given them opportunities which they have been willing to avail themselves of. The preamble of the Constitution of the United States assigns as reasons why it was framed: "To form a more perfect union, establish justice, insure domestic tranquillity, provide for the common defense, promote the general welfare, and secure the blessings of liberty to our-

selves and our posterity." Most excellent reasons for framing such a charter of liberty, and every officer who acts under it should keep these objects in view. But many of the officers sent here have acted as though they were determined that none of these blessings for which the Constitution was framed should reach us. The sanctity of home, the liberty of person, the modesty of maidenhood, have all been wantonly violated in the effort to punish the Latter-day Saints for their integrity to God and His laws. Instead of seeking to establish justice and insure domestic tranquillity, they have sought to array neighbor against neighbor, friend against friend, brother against brother, wife against husband and children against parents, and to loosen and destroy all the bonds which bind man to his fellowman. Their mission has not been to build up and cement society, but to tear down and break it up. They have taken delight in their efforts to sow dissension and strife, to tempt wives to betray their husbands and to induce husbands, by threats of severe punishment if they refused to comply with their wishes, to disown and forsake their wives, and to discard and bastardize their offspring, and to turn loose, as forlorn outcasts, those whom they had solemnly covenanted to provide for and protect.

21. When these officials commenced their attack upon us and our religion they found our homes filled with love and affection—husbands and fathers devoted to their wives and children, and doing all in their power to make them comfortable and happy; wives and mothers contented and at peace, honoring their husbands and proud of their relationship to them; and children whose respect and obedience testified to the reverence and esteem in which they held their parents. Husbands and wives and children dwelt together without compulsion or coercion. Nowhere on all this broad earth, where matrimonial ties are held to have binding effect, did such complete liberty exist as among the Latter-day Saints.

22. It is true, wives were sealed to husbands by the eternal Priesthood of the Almighty, for time and all eternity; but this union in the first place was only made possible by love, and by love the tie is perpetuated. Women knew their rights, and they knew they could not be compelled to live with an unworthy

man. Happiness reigned in our homes, because freedom reigned there, and all had their full agency. No better proof of this need be adduced than the fact that in the midst of all this persecution, and the many inducements there are offered to women to dissolve their family relationship, but few men have accepted the proffered terms and discarded their wives; and to the honor of our sisters be it said, not one woman that we know of up to the present writing has broken her marriage vow and dissolved her relations with her husband and children.

23. Yet it is to the destruction of these happy homes that all the efforts of these officials have been directed. In the sacred name of law, and under the guise of a pretended desire to enforce it, they would convert this condition of society, so peaceful and so admirable, into a pandemonium. They have worked to this end with such malignant cunning, such heartless persistence, and such unscrupulous disregard of the principles of justice as have no parallel in American history; and that they have not accomplished this result has not been for the want of effort on their part, but because God has been with His people, and His Spirit has been poured out upon them to strengthen and sustain them.

24. No man-made system or organization could have withstood the concentrated hate and violent assaults which have been directed against the Church of Jesus Christ of Latter-day Saints. Division and weakness would have shown themselves, fatal breaches would have been made in the framework of the system, and the imprisonment or enforced concealment of the leading men would have been followed by a decay of faith and the disintegration of the organization. But the Lord, in establishing His Church, provided against such contingencies as these. He promised—and all have been urged to claim the fulfillment of the promise—that He would give to those who entered sincerely into covenant with Him, a testimony of the truth for themselves, and to bestow His Holy Spirit upon all. It is this promise and its fulfillment that today constitutes the strength of the Church of Jesus Christ of Latter-day Saints.

25. The Prophet Joseph Smith was once asked by a visitor to the city of Nauvoo, the good order and prosperity of which struck him with surprise, how it was that he governed the people so as to produce such admirable results. The memorable reply of the Prophet of God was: "I teach them correct principles and they govern themselves." This was the secret of the good government at Nauvoo, and it is still the secret of the good order and freedom from strife and other evils which prevail among the Latter-day Saints in Utah and throughout all this mountain region where they have control. In what other community in the world could a governor, judges and other appointees act as these officials have done in Utah, without producing anarchy and the complete overthrow of all barriers which are erected for the protection of society and the rights of men? Our enemies are loud in their denunciation of the Priesthood and its influence upon the Latter-day Saints; but that violence and confusion do not reign in this fair Territory today is due to the teachings of that Priesthood and their influence upon the people who give heed to them. The people have been taught correct principles, and they govern themselves.

26. Do we overstate the truth when we say that every good, peaceably inclined citizen of Utah, Jew, Gentile and "Mormon" would enjoy more peace, more prosperity, more kindly feelings towards each other today if we had no Federal officials at all of the class of many who are now among us? When a governor introduces himself to the world and to the people he is sent to govern, in all his public utterances from the platform, and through the press, as the latter's avowed and bitter enemy, and prostitutes the powers of his high office to defame, malign and injure them, would not the Territory be better without such an officer? When judges openly announce from the bench that a law which is general in its language is to be made special in its application, and so instruct attorneys and juries, and punish with all the severity possible one class of citizens under its provisions while notorious offenders of another class go scot free, and, not stopping at this, go on to the public platform and denounce with voluble and unbridled truculence the class of citizens whose cases they expect to come before them to decide upon—had not the temple of Justice better be closed awhile, than such judges

should sit therein? Instead of seeking to insure domestic tranquillity, these officers have fomented strife, they have fostered religious hate, they have embittered class against class, they have sought in every way possible to destroy that charity which should exist in every community composed of citizens of different religions and politics. They have adopted and enforced a policy of non-intercourse between citizens. A Gentile citizen who has dared to speak of or treat a "Mormon" citizen as a friend and associate has been denounced and ostracized, and an impassable gulf has been created between them.

27. Is it any wonder, then, while some of the principal officers sent here to govern and maintain law, are the people's greatest enemies and the most deadly foes to law and order, that prejudice upon all questions affecting us and our Territory should prevail? Or that Congress should be induced, regardless of the Constitution and its guarantees, under the pressure brought to bear upon it by the incessant clamors and misrepresentation of this class to enact measures that would reach such a people as we are described to be? The Edmunds Law was begotten by prejudice, conceived in ignorance, and brought forth in hate. But its enforcement in these Territories is in the spirit of merciless severity and undiluted malice, and those who prosecute under it have not the excuse which a deceived and blinded Congress might plead for its enactment.

28. The officials here have gone far beyond the letter and spirit of the law itself, and strained it for the purpose of inflicting punishment; this was conspicuously so in the case of Elder Lorenzo Snow, one of the Twelve Apostles, whose trial upon the evidence presented would undoubtedly have resulted in his acquittal had he been tried before a righteous judge and an unbiased jury. If any one fact was more clearly established than another at his trial, it was that he was innocent of any violation of the law as charged against him. But he is a prominent man—one of the Twelve Apostles—and could not be permitted to escape. His case is now on appeal to the U. S. Supreme Court at Washington. In order to have it put forward on the calendar, he surrendered himself to the officers, and is now in the penitentiary.

The court has fixed a day when his case will be heard; and, as in every case that has gone to Washington, we hope, notwithstanding previous disappointments, that this will receive favorable consideration. It is of such trials as his—and his is but a sample of many others—that we justly complain.

29. The law, as it passed Congress, was harsh and cruel and sufficiently destructive of our rights and liberties to satisfy the implacable author, but by packing grand and petit juries with jurors who are selected expressly because they are the pronounced opponents of the accused and their religion—by strained constructions of the law—by extraordinary rulings framed to suit each case without regard to preceding rulings on the same points—and by charges to juries which amount to direct instructions to convict, this law is made an instrument of the most frightful wrong, and in the torture which it inflicts goes far beyond anything ever conceived of by the men who voted for its passage. It is to be remarked of many of the officers who enforce the law, that they seem to take delight in the misery which they think it brings.

30. As to justice in these courts as now constituted, and with the animus the officials manifest, it is out of the question. Every one knows before a trial commences what the sentence will be. Not one escapes, no matter how flimsy or insufficient the evidence may be, who is indicted if the prosecuting officer has made up his mind there shall be a conviction. He finds a willing judge and a pliant jury ready to execute his decree. As to mercy the adamantine heart of the prosecuting officer is impenetrable to the sentiment. If he decides that a victim shall be sacrificed the agony of wives, the burning tears of innocent and helpless children touch him with no pity and have no more effect upon him than if he were made of stone. Impudence and ferocity sit upon his brow. In all his proceedings he has a ready coadjutor in the judge of the third judicial district, who browbeats the accused, and evinces an inhuman exultation in pronouncing sentence, his only regret being, as he has expressed himself, that the law does not permit him to inflict sentences of greater severity. When these men decide upon the punishment which an accused man shall have, neither the eloquent arguments of

counsel, nor the insufficiency of evidence, nor the scantiness of the law, is allowed to stand in the way of the pre-arranged sentence. If they decide upon one indictment or three, upon six or twelve, they have only to intimate to a grand jury that such is their wish and they can be gratified. The more distinguished the man the more certain his fate.

31.No grand or petit jury has failed to find an indictment or a verdict against any man whom the prosecution and court have selected as a victim. The marshal, the prosecuting officers and the court, by the exclusion of all who have not been avowed enemies of the religion professed by the accused, and by the aid of the open venire, have been able to pack the juries to execute their will with unquestioning servility.

32.Seeing, therefore, how useless it is to make defense, many of the accused have made none, but have pled guilty. In doing so they did not acknowledge the rightfulness of the law, nor the justice of the punishment: for they viewed the law as unconstitutional and destructive of religious liberty and the punishment as an act of persecution; but by pleading guilty they saved costs, and what was of still greater importance, they saved their wives and children the humiliation of going into the witness stand and being plied with indecent questions by the brutal prosecutors. The majority of the accused, however, have felt it to be a duty to contest every inch of the ground and to let the world see how utterly destitute of justice these courts are in their treatment of these cases. For this reason they have suffered their families to be exposed to the rudeness of deputy marshals and the insolence of prosecuting attorneys; though to have saved their loved ones from these indignities they would otherwise have been willing to endure the full punishment of the court for the offense with which they were charged.

33.Against the brutalities, usurpations and falsehoods of men dressed in a little brief authority, we have appealed and apparently, until quite lately, appealed in vain. Our request has been a very modest one; it was simply that the wrongs under which we were suffering might be investigated; but investigation was the last thing that the foes to our liberties desired. A few weeks since our sisters followed in the wake of the brethren, and

in mass meeting assembled, at Salt Lake City, offered the same simple petition, sent up the same fervid cry for investigation, that the truth might be known and the real facts of the situation be made public. In their memorial to the President and Congress of the United States, they very consistently, and with the best grace in the world, modestly asked as follows:

34."We respectfully ask for a full investigation of Utah affairs. For many years our husbands, brothers and sons have appealed for this in vain. We have been condemned almost unheard. Everything reported to our detriment is received; our cries to be heard have been rejected. We plead for suspension of all measures calculated to deprive us of our political rights and privileges, and to harass, annoy and bring our people into bondage and distress, until a commission, duly and specially authorized to make full inquiry into the affairs of this Territory, has investigated and reported."

35.Is there anything unwise, imprudent or un-American in this? Do we injure man, woman, or child by such a request? Are any person's rights or liberties jeopardized or infringed upon by such a demand? We answer unhesitatingly, No! We simply ask for our own. Will not our fellow citizens grant it? We desire to infringe upon no one, in person or property, in rights or liberties, in privileges or immunities. All we ask is that they will grant us the same blessings they claim for themselves, and, if granted, we shall be abundantly satisfied.

36.Our sisters have had ample reason for their remonstrances and petitions. Nowhere else on this broad land have the officers of the law treated women with the same indignity, inhumanity and indelicacy that they have in Utah and regions adjacent. Lady witnesses have been arrested, placed under heavy bonds, guarded by impure men, carried on long and unnecessary journeys at unseasonable hours of the night, harassed and perplexed by improper and, occasionally, indecent questions, and treated frequently as though they were criminals convicted of the blackest crimes. A number have been committed to the penitentiary for refusing to answer questions that reflected on their virtue, or tended to criminate those to whom they were joined by the most sacred ties of affection and duty: The first wives—those recognized by the law under which the officers were acting, as the legal wives—have, contrary to all precedent, been compelled to testify against their husbands. We do not mention this fact to draw any line of demarcation between the first and plural wives. If joined to their husbands by the eternal covenants of God's house, all are alike honorable in His sight; His ordinances stamping their union as equally legal and lawful before Him. Their feelings are as acute, their affections as strong, their susceptibilities as delicate, one as the other. We simply mention this fact to show how utterly the judges and their aids ignore all precedents, ride over all well-established usages and make all things subservient—law or no law—to their effort, which, to use the expression of one of their leaders, uttered from the bench, is "to grind to powder" us and our institutions.

37. In Idaho Territory the usurpations of the officers have gone from bad to worse. They there out-Herod Herod in their disregard of the people's liberties. One of the latest movements has in view the revocation of all certificates given to school teachers who are members of the Church of Jesus Christ, which means the placing of our children, by the help of our taxes, under the tuition of those who would gladly eradicate from their minds all love and respect for the faith of their fathers. The duty of our people under these circumstances is clear; it is to keep their children away from the influence of the sophisms of infidelity and the vagaries of the sects. Let them, though it may possibly be at some pecuniary sacrifice, establish schools taught by those of our faith, where, being free from the trammels of State aid, they can unhesitatingly teach the doctrines of true religion combined with the various branches of a general education.

38. And in this connection permit us to urge upon the Saints in all the Stakes of Zion the necessity of caring well for the education of our youth. If we are to be a powerful people in the near future, wielding potent influence for good among the peoples of the earth, we must prepare ourselves for those responsibilities, and not expect that ignorance will avail us in that day; but a knowledge of true principle, of doctrine, of law, of the arts and sciences, as well as of the Gospel, will be urgently necessary to enable to fulfill, to God's glory and the renovation of the world, the responsibilities which we believe will, by right of our calling, at that time be most assuredly ours.

39. If the threats which are uttered and the war that is made against the Latter-day Saints were made against any other people, they would become unsettled and discouraged. A session of Congress has not been held, and scarcely a President's message been published for years, without some threatening and inimical action or words against the majority of the people of Utah. But we have had this kind of opposition in various forms to contend with from the beginning. We should scarcely have built a house, planted a tree, opened a farm or formed a settlement, if we had allowed menaces or attacks to have deterred us. We have had to live by faith, as all the just must do. The present persecution should not be allowed to weaken us in our exertions to improve.

40. We should live together in love; there should be union in every family circle, and harmony in every neighborhood and city. We should be cleanly in our persons, in our dress and in our habitations and surroundings. Industry should be habitual with the adults of our community, and the rising generation should be taught its lessons and be impressed with its value as a means of happiness.

41. God has given us the earth as a dwelling place, and when mankind live as they should do, it is a delightful residence. It is our duty to adorn and beautify it—to make it so lovely and attractive that angels may condescend to visit it. We should, therefore, have fruitful farms, choice orchards, well arranged gardens, and if every dwelling is surrounded by flowers it will neither detract from its beauty in the eyes of visitors, nor make it less attractive as their home to the children of the household. In some quarters there has been ruinous neglect on the part of parents in making their homes attractive to their children. A well-ordered, lovely home, in which peace and good-will prevail, is a place of perpetual delight to those who reside there, whether old or young. Where such homes exist the young who live there are not found loafing at street corners or stores, nor spending company at late hours.

42. Books and musical instruments are now so cheap as to be within the reach of the most humble. By furnishing means of instruction, amusement and enjoyment at home, parents can, by adding kind words and loving deeds to their children tie them by bonds of affection that can never be broken; and in after years those children will think of that home as the brightest and dearest spot in their memories; in their minds it will always be surrounded by a heavenly halo.

43. The aim of every farmer, orchardist and gardener should be to produce the best grains, fruits and vegetables. So also with our stockmen; they should raise the best horses, horned stock and sheep; and those who pay attention to poultry should take pains and secure the best breeds. The trouble in raising the best qualities of grain, fruit and vegetables, is no greater than in raising inferior articles of the same kind. A good colt, calf or lamb costs but little, if any, more to raise it than a poor one does—and then how much more valuable and saleable first class grains, fruits, vegetables and animals are than those which are inferior! The Lord has given us a land in which grains, fruits, vegetables and animals can be raised to the utmost perfection; and we should appreciate and take full advantage of our climate, soil and water. With the exercise or good judgment, proper care and well applied industry, we can have the best productions of the vegetable and animal kingdoms at our disposal, and the poorest man in the land can have on his table such bread, fruits and vegetables as would be difficult, if not impossible, to find on the tables of the wealthy and noble of lands less favored than ours.

44. Our cities are generally well laid out. Our city lots are roomy. But we should provide for the increase of population. Sanitary regulations should be strictly enforced. Care should also be taken to secure plenty of unoccupied space for public grounds. They act as lungs for large and crowded cities; but it is in the early settlement and laying out of cities they can best be secured. Then land is cheap, settlers are not so numerous, and the struggle for eligible sites is not felt. That is the time to secure and lay out squares for public grounds; trees should be planted as quickly as possible, and be carefully protect-ed, and, as population increases, the grounds should be made attractive. And in this connection permit us to call attention to the burial places of our dead. For a people whose reverence and labor for their dead are as great as ours, we are strangely neglectful of their last resting places. One reason for this is the scarcity of water, and the difficulty of getting it to the cemeteries. But this is no justification for the neglect shown in many places—the grounds left unfenced and uncared for, and cattle frequently allowed to roam at will over the tombs of the loved ones. Artesian wells in many localities are being bored with great success, and in many burial places water may yet be secured by this means for their adornment with trees, shrubs and flowers—change which will be gladly welcomed by all.

45. In the construction of our residences, school rooms, meeting houses, tabernacles and other public buildings, there is room for the employment of the most cultivated and unlimited taste. With the increase of facilities during the past few years, there is no longer any need for such structures as we formerly had to be content with. The principles of architecture should receive attention in all our settlements, and there is no good reason why convenience, a regard for health, and beauty should not go hand in hand in the erection of all our private and public buildings. The construction of our Temples at St. George, Logan, Manti and Salt Lake City has furnished opportunities for many of our young men to obtain a knowledge of skilled branches of mechanism, the effects of which are visible in their own homes and the homes of their neighbors. And while we should impress upon the rising generation, as qualities of incalculable worth, that they should be pure in their morals, and have a high standard of honor, of truth, virtue and integrity, that they should be obedient to their parents and their God, and cherish a reverence for everything holy, be loyal to their country, and respect all constitutional laws; we should not neglect to instruct them in those branches of industry which will make them self-supporting, valuable citizens. All industrial pursuits claim our attention, and we should endeavor to impart to our young people knowledge, skill and good management in

farming, stock-raising, manufacturing, mechanism, trade, commerce and the arts and sciences. Give our young people an opportunity, and they will excel as missionaries abroad and in every branch of skilled industry at home, and be behind none in the practice of the leading and useful professions. This they have demonstrated in every instance when they have gone out of the Territory to colleges and schools, and to receive technical instruction in the profession or branches of art.

46. As the world must yet know, the faith that was taught by the Lord Jesus to the Apostles, and by them to the world, and that brings forth the same fruits now as then, can only be extinguished in a pure people by their destruction. It is this faith that the Lord has restored to the earth, and that we possess. So long as men and women who receive it remain pure, that faith will live and thrive and bring forth the fruits of righteousness. This every Latter-day Saint has proved. But faith should be cultivated. By cultivation it increases. The present is a time when the Latter-day Saints should devote themselves to their religion with all the ardor of their souls. They should so live as to enjoy the Holy Ghost and its gifts for themselves. These are needed by every man and woman to enable them to endure the trials which they have to meet.

47. At this point it may not be improper to again solemnly warn the officers and members of the Church against all conduct that tends to immorality and unchastity. We are being continually, though most falsely, accused of teaching and practicing sexual vice under the garb of religion. No charge could be more utterly false; for no system of philosophy, no code of ethics, no articles of religion since the world was first peopled, ever taught more strictly and emphatically than does the Church of Jesus Christ of Latter-day Saints the paramount necessity of personal purity in the relations of the sexes. Of this the Saints are well aware. Let us see to it, then, that our actions correspond with our faith; for we may rest assured that no prominence of opposition, no ties of family, no influence of wealth can save us from the penalty if we break the law of God in this regard. But a few weeks ago it became the

sad duty of the Quorum of the Twelve Apostles to sever from the communion of the Saints one of its members who had violated the law of chastity. He was a man of education, of experience, of judgment, of long standing in the Church, but neither these nor his exalted position to the Priesthood could save him from the penalty of the law he had so flagrantly broken. And as with him, so with all others. The law must be administered by the officers of the Church with justice and impartiality, with malice towards none, but with due regard to the commands of God and the honor of His holy name. Hear it, O house of Israel! ye who are seeking to attain to the Celestial Kingdom of our Father—none but the pure in heart can see God; none but those who have sanctified all their affections and passions by entire and complete subservience to His laws can dwell in His eternal presence!

48. Let us also remember that the condition of a community, as a whole, depends upon the condition of the individuals composing it; as are its components parts, so is it in its entirety. If the individual members of a people are wise, just, intelligent, honest, honorable and pure, that community will be distinguished among its fellows by those peculiar virtues.

49. To apply the lesson to ourselves, each one for himself, if we wish to see the Church of Christ prepared as a bride for the Savior, we must, individually, live our religion and exemplify in our own lives those virtues which we know must adorn the bride before she can enter the presence of her Lord. This matter of personal purity, faith, diligence and good works is one that we cannot delegate to our neighbor, or place on the shoulders of other men and women; but each must do his own duty, each bear his own responsibilities, each set his own house in order, each magnify his calling, each live near unto God, if he expects God to draw nigh unto him.

50. We are pleased to be able to report that the Lord is abundantly blessing the labors of the brethren and sisters engaged in the performance of ordinances pertaining to the Temples of our God; and a great work is being done therein in the interest of both the living and the dead. We have been pained, however, to learn that in some few instances, either through misunderstanding, carelessness, or

partiality, recommends have been given to unworthy persons. This is a grave error—one that should be guarded against with every possible care. The Bishops and Presidents of Stakes should take every precaution that the House of the Lord is not defiled by the intrusion of the unworthy through their recommendation. We strongly advise more caution and greater care in this regard.

51. To the Saints we say that those who desire the blessing of entering into and officiating in these houses dedicated to the Most High should render themselves worthy thereof. They should live in harmony and peace at home, they should settle all their differences before attempting to enter this holy place, which should be a house of peace, a house of order. They should pray with their families morning and evening, and not neglect secret prayer; they should honestly pay their debts to all men, and not only to man, but remember also that which is due, as tithes and offerings, to the Giver of all. They should observe the Word of Wisdom in the spirit and meaning thereof, for it is most inconsistent to carry the smell of whiskey and tobacco into the sacred precincts of the Lord's House. Or in a word, they should observe to do and to keep all God's holy laws and commandments, that when they enter His House they can enjoy that spirit which gives zest, power and efficacy to their administrations.

52. The reports from the Elders engaged in the active field of missionary labor are far from discouraging, though the results in baptisms in those lands where our brethren have labored the longest, will not equal the showing of former years. The annual number of baptisms, as well as the total membership of the Church in Scandinavia, now exceeds those in Great Britain. But the most marked results of our labors, of late, have manifested themselves in New Zealand, amongst the Maories, the aborigines of those islands, who being a remnant of the house of Israel, nearly allied to the Sandwich Islanders, have received the Gospel with gladness, and show great firmness and integrity in cleaving to its truths.

53. In the present depressed state of business, and consequent lack of employment, the Bishops must not forget the duty which, as fathers of the people, they owe to the poor and inexperienced. None must be permitted to suffer. But we have learned long since that benevolence to be worthy of its name must be guided by reason as well as by sympathy; and aid should be given primarily with the view of doing real and lasting good to the recipients, and must be bestowed in a manner to discourage improvidence and the growth of a spirit of pauperism. Our aim should be to develop the powers of the worthy poor through that thoughtful help which will utilize the resources of the new-comer or unfortunate, and assist those who, if able, are willing to help themselves. In these labors of love we trust the fullest cooperation and most perfect harmony will exist between the Ward authorities and the Relief Societies, that thereby they may mutually strengthen and enhance the value of each others' efforts.

54. Nor must the families of the missionaries be forgotten; those whose whole time is spent in proclaiming the truths of the Everlasting Gospel must not have reason to complain of want of consideration by their brethren and sisters. If the counsel heretofore given to the Presidents of Stakes and Bishops with regard to the establishment of missionary farms had been more widely carried out, we believe the results would have been more encouraging. Brethren, there is still time for action in this matter.

55. In these times, when many men, because of being faithful to religious convictions, are immured in prison, if proper precautions are not taken, there is danger of their families suffering on account of their absence. Great care should therefore be taken by the Presidents of Stakes, the Bishops of Wards, the Priests and Teachers, and by the people generally, to see that, in the absence of their natural guardians and protectors, they are protected in their persons and property. Where there is any lack of means, they should see that it is amply supplied; not in the shape of charity, but as a duty we owe to our brethren who are persecuted for conscience sake, and who are immured in prison for their adherence and fidelity to their wives and families.

56. The so-called Christians are most egregiously ignorant of the relations of man and wife; and while they talk quite flippantly of the eternity of matter, they know nothing of the eternity of matter and spirit of which man

and woman are composed, nor the eternity of the marital relation, nor the eternal covenants entered into between men and women, husbands and wives, parents and children. The acme of all their hopes in relation to matrimony and its continuance, as expressed in their covenants, is "UNTIL DEATH DO YOU PART." What a gloomy picture! What, nothing more? No; this is the general formula of all the churches, of all the millions of so-called Christians who dwell on this continent, and the hundreds of millions of professed Christians throughout the world. What in this case becomes of all our hopes of eternal life, eternal exaltations in the mansions of the just? Does God indeed "join them together," as they say; and then does death divide them and sever the covenant? No, indeed; they make no such covenant, and therefore cannot break it. Their covenant is until death does them part—no further, no more. When this is accomplished all is ended in regard to their matrimonial relations. What of the resurrection from the dead? What of the New Jerusalem—the celestial glory—the eternal union that the authors of fiction write about? To them, as to the professed Christians, it is all fiction—a beautiful dream which death dissolves.

57. We have other views, other ideas, other hopes. We believe in death being swallowed up in victory, in "a new heaven and a new earth, wherein dwelleth righteousness;" in the resurrection of the just, both men and women, parents and children. Our Gospel, "The Gospel of the Son of God, brings life and immortality to light." We believe in Jerusalems, such as the one which John saw when banished as a slave to the Isle of Patmos because of his religion, where the promises made to Abraham, Isaac and Jacob are to be fulfilled; which had a wall great and high, and had twelve gates, and at the gates twelve angels—"and the twelve gates were twelve pearls; every several gate was one pearl." Its walls were of jasper, its streets and the city were pure gold. The foundations of the wall were garnished with all manner of precious stones, and the glory of God did lighten it, "and the Lamb is the light thereof." Its pearly gates had written upon them the names of the twelve tribes of the children of Israel, and the foundations of its walls "the

names of the Twelve Apostles of the Lamb." "The throne of God and of the Lamb shall be in it, and His servants shall serve Him; and they shall see His face; and His name shall be in their foreheads." The porters of its gates were angels and its light the glory of God.

58. What was written on those pearly gates? The names of the twelve tribes of Israel. Who was Israel? Jacob. From whom did the twelve tribes descend? From Jacob. What were their names? The names of the sons of Jacob, which he had by four wives. Jacob, then, was a polygamist? Yes; he was one of those barbarians of which the Judge of the Third Judicial District says: "These practices might have been proper in a barbarous and primitive time—in crude times—but they won't do now. Civilization has thrown them away. It won't do to gather up these old customs and practices out of the by-gone barbarism and by-gone ages, and attempt to palm them upon a free and intelligent and civilized people in these days."

59. How free the people are in Utah today needs no discussion. If the judge cannot stand these things it would seem God and the Lamb can, for He is the light of the city on the gates of which are written the names of twelve men, the sons of one man, by four women—a polygamist. Had Jacob lived now, the judges would have sent spies, spotters and deputy marshals after him, and if caught would have sent him to the penitentiary with other honorable men who had the courage of their convictions, and for whom "God is not ashamed to be called their God, for HE HAS PREPARED FOR THEM A CITY."

60. And what of his handmaids; will they be there? Yes; where there is so much beauty and glory and so many of his servants the women are sure not to be absent. Besides are they not one? Has not "God joined them together?" It would not be a heaven without them; they have entered into covenants with the men for time and eternity in the Lord; "They twain are one flesh." "The man is not without the woman nor the woman without the man;" but the corrupt have no place therein. For without are dogs and sorcerers and whoremongers and murderers and idolaters and whosoever loveth and maketh a lie.

61. Speaking of the sexes, the same God who created Adam, created Eve, "male and

female created He them; and blessed them and called their name Adam." Who are women? The mothers of the whole human family. They were all born of women, who were created and prepared as companions and helpmeets for man. To Eve God gave another seed in the place of Abel. "For God said, He hath appointed me another seed instead of Abel whom Cain slew." Who made this appointment? God. From whom came kings, emperors, prophets, seers and revelators? They came through women who were often Prophets themselves, and who were frequently ministered to by angels. Jesus was born of a woman; they were His companions on earth, were with Him at His death, and were first at His sepulcher, and will be His and His saints' companions in heaven.

62.Polygamy is not understood nor our relations thereto. There is nothing secret about it. When it was first proclaimed in Salt Lake City, in 1852, Elder Orson Pratt went shortly after to the city of Washington and published it to the world in a paper called The Seer; after that President Brigham Young, who was a known polygamist, was reappointed, by the President, Governor of the Territory of Utah.

63.It is alleged that we are in danger of perverting the nation's morals. But how much danger there is of this may be judged by the morality of those in our midst who endeavor to make us believe they represent the government and nation, as exhibited in the following:

CRIMINAL STATISTICS OF SALT LAKE CITY FOR THE YEAR 1885

Total estimated population 26,000
Mormons .20,800
Non-Mormons 5,200
Or 5 Mormon to 1 non-Mormon.

There were during the year 1,276 arrests
Adult males 1,126
Adult females 134
Boys under 10 years old 16
                                          1,276

The 20,800 Mormons produce arrests . . .96
The 5,200 non-Mormons
    produce arrests . . . . .1,180.or 1 to 12 1/3.

64.There are now in the city some six Brothels, forty Tap Rooms, a number of Gambling Houses, Pool Tables, and other disreputable concerns, all run by non-Mormons. But for the presence of those who are constantly making war upon us, our city would be free from the contaminating influences of houses of prostitution, gambling houses, dram shops and other such death-dealing concerns, and the taxes would be greatly reduced. But, as it is, the "Mormons" are forced to pay a liberal tax in support of the laws against the lawlessness of their non-tax paying enemies. Every other town, city and county in the Territory, and all the jails and the Utah penitentiary, show even a much cleaner record in favor of the "Mormons" than the foregoing exhibit portrays.

65.If it should be said that these convictions were made by "Mormon" judges and justices, it must also be remembered that the District Court always stands open and gladly extends relief to any who consider themselves wronged by "Mormon" officers.

66.It is a remarkable fact that in all these years since the introduction of polygamy among us, not one Gentile has ever entered into it through our agency; those who are corrupt have easier methods which are furnished and approved by the professed Christian world. These are not "Mormon" institutions; but the practical outgrowth of monogamy.

67.The question arises, if in thirty-four years not one Gentile has adopted polygamy, how many years will it take to demoralize the fifty-five millions of the United States? The fact is, our Elders could not thus introduce it if they would, and any one so doing would be immediately severed from the Church. The question arises, What shall we do? Shall we, because of the inconsiderate action of Congress, of the judiciary and of other Federal officers, array ourselves against the nation, and sacrifice our loyalty to the greatest nation which is now in existence? Certainly not. Joseph Smith told us that "the Constitution of the United States was given by inspiration of God." Is it less true today than it was then? What shall we do? Have they passed "test oaths" which are forbidden in that Constitution? Yes. Have they not "prohibited the free exercise of" our "religion?" Yes. Have they not passed ex post facto laws?

Yes. It is not only said that no ex post facto law shall be passed, but also no "law impairing the obligation of contracts." Some thousands of people in this Territory have entered into sacred contracts for time and for all eternity; Congress has passed a law making this a crime, and many men, who will not violate their contracts, are in prison today for a violation of the law of Congress which is ex post facto, making that a crime which was not a crime when the law was passed. This, then, is another violation of the Constitution. What about the "religious test oaths" instituted in Idaho, Arizona, and in certain forms in Utah? What about the 4th amendment to the Constitution, which says: "The right of the people to be secure in their persons, houses, papers and effects, against unreasonable searches and seizures, shall not be violated; and no warrant shall issue but upon probable cause, supported by oath or affirmation, and particularly describing the place to be searched, and the persons or things to be seized?" In article 8 of the Constitution it is stated, "Excessive bail shall not be required, nor excessive fines imposed, nor cruel and unusual punishments inflicted." In George Q. Cannon's case lately, in an offense for which the law provides $300 fine and six months' imprisonment, a bail of $25,000, and an additional $20,000 for two complaints which were not at the time supported by any evidence, was required: thus he was made subject to a $45,000 bond. Is this excessive bail? If so, it is a violation of the Constitution. Thus we have six different violations of the Constitution of the United States, sanctioned, approved or winked at by those who have sworn to sustain that charter of liberty.

68. These are no fictions, but veritable facts that we have had to meet and put up with. But because of this misrule and perversion of the Constitution, and of the rights of American citizens shall we be inimical to that Constitution or to the institutions of the country to which we owe allegiance? Certainly not. These errors have to be corrected, and it is our duty, so far as lays in our power, as it is the duty of all honorable men in these United States, to sustain the Constitution thereof, and to oppose in all legitimate ways any infringement of that instrument.

69. We are inconsiderately asked to rend our family relations and throw away our ideas of human freedom, political equality and the rights of man, and "to become like them." Be like them for what? Like them in sapping the foundations of human liberty, like them in violating our constitutional oaths, like them in covenanting with wives and children till death parts them, and no more but a dead blank? What does it mean to be like them? It means that E pluribus unum is a fiction; it means that we tamper with and violate that grand palladium of human liberty, the Constitution of the United States and substitute expediency, anarchy, fanaticism, intolerance and religious bigotry for those glorious fundamental principles of liberty, equality, brotherhood, human freedom and the rights of man. It means judicial corruption, perverted justice, missionary judges, class rulings and minority representation; it means judicial tyranny and oppression, the introduction of spies and spotters, of packed juries and intolerance, of prisons, chains and terrorism; and introduces cruelty, oppression and despotism, in the place of liberty, equality and brotherhood. We cannot do it. We will rally around the flag of our country and maintain the glorious Constitution for weal or woe. We cannot and will not lay aside our fealty to the nation at the bidding of political demagogues, religious fanatics or intolerant despots.

70. To you, Brethren, who as Presidents of Stakes, High Councilors and Bishops, hold in your keeping the purity of the lives of the members of the Church, we again repeat the warnings and admonitions of our former epistles and say, upon you lays the responsibility of the keeping of God's house in order, each according to his calling, ordination and appointment, and to the extent and scope of the duties imposed upon him. In these duties you cannot be negligent without incurring the displeasure of the Lord and losing His Spirit. The Lord holds each man responsible for that portion of the flock which is placed in his care. The Relief Societies, the Young Men and Young Women's Mutual Improvement Associations, the Sunday Schools, and the Primary Associations should all receive your hearty encouragement and support. Each of these organizations can be of great benefit to all of you in your labors. All of these Presidents are or

should be subject to the authorities of the Wards and Stakes where they reside.

71. It devolves upon the Twelve Apostles and the Seventies to see that the Gospel is carried, and to carry it themselves, to all the nations of the earth—first unto the Gentiles and then to the Jews. This is their especial calling, and they should keep it constantly before them.

72. Like the First Presidency, the most of the members of the Council of the Twelve Apostles have been greatly restricted in their movements. One of their number, Elder Lorenzo Snow, is in prison. He bears his imprisonment with equanimity and fortitude; and so far as we know all of the Apostles feel cheerful and full of faith, and determined to magnify their calling.

73. Our latest advices from President Joseph F. Smith report him as enjoying good health and to a goodly degree the spirit of his office and calling. From his letter, recently published in the *Deseret News*, the Saints have learned his sentiments concerning the work of God, and the present situation of affairs.

74. In conclusion, we say to all the officers and members of the Church, be diligent in reading the word of God, contained in the Bible, the Book of Mormon and the Doctrine and Covenants; search the prophecies and let your hearts be comforted by their precious promises. God has said concerning Zion, that "no weapon that is formed against thee shall prosper; and every tongue that shall rise against thee in judgment thou shalt condemn. This is the heritage of the servants of the Lord, and their righteousness is of me, saith the Lord."

75. Our history is one continued illustration of the fulfillment of this word of our God. We can truthfully ask, where is the weapon that has been formed against Zion which has prospered? or where is the tongue that has risen against Zion in judgment which has not been condemned? Her enemies have been very numerous; in many instances they have been prominent and powerful. They have strutted their brief hour upon the stage and have thought they were performing doughty deeds; but where are they? If their names were not kept in remembrance in our history, as enemies of the work of God, the most of

them would be as utterly forgotten by the world as if they had never lived. But Zion will prosper and prevail. There may be storms to be endured; there may be trials to be encountered and difficulties to be overcome; and there may be seasons when clouds of darkness may envelop us and shut out the horizon from our view; yet if we humble ourselves before our God and keep the covenants we have made with Him, He will neither desert nor neglect us.

76. The Lord has said, through one of His Prophets, "Hear, ye that are afar off, what I have done; and, ye that are near, acknowledge my might. The sinners in Zion are afraid; fearfulness hath surprised the hypocrites. Who among us shall dwell with the devouring fire? Who among us shall dwell with everlasting burnings? He that walketh righteously and speaketh uprightly; he that despiseth the gain of oppressions, that shaketh his hands from the holding of bribes, that stoppeth his ears from hearing of blood, and shutteth his eyes from seeing evil. He shall dwell on high; his place of defense shall be the munitions of rocks; bread shall be given him; his waters shall be sure."

77. These are the kind of people we should be; for it is such people who will build up and be counted worthy to stand in Zion. Then it can truthfully be said: "That the Lord hath founded Zion, and the poor of his people shall trust in it."

78. Be it our lot to live as Saints, to maintain every principle of virtue, of honor, of truth and integrity, to keep sacred the covenants we have made with God and with each other, and to obey in all things the word of the Lord. So shall we and our families be blessed of the Lord in time and throughout the eternities that are to come.

79. God bless you and all the friends of Zion and peace and happiness in this world and, in the world to come, with life everlasting, in the name of Jesus Christ. Amen.

Your brethren in the Lord,

JOHN TAYLOR,

GEORGE Q. CANNON,

Of the First Presidency of the Church of Jesus Christ of Latter-day Saints.

March, 1886.

ADDRESS 35

Due to the question over the legality of polygamy and the desire of certain federal officials to imprison, prosecute, and/or otherwise hound church leaders into compliance, many of the Brethren, notably members of the First Presidency, were forced to go underground to avoid any public appearance. Unable to attend the 56th Semiannual General Conference of The Church of Jesus Christ of Latter-day Saints, and in lieu of what they might have said had they been able to attend, President John Taylor issued the following epistle which was read to the conference by Heber M. Wells on October 8, 1886. As a number of the Brethren were experiencing the same difficulties with the law, it was thought advisable to hold general conference in Coalville, Utah, rather than in Salt Lake City as was the usual place.

AN EPISTLE of the First Presidency to the Church of Jesus Christ of Latter-day Saints.

BELOVED BRETHREN AND SISTERS:

1. Six months have passed away since we last had the pleasure of addressing you through our General Epistle, and we find ourselves face to face with the Fifty-sixth Semi-Annual Conference of the Church in this dispensation. The past six months have been very fruitful in events in which all of us have been deeply interested. The season has been a healthful one; no sickness worthy of note has affected our people unpleasantly. The summer has been both unusually dry and hot, and many of the crops have not yielded as good a return as usual. Nevertheless our land is still filled with plenty, and man and beast have sufficient to supply their wants.

2. Our enemies during the past half year have not slackened their activity in the work of persecution. If there has been any difference, it has been pursued with greater vindictiveness and more flagrant disregard of law and justice than at any time previous. Those who have been compelled to endure the penalties inflicted upon them have submitted, in nearly every instance, with a cheerful equanimity and fortitude that must have won the admiration of heaven and of all just men. That which has been accomplished furnishes but little cause for gratification to those who have been engaged in the inhuman task of persecuting a people for the practice of their religion. There have been but few persons in all who have been tried and convicted who have felt sufficiently terrified at the prospect of punishment to express a willingness to accept the rulings of the court instead of the law of God, as the guide for their consciences.

3. The faith of the Latter-day Saints seems to grow stronger from these efforts to destroy it; and men, women and children who have been living in the practice of the requirements of their religion feel more determined than ever to maintain their integrity and to do all that the Lord requires at their hands with cheerful willingness, whatever may be the consequences from a worldly point of view.

4. This persecution is not without its effects upon those who have made a pretense of being faithful members of the Church. Iniquity is being brought to light. The wrong-doer is being made to feel, in a most remarkable manner, that his sin will find him out; and the evidence that God is pleading with and awakening the consciences of those who have been living in sin is frequently furnished to us. There have been many violations of the law of God practiced among us which have been hidden from the public gaze. The trials through which we are passing have the effect of causing these evils to be brought to light. It seems as though the Lord is tearing the covering, not only from the nations of the earth, but from the Latter-day Saints; and the time is not far distant—in fact, it has reached us already in part—when

the sinner in Zion shall tremble, and fear shall seize upon the hypocrite.

5. So far as we can learn there is an increased disposition on the part of the faithful officers of the Church to do all in their power to cleanse the Wards and Stakes in their charge from those who will not conform to the requirements of the Gospel. Greater strictness is being shown, and the Saints who have the love of the truth within them feel that the time has come to put away their follies and their sins far from them and to conform to a higher standard of righteousness.

6. The great, crying sin of this generation is lasciviousness in its various forms. Satan, knowing how powerful an agency this is in corrupting men and women, and in driving the Spirit from them, and bringing them under condemnation before the Lord, uses it to the greatest extent possible. It requires an incessant warfare to check its spread and to prevent the people of God from becoming its victims. No people who practice or countenance these sins can be accepted of the Lord or find favor in His sight. His anger will fall upon them unless they thoroughly and heartily repent of every such evil. When we take into consideration the teachings we have received upon this subject, the holy covenants into which we have entered, and the professions which we make, unchastity should have no existence among us. It is sorrowful to contemplate that Satan finds those among us who are willing to yield to his temptations, and thus bring misery upon themselves and all connected with them.

7. We solemnly call, as we have done so often before, upon all the officers of the Church to set their faces like flint against practices of this character. Those who indulge in them must be dealt with according to the laws of God, and they must be made to feel that if they do indulge in this wickedness they cannot have the fellowship of the Saints nor a standing in the Church of Christ. If men and women would only profit by the experience of those who have fallen, they would resist the allurements of sin and walk in the path of righteousness. "The wages of sin is death." The misery which it brings upon the guilty, and upon all connected with them, furnishes

some idea of the dreadful condition of the wicked who die in their sins and do not obtain the forgiveness of their God. Oh! that men and women could be warned, and that they would turn to the Lord and seek unto Him, humble themselves before Him, put away their sins, and obtain His Holy Spirit to be their guide and their companion, then no matter what the circumstances might be in which they were placed, they would have the peace of heaven, the joy of the Holy Ghost, and a conscience void of offence towards God and man! And this is the condition in which every Latter-day Saint should live.

8. The circumstances which surround us, though in many respects painful and trying, are not such as to discourage the faithful Saint. We have been taught to expect just such scenes as these through which we are passing, or, at least, just such opposition as we now have to contend with. What we now behold is in direct fulfillment of the predictions of God's servants to us in this generation, and unless these events take place His word could not be fulfilled.

9. Not only have the Prophets in our day spoken about the events which should take place in connection with the latter-day work and the opposition it would have to contend with, but the Prophets of old foretold with accuracy and minuteness that the people of God should be few and their dominions should be small, because of the wickedness of "the great whore" which should make war against them. But notwithstanding that the multitudes of the earth should fight against the Church of the Lamb of God, the power of God would descend upon the Saints and upon His covenant people; and they should be armed with righteousness and with the power of God and great glory. The scenes in which we are now taking part were known to men of God, by the spirit of revelation, thousands of years ago. But while they predicted the troubles and difficulties with which the people of God would have to contend in the last days, in every instance they broke out in language of encouragement respecting the result of the struggle and predicted the complete triumph of God's kingdom over all the opposing powers of evil.

10.Therefore, in this contest which is forced upon us we do not wage a defense that is hopeless. The God of heaven is on our side. He has made promises to Zion which cannot fail. He is mightier than all of earth's hosts, and by His wonderful providence can bring to pass, in His own way, the fulfillment of all the words of His inspired servants. Upon this foundation we can rest secure. No weapon that is formed against Zion can prosper; and every tongue that shall rise against her in judgment shall be condemned. Our enemies gloat over the prospect of our destruction. Even those who feel inclined to be friendly can see no prospect for our deliverance except by the abandonment of our religion. But it is better for us to die than to abandon our God! We cannot do this without throwing away all hope respecting the future and the great eternity that awaits us. We know that there is no faithful Latter-day Saint who feels for one moment like yielding to the demands of the wicked.

11.Our religion is given to us from our God. We have received it by the revelations of Jesus to us. When all the world was in darkness and struggling and contending about doctrines and ordinances, He condescended to restore the Everlasting Priesthood from the heavens and His Gospel in its purity and fulness and power. We were left no longer to grope in the dark and to follow the traditions of our fathers or the false teachings of uninspired men. The path of salvation was plainly marked before us, confirmed to us by the unerring testimony of God's Holy Spirit. Our souls, in walking in that path, have been filled with ineffable joy and peace. While others who have rejected the truth have been apprehensive and fearful concerning the events that were taking place and that were likely to take place, we have had a peace, a satisfaction of mind, and a contentment that have made our position unique. God has given unto us the fruits of His Gospel in great abundance. We behold them in our family organizations. We behold them in our Wards, and in our Stakes, and in our entire Church. His blessing has visibly rested upon us, and His power has been displayed in our behalf. Every faithful Latter-day Saint has rejoiced in the abundance of

the gifts of the Spirit which He has bestowed; and no promise that was made to the ancient Saints, or that has been made to us, upon the condition of our faithfully obeying the Gospel, has been withheld from us. We have been a people greatly blessed of the Lord, and our hearts should swell with gratitude and thanksgiving to our God for His abundant mercies.

12.We again call upon the Presidents of Stakes and the Bishops of Wards to look carefully after the wants of all who are within their jurisdiction and stand in need of assistance. Especially should the families of those who are in prison, or who have been compelled to flee, or who are upon missions, be tenderly cared for. They need both aid and sympathy. Those upon whom the heavy hand of persecution does not personally rest should be willing to share the burdens of their afflicted brethren and sisters, by contributing to the comfort and sustenance of those who are deprived of the society and guidance of husbands and fathers for righteousness' sake. By so doing they will lay up treasures in heaven, and share the reward for these trials. The weight of this persecution falls upon the women and children. Deprived of the presence and support of their husbands and fathers, upon whom they have been accustomed to rely, they are comparatively helpless and naturally a prey to deep anxiety. The care and training of the children thus bereaved devolves upon their mothers, whose burden is made doubly heavy to bear. The Teachers should be particularly diligent in visiting such families, and in watching over their welfare. Thus the hands of the mothers should be strengthened, the young encouraged, the wayward admonished, and the heroic example of heads of those households held up for admiration; and everything possible should be done to make their situation tolerable and pleasant. In this way we can bear each other's burdens, and so fulfill the law of Christ, and witness to our God and to the world, that though we may not personally suffer persecution, our sympathy and faith are with those who are afflicted for adherence to their religion, and that we are ready and willing to do our part and manifest our devotion to the cause of Christ.

13.The District Courts of Utah still pursue their extreme, vindictive and unrelenting course. The law is perverted, not justly administered; the object appears to be, not the maintenance of social purity nor the rectification of alleged evil, but the oppression and distress of individuals because of their religious position. The Latter-day Saints are under the most sacred obligations to do the will of God. At the same time they wish to obey every valid law of the land. But by the strained interpretation and the unwarrantable application of the Edmunds Act, men are made offenders because of their religious scruples, and rendered criminals when they are not fairly amenable to the law. Defendants who, according to the evidence, have only lived with one wife, are "presumed" to have cohabited with another wife, and thus are convicted of "cohabiting with more than one woman," when the presumption is obliterated by the proof.

14.In other cases when parties, in their desire to observe the requirements of the Edmunds Act, have privately agreed to the voluntary relinquishment of association as husband and wife, the husband has not escaped the vengeance of the law. Though there are numbers of instances where such parties have honestly endeavored to live within the law, yet whenever indictments have been found, husbands have almost invariably been convicted and sentenced to the full penalties of fine and imprisonment.

15.We take this opportunity of recording our high appreciation of the spirit of self sacrifice which has been manifested by our sisters throughout the entire crusade. They have shown a fortitude, a courage, a devotion and love which must be the admiration of posterity. They have not faltered in their devotion to the principles of righteousness, have not shrunk from the consequences attending obedience to God's law, and have been a source of strength and encouragement to their sons, their husbands and their fathers. There are numerous instances which have come to our knowledge of wives offering to make the most heroic sacrifices to save their husbands from the penalties of the law.

16.Contrary to the jurisprudence of centuries, legal wives are compelled, under threats of imprisonment, to testify against their lawful husbands and disclose family secrets that should never be bared to the public eye. This is a gross violation of the law under which they act, and opposed to recognized public polity and family rights. And by the system of "segregation" an offense which, according to the law, is punishable at the utmost extent by six months imprisonment and a fine of $300 is multiplied into many offenses and the full sentence inflicted for each fraction of that offense.

17.The plan of finding several indictments for the one offense has been discarded and the scheme adopted of making several counts in the one indictment. The number of these counts is not regulated by law, but is left to the arbitrary disposition of a grand jury selected from the class in hostility to the defendants, and usually subject and pliant to the will of an extremely bitter and unscrupulous Prosecuting Attorney. The petit juries empanelled for the trial of persons thus indicted, are also picked out for their known antagonism to the society to which the accused belong. And in almost every instance they find verdicts as requested by the Prosecuting Attorney, oblivious of the exculpatory portions of the evidence. Juries are thus selected, not only for the trial of cases under the Edmunds Law, which permits challenges of "Mormons," but by the open venire process strong anti-"Mormons" are chosen to try "Mormons" accused of offenses not included in the Edmunds Act, and thus again is the law perverted and prostituted to work oppression and injustice. The Courts, as a rule, decide on questions of law and procedure as desired by the District Attorney, and ignore the request of defendant's counsel for legal instructions to the trial jury. Thus the victims marked for the sacrifice on the altar of hate, are, humanly speaking, entirely at the mercy of their persecutors.

18.Another new step in the progress of this iniquity is the rule, recently enforced, of compelling persons charged with violations of the Edmunds Act to plead guilty or else have their families forced upon the witness stand, to be plied with shameful questions concerning the most private acts and relations of their husbands and fathers.

Children of tender years are compelled to give evidence on subjects unsuited to their immature minds, and to become the instruments of their parents' incarceration. Formerly, defendants were permitted to plead not guilty and then go upon the stand and testify against themselves, declaring the facts and leaving the result with the jury and the court. By this means a conscientious man who did not consider himself guilty of crime, could explain his position, and meet the issue without doing violence to his convictions. But this poor consolation is now denied by the malevolent District Attorney. The unfortunate defendant must do violence to some extent to his conscience by pleading guilty, or suffer the anguish of witnessing the tortures of his wives and children when subject to the legal rack of a brutal cross-examination, in which no regard is shown for a wife's affection or a daughter's love, the sensitive shrinking of a virtuous woman from exposure of her marital associations, or a child's tearful aversion to disclosing the secrets of home for the conviction of a father. Such proceedings prove that the object is not the vindication of the law but the promotion of human suffering, providing the victims are members of the "Mormon" Church. Many of the objects of this malevolence are aged men who have passed the allotted three score years and ten, who have contracted no new marital obligations, but are engaged in caring for their families as honor and righteousness dictate. The heartless severity with which such defendants are pursued is also evidence that the object is not the public benefit but the wreaking of vengeance upon members of a Church.

19. Another indignity which has been heaped upon the heads of Latter-day Saints is the charge of perjury which the reckless District Attorney has publicly but not legally made. Witnesses who have been compelled to testify against their dearest friends, when answering "I do not know" to questions concerning matters of which they were not cognizant, have been insulted and abused and branded with perjury. All evidence they disclose which suits him he uses as undeniable truth before a commissioner or a jury, but everything elicited from the same witnesses that does not suit his purpose he denounces as perjury. And he has the hardihood to claim that this crime is taught and encouraged by the "Mormon" Church. The refutation of this atrocious calumny is found in the standards of Church doctrine, and in the fact that the brethren who are now lingering in prison for declining to repudiate their wives, have been sent there, in nearly every instance, through their own testimony or the testimony of their families. And it is well known that every one of them could have escaped the penalties of the law if they would but promise to obey the law, in future, as construed by the courts. It would have been easy to make the promise and avoid imprisonment. But their regard for their word was such that they would not make a promise which they did not intend to keep, so they accepted a loathsome prison and pecuniary loss in preference to the appearance of falsehood.

20. It may seem to those who do not understand the situation that the requirement of future obedience to the law is but reasonable and that every good citizen should make this agreement. But an explanation of the facts will speedily dissipate this conclusion. Obedience to the law as construed by the courts, would be difficult of comprehension if the numerous and diverse definitions of the law were considered. But according to the latest rulings, a promise to obey the law signifies an agreement to violate the most solemn covenants of marital fidelity that mortals can make with each other and their God. It means the utter repudiation of loving wives and the separation either of the father and some of his children or of the mother and her children. It is a promise not to visit, go to the same place of worship or amusement, or recognize, associate with, or even call on when sick or dying, or when her child is sick or dying, the plural wife who has been faithful in all things. It means dishonor, treachery, cruelty and cowardice. It places not the law but a gross and wicked perversion of the law, above the revealed will of God and the noblest promptings of the human heart. It is a promise that no true Latter-day Saint can make, and that no humane being would demand.

21.Thus the legal difficulties that surround the Saints are not so much the effects of a special and partial law aimed at a feature of their religion as of the wicked and absurd constructions of that law and its improper and unprecedented administration, prompted by malice, inspired by Satan and intended to crush out a system of religion which cannot be overcome by truth, reason and the agencies of enlightened humanity.

22.Before leaving this uninviting subject we desire to say to the Latter-day Saints, that though we are suffering so acutely from the inhumanity of our fellow men, we must not descend in the slightest degree to acts that would savor of retaliation, or in the least seek to curtail any man in his individual rights. We wish it fully understood by the Saints and by all the world that we have a profound respect for all wholesome and constitutional laws. We are the firm and unequivocal advocates of law and order, and of every principle associated with human freedom, and though we regard the Edmunds Act, in its provisions and its administration, as ex post facto, cruel, oppressive and unconstitutional, yet we are not contending against it in our own interests alone, but we are also fighting the battle of civil and religious liberty, and of freedom of conscience in behalf of our common humanity and in the interest of every people. We feel assured that, as the founding of these United States formed an epoch in the history of human liberty, so this action of ours will have due weight in restraining the tendency to intolerance and oppression that today uprears its head to stay the progress of human freedom. We say, as Elder Parley P. Pratt very forcibly expresses it in one of his political effusions:

"Come ye Christian sects; and Pagan,
    Pope and Protestant and Priest,
Worshippers of God or Dagon,
    Come ye to fair freedom's feast.
Come ye sons of doubt and wonder—
    Indian, Moslem, Greek and Jew,
All your shackles burst asunder;
    Freedom's banner waves for you."

23.Probably at no period in the world's history has Satan had such power over the hearts of the children of men as he appears to wield at the present. He has flooded the earth with lies, endeavoring by means of these deceptions to retard the work of God, to destroy its influence, and to make victims of its believers, especially those who have the authority to administer the ordinances of the Gospel. A more striking illustration of his power in this respect has not been furnished us than was witnessed at the meetings which were attended by some of the members of the Grand Army of the Republic who were passing through here. It would be incredible to believe that people could be so deceived by the false statements which were made to them by our enemies who reside here, had it not been witnessed. The most abominable falsehoods, which could be disproved with the greatest ease, were told with an unblushing effrontery that was Satanic; and though many of the visitors had opportunities of seeing for themselves, and of mingling with the people, some went away fully imbued with the idea that the Latter-day Saints ought to be exterminated from the face of the earth. But to the credit of humanity be it said, others became thoroughly disgusted with the proceedings, and denounced unsparingly the folly and wrong of condemning a people affording so many evidences of the qualities that go to make excellent citizens, from the one-sided statements of their avowed enemies.

24.The course of the former class is an illustration of the malignant power of falsehood wielded by Satan in other directions and places. If lies could overwhelm the work of God, we should be completely crushed under their weight. It is this great influence upon which Satan depends to thwart the purposes of God and check the spread of truth; and, unfortunately for the world, it appears willing to drink in his spirit and to believe his fabrications. It is this that arouses mobs and causes them to indulge in acts of violence and hostility against unoffending servants of God, and that has incited them to shed the blood of innocent men in the most cruel and barbarous manner.

25.By means of this incessant stream of falsehood which is continually being sent forth, the rulers of our nation are urged to adopt the most extreme measures against us. It appears vain to point to our works, to show what we have done in reclaiming this land from its original sterility, and building up a grand commonwealth in these mountains—a commonwealth, rich in all the elements of greatness, lightly taxed, free from debt, with peace and union prevailing to an unparalleled extent throughout all these mountains where Latter-day Saints reside. It is in vain that we point to our frugality, our temperance, our comparative freedom from crime, and the peace and good order which exist wherever we are in the majority. All these evidences of thrift and virtue go for nothing, and the National Legislature feels that it is under the necessity of devising schemes to take away from us the rights we have inherited, and which belong to us as a free people, and to bring us into bondage to those who malign us, and who would take delight in destroying us.

26. Every effort possible was made during this last session of Congress to secure legislation of the most proscriptive and sweeping character against the Latter-day Saints. Not only was it the design to reach persons who believed in and practiced plural marriage, but our enemies went so far as to propose the complete annihilation of every political right belonging to those who were free from the charge of polygamy, and whose only crime was that they were members of the Church of Jesus Christ of Latter-day Saints. Congress adjourned without acting upon this measure. Already we hear the notes of preparation for a renewal of the campaign against us. Filled with anger at their non-success at the last session, our opponents are preparing for the onslaught at the coming session of Congress, and we are threatened with vengeance of the most dreadful description.

27. But in this, as in all other circumstances and conditions, our trust is in God. This is His work. He has thus far taken care of it and preserved it, and has delivered us from the many plots which have been framed against us. It has progressed thus far only by His power, and not by the power of man. Whatever glory there is connected with the establishment and progress of this great work is due entirely to Him. Man's wisdom, education, shrewdness, wealth and ability have not been the factors that have produced success; but it has been the blessing, the power, and the overruling providence of our God.

We have had to trust Him in the past in the midst of unnumbered foes; we must trust Him in the future against the terrible odds that are pitted against His work and His Gospel. We know, and can boldly testify to the Latter-day Saints, and to the whole world, that the Lord hath founded Zion, and that no power beneath the Celestial Kingdom can prevail against it.

28. But those who fight against it will share the fate of all who have ever fought against it. Who is there that has prospered in his warfare against Zion. Who can point to the laurels which have been won in fighting the work of God? What man or what nation has gained credit and glory in the earth for successes achieved over the feeble Latter-day Saints? We have seen generation after generation of our opposers pass, one after another, into cold oblivion. They have strutted their brief hour upon the stage, appearing to think that they were accomplishing wonders. But they have passed away, and the memory of their deeds only lives in our historical archives. So it will be with those who now occupy so large a portion of public attention as crusaders against the Saints, and who imagine themselves to be such doughty heroes.

29. Not only has Satan sent forth his lies outside of our society, but he uses his influence in this direction among us. The tendency in our settlements and cities to listen to and believe in every wild and slanderous rumor which may be put in circulation is to be deeply deplored. No matter how unfounded and destitute of even the semblance of truth such reports may be, there are those among us so silly and credulous as to readily believe them. The injury that is thus wrought is not easily measured. Many of the evils from which we have suffered have been greatly aggravated by this disposition on the part of some who call themselves Latter-day Saints. The man who frames a lie is a great sinner; but the one who loves a lie, and who circulates a lie after it is told, is also under condemnation. Many stories go from mouth to mouth concerning the truth of which those who repeat them know nothing. But it seems as though the constant repetition of a falsehood impresses many people as though it were a fact.

30.Where Latter-day Saints, so-called, are found telling that which is untrue, they should be called to an account. It is written that whosoever loveth and maketh a lie shall not be permitted to enter into the Holy City, nor to have a right to the tree of life, but they are to be without, with dogs, sorcerers, whoremongers, murderers and idolaters. The Lord has said, "He that telleth lies shall not tarry in my sight." Latter-day Saints should be warned upon these points, that they may not grieve the Spirit of the Lord, nor do injury to their friends and neighbors, by indulging in this pernicious habit of repeating and attaching credence to every slander and false rumor that may be put in circulation. But every one should be careful, when they hear a story about their brethren and sisters, to refrain from repeating it until they know it to be true, and then not to do so in a way to injure the person about whom it is told. The reputation of our neighbors and the members of our Church should be as dear to us as our own, and we should carefully avoid doing anything to another or saying anything about another that we would not wish done or said about ourselves.

31.We testify that those who give way to this influence, who take delight in reading lies which are published about us in papers circulated in our midst or outside of our Territory, who delight in listening to the false and malicious representations which are made concerning the servants and people of God or His work, or who themselves gossip about and aid in the dissemination of these things to the injury of their fellows, will, unless they speedily repent, lose the Spirit of God and the power to discern between truth and falsehood, and between those who serve God and those who serve Him not. Their own minds will become so darkened by the spirit of falsehood that the Spirit of God will cease to have power with them and will flee from them.

32.Among the sins into which some who are called Saints have been betrayed is Sabbath-breaking and over indulgence in useless pleasure. "The Sabbath was made for man, and not man for the Sabbath." But it is the Lord's day and should be spent as he directs. We are not left to the doubts and queries which enter into the polemics of sec-

taries on this important matter. We have the word of the Lord upon it, direct. He has declared to us through His Prophet:

33."And the inhabitants of Zion shall also observe the Sabbath day to keep it holy.

34."And that thou mayest more fully keep thyself unspotted from the world, thou shalt go to the house of prayer and offer up thy sacraments upon my holy day;.

35."For verily this is a day appointed unto you to rest from your labors, and pay thy devotions to the Most High;

36."Nevertheless thy vows shall be offered up in righteousness on all days and at all times;

37."But remember that on this the Lord's day, thou shalt offer thine oblations and thy sacraments unto the Most High, confessing thy sins unto thy brethren, and before the Lord.

38."And on this day thou shalt do none other thing, only let thy food be prepared with singleness of heart that thy fasting may be perfect, or, in other words, that thy joy may be full."

39.These commandments of the Lord do not admit of Sunday excursions to the lake or the canyons or other places any more than manual labor. That day will be held sacred to the service and worship of God by every true Latter-day Saint. Those who desecrate it reject the word of the Lord and will not be held guiltless. We admonish all members of the Church to obey this commandment and the officers of the Church to see that it is not broken with impunity.

40.The mania for recreations of various kinds which has seized upon many of the people is harmful in several ways. It unfits them for the regular duties of life. It renders them restless and impatient of proper restraint. It obstructs business. It tends to contract habits of dissipation. It throws our young folks into the company of persons whose society should be shunned. It cultivates worldliness. It conduces to many evils, and the spirit of purity, temperance, holiness and peace will not abide in resorts such as have been established for the purpose of enticing the Saints into folly. Many thousands of dollars have been worse than wasted during the past summer on excessive amusements and sometimes unseemly diversions. The influential men and women of the Church should discountenance this evil, and with all wisdom and prudence endeavor to check it and prevent its increase among the Saints.

41. We have no disposition to deprive either young or old of proper amusement. It is necessary to perfect health and rational enjoyment. It should be provided by those who have the watchcare of the people, especially for the young, and conducted without sinfulness and without excels. But in these times of trial and distress to many, is it seemly to indulge in frequent and hilarious junketings and to act as though we disregard the afflictions of our brethren and sisters who are placed in difficulty and jeopardy? When most of our leaders are in exile, when good men are thrust into prison, when many families are plunged into grief at the enforced absence of those who are dear to them, when the cords of oppression are being drawn more tightly and the small liberties remaining to us are being gradually taken away, when our enemies are forging fetters for our feet and planning for our utter destruction, and when Satan is working with all his forces to weaken our ranks by leading the Saints into sin, is it a time to waste our days in useless pleasure and spend our nights in noisy revels? Rather, should we not humble ourselves before the Lord and seek by faith and devotion to good works to obtain power that we may prevail against our foes? We do not believe in a long-faced sadness or the piety that consists in a sanctified appearance. There is no need for drooping heads or a sad countenance. A cheerful spirit should be cultivated and hearts should be gladdened by words of cheer. But these are serious times and the sorrows of the afflicted and the carousings of the thoughtless seem utterly incongruous when all profess to be brethren and sisters. Let unseemly levity be abandoned and let the solemnities of eternity rest down upon those who are called the Saints of the Most High God.

42. Notwithstanding the violent and unabating opposition which is arrayed against us the work of ministering in the ordinances of the Lord's House continues, and the blessing of the Heavens still follows these administrations. As we have so long expected and so frequently been warned, Satan rages as he views his domain trenched upon, his captives delivered, and the souls of men wrenched from his grasp by the labors of the living for the dead in and through those sacred ordinances that belong alone to the Gospel of the Son of God, administered in holy places by His chosen servants and handmaidens. And it must not surprise us if the rage of the archenemy of mankind increases and his emissaries grow more relentless and cruel, more brutal and inhuman in their efforts to stay this work, as the number of temples increases and the thousands of Israel go in thereto to minister the ordinances of salvation for their ancestors and departed friends. We further rejoice that the work of erecting the Salt Lake and Manti Temples goes steadily forward, and that the latter is nearing its completion with all the rapidity that could reasonably be expected when we consider the condition of the Church and the people and the difficulties under which they labor.

43. It is pleasing to notice the increased feeling of anxiety on the part of the Saints to have their children educated in schools where the doctrines of the Gospel and the precious records which God has given us can be taught and read. Our children should be indoctrinated in the principles of the Gospel from their earliest childhood. They should be made familiar with the contents of the Bible, the Book of Mormon and the Book of Doctrine and Covenants. These should be their chief text books, and everything should be done to establish and promote in their hearts genuine faith in God, in His Gospel and its ordinances, and in His works. But under our common school system this is not possible. In Salt Lake City, we understand, an effort is now being made to establish a school of this character, and, we are informed, the prospect for its success is very encouraging. The Brigham Young Academy, at Provo, and the Brigham Young College, at Logan, are both doing excellent work in this direction and should be patronized and sustained by the Latter-day Saints. In no direction can we invest the means God has given us to better advantage than in the training of our children in the principles of righteousness and in laying the foundation in their hearts of that pure faith which is restored to the earth. We would like to see

schools of this character, independent of the District School system, started in all places where it is possible.

44. The life of a Saint is not simply a personal perfecting, it is also a factor in the entire scheme of earth's redemption. No one can be saved alone, by himself or herself, unassisted by or unassisting others. The weight of our influence must be either for good or harm, be an aid or an injury to the work of human regeneration, and as we assume responsibilities, form ties, enter into covenants, beget children, accumulate families, so does the weight of our influence increase, so does its extent broaden and deepen. The Scriptures inform us that God created this earth as a habitation for man and he placed man on it that he might have joy, a joy that is to be eternal.

45. To accomplish these purposes, the preparatory one of peopling the earth, and the ultimate one of man's eternal happiness, He, the Creator, established marriage, and commanded those he first placed here on earth to be fruitful and multiply. This institution he regulated by strict laws given through his servants to His people in their various dispensations; and His Son, our Savior, emphasized these commandments, by most unequivocal teachings with regard to the sacredness of the marriage covenant, and of the sinfulness of divorce for other than the most grave departures from the spirit and intent of that covenant. In this is wisdom, for the experience of the world, in all its ages, proves that where lax ideas exist with regard to marriage and divorce, more especially where those ideas find expression in lax legislation, there we discover peoples and nations whose code of morals is inferior, and where sexual irregularities and sins increase, until that righteousness, which has been so truthfully said "exalteth a nation," ceases to have an existence in their midst.

46. To a people who believe as we do, that true marriage was divinely instituted for the multiplication of mankind, and is not a union for time alone, but reaches into the eternities, the disruption of families by divorce is an evil of no ordinary character, not only bearing a harvest of sorrow and suffering in this life, but also having a far reaching influence into the world beyond the grave, and by involving others in ruin who had no voice in the separation or power to avert its occurrence. For this reason the Latter-day Saints of all people should be most loath to sunder sacred ties once formed, and most determinedly opposed to the severance of unions made in holy places in God's appointed way, for light and trivial causes; and the efforts of Teachers and Bishops in their labors amongst families where differences, alienation or quarrels exist, should always be to effect reconciliation, promote union, inspire mutual forbearance and increase love. Only when every kindly counsel and ministration fail should that last resort, a divorce, be permitted. And in such cases those who have received of the sealing power of the Church should also be separated by the same authority that bound them together: until this is done new alliances are sinful.

47. There is another evil that is growing amongst the peoples of the world that is not unfelt amidst the Latter-day Saints. It is the crime of self-murder. Suicide should be made odious among the people of God—it should be emphasized as a deadly sin, and no undue feelings of tenderness toward the unfortunate dead, or of sympathy towards the living bereaved, should prevent us denouncing it as a crime against God and humanity, against the Creator and the creature. It is true that the exact enormity of the act is not defined with minute detail in the Holy Scriptures, or the limits of its punishment given; but to believers in the God whom we worship it has always been regarded as a sin of great magnitude; and in many countries especial pains have been taken to discourage it, by refusal to bury in consecrated ground, by indignities offered to the lifeless remains, or by such lack of funereal observances as would produce a peculiar and horrifying effect upon the survivors.

48. Now, while not advocating measures of this description, we do not think that the same laudations and panegyrics should be pronounced over the self-murderer as are so freely uttered over the faithful Saint who has gone to his eternal rest. There is a difference in their death, and that difference should be impressed upon the living, unless the deceased, at the time of the rash act, was in such a mental condition as not to be wholly

responsible for his actions; but again, if this condition be the result of sin, of departure from God's laws, then the unfortunate one, like the inebriate, is not altogether free from the responsibility of acts committed while in this state of mental derangement; if he is not censurable for the act itself, he is for the causes that induced it. In such cases the mantle of charity must not be stretched so widely, in our desire to protect our erring friends, as to reflect dishonor on the work of God, or contempt for the principles of the everlasting Gospel. There is an unfortunate tendency in the natures of many to palliate sins by which they are not personally injured, but we must not forget that such palliation frequently increases the original wrong, and brings discredit on the Church and dishonor to the name and work of our blessed Redeemer; in other words, to save the feelings of our friends we are willing to crucify afresh the Lord of life and glory.

49. The reports of our Elders engaged in missionary labors in foreign lands are far from discouraging, when we consider the tempest of misrepresentation and abuse that has flooded the lands of civilization with regard to ourselves, our objects and our methods of evangelization, as well as the prejudices that have to be overcome and the persecution which has to be met by those who have sufficient moral courage and stamina to obey so unpopular a doctrine as the fullness of the Gospel of our Lord Jesus Christ. Yet were the results even less encouraging than they are, we have still imposed upon us the duty of warning the peoples of the earth of the judgments of Almighty God, which in his own due time must surely come. The divine injunction given to the servants of God in former dispensations and reaffirmed in this, "Go ye into all the world and preach the Gospel to every creature," has never been abrogated nor annulled; and our duty to carry the Gospel's warning voice to all nations, kindreds, tongues, and peoples, to the Gentiles first and then to the House of Israel, still remains unchanged.

50. President Woodruff and the members of the Council of the Twelve Apostles still continue in the active performance of the duties appertaining to their Priesthood and calling, occasionally hampered, it may be, in certain directions by the unrelenting attacks of our persecutors. Almost without exception they have enjoyed good health, while the more aged ones, including Elder Lorenzo Snow, in prison, have been blessed with a vigor and with powers of endurance remarkable for men of their years. Brother Lorenzo Snow bears his unjust imprisonment with much fortitude and patience and is a source of great comfort and strength to his fellow-prisoners, deprived of liberty for their obedience to the requirements of God's law.

51. President Joseph F. Smith continues to send us words of faith and encouragement, of patience and brave endurance, and, so far as his position and surroundings will admit, he is zealously furthering the interests of God's holy Church and Kingdom.

52. We hear favorable reports of the good done by our Sunday Schools, Primaries, Improvement Associations and Relief Societies, and we feel to abundantly bless the brethren and sisters who so diligently and faithfully labor therein for the instruction of our youth and the benefit of the poor. We desire to encourage all engaged in these duties to continue with unabated zeal and disinterestedness in these labors of love and mercy, that the institutions under their charge may rise to yet greater heights of excellence and usefulness, and the scope of their influence for good in the midst of the Saints continually increase, and upon parents we urge the wisdom and desirableness of fostering by their faith, influence and example these admirable institutions for the benefit of their children.

53. In consequence of the unusually dry summer the crops have not been so abundant as in some former seasons. Although the yield of wheat is comparatively small it commands but a low price in the market. Wisdom and economy suggest that our farmers should not be anxious to make immediate sales. Every kernel of wheat is precious. It should be stored carefully for future use, in such a manner as to preserve it from destructive insects and the action of the elements. The warnings which have been given to Israel on this point were not uttered in vain, as coming time will abundantly establish. Let no grain be wasted nor thrown heedlessly upon a depressed market to continue the depression

and fritter away the fruits of arduous toil.

54.Preparations should be made for the proper care of stock during the approaching winter. Too many animals are permitted to perish for the lack of food and shelter. After the Lord has blessed the flocks and herds of His people, it is sinful to allow them to wander on the bleak prairies or snow-covered benches to die of cold or starvation. Unless provided with shelter from storm and inclement weather loose stock should be gathered up and sent to warmer localities for winter range.

55.The wool crop of the past season has been very large and sheep-owners have made fair profits on their products. But domestic economy recoils at the spectacle of 7,000,000 pounds of wool being shipped out of the Territory to be returned in the shape of inferior cloth; and be purchased at high prices by woolgrowers and others. Factories among our own people should utilize the whole of this product, employing hands that are now idle to manufacture honest goods, and thus retain in the Territory much money that goes to build up industries afar off. Our home factories are turning out most excellent articles at reasonable prices; these should be purchased in preference to foreign made goods, because they are more durable and because home industries ought to be patronized.

56.On the same principles and for the same reasons the hides and pelts which are now shipped away to be brought back manufactured into articles that can be made in this Territory, ought to be retained and worked up for home use. Factories for this purpose, carefully conducted, would soon return fair profits, while the whole community would share in the resultant benefits.

57.In conclusion, we say to the Latter-day Saints: Put your trust in God, as you ever have done. He will not fail you. Continue to live in strict conformity to His Gospel. Humble yourselves before Him in mighty faith and prayer. Confess your sins one to another; and go to your God and confess to Him, and obtain His forgiveness therefor. Live in close communion with the Holy Ghost, that it may be your constant companion, and that through its heavenly influence you may be prepared for every coming event. The Lord is holding a controversy with the nations, and He has said, "After your testimony cometh the testimony of earthquakes. * * * And also cometh the testimony of the voice of thunderings, and the voice of lightnings, and the voice of tempests, and the voice of the waves of the sea, heaving themselves beyond their bounds. And all things shall be in commotion; and surely men's hearts shall fail them; for fear shall come upon all people." Already His words upon this subject are being fulfilled. The elements are joining their voices with the voice of His Elders in testimony of the near approach of the end. And woe! to the people or the nation that fight against Zion, for, as we have often had occasion to say, God will fight against them. His wrath will be poured out upon them. Babylon will fall, and the refuge of lies will be swept away; and truth and righteousness will cover the earth as with a flood, in fulfillment of the words of the prophets. Greater signs will appear in the heavens above and on the earth beneath, bearing awful testimony of the near approach of that great day when our Redeemer will be revealed from heaven in power and in great glory.

58.With continued prayers for your safety, and for your posterity in the work of God, and with most earnest desires that every man, woman and child will he faithful to the trust which God has reposed in us, we remain,

Your brethren and fellow servants,

JOHN TAYLOR,

GEORGE Q CANNON,

Of the First Presidency of the Church of Jesus Christ of Latter-day Saints. President's Office, October 6, 1886.

ADDRESS 36

Due to the question over the legality of polygamy and the desire of certain federal officials to imprison, prosecute, and/or otherwise hound church leaders into compliance with questionable civil law, many of the Brethren, notably members of the First Presidency, were forced to go underground to avoid public appearances. Unable to attend the 57th Annual General Conference of The Church of Jesus Christ of Latter-day Saints, and in lieu of what they might have said had they been able to attend, President John Taylor issued the following epistle that was read to the conference by Bishop G. F. Whitney on April 8, 1887. As a number of the Brethren were experiencing the same difficulties with the law, it was thought advisable to hold General Conference in Provo, Utah, rather than in Salt Lake City as usual.

AN EPISTLE of the First Presidency to the Church of Jesus Christ of Latter-day Saints in General Conference Assembled.

BELOVED BRETHREN AND SISTERS:

1. Once more, in the providence of the Almighty, we are permitted to address you in an Epistle. It would give us very great pleasure to be able to communicate to you our views orally; but through circumstances with which you are all familiar this gratification is denied us. We rejoice, however, that the privilege of communicating a few of our thoughts in writing is still at our disposal. We have profound feelings of thanksgiving to our God for His goodness and mercy unto His people. Personally we have reason to be very grateful to Him for His preserving care in our behalf.

2. Zion has been passing through a series of trials which God will undoubtedly overrule for our good. The experience of the past two years and a half has convinced us that there has been a divine providence in all that has taken place, and in the shaping of ordeals to which the Saints have been subjected. Painful as they have been to very many, the day will come when they will be acknowledged as having been the means of bringing great benefits to Zion.

3. The Twelve Apostles and their Counselors have labored with great efficiency, as far as they have had opportunity, among the people, and have been active in attending to the duties devolving upon them. The health of all has been good. Recent letters from those outside the Territory convey the intelligence that they are enjoying their labors and are successful in the performance thereof. The latest advices from President Woodruff assure us of his good health. Though he is now past 80 years of age, his bodily and mental vigor appear unimpaired.

4. We ourselves are in the enjoyment of good health, and able to perform our duties with satisfaction to ourselves and pleasure in the liberty that we enjoy. President Joseph F. Smith's health has been somewhat impaired, but he is now fully restored.

5. The most gladdening news we can communicate to the Conference of the Church in our Epistle is that from every part of the land which we inhabit, gratifying reports have been received of the zeal and diligence of the people in attending to the duties of their religion. Probably at no time in our history has there been a better disposition manifested by the people to attend their meetings on the Sabbath day, and on fast days, and the prayer meetings which have been held during week day evenings. Meetings have been held at suitable residences on many of the blocks in the city and country wards throughout these mountains. These have generally been crowded, and have been occupied by the Elders in giving instruction, and by the Saints in bearing testimony and in prayer. All the Elders who have been free to travel who have reported the results of their labors to us, agree in saying that at no time in their experience have the meetings which they have held been so crowded as during the past winter. These evidences of the faith and diligence of the people are exceed-

ingly gratifying to us. We have been cheered in listening to them, for we know that when the Latter-day Saints repent of their sins and devote themselves assiduously to keeping the commandments of God, their enemies cannot have much power over them.

6. As a people, in times past we have been careless and indifferent in many directions. Neglect of duties has been too common everywhere. Hypocrisy has been indulged in to some extent, and a laxity has prevailed in many quarters concerning the keeping of the laws of God which is not in accord with the spirit of the Gospel. Under these circumstances the Lord has permitted persecutions and trials to come upon His people that have had the effect of stirring them up to greater diligence. When the Lord, for any reason, turns His face away from His people, and is slow to hear their cries, thorough repentance on their part and a complete abandonment of their evil ways are sure to bring back His favor, and to cause His countenance to shine upon them. This has been the case in every age when God has had a people upon the earth. In our own day we have seen frequent illustrations of this. We have never feared for the people, nor for the prosperity of the work, when the Latter-day Saints have been fully alive to the duties and requirements of their religion. But when they have been careless and neglectful, or disobedient and hard in their hearts, then we have trembled; for when the Saints are in such a condition the displeasure of the Lord is sure to be awakened against them, and His scourges are likely to fall upon them. The Lord does not permit His enemies, nor the enemies of His people, to prevail over them for any length of time when they are living near unto Him and complying strictly with His will. All His promises, of the brightest and most glorious character, encouraging and hopeful, are given to those who keep His commandments and who seek earnestly to carry out in their lives the principles of salvation which He has revealed. When a people are in this condition their enemies cannot have much power over them.

7. We attribute the failure on the part of our enemies to accomplish their wicked purposes during the last session of Congress to the fact that the Saints were more true to their professions, and were offering up, in sincere humil-

ity and faith, their petitions to the God of heaven for His interposition in their behalf. When we consider the character of the measures which were framed in the first place, and which it was the evident purpose of our enemies to force through and make law, it is clearly to be seen that our Father in heaven has restrained the efforts of the wicked and defeated them in their iniquitous designs. For a while it seemed inevitable that every liberty would be wrested from us, and that we should be brought into subjection to a most odious tyranny and be stripped of every right which belongs to free men. And though the measures which have been enacted are odious to the principles of true republicanism, still our enemies are disappointed in their schemes and feel that they have been defeated; while the Saints rejoice in the goodness of God, and feel assured that by His help and their continued faithfulness in keeping His commandments and relying upon Him, they will be able to endure, with patience and without grievous loss, all that the enemies of His Kingdom shall have power to bring upon them.

8. It is of the utmost importance that the teachings which have heretofore been given to the officers of the Church, and which it is not necessary to repeat at length here, should be kept in mind and carried out in the spirit in which they were given. Great responsibility rests at the present time upon those Elders who have liberty of action, and they should be untiring in their efforts to magnify their Priesthood and to do everything possible towards building up and strengthening the Saints in the practice of those holy principles which God has revealed.

9. Much depends in these days of trial upon those who bear the Lesser Priesthood. They have opportunities which are of unequaled advantage. They visit, or should visit, the people at their homes. They talk to them by their firesides. They can see their inner lives, and learn wherein they need strengthening and guiding, in order to be more efficient Latter-day Saints. When Priests and Teachers understand their duties and seek to enjoy the spirit of their offices, they can do an immense amount of good, for they are brought directly in contact with the people; they learn their wants, are made familiar with their weaknesses, and are in a position to check the growth of

evil tendencies in parents and in children. There is, in many instances, doubtless, too much formality in the character of these visits—a disposition to drop into routine and to ask stereotyped questions, without conversing in a way to bring out the real feelings and spirit of the households which they visit. Visits of this character are comparatively barren of results. To make them as productive of good as they should be, live, active men should be used as Priests and Teachers. The best ability in the various wards can find ample field for usefulness in performing these duties. Young men who have not had experience should be associated with those who have had experience, and they should be impressed with the importance of seeking for the Spirit of God to rest upon them in power, to dictate to them the very things that should be said to the family which they visit. The teachings which might be appropriate to one family, and be the very instruction which they might need, would not perhaps be so suitable for another family. Therefore, the necessity of having the guidance of the Spirit of God is apparent.

10. There is a tendency, almost amounting to an epidemic in some places, among the young people, to indulge in cigarette smoking. The habit is filthy, unhealthy, and pernicious generally. God has spoken so plainly on this subject that there is no room to question the impropriety of this practice. The Teachers should make it their especial business, in all kindness and in a mild, instructive spirit, to reason and remonstrate with young people upon this habit. Every effort should be made to check its growth amongst us. The habit, also, which some young people fall into, of using vulgarity and profanity, is one which should receive the attention of Teachers. This practice is not only offensive to all well-bred persons, but it is a gross sin in the sight of God, and should not exist among the children of the Latter-day Saints.

11. At the Priesthood meetings of Wards, Bishops and Counselors and other experienced Elders can do great good to the young men by imparting to them instruction upon these points and giving them explanations concerning questions which they may be asked upon the live issues and topics of the hour. There is a body of young men growing up in Zion, who, if taught as they should be, can be made most efficient in building up the Church and in strengthening its members against the various temptations to do wrong to which they are exposed. These young men are generally full of zeal and energy and good desires, and only need to be directed aright to accomplish immense results.

12. Connected with our temporal labors there is probably no point of more importance than the providing of employment for our people. The spirit of the Gospel of the Lord Jesus Christ is opposed to idleness. We do not believe that a man who has that spirit can rest content if he is not busily employed. There are many who come from other parts who have been accustomed to following branches of trade at which they cannot find employment here. There are a great many young men and young women growing up also, who do not have the necessary experience or knowledge to employ themselves. These cases should receive the attention and consideration of the Bishops and Presidents and other officers of the Church. We should aim to create industries at which the people can find employment. If all who have the influence of position, or the power that the control of means gives, would keep this subject constantly before them and work unitedly in the proper direction, a great many industries might be started in this Territory that would result in profit to their founders and give fixed employment to many who are now in want of it. In every Ward or Stake where there are opportunities of this character, judicious men should be selected to take the direction of such affairs and to make wise investments, so that discouragement will not follow through the loss of means or the unskillful handling of the business.

13. From the day of the organization of the Church of Jesus Christ of Latter-day Saints, the adversary of souls has stirred up the wicked to accomplish its destruction. Various agencies have been employed to effect this purpose. Falsehood, tradition, deep-rooted prejudice, the learning, wealth and power of Christendom, mob violence, fire, fetters, the rifle and the sword, wholesale expulsion and military force having been tried in vain, a new crusade has been inaugurated in the form of legislative and judicial tyranny, prompted by Satan and carried on by cunning adventurers and reckless fanatics.

14. Perhaps the most shameful and unrepublican attempt of this character was the latest scheme devised by the local conspirators. What is known as the Edmunds Law—the act of March 22nd, 1882—was hoped to be broad enough in its intended scope to secure the political control of the Territory to the anti-"Mormon" voters. A large number of both sexes were by that act deprived of the franchise. That it did not wrench the control of the Territory out of the hands of the majority of its residents, is not to be credited to the absence of such a wish and design on the part of its authors and promoters, but to the overruling providence of the Almighty. The ground which those who favored this measure seemed to take was, that it was both praiseworthy and justifiable to violate the soundest political principles, and even the Constitution itself, to take the political control of the Territory of Utah from the "Mormon" majority and concentrate it in the hands of the anti-"Mormon" minority. Having gone thus far to accomplish this end, it was scarcely to be expected they would hesitate to make other and more outrageous attempts, when they found that the Edmunds Law had not answered the full purpose for which it was intended. It appears to be one of the effects which follow a departure from sound republican and constitutional principles like the enactment of such a strange piece of legislation as the Edmunds Law, that every future attempt in the same direction will be more regardless of the settled principles of political liberty than its predecessor.

15. The Edmunds Law, instead of appeasing the anti-"Mormon" appetite for power, only whetted it. The success of its promoters in securing its passage, and the results which have followed, emboldened them to make the most extraordinary demands upon Congress for further legislation. Emissaries from Salt Lake City were employed and sent to Washington, sustained by funds levied upon and collected from the non-"Mormon" population of the Territory, to secure the passage of a law which would bind the "Mormon" people hand and foot, and leave them, their liberties, their property and all that makes life valuable and desirable, at the feet of their deadly enemies. They did not appear to doubt that their demands for legislation of this character against us would meet with ready

acceptance on the part of the National Legislature and the public generally.

16. On the first day of the first session of the Forty-ninth Congress, Senator Edmunds introduced a bill (numbered 10 on the Senate calendar) which contained shameful unrepublican features, the evident purpose of which was to entirely destroy all the liberties of the majority of the people of Utah. There were a few Senators who stood up manfully and resisted the passage of this measure as an attack upon religious liberty; but their protests and arguments were in vain. The bill passed the Senate and was sent to the House. It was ably discussed before the Judiciary Committee of the House by our friends, and everything was done that was possible to enlighten that committee concerning the affairs of Utah and the conspiracy which existed here to obtain the political control of the Territory. A new bill was reported by the chairman of that committee, as a substitute for the Senate bill, and the provisions of the new bill were found to be equally objectionable with the bill for which it was a substitute. The measure was modified and changed by wiser and more conservative legislators, in spite of the efforts of those who inspired it—a result which we view as due to the overruling power of Providence and the reluctance of some reasonable public men to sanction a measure so utterly subversive as this was of the rights of citizens. An agreement was reached by the Conference Committee, composed of members of the Senate and of the House, and in amended form the bill was reported to both houses, and passed without alteration. It finally became law, without the signature of the President. In its original form the palpable intention was to destroy the Church.

17. It is generally admitted that no such law was ever enacted in this country before; and to find its parallel one must search the records of medieval times, when men's ideas of liberty were confined to such giants as despotic governments and rulers reluctantly chose to give them. The provision interfering with the property of the Church, and looking to the escheating or other disposition of its funds in a manner contrary to the intention of the donors, are in violation of ecclesiastical rights and in the nature of confiscation and spoliation.

18. The disfranchisement of all the women

voters, without cause and without even the allegation of crime against them, is an arbitrary exercise of despotic power without parallel in republican history. No reasonable excuse can be offered for such an invasion of political rights exercised without hindrance for seventeen years; and the vain pretense of the enemies of the Latter-day Saints that they wish to rescue the woman of Utah from bondage has, by this outrage upon freedom, been effectually silenced for ever. Taken with other portions of the law it betrays an attempt to pave the way for the domination of the majority by the minority, because the former is composed of members of an unpopular Church.

19. It should be the purpose of good citizens and faithful Latter-day Saints to maintain the liberties which are dear to every citizen, by all legal and consistent means within their power. And while many of the men and women who, with divine assistance, opened this region to human occupation and fitted it for civilized existence, are arbitrarily deprived of any personal participation in its government, it becomes the duty as well as the privilege of those who can do so under the operation of unjustly discriminating laws, to stand up manfully and use all diligence and vigilance in the retention and prevalence of the local rule of the local majority. In thus sustaining the right and assisting in the prevention of wrong, they will have the blessings of a just God and the approval of an enlightened conscience.

20. A redeeming feature of the new law is the exemption of wives who are viewed as legal from testifying against their husbands in cases arising under the Edmunds Act. This and the decision of the Supreme Court of the United States condemning the segregation system, by which the extreme penalties imposed by law were unlawfully multiplied upon "Mormon" defendants, are cutting rebukes to the Utah Courts and District Attorney, for their excesses and malice in pursuing persons acting under the strongest religious convictions. The relief thus afforded to many subjects of judicial persecution would doubtless be considerably extended, if other extreme rulings of the Utah Courts were reviewed by the highest tribunal of the land.

21. As to whether the Church is a corporation, grave doubts are entertained. This is a question yet to be determined. But if it should be decided that it is a corporation, is it possible that after a Territory has granted a charter of incorporation, and Congress has for long years permitted the Territorial act to stand unchallenged and unquestioned, the latter body can now revoke the charter and appropriate the proceeds of the property to such uses as the majority of Congress may designate? If this be possible, well may we, with all the people of the Territories, ask: Are we living under a government of law, or are we and all our rights as free men subject only to the whim and caprice of Congress?

22. The Supreme Court of the United States, in 19 Howard, page 499, said: "The power of Congress over the person and property of a citizen can never be a mere discretionary power under our Constitution and form of government. The powers of the government and the rights and privileges of the citizen are regulated and plainly defined by the Constitution itself, and when a Territory becomes a part of the United States, the Federal Government enters into possession in the character impressed upon it by those who created it. It enters upon it with its powers over the citizen strictly defined and limited by the Constitution from which it derives its own existence, and by virtue of which alone it continues to exist as a government and sovereignty. It has no power of any kind beyond it, and it cannot when it enters a Territory of the United States put off its character, and assume discretionary or despotic powers which the Constitution has denied to it. It cannot create for itself a new character separate from the citizens of the United States, and the duties it owes to them under the provisions of the Constitution."

23. To appropriate the property of a private corporation by saying that all beyond a certain value shall escheat to the Government, is an act worthy of the dark ages when the right of the state to such property was maintained by feudal theories. In latter days the more equitable doctrine prevails, even when corporations are dissolved for violation of law, that the property of the defunct corporation goes to the corporators.

24. As has been well said by the court in the case of Wilkinson vs. Leland, (2 Peters 65) in dealing with the question of taking the property of one and giving it to another, without

judicial inquiry and by legislative enactment: "That government can scarcely be deemed free, where the rights of property are left solely dependent upon the will of the legislative body, without any restraint. The fundamental maxim of all free governments seems to require that the rights of personal liberty and of private property should be held sacred. * * * A different doctrine is utterly inconsistent with the great and fundamental principles of a republican government and with the right of the citizens to the free enjoyment of their property lawfully acquired."

25. In a case which was appealed to the United States Supreme Court, (Terrett vs. Taylor, 9 Cranch), which involved church property, that the Legislature of the State of Virginia had undertaken to take from the corporations holding it and turn over to trustees, as this law attempts to do, Judge Story said: "But the property was, in fact and in law, generally purchased by the parishioners or acquired by benefactions of private donors. The title thereto was indefeasibly vested in the churches, or rather in their legal agents. It was not in the power of the crown to seize or assume it, nor of the Parliament itself to destroy the grants, unless by the exercise of a power the most arbitrary, oppressive, and unjust, and endured only because it could not be resisted. It was not forfeited, for the churches had committed no offense. The dissolution of the regal government no more destroyed the right to possess or enjoy the property than it did the right of any other corporation or individual to his or its own property. * * * * We think ourselves standing upon the principles of natural justice, upon the fundamental laws of every free government, upon the spirit and letter of the Constitution of the United States, and upon the decision of the most respectable judicial tribunals, in resisting such doctrine."

26. It seems to plain men that this new law, in its attempt to seize and dispose of our property, lawfully acquired, is in direct conflict with the provision of the Constitution which declares that "no person shall be deprived of life, liberty or property without due process of law." A well known writer has said: "They have first of all to remove a very stubborn prejudice which has been confirmed by immemorial usage that what a person honestly acquires and legally possesses is his own and not another's."

27. Probably no portion of this law has received so much attention since its passage as the section containing what is known as the "test oath." The municipal election at Brigham City, immediately after the bill became law, and the pressing necessity for a decision on the part of those who are eligible to vote in order that they might register, forced this point in the law into immediate prominence. Our enemies have circulated the most atrocious falsehoods, accusing our people of resorting to perjury when by so doing they could shield themselves and friends from punishment; but none knew better than they that in making these charges they were uttering deliberate untruths. The proof of their falsity has been witnessed in the Federal Courts every day during the past thirty months, when Latter-day Saints were being tried for taking care of and acknowledging their wives and children, and refused to give the promise which the courts endeavored to extort from them under an assurance that if they would only make it—which they were told they might easily do—they should be permitted to go unpunished.

28. Having tender consciences upon the subject of saying or doing anything that could have even the appearance of relinquishing any principle of their religion, our people have carefully examined this oath and fully weighed the effect the taking of it would have upon themselves, their children and the world at large. Understanding fully, therefore, all its consequences, they who can do so have generally resolved to take the oath. But their willingness to do so does not divest it of its enormity or unconstitutional character. The rule of law is that a man is presumed innocent of offenses and of the intention to commit offenses until he is proven guilty. But by this law it is presumed that the citizens of this Territory are disposed to violate the law and they must therefore rebut the presumption by taking the oath! If the oath was expurgatory, and to be required of people who had been in rebellion, it might have a show of justifications; but to require such an oath as this from citizens who have violated no law is without a parallel even among despotic governments.

29. It is extraordinary to what extremes men will go in their eagerness to strike a blow at

the Church of Christ. We felt this when the Edmunds Law of 1882 was enacted; but this feeling became one of amazement when the second Edmund's Bill was rushed through the Senate at the first session of the 49th Congress, and afterwards, in a remodeled form, through the House of Representatives in the second session of the same Congress. That a powerful government like ours, representing a population of fifty-five millions of people, should magnify the words and acts of a community numerically as weak as our Church is, and exert itself in so tempestuous a manner to destroy its influence and growth, is sufficiently remarkable to excite surprise; but when to effect this the very principles upon which the whole superstructure of government rests are disregarded, and the Constitution itself and its guarantees are trampled upon, then the feeling becomes one of wonder at the madness which seems to take possession of men when what is called the "Mormon question" comes up for discussion and action. In the haste and zeal of this madness to destroy our religion, settled principles of jurisprudence are disregarded, evil precedents are established, and men talk and act as if it were absolutely essential to the happiness of the people of the republic to override every true principle of government to strike down the majority of the people of Utah. It is easy to predict what this contemptuous disregard of the rights of citizens and the written pledges of the Constitution will result in. The precedents now being made will, in the not distant future, be inconceivably fruitful of evil to the people of this republic. No people or government can defy the sound principles of law which are essential to the correct administration of justice and to the maintenance of the rights of its citizens, without calling into existence forces which are calculated to lead to its destruction.

30. There has been no cessation in the annoyances, persecutions and unjustifiable conduct from which our people have suffered at the hands of those clothed with a little brief authority as officials in our midst. Unlawful cohabitation, an offense which, under the law, is a misdemeanor, is magnified into a crime of great turpitude, and more zeal is manifested in seeking to ferret out and punish those who are accused of it than there is in dealing with all the other crimes on the calendar. All other offenses, however gross and horrid, appear to sink into insignificance in the eyes of the Federal officials in comparison with the act of a man's caring for, furnishing, or even visiting his wives, taken by him, as he believes, in accordance with a command of God, and his children born to him in such wedlock. In former epistles we have described the conduct of some of these officials in fitting language. Upon slight pretexts, and where presumption merely exists, men are still arrested and treated with an indefensible severity which is nothing less than persecution, and which lifts those who endure it on to the plane of martyrs.

31. The treatment of the Latter-day Saints in these Territories under the Edmund's Law will yet be read with surprise and wonder, when the facts all become known. That American citizens should receive such usage in a government like ours professes to be, would appear incredible if it were not substantiated by convincing proofs. Aged men, whose lives have been upright and honorable, and against whom not a word of reproach can be uttered, have been ruthlessly and barbarously consigned to prison cells because they were too manly to disavow their families and to break the solemn covenants which they made in the presence of heaven with their wives.

32. But this has not been the extent of the inhumanity of those who have taken upon themselves the role of persecutors. Blood has been shed, and that in a most dastardly and cruel manner. Edward M. Dalton, a respectable young man, of good family and connections, while unsuspectingly riding in the streets of Parowan, was hailed by a deputy marshal William Thompson, Jr. concealed behind a fence, and simultaneously shot in the back. He fell from his horse and died shortly after. His slayer was indicted for manslaughter by a grand jury which he himself had summoned on open venire, and was tried in the Second District Court, at Beaver, the prosecuting attorney making what was virtually a plea in his behalf, and he was acquitted. No other result could have been expected under the circumstances, with such a jury, such a court, and such a prosecuting officer; for, it is only the truth to say, the deed was viewed with satisfaction and approval by many, and defended as an act that was entirely justifiable. It might be thought that, after such an occurrence, such a

man would be quietly set aside and kept from public notice. But, alas! for our country and the evil days upon which we have fallen, this man is now retained in the employ of the government and acts as a deputy marshal!

33. Edward M. Dalton died, it may be said, a martyr to the principles of religious freedom. His innocent blood was shed without provocation. His name will yet stand out in history as that of a victim to religious hate, and his memory will be cherished by his family and friends and our entire community with loving veneration.

34. Elder Lorenzo Snow, one of the Twelve Apostles, was sentenced by the First District Court to eighteen months' imprisonment in the penitentiary and $900 fine and the costs of his trial. It was felt that this was an unjust sentence; that the grand jury, under the direction of the District Attorney, violated the law in segregating the offense with which he was charged and bringing in three indictments against him. After some trouble an appeal was secured to the United States Supreme Court, which reversed the decision of the lower court and declared segregation to be unlawful. After eleven months confinement in the Penitentiary, which he endured with great patience and equanimity, he was released from confinement. The joy felt at this action of the Supreme Court was universal throughout the Territory; not only because of its effects on other cases, but because of the deep interest which was taken in the case of our venerated brother. Though upwards of 72 years of age and of a delicate frame, the Lord sustained him during his imprisonment in a remarkable manner, and he is now at large and able to travel and visit the Saints in their meetings and Conferences.

35. Respecting amusements: We have given the religious world a lesson upon this point. We have shown that social enjoyment and amusements are not incompatible with correct conduct and true religion. Instead of forbidding the theater and placing it under ban, it has been the aim of the Latter-day Saints to control it and keep it free from impure influences, and to preserve it as a place where all could meet for the purpose of healthful enjoyment. Our leading men have, therefore, gone to these places with the view, by their presence, of restraining all practices and influences that would be injurious to the young and rising generation. Too great care cannot be exercised that liberty shall not degenerate into license, and not to convert that which should furnish enjoyment and simple pleasure into a means of producing unhealthful excitement or corrupting morals.

36. Our social parties should be conducted in a manner to give gratification to all who attend them, however delicate and refined they may be in their feelings. Rude and boisterous conduct and everything of an improper character should be forbidden at such assemblages. It is not always convenient for the Bishop and his counselors to be present themselves on such occasions. It would be well, therefore, to select in every ward a committee of judicious, wise, good-tempered and firm men to take charge of the social parties, and to see that order is maintained, and that no improper persons are allowed to obtrude themselves into the party to disturb the peace and enjoyment of those who go there to meet with their friends and neighbors. We think round dances should not be encouraged. And while there may be no harm in granting the permission which was given by a circular of the Twelve Apostles some time ago, in which it was stated that one or two round dances might be held during the evening, care should be taken that this is not abused or carried to excess. This style of dance has been taken advantage of by many impure persons, and respectable people have been annoyed and grieved thereat, and have felt that it should be entirely prohibited. Committee-men and officers in charge of parties should see that dances of every kind are conducted in a modest and becoming manner, and that no behavior be permitted that would lead to evil or that would offend the most delicate susceptibilities.

37. As the summer months are approaching, when open air recreations will become common, we deem it necessary to warn the Saints, and especially our young people, against the excesses and improprieties that often attend such public entertainments. In the inordinate desire to make money, attractions are devised to draw crowds of people together where the usual restraints that regulate good society are greatly relaxed, to the detriment of pure morality, and the breaking down of those safeguards which should pro-

tect sobriety and virtue. Pleasure and relaxation which in themselves may be not only harmless but really beneficial to mind and body, are often rendered evil in the extreme, because of their surroundings and associations. The thoughtless and inexperienced are frequently oblivious to the harm thus attending something in which there is no essential wrong, and are led to look with allowance, if not actual approval, upon things that would shock them under other circumstances. The indiscriminate commingling of the Saints with persons not of their faith whose habits, history and purposes are bad or unknown to them, is fraught with evil and to be strongly deprecated. To expose our youth to the contaminating influence of vile men and women such as often congregate in places of public amusement, where they are thrown together in social intercourse, is more than folly; it is wickedness. It is proper that strangers should be treated with courtesy and respect but intimacy with them is not desirable, and our young people should be cautioned and guarded against casual acquaintanceship and the society of persons whose intentions and influence may be of the very worst character.

38. Excursion parties should be conducted by persons of standing and wisdom and under regulations that will preclude the evils that frequently attend such gatherings. When arranged for purposes of speculation, the promoters are often too heedless of consequences in their anxiety for profits, and will mix together the worst of characters and the good and unsophisticated, with results that can but be lamentable. Sunday excursions to lake or canyon, moonlight trips and late bathing trains should be emphatically discouraged.

39. The society of persons who place themselves under the baleful influence of intoxicants should be avoided. Order should be maintained in the midst of merriment. Indecorous language and conduct should be frowned down. All excess is detrimental. Temperance should govern in everything. Amusement is not the purpose of life, it should be indulged in only by way of variety. When people accustom themselves to constant or oft-repeated rounds of pleasure, the true objects of human existence are forgotten and duty becomes irksome and detestable. Children should not be permitted to attend

public gatherings without older persons accompanying to guard them from accident and from the contamination of the ungodly. The responsibility for the evils attending violations of these instructions will rest upon parents, guardians and the local Priesthood in the various wards and settlements.

40. Persons who habitually desecrate the Lord's day cannot be held in fellowship, and members of the Church who neglect public worship and the partaking of the Sacrament and do not remember the Sabbath day to keep it holy, will become weak in the faith and spiritually sickly, and will lose the Spirit and favor of God, and ultimately forfeit their standing in the Church and their exaltation with the obedient and faithful.

41. Among the pressing requirements of the summer months is special attention to sanitary measures. The Saints ought always to be cleanly in their habits, persons and surroundings. But during the heat of the summer this becomes particularly needful. Much disease can be avoided by frequent ablutions, simple diet and the destruction or removal of all refuse. Cleanliness is part of godliness. Filth is obnoxious to the spirit of the Gospel. It is the breeding place for epidemics. Our bodies, our houses, our gardens and outhouses should all be kept free from uncleanly accumulations. Individual effort in this direction is a necessity, and this should be supplemented by organized regulations in the various wards so that the atmosphere may not become charged with the germs of disease and death, arising from decaying vegetable and other matter festering in the sun, and from unwholesome vapors arising from dirt and neglected refuse. Let pure air and bright sunshine have free circulation in every apartment; remove everything in the house or around it that sends forth sickening odors; avoid the use of much animal food and of stimulants; preserve a cheerful spirit and a serene mind, and under the blessings of our Heavenly Father health and peace will abound and joy will dwell in the habitations of the Saints.

42. We are constantly calling for missionaries to go to the various fields of labor in this country, in Europe, and in other parts of the world. The greatest care should be taken to select suitable persons for this duty. It often

costs a considerable sum to send men to the field of labor for which they are selected; hence it is important that proper persons should be chosen, that their time and the means necessary for their transportation be not wasted. We have a large number of young men who ought to be very suitable for missionaries. Our Sunday schools and theological classes, and our young men's mutual improvement associations, should give our young men who avail themselves of these facilities an excellent preparation for missionary labor. Every young man who has faith should be taught to consider a mission to the world as an honorable event in his life, for which he will diligently prepare himself, and which he will look forward to with pleasure. There is an immense field lying before us, which must be occupied by our Elders in order to fulfill the obligations God has laid upon us. Presidents of Stakes, Bishops of Wards, and Presidents of Quorums should exercise a wise discretion in selecting for missions worthy persons who will do the cause they represent no discredit, and who will be useful in the labor assigned them.

43. We suggest to the Bishops and others whose duty it is to appoint Sunday School Superintendents the great necessity of care in the selection of these officers, as on them depend, more than on any other persons, the conduct, progress and well-being of the schools. An efficient superintendent implies a good school. Three characteristics, wherever obtainable, are most desirable in the Sunday School Superintendent—a love of his work, an aptness for control, and a devotion to the cause of God. In the last named we include, as a matter of course, a life consistent with his professions, that there may be no jar in the minds of his scholars between the force of his teachings and the influence of his conduct. It is also desirable that the superintendent be furnished with the most experienced and devoted help that the ward affords; as that officer is placed at a great disadvantage if he have an inefficient corps of teachers, and the progress of our children is materially retarded, and much valuable time and effort ill-spent, if his labors are not sustained by his associates.

44. Our brethren and sisters should always remember that the work of teaching in our Sunday schools imposes upon them a moral obligation to make their daily walk and conversation accord with their teachings. Of all lessons, the living lesson is the best. Children are surprisingly shrewd in detecting inconsistencies between the instructions and habits of their instructors. Besides, the teacher who seeks to live up to his own advice, not only benefits his scholars, but his teachings exert a salutary influence upon himself, and he profits by his own lessons.

45. The winter which has passed has been remarkable for its mildness in the central and southern parts of the Territory. In the extreme north storms have been more frequent and the seasons been more severe. But, taken as a whole, the winter has been an extremely favorable one. The open weather of the past two months has enabled farmers to get in their crops with a facility and to an extent rarely equaled. Good health has generally prevailed throughout our settlements, and food for man and beast has been generally abundant.

46. In former Epistles we have dwelt upon the necessity of improving our system of agriculture. The Saints have been counseled to select the best kinds of grains, fruits and vegetables. Our soil is admirably adapted for the production of the best varieties of these articles, and there is no reason why we should not have them of as good quality as can be raised anywhere in our zone. The same remarks apply to horned stock, horses and sheep, and all kinds of poultry. It is only repeating a truism to say that it is as easy to raise a good colt, a good calf, or a good sheep, as to raise a poor one.

47. Tree planting should be systematically followed throughout these treeless regions which we occupy. The best varieties of trees should be sought for. In the early days we had to use quick-growing varieties that were easily procured. But with our present railroad facilities we can select trees which are best adapted for future use in building, for manufacturing purposes, and for ornament. In some of the prairie States a day has been set apart in the spring of each year for the planting of trees, which is called Arbor Day. The results which have followed the devotion of one day to this purpose are said to be very marked in regions where it is observed. But we should not confine our tree-planting to one day. Every man who owns a piece of

ground should increase its value by planting fruit and shade trees, and make his selection of the latter from those kinds that will prove valuable as timber. The general planting of dark-wood trees would be attended with greater profit and much more satisfactory results than the wide-spread cultivation of varieties of the cottonwood and poplar. These latter grow readily and afford shade, but are of very little further use except for firewood.

48. It is beyond doubt that the exportations and general marketing of the surplus products of our Territory form quite an addition to the financial resources of the people. More care however, should be exercised in putting up and taking care of articles intended for shipment to points within the Territory, or outside its borders.

49. The manufacture and care of butter should receive attention. This article is among the most sensitive to its surroundings, so that cleanliness in every stage is of vital importance. In this direction great improvement has been made in the Eastern States and it would be well for neighborhoods to combine and purchase suitable plant and machinery and acquire skill in the improved method of manufacturing butter.

50. Many of our cheese factories now turn out an article that is very desirable and which commands ready sale and the full price in the market. There is room for the increased manufacture of this product.

51. The income of the Territory from the sale of eggs is not an inconsiderable item. If any economical method could be devised for preserving them when abundant it would be a great advantage, and the price would be more nearly equal at different seasons of the year.

52. The dried fruit business has been quite remunerative in the past, but our people need to be more careful in drying. Cleanliness is essential, and the adoption of the Alden or other process would help us to maintain the old credit which our Territory had for the excellence of its dried fruit.

53. The shipment of hides from our Territory ought to cease and tanneries should be fostered in every locality where they can be maintained.

54. The same may be said about wool. Wise economy would prompt the establishment of a sufficient number of woolen mills to purchase and manufacture all our home grown wool, so that instead of exporting the raw material we should manufacture it ourselves and pay our own people the wages therefore that we otherwise have to pay to workmen in other places.

55. The Territory exports considerable grain, lucerne seed and potatoes. These products have sometimes been poorly cleaned and not been properly assorted, and this negligence injures our credit and spoils our market. Making the professions which we do as Latter-day Saints, and having the promises of the Lord concerning the aid which He will give unto us, our business affairs should be conducted in a way that will show that our professions are not vain.

56. The Church is now passing through a period of transition, or evolution, as some might be pleased to term it. Such periods appear to be necessary in the progress and perfecting of all created things, as much so in the history of peoples and communities as of individuals. These periods of transition have most generally their pains, perplexities and sufferings. The present is no exception to the rule. But out of apparent evil, Providence will bring abundant good, and the lesson which the signs of the times should teach us is one of patience, endurance, and calm reliance on the Lord. The result will be that we shall be stronger, wiser, purer, happier, for the experience gained, and the work of the Lord, delivered by His Omnipotence from all the snares set for its retardation, or plans laid for its destruction, will yet triumph gloriously over all its foes, and the infinite atonement of the Redeemer will accomplish its perfect work. The final victory of the Saints is certain; after the trial comes the reward.

57. We cannot close our Epistle without expressing, as we have often done before, our faith and hopes concerning the great work in which we are engaged. "The Lord hath founded Zion, and the poor of His people shall trust in it." Our hearts are filled with gratitude and thanksgiving to our Great Creator that we have the privilege of living in this age of the world, and taking part in this great work. We feel that all who have entered into covenant with God and who suffer persecution for His cause, have reason for rejoicing, even as Jesus told His disciples when He was upon the earth: "Rejoice and

be exceeding glad, for great is your reward in heaven: for so persecuted they the prophets which were before you." If we are persecuted for our religion, it is no more than we have been taught to expect. All who have been baptized into this Church, and who were properly taught at the time, were led to expect that they would have to suffer as our Lord and Master and His disciples did. Our Savior has given us ample testimony upon this point. We need not, therefore, be surprised nor disappointed when persecution comes. We have, however, many great and glorious promises made to us. God has established Zion, nevermore to be thrown down, nor to be given into the hands of another people. The most encouraging words that could be uttered by Our Almighty Father to His children have been given to us. We have proved them to be true up to the present, and we know every word will be fulfilled that has been spoken concerning the future. They who fight against Zion shall be destroyed; and the pit which has been digged for our destruction shall be filled by those who digged it, unto their utter destruction.

58. The enemies of righteousness may gather themselves together, and plot evil, and effect secret combinations, and say concerning Zion: "Let her be defiled, and let our eye look upon Zion. But they know not the thoughts of the Lord, neither understand they His counsel." The Lord has stretched forth His hand and He has spoken His word. He will not withdraw it, either, until His purposes concerning the earth and its inhabitants shall be completely fulfilled. We need not fear nor tremble. The afflictions which our Father permits to come upon us will be made light unto us, and they will be made to appear as very trifling in comparison with the calamities that He has said shall come upon the ungodly inhabitants of the earth. Great judgments are pronounced upon Babylon, and they will be fulfilled to the very letter. But if we do as the Prophet says: "Seek ye the Lord, all ye meek of the earth, which have wrought His judgment; seek righteousness, seek meekness; it may be ye shall be hid in the day of the Lord's anger;" we shall be saved from impending evils.

59. The Lord has given unto us an inheritance upon this land, which He declares is a choice land. He has told us that whatsoever nation shall possess it shall be free from bondage and from captivity, and from all other nations under heaven, if they will but serve the God of the land, who is Jesus Christ. These words have been fulfilled in the fate which has befallen nations in the past; they will be fulfilled in the future. If we keep the commandments of God, if we serve Him with diligence and full purpose of heart, the Lord will not suffer us to be brought into bondage to our enemies, but will give us freedom, and maintain it upon the land to which He has led us. We may rest confidently upon His promises to Zion, and be assured that the time will come when it shall be "a land of peace, a city of refuge, a place of safety for the Saints of the Most High God; and the glory of the Lord shall be there, and the terror of the Lord shall be there, in so much that the wicked will not come unto it and it shall be called Zion. And it shall come to pass among the wicked, that every man that will not take his sword against his neighbor, must needs flee unto Zion for safety. And there shall be gathered unto it out of every nation under heaven; and it shall be the only people that shall not be at war one with another. And it shall be said among the wicked, 'Let us not go up to battle against Zion, for the inhabitants of Zion are terrible; wherefore we cannot stand.' And it shall come to pass that the righteous shall be gathered out from among all nations, and shall come to Zion, singing songs of everlasting joy."

60. These promises are made to us directly, and the Spirit of God bears testimony to us today that they are true.

61. With full confidence that the dense clouds which have darkened our horizon during the past two or three years will be soon dissipated by the bright rays of the sun of righteousness, and invoking the blessings that come through patient endurance of affliction and faithful adherence to the right, upon the Saints of God in all the world, we subscribe ourselves your fellow servants in the great work of the latter days,

JOHN TAYLOR,
GEORGE Q. CANNON,
JOSEPH F. SMITH,
First Presidency of the Church of Jesus Christ of Latter-day Saints. April, 1887.

SOURCES

ADDRESS

1. *Deseret News*, December 12, 1877. See also Journal History March 24, 1877—Oct. 8, 1877, frames 2-3 and *Journal of Discourses*, Vol. 19, pp. 119-121.
2. *Journal of Discourses*, Vol. 19, pp. 122-129. See also Journal History, Oct. 7, 1877.
3. *Deseret News*, 27:274. See also *Journal of Discourses*, Vol. 19, pp. 300-311.
4. *Journal of Discourses*, Vol. 20, pp. 174-180.
5. *Ibid.*, Vol. 21, pp. 29-38. See also *Deseret News*, March 17, 1880.
6. *Ibid.*, Vol. 20, pp. 316-321.
7. *Ibid.*, Vol. 22, pp. 1-4.
8. *Millennial Star*, Vol. 41, Oct. 8, 1879, pp. 709-710.
9. General Conference Addresses 1880, LDS Church News, *Deseret News*, Excerpts, pp. 61-65.
10. *Ibid.*, p. 67.
11. *Ibid.*, pp. 74-79.
12. *Ibid.*, pp. 99-103.
13. *Journal of Discourses*, Vol. 22, pp. 38-41.
14. *Millennial Star*, Vol. 43, April 3, 1881, pp. 273-274.
15. *Ibid.*, April 4, 1881, pp. 279, 283-285.
16. *Ibid.*, April 5, 1881, pp. 305-307.
17. *Ibid.*, Oct. 6, 1881, pp. 705-706, 709.
18. *Ibid.*, Oct. 7, 1881, pp. 723-725.
19. *Journal of Discourses*, Vol. 22, pp. 290-297.
20. *Millennial Star*, Vol. 44, April 6, 1882, pp. 273-274.
21. *Ibid.*, April 7, 1882, pp. 293-294.
22. *Ibid.*, April 9, 1882, p. 327.
23. *Journal of Discourses*, Vol. 23, pp. 47-68. See also *Millennial Star*, Vol. 44, May 29, 1882, pp. 337-342.
24. *Ibid.*, pp. 257-270.
25. *Ibid.*, Vol. 24, pp. 123-129.
26. *Ibid.*, Vol. 26, pp. 128-135.
27. *Ibid.*, Vol. 24, pp. 287-296.
28. Journal History, April 4, 1884, frame 7.
29. *Millennial Star*, Vol. 46, April 6, 1884, pp. 293—294.
30. *Ibid.*, Oct. 4, 1884, pp. 673-675.
31. *Journal of Discourses*, Vol. 25, pp. 303-317. See also *Millennial Star*, Vol. 46, Oct. 6-7, 1884, pp. 709-712.
32. *Millennial Star*, Vol. 47, April 4, 1885, pp. 290-296.
33. *Ibid.*, Oct. 6, 1885, pp. 705-717.
34. *Ibid.*, Vol. 48, April 6, 1886, pp. 305-314, 321-329.
35. *Ibid.*, Oct. 8, 1886, pp. 705-719.
36. Journal History, *Deseret Evening News*, April 8, 1887, frames 2-5. See also *Millennial Star*, Vol. 49, May 9, 1887, pp. 289-301.

INDEX

Taylor 34:24; those who persecute will always fail in their ultimate objectives and will be remembered only in historical archives, Taylor 35:28.

CITIES, advice in the building of, Taylor 34:44.

CIVIL WAR, predicted by Joseph Smith— much worse seen for the future, Taylor 6:8.

CLEVELAND, GROVER, appeal to the President for redress of grievances regarding persecution over the institution of polygamy, Taylor 33:33.

COMMANDMENTS, when Saints become lax in the keeping of, the Lord allows the enemies of the Church to prevail over them for a time to bring them to repentance, Taylor 36:6.

COMMUNISM, to roll on until it will be a vexation to hear the reports thereof, Taylor 19:24; we want nothing like it or nihilism that are beginning to vex and perplex the nations, Taylor 19:24; seen as a secret or illegal combination, Taylor 23:67.

CONSTITUTION, when deserted by all, the elders will rally around its shattered fragments, Taylor 5:11; this nation abounds with traitors who ignore that sacred palladium of liberty, Taylor 5:11; the good and holy principles of may be perverted by corrupt and wicked men, Taylor 5:11; a stepping stone to a future program God alone can impart, Taylor 5:12; politically Saints to be united in seeing that the Church is not in violation of what the fathers of the country instituted, Taylor 5:13; the law against polygamy seen as at variance with the C.; therefore obedience to is not obligatory, Taylor 6:3; Saints not to be surprised that the C. should be trampled underfoot of man, Taylor 6:6; those who violate are enemies of mankind and will be held accountable before God, Taylor 11:12; administrators apostatizing very fast from the principles that the fathers of this nation instituted, Taylor 19:19; an embodiment of principles contained therein calculated to bless and benefit mankind, Taylor 19:19; many profess to believe in until applied, Taylor 19:19; let all men be free in their business relations, Taylor 19:22; an inspired document, Taylor 23:21; Congress cannot afford to trample upon, ere long they will need all its protecting influence to save this nation, Taylor 23:70; already agencies are at work in the land cal-

culated to subvert and overthrow every principle of rule and government, Taylor 23:71; some of the violations of include ex post facto laws and bills of attainder, Taylor 24:31; the despised often end up the deliverer of those who despised—such is the case with the, Taylor 24:33; Saints to uphold and sustain every law that is constitutional, Taylor 33:29; attacks upon the policy of the Church regarding the, Taylor 33:30; the anti-polygamy legislation demonstrably unconstitutional, Taylor 33:31-32; six specific violations of the C. noted in the enforcement of anti-polygamy legislation, Taylor 34:67; legal argument clearly showing the unconstitutionality of the second Edmunds Law, Taylor 36:21-28.

COOPERATION, making great stride toward self-efficiency, Taylor 12:3.

COURTS, Saints to take disputes to the various Church courts, Taylor 12:7.

CRIME, statistics comparing Mormons and nonMormons in Utah concerning, Taylor 23:50-61.

DANCES, suggestions regarding the proper conduct at, Taylor 36:36.

DEAD, advice in the care of grave sites, Taylor 34:44.

DEBT, Saints encouraged during jubilee year to release the indebtedness of the poor by fifty percent, Taylor 9:14, 16.

DECLARATION OF INDEPENDENCE, no government has the right to deprive man of his inalienable rights embodied in the, Taylor 24:24.

DEGREES OF GLORY, compared to the sun, moon, and stars, Taylor 31:10, 12.

DELIVERER, the despised often end up being the deliverer of the despised, Taylor 24:33.

DEVIL, everything which tends to divide the Saints comes from the, Taylor 3:18; a pretended advocate of freedom, Taylor 16:5; did not secure the whole of the people destroyed in the great flood, Taylor 18:4; a great war yet to be fought between Adam and Satan before the latter is cast out, Taylor 18:9.

DISCIPLES, all killed except one who was banished to work as a slave on the Isle of Patmos, Taylor 33:38.

DISPUTES, between Saints to be handled in Church courts, Taylor 12:7.

DIVORCE, if married in the temple should be divorced by the same authority; until this is done, new alliances are sinful, Taylor 35:36; the disruption of families by d. is an evil of no ordinary character, Taylor 35:46.

EARTH, man not placed upon to follow the devices and desires of own heart, Taylor 3:9; created as a place for men to propagate his species and have bodies formed, Taylor 31:3.

EDMUNDS BILL, the Saints reaction to the initial bill, Taylor 23:63; honor to members of Congress who saw this bill in its true light as destructive to the Constitution, Taylor 23:75, 77, 79; Saints advised regarding their obedience to, Taylor 23:93; the test oath resulting from was odious, unjust, and unconstitutional, Taylor 24:37-39; tribute to the members of Congress who opposed, Taylor 25:13; course of resistance to, proposed by the Church, Taylor 25:15-16.

EDMUNDS LAW, Saints prevented from voting while adulterers, prostitutes, etc. seen as respectable voters, Taylor 31:51; the enemies of the Saints established as judges in cases dealing with polygamy, Taylor 31:64; general attitude toward treatment under, Taylor 31:65; enforcement of, caused persecution to descend upon the Saints more fiercely than ever, Taylor 33:2, 4-6; under the law the most flagrant sexual crimes of nonmembers overlooked, and Mormons who agree to discard their wives excused, Taylor 33:7; demonstrably unconstitutional, Taylor 33:31-32; begotten by prejudice conceived in ignorance and brought forth in hate, Taylor 34:27; excellent summary of the violation of the Constitution and human rights under, Taylor 34:29-32; distorted and perverted to secure conviction in polygamy cases, Taylor 35:13-14, 16-19; tribute to the sisters undergoing persecution as a result of, Taylor 35:15; trials under required wives and children to testify against their husbands and fathers, Taylor 35:18; failed in its design to seize political power from the Mormons and give it to the non-Mormons, Taylor 36:14; instead of appeasing the anti-Mormon appetite for power, it only whetted it, Taylor 36:15; a second one enacted, the provisions of and effect upon the Church explained, Taylor 36:15-18, 20-21; legal argument clearly showing the unconstitutionality of the second law, Taylor 36:21-28; the treatment of the Saints under will yet be read

with surprise and wonder, Taylor 36:31; innocent blood shed by territorial officials involved with, Taylor 36:32-33.

EDUCATION, children to be provided every branch of e. calculated to promote their welfare, Taylor 3:34; children to be instructed in the schools by LDS teachers, Taylor 4:22; statistics comparing level of e., in Utah with the national average, Taylor 23:47-49; Saints advised to pay close attention to e. of the youth for the future, Taylor 34:38; Saints encouraged to patronize and establish where the principles of the gospel can be taught, Taylor 35:43.

ELIJAH, committed the keys causing the living to seek after the dead and the dead to feel after their children the living, Taylor 2:15, 18.

ENDURANCE, faith promoting examples of, Taylor 6:11.

ENEMIES, when the Saints become lax in adhering to the commandments, the Lord allows the e. of the Church to prevail over them for a time to bring them to repentance, Taylor 36:6; the pit dug by the enemy of the Church for Zion will be filled by those who dug it, Taylor 36:57.

ENOCH, CITY OF, underwent a similar gathering as did the Latter-day Saints, Taylor 31:6-7; the two Zions—the City of Enoch and the Latter-day Saints to meet and fall upon each others' necks, Taylor 31:7; Saints belonging to the city of and Latter-day Saints have much in common, Taylor 31:8.

FAITH, examples of great faith and endurance, Taylor 6:11; purity begets righteousness, Taylor 34:46.

FAMILY SIZE, answer to mothers who refuse to have but one or two children, Taylor 23:88.

FARMERS, advice to, Taylor 34:43.

FEDERAL OFFICERS, behaved as though the blessing of the Constitution did not apply to Mormons, Taylor 34:20, 26.

FIRST PRESIDENCY, the twelve to assume the leadership of the Church in the absence of the, Taylor 13:1, 3, 8; the organization of the, Taylor 13:1-4, 8-10.

FLOOD, Satan did not secure the whole of the people that were destroyed in the, Taylor 18:4; wicked were destroyed in the great f. because it was unjust to send holy spirit children into filthy bodies, Taylor 27:14;

inhabitants of the earth warned for nearly 300 years of impending f., Taylor 27:16.

FOOD STORAGE, Saints to prepare for the time when there will be a howling among the merchants in Babylon, for men will not be found to buy their merchandise, Taylor 5:20; because the brethren refused to comply with Young's request to store wheat, the sisters were asked to do so—in 1880 the Church found itself in need of that wheat, Taylor 9:11-13.

FOREORDAINED, many to hold particular positions among the children of men, Taylor 26:6.

FREE AGENCY, every Saint committed to the perpetuation of, Taylor 23:73.

FREEDOM, the devil is a pretended advocate of, Taylor 16:5; the principles of to be transmitted unimpaired and undiminished to those who follow, Taylor 34:14.

FUNERAL SERVICES, the same laudations and panegyrics should not be pronounced over the self-murderer as over the faithful, Taylor 35:48.

GATHERING, Moses committed to Joseph Smith the keys of the g.; otherwise the spirit of would not be present today, Taylor 2:14; reasons for given, Taylor 3:8; 7:4; 24:20; 26:8; the U. S. government attempts to halt Mormon emigration, Taylor 24:19.

GENEALOGY, Elijah committed the keys which caused the living to seek after the dead and the dead to seek after their children the living, Taylor 2:15, 18; the living and the dead ought to be operating closely together for the betterment of mortal man, Taylor 3:16; designed to provide the saving ordinances for those who accept the gospel on the other side, Taylor 18:7-8; priesthood is active on both sides of the veil to provide the saving ordinances for the dead, Taylor 18:8; 19:10, 13; answer to the question "we won't let you do it," Taylor 19:15; by the labors of the living for the dead the souls of men are wrenched from the grasp of the Devil, Taylor 35:42.

GOD, all nations are under his direction and control, Taylor 3:3; everything that unites exalts and ennobles, man comes from, Taylor 3:18; it is better to die than abandon, Taylor 35:10.

GOSPEL, not the work of man, did not originate with man, Taylor 3:5-6; not being of

man, no part thereof can be dispensed, Taylor 4:7; description of the proper attitude in the, Taylor 4:14; persecution regarded as a natural thing for those who preach the gospel, Taylor 7:7; those who lived on the earth without having a chance to hear the g. will have the opportunity on the other side, Taylor 18:7; he who is possessed with the love of the g. will seek to save man almost against his will, Taylor 19:3; the restoration of reviewed, Taylor 23:4-9; built upon the rock of revelation, Taylor 23:18; Saints commissioned to preach the g. but after doing so not responsible for the reception or rejection of the world, Taylor 27:8; the prophets do not have the authority to change it to harmonize with the view of the day, Taylor 31:37; some Saints show a disposition to creep or slip around this principle and that in the g., Taylor 31:38-39.

GOSSIP, the spreading of rumors to be deplored, Taylor 35:29-30.

GOVERNMENT, politically Saints united in that which is not in violation of what the Fathers of the country instituted, Taylor 5:13; attitude of the Saints toward the g. while undergoing persecution by them, Taylor 12:13.

HAYES, RUTHERFORD B., conversation with over the institution of polygamy, Taylor 23:78.

HEALTH, suggestions for better h. in the summer months, Taylor 36:41.

HEAVEN, the celestial city in h. described, Taylor 34:57.

HIGH COUNCILMEN, duties of, Taylor 23:8.

HIGH PRIESTS, duties and early history of, Taylor 3:23-24.

HOLY GHOST, there is an irrevocable law of heaven that when you yield obedience to the Laws of God the H. G. is received, Taylor 23:16; follow even though it does not always seem the right way, Taylor 26:11.

HOME, Saints to adorn and beautify their surroundings, Taylor 34:41.

HOME TEACHERS, apostles and prophets have a right to be instructed by their, Taylor 26:14; every ward to have teachers looking after the people, Taylor 31:20; advice to those called to visit the homes of the Saints, Taylor 36:9-10.

HUMAN RIGHTS, Saints strongly committed to protect human freedom, Taylor 24:32.

IMMORALITY, the laws of the Church regarding must be administered with justice and impartiality, Taylor 34:47; no prominence of position, no ties of family, no influence of wealth can save us from the penalty for, Taylor 34:47, 49; the great crying sin of this generation is lasciviousness, Taylor 35:6-7.

INALIENABLE RIGHTS, no man or government has the right to deprive one of his, Taylor 24:24.

INSANITY, if caused by sin, the person is not altogether free from the responsibility for his acts, Taylor 35:48.

INTELLIGENCE, we ought not to accept only the light and intelligence we wish to obey, Taylor 26:7.

JERUSALEM, the vision of the J. in heaven as seen by John on the Isle of Patmos, Taylor 34:57.

JESUS CHRIST, generally religious people who persecuted the Savior the most, Taylor 19:16; frequently selects the most unlikely of men to carry out his purpose, Taylor 24:8-9.

JOHN, vision of the Jerusalem in heaven, Taylor 34:57.

KINGDOMS OF GLORY, general thoughts regarding, Taylor 26:18.

KINGDOM OF GOD, description of how it was built up in early Utah through the Perpetual Emigration Fund, Taylor 2:23-25.

LATTER-DAY SAINTS, no greater benefactors to the world in existence than the, Taylor 2:22; children of, to be instructed in the schools by, Taylor 4:22; God has none other who will listen to his laws, Taylor 7:6; too fond of catering to the world, Taylor 7:18; the mission is to learn their duties relative to saving themselves and mankind, Taylor 24:2; God interested in the welfare of all, not just, Taylor 27:4; ought to feel toward the world as God does, Taylor 27:5; have much in common with the City of Enoch, Taylor 31:8; have much in common with the apostles of Jesus commanded to preach the Gospel, Taylor 31:11; many members of will not gain entrance into the Celestial Kingdom, Taylor 31:14-15; Some ideal characteristics to be sought by, Taylor 34:40-42; to adorn and beautify their surroundings and dwelling areas, Taylor 34:41.

LAW, God has none other except the Latter-day Saints who will listen to his laws, Taylor 7:6; Saints to uphold and sustain every l. which is constitutional, Taylor 33:28; purposely distorted and perverted to secure convictions in polygamy trials, Taylor 35:13-14, 16-19.

LAW SUITS, Saints to take disputes to the various Church courts for settlement, those who act contrary to this not to receive temple recommends, Taylor 12:7.

LEGAL ADVICE, Saints to take disputes to the various Church courts, Taylor 12:7.

LIE, whosoever loveth and maketh a l. shall not be permitted to enter the Holy City, Taylor 35:30; those who continue to tell lies lose the power to discern between truth and falsehood, Taylor 35:31.

LORD, man can do nothing without the assistance of the, Taylor 26:2.

LORD'S PRAYER, thoughts on the, Taylor 25:17, 19.

LUCIFER, has no power or dominion over children under eight years of age, automatically redeemed, Taylor 18:5.

MAN, not placed upon the earth to follow the devices and desires of own hearts, Taylor 3:9, 15; in a state of probation while on the earth, Taylor 3:14; every m. given a portion of the spirit of God which accounts for the general aversion to murder, dishonesty, etc., Taylor 27:9-13.

MARRIAGE, thoughts regarding the wedding vow of the Christian world, Taylor 34:56; where lax ideas exist with regard to, we discover nations whose code of morals is inferior and whose sexual irregularities increase, Taylor 35:45.

MAORIES, a remnant of the House of Israel and highly receptive to the gospel, Taylor 34:52.

MEEK, the prophecy that the m. will inherit the earth explained, Taylor 25:2.

MELCHIZEDEK PRIESTHOOD, to preside more especially over spiritual affairs of the Church, Taylor 5:29.

MISSION, every young man who has faith should be taught to consider a mission, Taylor 36:42.

MISSIONARIES, instructions regarding the type of men desirable as, Taylor 4:17; 7:10; the background of, very diversified, Taylor 23:15.

MORALS, where lax ideas exist with regard to m. we discover nations whose code is inferior and whose sexual irregularities increase, Taylor 35:45

MORMON EMIGRATION, U.S. Government attempts to halt, Taylor 24:19.

MOSES, committed the Keys of the gathering of the dispensation to Joseph Smith, Taylor 2:14.

MOTHERS, strongly admonished to keep the sons and daughters from the contaminating influences of immoral characters, Taylor 16:4-5.

NATIONS, warning to the n. of the earth unless they repent, Taylor 23:72.

NOAH, wicked were destroyed in the time of N. because it was unjust to send holy spirit children into filthy bodies, Taylor 27:14; wicked of in the day of Noah in prison about 2,400 years before Christ visited them, Taylor 31:13.

OBEDIENCE, the less one is in o. to the laws of God, the more light he loses, thus becoming critical of the brethren and fighting against God, Taylor 26:10.

OPPOSITION, the powers of God have always been opposed by the powers of the Evil One, Taylor 7:3.

PARENTS, strongly admonished to protect sons and daughters from the contaminating influences of immoral characters, Taylor 16:4-5; warning to in the raising of children, Taylor 33:55; urged to send children to school where the principles of the gospel are taught, Taylor 35:43.

PARTIES, proper conduct of the youth at social gatherings, Taylor 36:36-39.

PERPETUAL EMIGRATION FUND, indebtedness to nearly a million because Saints using the services of unwilling to repay, Taylor 2:28; the amount owed by the poor reduced by fifty percent, Taylor 9:4, 6; repayment of debt by Saints to the, disgraceful, Taylor 16:2.

PERSECUTED, words of consolation to those who feel, Taylor 7:7.

PERSECUTION, the powers of God have always been opposed by the powers of the Evil One, Taylor 7:3; regarded as a natural thing for those who preach the gospel, Taylor 7:7; attitude of the Saints while enduring p. from the government, Taylor 12:13; some general thoughts regarding, Taylor 27:19; to be imprisoned, persecuted, discriminated against and abused are not

causes of sorrow to true Saints, Taylor 33:8; each of the great prophets had the option of escaping p. by denying the faith, Taylor 33:9; if man expects to inherit the Celestial Kingdom, he must be tested to the very uttermost, Taylor 33:12; the policy of the Church historically has never been to resort to revenge in the face of, Taylor 33:27; a general tendency has always existed to garnish the tombs of the dead prophets and saints while persecuting and killing the living ones, Taylor 33:38; the good effects of p. noted, Taylor 34:9-10, 12-13; the Church an example of the fulfillment of the promise to Zion that no weapon formed against shall prosper, Taylor 34:74-75; that of the last days foreseen by the prophets of old, Taylor 35:8-9; Saints not suffering from p. should help share the burden of those who are, Taylor 35:12; those who persecute the Church will fail and only be remembered in historical archives, Taylor 35:28; Saints have been taught to expect p. for their religion, Taylor 36:57; afflictions God permits to come upon the Saints but a trifle in comparison with the calamities yet to fall upon the ungodly, Taylor 36:58.

POLITICS, as it is with us in our religion, so it ought to be with our p. etc., Taylor 5:7; politically Saints to be united in the ideas embodied in the Constitution by the Founding Fathers, Taylor 5:13.

POLYGAMY, the law against seen by Pres. Taylor as a violation of the Constitution; therefore obedience to was not obligatory, Taylor 6:3; testimony of Taylor regarding, Taylor 6:4; party politics and the desire to please the clergy for vote getting power seen as the major forces for the anti-polygamy legislation, Taylor 6:13-14; critics of p. often were found seducing females then going to church or courts talking about the impurities of the Mormons, Taylor 19:20; advice on how to weather the storm against those who practice p., Taylor 21:2, 5; conversation with Pres. Hayes over, Taylor 23:78; the type of person eligible to enter into the practice of described, Taylor 23:80; reasons given why the practice of could not be extended to the gentiles, Taylor 23:81; regarding obedience to the Edmund's Bill prohibiting the practice of, Taylor 23:93; many honorable men have been deceived into persecuting the Saints

over, Taylor 24:41; course of action proposed by the Church in warding off resistance to, Taylor 25:17; laws designed to discourage p. ended up promoting prostitution,
Taylor 31:42-49; avowed enemies of the
Saints were established as the judges in
cases dealing with, Taylor 31:64; those practicing p. denounced as criminals unable to
receive a fair trial, become fugitives before
the law, Taylor 32:3-3; three from Arizona
sent to the House of Correction at Detroit for
sentences of 3 1/2 years, Taylor 32:5;
because of legal persecution many left their
homes to seek freedom in foreign lands,
Taylor 32:5; Pres. Taylor forced to go underground because of legal persecution, Taylor
32:6; argument that Jesus himself was born
through polygamic lineage and that most of
the renounced prophets were in obedience
to, Taylor 32:10; laws against the practice of
a violation of obligation of contract, Taylor
32:14; only about two percent of the Church
in practice of, Taylor 32:18; Saints admonished not to retaliate in kind to persecutions
over, Taylor 32:20; the enforcement of the
Edmunds Law causes persecution to
descend upon the Saints more fiercely than
ever, Taylor 33:2, 4-6; under the Edmunds
Law the most flagrant sexual crimes of nonmembers overlooked and Mormons who
agree to discard their wives excused, Taylor
33:7; well meaning nonmember friends
appeal to the Church to do away with p.
because of the opposition to it, Taylor 33:10;
appeal sent to Pres. Cleveland for redress of
grievances resulting from anti-polygamy
legislation, Taylor 33:33; those willing to
endure imprisonment for their belief in, will
show the good of the world that there must
be a principle in the practice of, Taylor
33:39-42; idea that the practice of is a menace to the monogamous system in the world
is fallacious, Taylor 33:46; all elements of
the world the proper and well bred and
pimps and harlots united to stamp out,
Taylor 34:16; condition of women under,
Taylor 34:22; Lorenzo Snow imprisoned in
the penitentiary for, Taylor 34:28; excellent
summary of the violation of the Constitution
and human rights for those charged with,
Taylor 34:29-32; the attempt to get the government to investigate the falsehoods etc.
stemming from the practice of, Taylor

34:33-34; sisters involved in the practice of
treated by the law as though criminals, lewd
and indecent, Taylor 34:36; Idaho Territorial
Federal Officials to eliminate LDS teachers
from the classroom because of their support
of the practice of, Taylor 34:37; bishops to
see to it that families of the brethren imprisoned for the practice of p. are well taken care
of, Taylor 34:55; answer to the charge that
polygamy would pervert the nation's morals,
Taylor 34:63, 66; six specific violations of
the Constitution noted in the enforcement of
anti-polygamy legislation, Taylor 34:67.
POOR, beef and flour need to be added to
our prayers for the poor, Taylor 21:1; aid
should be given to with the view of doing
real and lasting good, Taylor 34:53.
POSSESSIONS, God responsible for all our,
Taylor 12:15.
PRATT, ORSON, funeral services of a part
of General Conference, Taylor 17:2.
PRAYER, some would rather pray for the
poor than to relieve them, Taylor 10:2; beef
and flour need to be added to our prayers
for the poor, Taylor 21:1.
PRIESTS, Saints literally a kingdom of,
Taylor 3:15.
PRIESTHOOD, certain manifestations and
powers in addition to the p. must be given
individually, Taylor 2:9; we are literally a
kingdom of priests, Taylor 3:15; not conferred upon man to exercise any degree of
unrighteousness, Taylor 12:6; active on
both sides of the veil for the work of the
dead, Taylor 18:8; should be a chosen communion between the p. on the earth and the
one in heaven, Taylor 31:17; those holding
positions in the p. not to act as autocrats,
Taylor 31:21.
PROPHECY, time will come when calamity,
bloodshed, confusion and strife will spread
among all nations, Taylor 3:21; time will
come when there will be a howling among
the merchants in Babylon, for men will not
be found to buy their merchandise, Taylor
5:20; he that will not take up his sword
against his neighbor must needs flee to Zion
for safety, Taylor 5:20; Saints yet to see in
this country more bloodshed, more ruin,
more devastation than seen in the Civil War,
Taylor 6:8; a war to come with brother
arrayed against brother, mother against
mother, etc., Taylor 6:8; communism will roll

on until it will be a vexation to hear the reports thereof, Taylor 19:24; destruction, desolation, war, famine and bloodshed promised for the nations which do not speedily repent, Taylor 23:72; the two Zions—the city of Enoch and the Latter-day Zion—to meet and fall on each others' necks, Taylor 31:7; those who persecute the Church will always fail in their ultimate objectives, and the memory of their deeds will only live in the historical archives, Taylor 35:28; concerning the fleeing of the inhabitants of the earth to Zion for safety, Taylor 36:59.

PROPHETS, tendency of people to garnish the tombs of the dead p. but kill the living ones, Taylor 33:38.

QUORUM OF THE TWELVE, decision made to allow members of to have a reasonable recompense for their services, Taylor 2:2; to assume leadership of the Church in the absence of the President, Taylor 13:1, 3.

RECREATION, useless and excessive amusements harmful in several ways, Taylor 35:32, 40-41.

RELIEF SOCIETY, especially good tribute to, Taylor 16:3.

RELIGION, Saints not to impose their religion on others, Taylor 24:26-27.

RESTORATION, before r. of the gospel there were no people that had a correct knowledge of God, Taylor 5:8.

REVELATION, most men believe only in their own theories, notions, ideas, etc. not in, Taylor 19:6; gospel built upon the rock of, Taylor 23:18.

REVENGE, never the policy of the Church when persecuted and driven to resort to, Taylor 33:27.

RUMOR, the spreading of deplored, Taylor 35:29-30.

SABBATH BREAKERS, cannot be held in fellowship, Taylor 36:40.

SABBATH-BREAKING, do not admit of Sunday excursions to the lake or canyons, Taylor 35:39; those who desecrate the Sabbath, reject the word of the Lord, Taylor 35:39; will become weak in the faith and spiritually sick, Taylor 36:40.

SAINTS, a general tendency has always existed to garnish the tombs of the dead prophets and s. while killing the living ones, Taylor 33:38.

SATAN, see devil.

SECRET COMBINATIONS, communism seen as a, Taylor 23:67; already are being entered into which are very ominous for the future of this republic, Taylor 23:69.

SECRET SOCIETIES, Saints not to associate with, distinctly spoken against in the Book of Mormon, Taylor 33:28.

SEVENTIES, some general thoughts regarding the duties and responsibilities of, Taylor 3:25-26.

SCRIPTURE, Saints admonished to study the prophecies for comfort, Taylor 34:74.

SCHOOLS, LDS children to be instructed by LDS teachers, Taylor 4:22; Saints encouraged to patronize and establish schools where the principles of the gospel can be taught, Taylor 35:43.

SOCIAL ACTIVITIES, proper conduct of youth at social gatherings, Taylor 36:36-39.

SODOM AND GOMORRAH, suffered the vengeance of eternal fire, Taylor 31:1-3.

SMITH, JOSEPH, thoughts on his role in the organization of the Church, Taylor 4:3-6.

SNOW, LORENZO, imprisoned in the penitentiary for polygamy, Taylor 34:28; as a fellow prisoner a great source of strength to those brethren in the penitentiary, Taylor 35:50; freed from prison after eleven months confinement, Taylor 36:34.

SPIRIT OF GOD, every man endowed with a portion of the, which accounts for the general aversion to dishonesty, immorality, and murder, Taylor 27:9-13.

STAKE PRESIDENTS, some thoughts regarding the duties of, Taylor 3:28; to see that drunkenness, Sabbath breaking, covetousness and other sins be not among the Saints over whom they preside, Taylor 26:19-20.

SUICIDE, a deadly sin, a crime against God and humanity, against the Creator and the creature, Taylor 35:47; if mental condition is the cause of, but such a condition is caused by sin the person is still in part responsible, Taylor 35:48.

SUNDAY SCHOOL TEACHERS, advised to make their daily walk and conversation accord with their teachings, Taylor 36:44.

SUNDAY SCHOOL SUPERINTENDENTS, qualities to be sought in the selection of, Taylor 36:43.

TABERNACLE, the building of a, Taylor 2:29.

YOUNG MEN'S MUTUAL IMPROVE-
MENT ASSOCIATION, first reference to,
Taylor 12:9.

YOUNG WOMEN'S MUTUAL IMPROVE-
MENT ASSOCIATION, the first reference
to, Taylor 12:9.

ZION, time will come when calamity and
bloodshed will encompass all nations, causing many to flee to z. or take up the sword
against their neighbor, Taylor 3:21; he that
will not take up his sword against his neighbor must needs flee to z. for safety, Taylor
5:20; the hand of God will be against any
who try to destroy, Taylor 6:15; the two
Zion's—the City of Enoch and the
Latter-day z.—to meet and fall upon each
others necks, Taylor 31:7; the Church an
example of the fulfillment of the promise to
z. that no weapon formed against shall prosper, Taylor 34:74-75; prophecy regarding
the fleeing to of all who will not take up the
sword against their brother, Taylor 36:59.

ABOUT THE COMPILER

Dr. Harold W. Pease and wife Jeannene are the parents of seven children, three of whom are presently serving on missions for The Church of Jesus Christ of Latter-day Saints. He received his doctorate from Brigham Young University in August 1974. Immediately thereafter he was employed as the historian on the B.Y.U. Centennial Committee. This was followed by 24 years of teaching political science and U.S. History at two California colleges. This time period was broken only to serve for a few months in 1979 as an advisor to the Constitutional Subcommittee of the Judiciary Committee of the U.S. Senate. At different times during those interim years he was a political columnist in about twenty newspapers and did a daily five-minute radio spot "In Defense of the Constitution," on several California stations.

Dr. Pease's most notable published work was *The Communist/Capitalist Alliance*. His most recent book is *The Mind and Will of the Lord: Brigham Young*.

With respect to his many awards, Dr. Pease was the first political scientist in the nation to receive the prestigious Leavey Award for Excellence in Private Enterprise Education—the Freedom Foundations highest award. Today Dr. Pease in a noted lecturer on the U.S. Constitution and New World Order politics.

Despite a very busy career, Dr. Pease has fulfilled many callings at both ward and stake levels in The Church of Jesus Christ of Latter-day Saints. He loves to serve. "The only award or honor that really means anything," he maintains, "is the one the Lord bestows on the other side."